Hegel's *Phenomenology of Spirit*

OXFORD GUIDES TO PHILOSOPHY

Series Editors
Rebecca Copenhaver, Washington University, St. Louis
Christopher Shields, University of Notre Dame
Mark Timmons, University of Arizona

*

Advisory Board
Michael Beaney, Ursula Coope, Karen Detlefsen, Lisa Downing, Tom
Hurka, Pauline Kleingeld, Robert Pasnau, Dominik Perler, Houston Smit,
Allen Wood

*

Oxford Guides to Philosophy presents concise introductions to the most
important primary texts in the history of philosophy. Written by top
scholars, the volumes in the series are designed to present up-to-date
scholarship in an accessible manner, in order to guide readers through
these challenging texts.

*

Anscombe's *Intention*: A Guide
John Schwenkler

Kant's *Doctrine of Virtue*: A Guide
Mark C. Timmons

Sidgwick's *The Methods of Ethics*: A Guide
David Phillips

Spinoza's *Ethics*: A Guide
Michael LeBuffe

Bentham's *Introduction to the Principles of Morals and Legislation*: A Guide
Steven Sverdlik

Mary Shepherd: A Guide
Deborah Boyle

Candrakīrti's *Introduction to the Middle Way*: A Guide
Jan Westerhoff

Vātsyāyana's *Commentary on the* Nyāya-sūtra: A Guide
Matthew R. Dasti

Hegel's *Phenomenology of Spirit*: A Guide
Terry Pinkard

Hegel's
Phenomenology
of Spirit

A Guide

TERRY PINKARD

OXFORD
UNIVERSITY PRESS

OXFORD
UNIVERSITY PRESS

Oxford University Press is a department of the University of Oxford. It furthers
the University's objective of excellence in research, scholarship, and education
by publishing worldwide. Oxford is a registered trade mark of Oxford University
Press in the UK and certain other countries.

Published in the United States of America by Oxford University Press
198 Madison Avenue, New York, NY 10016, United States of America.

Library of Congress Cataloging-in-Publication Data
Names: Pinkard, Terry P., author.
Title: Hegel's Phenomenology of spirit : a guide / Terry Pinkard.
Description: New York, NY : Oxford University Press, [2023] |
Series: Oxford guides to philosophy | Includes bibliographical references.
Identifiers: LCCN 2023005067 (print) | LCCN 2023005068 (ebook) |
ISBN 9780197663127 (hardback) | ISBN 9780197663134 (paperback) |
ISBN 9780197663158 (epub)
Subjects: LCSH: Hegel, Georg Wilhelm Friedrich, 1770–1831. Phänomenologie des Geistes.
Classification: LCC B2929 .P44 2023 (print) | LCC B2929 (ebook) |
DDC 193—dc23/eng/20230222
LC record available at https://lccn.loc.gov/2023005067
LC ebook record available at https://lccn.loc.gov/2023005068

DOI: 10.1093/oso/9780197663127.001.0001

To Susan

Contents

Prelude

Few books have been more celebrated and more vilified than Hegel's 1807 *Phenomenology of Spirit*. It has always attracted an enormous legion of admirers and another large group of detractors. It has also been repurposed any number of times in support some more recent trend or new wave of thought, and it has equally served as a paradigm to be rejected in some more recent trend or new wave of thought. Many times it has served both as support and rejection of the same recent trend or new wave of thought. For example, various strands of both Marxists and existentialists have used it to support their views or as paradigms of what their views are aimed at rejecting. All the while, new interpretations of Hegel's book appear with undulating regularity. For what it's worth, the famous title of Benedetto Croce's 1906 work, *What Is Living and What Is Dead of the Philosophy of Hegel*, might well serve as the title of just about every work on Hegel's book published since Croce's piece.

One of the initially puzzling things about such a famous work is that there has been and still is great disagreement about what the book is about. Even all the words in the title are disputed. What is the sense of "phenomenology" being used? And in German the title has to do with the phenomenology of *Geist*—but how is *Geist* to be rendered? As "spirit" or as "mind"? (Various English translations choose one or the other.) What does this have to do with Hegel's original title for the book, "The Science of the Experience of Consciousness," which he dropped in favor of the title it has now but which he also kept and which appears on different pages of the various versions of the original 1807 German edition? To add to the perplexity, Hegel developed his own very technical vocabulary in writing the book. He always insisted that this was absolutely necessary for the properly "scientific" nature of the enterprise to be given its proper expression, but the jargon he created never really fully caught on and thus there is no "common usage" for it to which an appeal can be made. As a consequence, all readers of the book, from the beginner to the Hegel specialist, have to make key decisions about to understand many of the basic terms of the book itself in order to read it at all.

This also has to do with another striking feature of the book. As Robert Stern, a prominent Hegel scholar, has noted, the normal authorial voice recedes in it. Much contemporary philosophy starts out with a statement about what one is trying to do (often expressed as "Here I want to argue that . . .") followed by an attempt to do just that with a reminder at the end that this was what one was trying to do. Hegel does not do that. Instead, there is a voice, as it were, setting a scene, and sometimes what one hears are the voices in the scene itself and sometimes the voice of a narrator who is describing the scene. At the end of the section, the narrator often brings us, the readers, into a union with himself in wondering just what just happened. One of the results of that kind of way of staging the argument is that we are never sure where we are going until we get there, and we are never quite sure what the argument is, nor, for some interpreters, are we ever sure that there was an argument and not something else. In some very general ways, this resembles Ludwig Wittgenstein's procedure in his *Philosophical Investigations*, where we also follow a set of scenes accompanied by a narrator (and also sometimes another interlocuter who is never identified) that is supposed to bring us to think not only about some key issues but also about the way we have been thinking about those issues and thereby follow the same circuitous process the author has himself gone through to get there. In such a book, there can be no preannounced lesson to be learned, and the idea is that whatever it is that one learns, one has to learn it oneself in going through the model cases laid out in the book. Hegel even begins his Preface to the book (itself written after he finished writing the book itself) by telling us that one cannot really write a preface to a book like this (although he goes on to write a very lengthy preface) since one has to go through the book on one's own in order to appropriate the lesson to be learned—or to know whether there is a lesson to be learned.

After publishing the book, Hegel would describe it to his own students as his own *Entdeckungsreise* (his own voyage of discovery). It was where Wilhelm, as he was known to his family and closest of friends, became Hegel, the famous and forbidding German philosopher. This aspect of the *Phenomenology* should be preserved, so that at every step of the way, even though in a commentary such as this one where one is told where one is going, one needs to be reminded that the "characters" in the book do not know that. Even calling them "characters" already begs several questions. Any number of commentators from Hegel's own day to our own have been struck by the way in which in giving such an account of the development of *Geist* (Mind? Spirit?), Hegel seemed to be writing a kind of sui generis Bildungsroman, a kind of "coming of age" novel in which the main character is, of course, *Geist* itself, which takes on various shapes as it comes to a realization of what it was seeking after having followed out some false early leads. However, Hegel does not describe these characters as characters but rather as "shapes of consciousness" (in the first part of the book) and as "shapes of a world" (in the second part). In all these cases, we have a description of a "shape of consciousness" or a "shape of a world" which is working its way to a conclusion that seems to rationally follow from what the characters (or maybe one character) take themselves to be doing but which ends with ultimately unbearable conclusions, none of which seemed predictable at the outset (unless our accompanying narrator has already tipped us off). Our narrator is also a commentator (he is Hegel himself) who tells us what is really going on in the logic of the situation which the participants themselves either cannot see or see only very dimly. A commentary on the *Phenomenology of Spirit* is already layering on another level of commentary in a book that already has more than one of them.

There is yet one more twist to all this. Hegel apparently changed his own mind about what book he was writing to the point that when he thought he had completed it, he decided that he had actually only completed half of it. He seems to have sent what was supposed to be the final copy to the printer only then to tell him shortly after the first run had been done that the book was only half finished. (As one could imagine, the printer was none too happy with this and exasperatedly threatened to scuttle the whole project. The whole thing was saved when one of Hegel's old friends basically told the printer he himself would help underwrite the cost.) When he finally got the book to the printer, he had a new table of contents, and the printer, now very confused and annoyed, more or less fused the different table of contents together and printed both of them. This has meant for those trying to understand the book that they have to make a decision on how to organize the oddly organized printed table of contents itself. The book started out as organized into three basic chapters: "Consciousness," "Self-Consciousness," and "Science," with various subheadings under the first two chapters. That changed with the additions, so one had things like the chapter called "Reason" becoming "C. Reason" or "AA: Reason." Basically, there are three options for making sense of this. The first option sees the book as organized into basically six separate sections: "Consciousness," "Self-Consciousness," "Reason," "Spirit," "Religion," "Absolute Knowing." The second option is to look at the roman numeral numbering Hegel gave it, in which case "A: Consciousness" consists of three chapters (1–3), "B: Self-Consciousness" consists of one chapter (4) with two subheadings, and it is followed by "C: Reason" (or "AA: Reason), which has chapter 5 within itself, followed in turn by 6: Spirit, 7: Religion, 8: Absolute Knowing (eight basic chapters altogether). Or one can see AA: Reason and BB: Spirit (and likewise CC: Religion and DD: Absolute Knowing) as subheadings of B: Self-Consciousness. (All very confusing.)

In this commentary, it will be argued that the structure of the book basically has two main chapters, which correspond roughly with one of the three options, that is, "Consciousness" and "Self-Consciousness," with everything that follows from "B: Self-Consciousness" as a subheading of that chapter.

Here is how that would go. We see the book as moving from within the following set of claims, which in turn generate the claims that follow, which will throw light on both the particular transitions between the various chapters and on the structure of the book as a whole. On that way of taking it, the book thus develops these six related claims:

1. All consciousness is self-consciousness. (Parts A and B)
2. Self-consciousness is social self-consciousness. (Parts B and AA)
3. *Geist* is self-conscious life, and this is to be conceived generically in terms of social self-consciousness. (Part BB, foreshadowed in Part B)

4. Self-conscious life has a history of that to which it collectively takes itself to be absolutely committed, which is as much ideal as it is material. (Part BB)

5. This history is progressive (and in that sense, teleological), and it culminates in modern life after the finalization of the French Revolution, with two different but related accounts of that teleology (the history of spirit and the history of religion). (Parts BB and CC)

6. The thesis about the centrality of self-consciousness is what the *Phenomenology* as a whole is about and at the end turns out to have both a theoretical and practical significance. The *Phenomenology* itself and the system to which it gives rise afterward is, we are supposed to realize, the very point of departure for modern life. It culminates with the experience of this being the book *you needed in particular* and *we needed in general*, and not just another book of philosophy. (Part DD)

On this reading, part DD, which took the place of the original final chapter, (which was originally simply "C: Science" but was discarded in the rewrite) is really the third (and very short) chapter of the book. "DD" should be "C: Absolute Knowing." The original plan for the book as "The Science of the Experience of Consciousness" had three basic chapters: A. Consciousness; B. Self-Consciousness; C. Science. The interpretation of the book being offered up here sees Hegel as more or less keeping faith with that original ordering but also as seeing that much more had to be added to it if it were to succeed in what it was setting out to do.

Still: why the little muddle in the table of contents? Or did Hegel not really know what he was doing?

Hegel's Path to the *Phenomenology*

Part of the reason for this confusion in the table of contents had to do with Hegel's own partial lack of clarity about the book, a lack that was filled out and resolved as he finished the book, and part of it had to do with the chaotic and depressing part of Hegel's life at the time of the writing. Hegel, born in 1770, went to the seminary attached to Tübingen university in 1788. The seminary's purpose was to train ministers for the Protestant church in Württemberg. He had wanted to go the university and study law, but his father's wishes (and the fact that he could go to the seminary on a full scholarship, relieving his father of the need to pay for a university education) sent him instead into training for the ministry. At Tübingen, he acquired a roommate, Friedrich Hölderlin, and the two of them a year later added another roommate, Friedrich Schelling, thereby creating a legend in itself of the possibilities of collegiate friendship. The three friends were each incredibly intellectually gifted, and together while students they worked out a common plan for a new way of thinking of philosophy and literature and the world in general. The French Revolution in 1789 gave them an additional passion, not just to change thought but to change the world itself. Hegel and Hölderlin graduated in 1793 and Schelling (born in 1775) graduated in 1795. All of three of them resolved with each other that they would never become ministers even though legally they were obligated to do so. (As things turned out, there were many more people qualified and actively seeking positions as ministers than there were available positions, so this legal obligation proved too weak to stop their nonecclesiastical ambitions). Schelling quickly became the boy wonder of German philosophy, managing to get a full professorship in Jena in 1798 as an already famous author and philosopher.

Hegel's career did not ignite so quickly. Soon after their graduations, Hölderlin was establishing a reputation as one of the up and coming of Germany's poets, Schelling had become a figure on the scene in German letters, but Hegel had little to show for himself. After his father died in 1799, Hegel came into a small inheritance, and he managed to get Schelling to finagle an invitation for him to come to Jena and teach as a private teacher—with no salary but the ability to get paying students to show up for lectures and to charge them for their examinations. Hegel arrived in Jena in 1801, only to gradually find out that his old friend and philosophical comrade regarded him as a kind of subordinate to Schelling's own philosophical position with a duty more or less to cement the Schellingian program. Schelling saw the program as shared, but it was Schelling's views that were supposed to be shared. If Hegel had his own views, they were not really what was at stake. Soon after his arrival, they together edited a philosophy journal devoted to propagating Schelling's ideas. Because of the deteriorating political conditions surrounding Jena at the time and because of some whispered scandals that were not scandals except to the people living there, Schelling departed in 1803, leaving Hegel stranded. Hegel found it impossible to get a fully remunerated position at the university or at any other university, and his small inheritance began to run out. Hegel needed a paying position at a university, and he needed a book to get it. Hegel had been writing drafts of his own system since he had arrived in Jena, but despite his declining fortunes and the threat of unemployment, he discarded them as unfit for publication. Starting in roughly 1805 (or 1804, according to his first biographer, Karl Rosenkranz), increasingly desperate for a position, Hegel set out again to write the first part of his own "system of philosophy." What was more or less a first draft was published in 1807 as the *Phenomenology of Spirit*. In the meantime, war between Napoleonic France and the various German lands had started and, as the legend has it, Hegel finished the book (although not the preface) on the night of the climactic battle of Jena, where Napoleon's forces shattered the Prussian army—a world-historical event that that also provoked the dissolution of the famous, long-lived, but by 1807 moribund Holy Roman Empire. Hegel had produced a new work of philosophy at the very moment when it seemed that Napoleon had finally brought the old political order of Europe down. Little good that did him: Hegel was out of a job with no visible future, had gotten himself into a further pickle when his landlady turned out to be pregnant with his child, and felt the world around him changing under his feet as one German university after another shuttered itself. Because of the battle at Jena, Hegel in fact missed his deadline for submitting all of the manuscript. (He was excused from the contract because it was determined the war had prevented him for meeting it.) It is no wonder that he submitted another table of contents and that the exasperated publisher threw the mismatched pieces together.

Why was it so important that Hegel produce not only a book but his own "system"? The quick answer to that question is that Hegel was writing in a period of system building in German philosophy, and in a system-building period, one had to have one's own system. But why was that?

By the 1790s, the university at Jena, which before that time qual-ified as one of the real backwater sites of the German university system, had blossomed almost overnight into one of the most vibrant intellectual centers in Europe. Jena's sudden rise to prominence was in part the result of the young Duke of Saxony-Weimar-Eisenach's appointment of the young literary star Johann Wolfgang Goethe as his key adviser and minister. Among Goethe's tasks was overseeing the university, which he quickly turned into a center for free thinking and advanced studies, even getting his comrade in the new German literary horizon, Friedrich Schiller, appointed as professor. The uni-versity quickly became the flashpoint for the discussion of Kant's phi-losophy in all of Germany. Kant had presented his views as a unified system and not merely a collection of independent pieces of philo-sophical reflection. His system was, he claimed, the means by which philosophy would finally become a science, a *Wissenschaft*. This term bore a slightly different meaning then than it does now. It meant something like a rigorous theory proceeding from a few stated prin-ciples that could furnish the basis for further research, rather than characterizing the procedures of the natural sciences and by analogy and courtesy those of the social sciences. The paradigm was that of Isaac Newton's elevation of physics to a new status, but the idea that other modes of inquiry could become sciences of their own did not at the time imply that they had to become empirical and predictive like physics. The idea was that fields such as philosophy and even theology could become sciences of their own if they could follow the new par-adigm of rigorous theory supplemented by observation. What Kant had so provocatively argued was that all prior philosophy—both metaphysical and practical—had failed simply because it had not es-tablished itself as a new science in keeping with the grand successes of Newton and his followers and, because of that, presented itself as a history of competing systems without having any real comprehen-sion of how to adjudicate among them. (Again, the hero was Newton, who had apparently solved the outstanding problems of the physics that preceded his own and had done so by putting physics on a firm, rigorous basis.)

Although Kant's system was dazzling and produced some very important results, it was not immediately clear how it all hung together or whether some of its parts might be extraneous and needed to be excised. Besides the intimidating machinery of Kant's 1781 (revised in 1787) *Critique of Pure Reason*, there were his views that all knowledge could only be of the world under the very specific and necessary conditions under which we could experience it and that any possible elaboration of these conditions burdened us with inescapable contradictions, so that we had to conclude that in addition to or behind or accompanying our experienced world was a realm of unknowable things-in-themselves. That seized the public imagination: our experienced world, so Kant claimed to have demonstrated, was a rigorously Newtonian deterministic world with apparently no room in it for human freedom or the soul or God, but it was a logical failure to conclude that this was true of things-in-themselves. We could have in principle no knowledge of things-in-themselves. Kant consoled his readers by claiming that if he had denied knowledge, it was to make room for faith. He then went on in other works to argue that in fact in our practical affairs, we had to assume that we were free, and this required we think of ourselves as capable of starting entire causal series on our own (such as moving one's body) that were not themselves the result of any prior causal series but of our own free willing. Theoretically, there was no place for freedom, but practically we had to assume we were free, and his distinction between the appearing world and the world of things-in-themselves made room for that assumption. "Science" seemed to rule out our freedom, but our practical faith that we were free as a "thing-in-itself" could not be overruled by "science," since to do so, it would have to make claims to knowing things it could not in principle know.

That only raised the cultural ante. If Kant's new "science" was necessary to resolve the apparent tensions between religion and modern scientific secularity, then it was really important to get the science all in order. In short succession, a number of contenders who wanted to put the finishing touches on Kant entered the scene. Karl Leonhard Reinhold accepted a professorship at Jena in 1787 and attempted to refound the Kantian system around what he called the "principle of consciousness" (which stressed the element of spontaneity in Kant's system) and the concept of "representation" (also central to Kant). But Reinhold's reframing itself ran into deep troubles, and in 1794 he left Jena and was replaced by another young rising star, J. G. Fichte, whose 1794 *Wissenschaftslehre* (*Doctrine of Science*), given initially in lectures there, attempted to refashion the Kantian system in terms of what the subject (the "I") needed to do to render itself consistent and coherent, remaking the Kantian system into a systematic progression that began with the "I" needing to posit something like a "Not-I" in order to hold its own self-relation together and a synthesis of the "I" and "Not-I" to stabilize the unity. (This was more or less the thesis-antithesis-synthesis model that has long been attributed to Hegel.) Along the way, Fichte also added some key elements to the system, such as making mutual recognition among agents as fundamental to morality rather than only what Kant had called simply respect for the moral law.

At the same time, around 1795, some of the audience for Fichte's lectures created a kind of post-Fichtean countermovement of an antisystematic conception of philosophy as having more to do with the arts and with religion. They reconceived Fichte's "I" as having more to do with the spontaneity and creativity of the "I" of an artist. This movement coined a term for itself—"romanticism"—and insisted on philosophy as fragmented, convivial, poetic, and attuned to nonconceptual sources of knowledge and to the idea of an "intellectual intuition" of the absolute. For them, life and thought were not matters of *Wissenschaft* and system so much as like a novel (a *Roman*, hence the term "Romantic"), and they began attracting as much attention as the Jena system builders. Thus, not only was the idea of a "system" now in the air, but also the countermovement of antisystematic philosophy represented by the Jena early Romantics, who took themselves to be working out some of the consequences of Fichte's works.

Fichte faced a series of spurious, trumped-up charges of atheism, and in 1799 Fichte was dismissed from the university and replaced by F. W. J. Schelling (Hegel's old friend). Schelling had arrived in Jena in 1798 and had immediately begun work on a synthesis of Fichte's version of Kantianism with a very Romantic conception of nature and a Romantic conception of the relation between natural science and the arts. Schelling also almost overnight became one of the leading figures in the formation of early romanticism, but he was also an exception since he was also focused on building his own system that would incorporate both the fragmentary, antisystematic, poetic program of the Romantics along with the *Wissenschaft*-oriented, system-building, post-Kantian philosophies while at the same time bringing in all the progressive dynamics of modern natural science.

If Hegel was to get anywhere in that hothouse atmosphere, he not only had to produce his own system but also had to contend with the sudden and growing influence of the early Romantics. Moreover, to the extent that anybody in the philosophical world knew anything of Hegel, they regarded him as a lesser Schellingian, so he had to make it clear how his views were different from Schelling's. Although he knew his own views were very, very different from Schelling's, virtually nobody else did. He himself was also personally convinced that only a system of the proper sort would provide an adequate way of keeping philosophy as vibrantly oriented to modern life as natural science had turned out to be. Like Kant, who had led the way, and like the others who followed in his wake, Hegel's insistence on "system" was not merely a taste for the ornately architectural but part of a deep conviction of his time that more than a collection of insightful but independent articles was needed if philosophy were to take its place in the order of the new sciences arriving on the modern scene.

His goals were now clear, but it was equally clear that he had to write the book in great haste. That also went against his own nature. He had already drafted several such systems but put them aside and started anew because he did not think they were ready yet for the public. Now, in 1805 or thereabouts, it was clear that he did not have that luxury. This left him with some small regrets. In 1807, as he was finally going over the page proofs for the finished book, he admitted in a letter to his friend, Niethammer, that he wished he could have slimmed it down, maybe streamlined it a bit and made the whole thing more seaworthy, voicing a hope for a second edition in which he could do that. However, no second edition was to appear. Shortly before he died, he was in fact at work a new edition in which he inserted a slip of paper into the original book with the note "Not to be redone," since he had come to see it as a work peculiar to him at the time in which it had been written. He never disavowed the *Phenomenology*, but as he began his storied career first at Heidelberg in 1816 and then at Berlin 1818, he began to think that the time now called for a slightly different approach to the issue of a scientific system of philosophy. However, his earlier work's fame continued to grow, and Hegel left the scene in 1831 before he had time to comment on how, in his mature years, he had come to view it.

Reading Hegel's *Phenomenology*

Because of Hegel's insistence on creating a technical vocabulary, getting used to reading Hegel is at first hard for us Anglophones—and for native German speakers as well. Nonetheless, once we get the terms down, we'll find the book easier going. In creating his "scientific" system, Hegel took German words and gave them more strict and technical meanings which he freely admitted were not what they meant in ordinary conversational German. He insisted, however, during his entire adult life that such a regimenting of vocabulary was necessary if philosophy was to be pursued as a science. Whereas many philosophers still subscribe to that view (although rejecting Hegel's own regimentation), many others think that philosophy should be written completely in the vernacular with as little artificial regimentation as possible. Hegel was perfectly capable of doing the latter, as his more popular and many of his earlier works attest. He simply did not think that it was appropriate or helpful in writing philosophy, and he left us, therefore, with the task of understanding just what his regimentation amounted to. Large parts of scholarly dispute about Hegel's philosophy in fact boil down to arguments about whether Hegel meant this or that when he used his more technical terms. There is no way out of coming to terms with his vocabulary.

First, to turn to the title a bit more: what is meant by *Geist*? As we have seen, the original title of the book was different, but Hegel changed his mind about the title and ultimately the book. The book was originally "The Science of the Experience of Consciousness," and it became the *Phenomenology of Spirit*. There has been much scholarly energy expended on what Hegel meant by *Geist*, why he introduced that term in addition to "consciousness," and the like, but there has been no definitively shared result. The term was floating around German philosophy at the time, and Hegel himself had used it in his writings from his early days up to the *Phenomenology*, so there is not much of a mystery about that. Since Hegel was drafting different "systems" between 1803 and the publication of the *Phenomenology* in 1807, and he was changing his mind on any number of issues, one has to step into fairly deep waters to work out just what he finally meant by *Geist* in 1807 (and whether he kept that sense of *Geist* for the rest of his career). In this commentary, *Geist* will be taken to be *self-conscious life*, and the case to be made for that will appear in the commentary itself. The concept of "life" as a category in Hegel's system takes on greater urgency in the period of Hegel's work leading up to the *Phenomenology*, so this is not a huge interpretative leap to take. The interpretive question that arises after this is whether Hegel takes *Geist* to be something beyond human self-conscious life and to be some kind of independent entity—perhaps God?

Second, there is the issue of "phenomenology" itself. The word was in common use in German philosophy by the 1800s. Kant, for example, uses it in his 1786 *Metaphysical Foundations of Natural Science*. The term has some but not much in common with the uses to which all post-Husserlian philosophy as "phenomenology" has put it. The term is still in use in physics, where it describes a way of relating theories to the concrete phenomena they claim to explain or predict and where it contrasts with a "pure" physics that is much more mathematical. Hegel's usage appears to be an offshoot of that sense of "phenomenology," although he gives it a special twist to make it more philosophically useful. This special sense has two facets. The first is logical, and the second is more experiential, even existential. Hegel will try to establish that there are certain ways in which what he will call "speculative" concepts relate to each other and have a logic to them—a logic in the sense that some kinds of statements will be well formed and others not; that some kinds of inferences drawn will be illicit, others permitted, and some required; and that certain conceptualizations require others. This logic manifests itself in concrete ways in the lives of people both individually and collectively. Faced with such oppositions, common sense naturally is led to think that it must show that one component of the opposition is more important than the other and that the less important must therefore be eliminated or subordinated as a lesser and untrue manifestation of the more important. "Speculative" or "dialectical" thought, on the other hand, shows that in fact such concepts that seemed to stand in exclusionary relations to each other are in fact both necessary components of a nonadditive whole. (It's an arguable point, but dialectical thought in this sense paves the way for the kind of philosophical pragmatisms represented by Charles Sanders Peirce, William James, and—especially—John Dewey that tend to look askance at earlier philosophical dualisms by showing how both components of the allegedly dualist scheme are actually functioning elements in some other complex whole of which they are parts.) "Phenomenology" in the Hegelian sense is thus the account of how these basic conceptual tensions manifest themselves and play out in the concrete lives of the self-creatures we are. This is the experiential or existential facet of his phenomenology. It is also part of this view that in a more rigorous treatment of these tensions, they do not simply show up in the lives of people, play themselves out, and then vanish in order to be replaced by other tensions that play themselves out in other, different shapes of collective life. In particular, the concepts with which such a phenomenology will be concerned are those that Hegel uses to define *Geist* itself: an I that is a We and a We that is an I (and as it will turn out later in the book, the relation between a "you" and another "you"). Hegel thinks that the chapters in his book are thus not merely ad hoc lists of different possibilities of life—although a number of different Hegel interpreters have thought something along these lines—but are about the way in which these concepts do not simply manifest themselves but also develop—and that is crucial—in certain ways so that the failures of one shape of life play a huge role in determining the shape of its successors. One could not, as it were, cut out the chapters and put them in a different order and still have the same book as the *Phenomenology* Hegel in fact wrote. Thus, if *Geist* is equivalent to self-conscious life, then the phenomenology of this *Geist* is the examination of how self-conscious life makes its appearance in the world, and that turns out necessarily to be not only developmental but developmental over time, that is, in its recollection of itself in its history. A phenomenology in the Hegelian sense cannot simply presuppose at the outset that there is such a logic to the concepts of the "I that is a We, and a We that is an I," nor can he presume that there is any particular order to the development he will be tracing. In this Hegelian phenomenology, we see the ways of concretely, even existentially, grappling with the "speculative," dialectical problem of a shape of life that seems to be determined by two (or more) competing terms that threaten to be mutually exclusive and to bring the entire shape into unsustainable contradictions and general incoherence. (This way of seeing "phenomenology" rejects some interpreters' attempt to argue that Hegel was presupposing his later *Logic* all along and thus just showing the ways that logic happens to be illustrated in the shapes of individual and collective life he sketches. Although he clearly says that this treatment is a way station to the rest of his "system" as a "science," he nonetheless insists that this phenomenology is a "science" unto itself.)

Here are some other key words and phrases from the Preface to keep an eye on:

Actual (*Wirklich*): the German (*wirklich, Wirklichkeit*) ordinarily means "reality," but Hegel gives it a technical meaning to bring it into line with Aristotle's use of *energeia*, which (following Aquinas's Latin lead) we usually translate into English as "actuality." It is what is really "at work," "real" in a given set of appearances. French translators generally render it as *effectivité*, and it would be better if we had that alternative.

Alienation (*Entfremdung*), as contrasted with *estrangement* (*Entzweiung*) and *relinquishing* (*Entäußerung*): there has been lots of ink spilled over how to render these terms. *Entzweiung* can refer to the way in which, for example, partners in a marriage or members of a family can become estranged from each other. It has people standing in some kind of relation that is dead to them. Alienation, *Entfremdung*, on the other hand, has people standing in a relation in which they cannot see themselves as related, as if they have been turned over to the will of an other. A third term used by Hegel is also joined with these two, that of *Entäußerung*. Luther uses it to translate the Greek *kenosis*, the activity by which God divests himself of—or pours out—many but not all his divine attributes in order to become man. The term clearly carries a lot of theologically freighted meaning in the German, and this makes rendering it in English all the more difficult. Here it is rendered consistently as "relinquishing" (and all its cognates). One way of taking this is that *Geist* must in its historical development relinquish itself and become more abstract to itself—as it moves from the "thick" concepts of the ancient world to the "thin" concepts of the modern world—before it is in a position to fill itself out again in a more human, "thicker" way. The terms here are also used by the young Karl Marx in his 1844 Paris manuscripts, where they have all traditionally been given much different translations than are being used here to render Hegel in twenty-first-century English.

Sublation: finally, there is a term over which almost all expositors and translators of Hegel gnash their teeth, and that is *Aufhebung* (and all its cognates). The term is ubiquitous in Hegel. It refers to the way in which certain "speculative" concepts are negated, negate others, or are transformed into some new set of concepts by the way they have mutually negated others or even themselves. Hegel discusses this term and why he uses it in two places (his *Science of Logic* and his *Encyclopedia of the Philosophical Sciences*), where he points out that it has two meanings. It can mean "save" or "preserve" (as in "Save me a seat if you get there early"), and it can mean "to cancel" (as in "Because of your failure to pay we are canceling your subscription"). The German term can also mean in some circumstances "to raise" (as in "All in favor, raise your hands"), but Hegel does not mention this third meaning as having any importance for his concerns. (Nonetheless, many commentators insist that in interpreting Hegel, one must include this third usage, which means that the terms that are canceling, being canceled and so on are also being raised to a higher level.) Since it is good to keep Hegel's sometime arcane technical vocabulary intact, here I have opted to keep an older translation of *Aufhebung*—"sublation." The term was once in use in English as a synonym for "negation," but it fell out of use early in the nineteenth century only to be brought back as a term for translating *Aufhebung* in Hegel. Even to this day, that remains virtually its only use in English.

There are others, and we will come to them as we need to in commenting on the text.

Now it's time to turn to the text itself. The goal here is to provide a paragraph-by-paragraph commentary on the text. Sometimes it is hard to get a handle on what Hegel is doing, why he is saying what he is saying, and how to make sense of it all. This commentary is supposed to help the befuddled keep up with what is going on and (one hopes) to provoke both the assured expert and the befuddled to think more about the ideas being argued and to form their own views (even if that means rejecting those being put forth by this commentator).

This commentary started out as a set of notes that I intended as an aid to class discussion, and its conversational tone is intended to keep it as an aid to discussion. It is a paragraph-by-paragraph conversation on what's going on in the book. (Yes, as conversations go, it's a bit one-sided, but you can provide the other side to the conversation.) It is thereby intended as an accompaniment to reading and discussing the book itself, not as a substitute for the great work on which it is commenting. The voice I try to assume in this book is that of just one among many readers (although I admit I've read the *Phenomenology* a few times before). In this guide, I engage almost not at all with the secondary literature. Alas. Doing so would turn it into more of a scholarly book than a reader's guide, and it also would be substantially longer. There are precious few notes.[1] For the most part, it also avoids bringing in the rest of Hegel's work to comment on the passages—although I do so a few times—and instead is supposed to be part of a conversation trying to make philosophical sense of the *Phenomenology* as if it were the only book Hegel ever wrote. (This is a limitation of my book.)

Think of this as a piece by one participant among several in a reading group of the book. If nothing else, it's meant to facilitate the conversation, not end it.

The translation of Hegel's text to which I will be referring is my own, published by Cambridge University Press in 2018.

1

The Preface

The Preface begins with a statement about why prefaces to this kind of book cannot really be written, followed by Hegel's exceptionally long preface. In the first seventeen paragraphs, there are lots of potshots at the state of contemporary philosophy in Germany in the period between, very roughly, 1798 and 1806, and mostly against the kind of sentimentalism, romanticism, and nature-philosophy trends at the time. The Preface was written after Hegel had completed the book, and it stands as a kind of calm reflection on what he had just done and why he had done it.

¶1. We are told that prefaces can't really be helpful for the kind of philosophy Hegel is proposing, although he doesn't immediately tell us here just what it is that he is proposing. One way of taking this would be to contrast it in terms of the way in which much philosophy (especially contemporary Anglophone philosophy) has understood things. On that view, philosophy is about "arguments," so that even if one states in a preface or an abstract that one will demonstrate such and such, what counts is not just that statement but the "argument" for it. If that were the case, then Hegel could easily state his conclusion at the beginning—one might imagine him saying something like "I will show that the absolute is the unity of the subjective and the objective" or something like that—but he does not. Instead, his point will be that in fact there is no preannounced lesson to be learned, so that the idea is that whatever it is that one learns, one has to learn it by oneself going through the model cases laid out in the book. There is no predetermined answer sheet to the book. One is not merely going to be going through the arguments. One is supposed to be appropriating the book and its themes for oneself.

¶2. Of course, Hegel might have started by comparing this work with others—in which case he would have said something like, "Unlike Kant and unlike Hume, I will say . . ."—but he does not. However, note

Hegel's Phenomenology of Spirit. Terry Pinkard, Oxford University Press. © Oxford University Press 2023. DOI: 10.1093/oso/9780197663127.003.0001

the veiled reference to Kantian antinomies and the nature of dialectical reasoning. Philosophy seems to generate incompatible positions that are not equivalent to the way in which ordinary assertions can be incompatible. In ordinary situations, faced with a contradiction, we either have to give up one of the propositions or reframe the whole matter so that the alleged contradiction is not really there. But there is something peculiar about such philosophical/metaphysical/conceptual problems. In philosophical problems, both sides of a debate seem to have good reasons on their side or at least seem to have compelling grips on us. Why is that? Hegel doesn't tell us immediately why, but that will emerge.

¶3. The whole of this book is the result (of the investigation or of the process itself) and the way it comes to be. However, if metaphysics rests on some kind of deep illusion about, for example, the relation of thought to reality, then there is no way we can ever come to a comprehension of the whole. Instead, we would just get a virtually endless set of oppositions or paradoxes, one after another.

It is also very apparent that Hegel thinks that philosophy has to answer to the felt needs of the time, yet philosophy usually takes itself to be timeless. How is it, as he put it in his later lectures, that something so timeless can yet have a history and take on a specific and different historical shapes?

The Preface contains lots of attacks on unnamed opponents in his own time. You have to dig a little into the history of the period to find out who some of those people are, and we'll mention a few of them later. However, you can see not who but what he is attacking in some of the sections.

1. Philosophy shouldn't be putting things into pigeonholes (¶¶14–16).
2. Philosophy shouldn't be a formalism. By "formalism," he means the repeated application of one or of a few abstract principles under which particular cases are subsumed.
3. Philosophy should not strive for edification (¶7).

¶4. Hegel introduces an important concept for him and classical German culture: *Bildung*. It means higher education, cultural formation, all in the service of forming a personality that is equipped conceptually and emotionally to be able to make good judgments. A man or woman of *Bildung* knows what's generally worth knowing, is able to discriminate the good from the bad, and has a good feel for the various arts. (They go to concerts, museums, gallery openings, etc.) You have to work at becoming a person of *Bildung*. Hegel makes the large claim that learning philosophy is at least to some degree necessary for becoming a man or woman of *Bildung*. Becoming such a person carries with it a kind of social authority that was crucial in the transitional time in which Hegel was writing.

¶5. Here is another large claim, not yet substantiated. Philosophy can only exist as a system. You can't really do piecemeal philosophy. Hegel says his task is to take philosophy from the love of knowing (enjoying doing the mental gymnastics necessary to doing philosophy) into real knowing, that is, an established system of rigorous, well-grounded theory (what the nineteenth century still called *Wissenschaft*, science). Philosophy at its most general explicates what it is to know anything, and that includes knowing something about what it is to know about what it is to know. And he follows this with a very large claim: this way of looking at philosophy is itself necessary. It's not just another department in the university; it is required for a university or college to be an institution dedicated to knowledge.

¶6. Hegel takes a swipe at some of the leading Romantic ideas that were gaining wide public acceptability at his time: knowing about the deeper things is only a matter of getting the right "feel," being in touch in one's own inwardness so that one is attuned to the absolute, etc. It's the view that all this is nonconceptual (nondiscursive), and that you can't argue about it. Supposedly all these people cannot tell us what it is to be on such intimate terms with the absolute, but they do seem to say that if we don't see it, we are simply showing that we are less knowledgeable than they.

¶7. Hegel's kind of historical approach gets a foreshadowing here. To the extent that "we" nowadays feel a need for a philosophical approach to tell us that we don't actually need philosophy already shows that the immediate faith we're hoping that philosophy might restore is already gone. It's like wanting to be argued back into childhood. This itself has to be conceptually grasped: Why do "we" want that?

¶8. Note that this kind of "edifying" approach to philosophy is often accompanied by a kind of wild moralism having to do with a tale about how we've lost our way, are in decline, and "we" need to be forcefully brought back to where we used to be. Note also the theme of "secularization": supposedly, religion used to hold us together, but it no longer suffices. When one looks at all the "new age" religions springing up around 1807, one is taken by how abstract they are, and that it takes so little to satisfy "us" about this shows how much we have thinned ourselves out.

¶9. Hegel makes it clear that he's fully opposed to such preaching.

¶10. The kind of "holier than thou" (or the "deeper than thou") approach is just pretentious nonsense. It claims to be in touch with that whereof one cannot speak, but it goes on and on speaking about it. These people are just displaying their own fancies and claiming it's all just so profound.

¶11. Here we come to one of Hegel's main ideas, that of birth and transition: the idea that *Geist* develops slowly and then suddenly reaches a point where it innovates and turns into a new world. There is a very striking claim here: we are at the birth of a new world. After 1789 (the French Revolution), things are going to be different. The change is going to be revolutionary.

¶12. The theme of *Wirklichkeit* (actuality) makes its appearance. It's clear that Hegel must mean something specialized by the term. The newborn child, he says, is not "actual." He hints at what he means. First, we have the "concept" of something (the child, in this metaphor) at the beginning. The concept is general, and we don't yet know what is to develop out of it. In particular, with regard to subjects (agents): they must seek to *adequate themselves* to the concept (or, more loosely, to their idea of themselves). The question: Does (and how does) anything follow from the "form" of such a concept? We come to see that the child in the species "normally" (not just statistically) develops into an adult. This is a fact-stating norm. The newborn is not yet, for example, a language user, but "user of language" lies in the form of the child who will develop into a language user.

(In ¶55, as an aside, Hegel notes that " 'Idea' means neither more nor less than 'kind,' or 'species.' ") Determining what Hegel means by "concept" is one of the fulcrums around which competing interpretations of this book and Hegel in general turn. At various points in other works, Hegel notes that his use of *Wirklichkeit* (more like just "reality" in everyday usage) is special. It is his preferred rendering of Aristotle's *energeia*, which we render typically in English as "actuality." *Wirklichkeit* also has to do with *Wirken*, to have an effect. *Wirklich ist das, was wirkt*, he says, in his *Philosophy of Right*. (Actuality is what works; or actuality is what is at work.)

¶13. The "concept" at first is there for us in its simplicity, and what follows from its "form" is not yet clear. It also seems to be a claim that not only do certain distinctions follow from the logical form of a concept (as expressed in a judgment), the form itself develops, and as the form develops, so does the content. But what does that mean? The book is supposed to show us by example how to answer that question. But do note: Hegel is not calling for an analysis of concepts. He is asking about the development of a concept.

¶14. It's unfair to criticize a philosophical science at its very beginning. In the background to this: Hegel is talking about the current (1781–1806) buzz in philosophy: What to do with the three Kantian *Critiques*? There are lots of objections, troubles with seeing how they all hang together, etc. He says what we need to do is to carry this impetus forward, and, sotto voce, he's saying that the way to do that is not for us all to become simply Kant exegetes but rather "post-Kantians." Note how he describes the buzz circa 1806: one side crows about all it has accomplished (the post-Kantians so far: Reinhold, Fichte, Schelling, et al.), and the other side is busy puffing itself up with its feelings about the absolute, etc. (e.g., some early Romantics). The one side crowing about what it's done is a bit undone by the fact that every year or so, somebody publishes a new "system" that claims to have finally resolved all the post-Kantian debates, only to be superseded by another claiming to do the same thing but differently and better. After a while, we all get bored with the new "systems" arriving at our doorsteps. Implicitly, Hegel is saying to his readers: Why take my "system" here any differently? I know by now you have good reasons to arch an eyebrow at mention of the arrival of yet another system.

¶15. We have the first of several swipes at Schelling, the Schellingians, and the odd assortment of *Naturphilosophen* of his day. The argument is that they more or less just have a formula which they apply to everything (as some later commentators thought that Hegel had a formula of thesis/antithesis/synthesis and applied it mechanically to everything). Against this, Hegel proposes what at this stage is still only a proposal, that we look at the concept of "development" and "unfolding" more carefully.

¶16. Here is the full and famous dig at Schelling's system as the night in which all cows are black. Schelling's so-called absolute is empty. If the absolute, as infinite, is the basis of all determination, then it must be indifferent to its finite determinations and thus be unknowable, and what is completely unknowable amounts to being a "nothing" at all. If such an "unknowable" has any determinateness on its own, then that determinateness is unintelligible. It just is what it is and can only be grasped in something like what Schelling called an intellectual intuition, something you either see or you don't. If you don't, you simply have an "incapacity to master the absolute standpoint." (Note Hegel's scorn for that.) Hegel also notes, again derisively, that this system and those like it look like they are including everything that is, but in fact they are doing little more than mechanically and superficially pigeonholing everything into a few tired, preestablished formulas.

Hegel and Schelling had been good friends in their seminary years, but in their time together in Jena, the friendship started unraveling. Schelling, already famous, began putting himself on a pedestal high above his not yet famous friend. Schelling left Jena for a better job, and Hegel had to stay behind with almost no job at all. After reading this, Schelling never really forgave Hegel, and the friendship cooled considerably.

¶17. "In my view, which must be justified by the exposition of the system itself, everything hangs on apprehending and expressing the true not just as *substance* but equally as *subject*."

Lots of interpretive energy has to be spent on that sentence, and the rest of the book is in one sense only a fleshing out of what is meant there.

But before we get to fleshing it out, here are some points to get us going.

Until Kant (or maybe Locke, who speaks of "thinking substance"), the highest category for most philosophers was the category of substance. Aristotle, in his *Categories*, says that everything is either a substance or an accident of a substance. Thus, we get the older questions about substance: How many of them are there? Mind, body, God? Just mind and body? Or only one substance with different appearances, à la Spinoza?

So we might take what Hegel is saying to be, roughly, that not only is the true system something like Aristotle's metaphysics (substance), the true system must also have an equally important place for self-consciousness (subject) in it. In the *Logic*, written a few years later, Hegel says: "It is one of the profoundest and truest insights to be found in the Critique of Reason that the *unity* which constitutes the *essence of the concept* is recognized as the *original synthetic* unity *of apperception*, the unity of the '*I think*,' or of self-consciousness."[1] The other major point about this is that once one finds a place for self-consciousness in the system, everything changes. Self-consciousness involves, as Hegel puts it elsewhere, taking purposes *as* purposes. The Kantian idea that all consciousness is self-consciousness is the idea that all thinking, all action must be accompanied by a sense that you know what it is that you are doing. Self-consciousness will thus not be "consciousness of an object." Hegel also speaks of the subject/predicate form. They are distinguishable but not separable. The judgment is not the mechanical bringing-together of two different things or as two different representations (taken as mental states or events). It expresses an "identity," that is, within the various semblances that the object of judgment takes. The "parts" of a judgment play an organic role within the judgment.

Hegel's question is Kant's question: What forms of thought are necessary for apprehending what is other than thought?

So what does it mean to say that everything hangs on understanding the truth not merely as substance but also as subject?

The true is the whole. The absolute is a result. One cannot in philosophy separate the conclusion from the process of reaching it. So what do these assertions amount to?

¶18. Living substance is subject: the living organism does what it does because of the kind of organism it is, which looks contradictory. The liver removes toxins, which is an effect of the liver, but removing toxins is the reason (actually, one of many reasons) the liver exists. It looks like an effect explaining the cause, but that's not the case. In a living organism, the organs can fail to do what it is that they are supposed to do, and the failure requires an understanding of the whole of the organism. The failing organ and the organ doing what it is supposed to do both obey the same physical/chemical laws. The difference between the organism and a machine is that the organism does this to itself, whereas the machine requires an artificer. This kind of teleology is unavoidable, so Hegel will later argue. The organism is thus the "subject" of its activities. "Life" is a substance of sorts that articulates itself into species, eventually into organisms that serve as the subject of their activities, and then eventually into self-conscious life, which is a subject of its activities in an altered sense.

¶19. Hegel can't resist heaping more scorn on the idea that this can all be understood through some kind of unmediated grasp of the absolute. He also makes a point about the "form" of a self-conscious life. That specific form is to be at odds with oneself such that one is compelled by virtue of the form to work out things for oneself (and one does that, so it will turn out, only by recognizing oneself in others). The "form" of self-conscious life is not something that is general and has some instances (in human shape). Rather, it is the form by which human agents shape themselves into the form of life of subjects (i.e., agents). To ignore the logical form of subjectivity is tantamount to falling into banality, pretentiousness, or worse. Our form is such that we develop into the kind of creature whose form is to be aware of and act self-consciously in light of our form. Our form, so we might say, is developmental. The next few paragraphs elaborate on this.

¶20. "The true is the whole. However, the whole is only the essence completing itself through its own development." Note how this has a structure similar to that of an action. X is doing something, X has done something, X will be doing something—except that there is no actor at work who has formed anything like an intention. We have purposiveness without there necessarily being action or an actor.

¶21. We have a shift of focus onto mediation: the Schellingians (and all who claim to have noninferential knowledge of the absolute) have misunderstood the conception of mediation. (Note the term indicates how you move in a syllogism: one looks for the "middle," the "mediating" term that links the premises and the conclusion.) Some form of mediation is self-conscious: one cannot be engaged in any form of activity without having a knowledge of what one is doing. This self-consciousness need not be reflective (as if in opening the door, one had to have another accompanying mental act, "I am opening the door," which would set off an infinite regress). The self-conscious subject ("I") is "pure negativity." It is what it is in distinguishing itself from itself and from others. It distinguishes itself while staying self-same. Hegel will call this "the difference that is no difference." Note too how something mediated can itself become a new immediacy, which is to say, something that works like an anchor for other things still on the move. It itself doesn't seem to be moving, but that is just because it is itself the result of previous movement.

¶22. Hegel's main point here in speaking of "purpose" is this: the sphere of the purposive is wider than that of the intentional-*geistig*, "minded." Plants may be purposive but not "minded." In our case, as self-conscious organisms, we act in light of our purposes. As the "self," it is "pure actuality" (*Wirklichkeit*, Aristotle's *energia*), it is what is really "at work" in the process. Otherwise, the phases of an action would be a mere heap, a bundle at best, of highly specific individual events. (Think: I'm [in the process of] cooking dinner; I'm not done yet, but by eight I will have completed it.) The self is "negativity," like Sartre's famous example of the waiter. At any given point, the waiter might embark on something else and cease to be "the waiter." The action of sustaining oneself as the "waiter" is such that one can succeed at it, then fail at it, or perhaps reject it. When you set out to be a "waiter," you haven't yet become one, you're in progress to being one, and then maybe you complete the project and "return into self," in Hegel's terms. ("Return into self" = action completed.) Maybe you really become a waiter. You're not ironic about it or anything like that. But you are never "completely" a waiter.

¶23. Hegel here makes a point about the grammatical and the logical form of propositions and how it can be, so he thinks, misleading. If we say, "God is the moral order of the world," it looks like we're using "God" as a referring expression (and thus picking him out by doing so). We then supply predicates to it to determine it. However, the point of saying something like "God is the moral order of the world" is to do no such thing. We are instead trying to develop a concept of what it is that we are talking about when we talk about God.

¶24. "Posited": the content of some such purposive activity spelled out in terms of what it is doing, what it is trying to accomplish, where it is in the process. You can be doing something with an implicit understanding, but when you "posit" that understanding, you have brought it out into a publicly observable realm that you and others can then scrutinize.

Note the way in which this can go wrong. As in ¶23, we can think of the subject as a fixed "point" of sorts and then ask what flows out of the subject. We might, for example, think of the subject as a material object with psychological states, and thus put the question in what has come to be called "Wittgensteinian arithmetic": What's the difference between an arm rising and an arm-raising? The supposed answer: raising = caused by a psychological state. Hegel rejects such a view. The explanation of events like actions have to take the subject's point of view into consideration. An action is a development with a goal to it, not just an event caused by some inner mental state.

¶25. Hegel realizes it is hard to state the issue he is after. What is the peculiar relation of self-consciousness? It is clearly not two "things" that stand in a relation to each other. Rather, *Geist*, self-conscious life, has a peculiar, specific form of self-relation. It "comports" itself to itself (it is the *sich Verhaltende*). When it comprehends this self-relation in the right way and "posits" it, it is *Wissenschaft*. That is, if self-conscious life (*Geist*) has a kind of purposiveness within its concept (and it does, since its purpose turns out at the end to be that of comprehending itself, determining what such a strange creature it is), then comprehending what it is doing in history has to take the form of a *Wissenschaft*. In particular, it will be the "science" of the *appearance* of spirit in history. A *phenomenology* looks at how the abstract *Geist* makes its appearance in the phenomenal world. At first, it looks like a kind of hidden essence underlying all the various appearances (*Erscheinungen*), which in turn suggests that perhaps these appearances are themselves only the semblance (*Schein*) of something else; but by the end of the book, we will see that it (*Geist*) *is* its appearances, there is no essence of *Geist* hiding behind the appearances, and this set of appearances is thus the unity of concept (or norm) and fact. How that works out is the subject of the book. Phenomenology is the study of appearances that turn out to be revelatory of the thing in itself (in this case, *Geist*), such that the factual development of *Geist* has these kinds of values embedded in it. This is *Geist* as "pure negativity," not another "thing" or "object" alongside all the other objects but a negation of them and a grasp of itself as their negative. As such, it is what is "minded," spiritual, *geistig*, that is doing the real work in the *Phenomenology*: "the spiritual alone is what is actual."

¶26. But if so, then the account of such a basic kind of self-relation (as *Wissenschaft*) would be a pure self-knowledge. It is "pure" in the sense of being nonempirical, not established as a generalization of observations. This makes it into a "purely" conceptual or metaphysical activity and raises the stakes for what counts as validating such conceptual activities. It would be the knowledge of the intelligibility of what is (the Greek ideal). Thus, we have a right, Hegel says, to be provided with a "ladder" to reach this point. So theory and "the natural consciousness" (that of everyday people as caught up in their present social assignments) have to be brought to bear on each other. How is that to be done? It can't be done just by showing "natural consciousness" that what it states implies something different, but that it itself needs whatever it is that this new "science" is promising to deliver.

¶27. Hegel gives us a preview of what is to come and why it may be difficult to make out what he's doing. He is presenting a *Wissenschaft*, but, as the *Wissenschaft* of *Geist*, it will be unlike other sciences. We can't simply lay down a "method" or a "research project" (or "set of instructions") and then see how things fit into it. *Geist* is aiming at itself, but the target itself keeps moving by virtue of the way it aims at itself. You can't just say: here's what *Geist* is, now let's see how other viewpoints get it wrong. The *Wissenschaft* can only be a *Wissenschaft* of *Geist* if it understands how it came to the very idea of itself as a *Wissenschaft* in the first place. This is one of the reasons that one can't write a "preface" to the book. Being on the developmental journey is the nature of this peculiar *Wissenschaft*.

¶28. Here we have a reference to the universal individual, the world-spirit. The thesis here is that we can view self-conscious life in terms of the needs of the species in various ways. The world-spirit is the most general way. But unlike other species (e.g., "the" goldfish, also a singular item, an "individual"), the most general way of speaking of the species *Geist* has to do with all the specificities of the history of the species. Before a certain point, there are only a few generalities one can make about the species as such, the universal individual. This comes to the fore in ¶29.

¶29. If in fact the *form* of existing subjects is to be distinguished from their existence, then the forms themselves—here this is no more than an assertion on Hegel's part, since the case for it has not been made—are historically and socially indexed. *Wissenschaft* is the study of these historical forms, and it is done for the sake of comprehending what spirit is. The stated thesis which is yet to be demonstrated is: what shape spirit now takes is a matter of how it got to the place it is—it is path dependent—and to understand why one shape gives way to another, we have to "linger" over each one. As he says, it "cannot have reached consciousness about itself in any lesser way." It will try to comprehend its own "substance," which will be a material world united in experience as falling under certain concepts and of itself as self-conscious, purposive life.

¶30. We mentioned that Hegel created his own technical vocabulary to make his points. Here a couple of his ordinary German terms come to take on specialized meanings for the purpose of his exposition. Hegel speaks here of *Vorstellung*, representational thought, which he will come to contrast with conceptual thought (or just "the concept," *der Begriff*). Because of the subject-predicate form of judgment, we are tempted to suppose that our explanations must always seek some kind of basic substrate that explains the appearances of which it is the substrate. *Vorstellung* as representational thought operates with "the understanding" (which Hegel contrasts with "reason"), which subsumes particulars (or data) under general concepts and then seeks to make those judgments consistent with each other.

Another feature of *Vorstellung* is that exclusive reliance on it leads us to think of judgment as "subsuming" judgment. Subsuming judgments works until one puts them to work at the level of the basic a priori concepts, and with other judgments that are not "subsumptions" but ways of showing what the general supporting meanings behind *Geist*'s activities are. Hegel notes that the sublation of the human forms of life—each human form of life is like a subspecies of the human unto itself in that the concept of "life" itself becomes embodied in practices in all kinds of different ways—does not mean that the *existence* of the individual is also sublated (canceled but still preserved). What is left is a *Vorstellung* of the forms and a familiarity with them. Overreliance on *Vorstellung* tends to see the human forms of life as general concepts under which things fall, and it treats those concepts as items in a subsumptive judgment, when in fact they function like a priori concepts setting the bounds of sense for a form of life. The "universal self" is *Geist*, self-conscious life as nominalized (in a way analogous to the way we nominalize species when we speak of "the gazelle" or "the oak").

¶31. The *Bekannte* (the familiar, the well known) is not for all that *erkannt* (known, cognized). We do not fully grasp the tensions in our thought, ultimately, our own way of life, until we think philosophically (or metaphysically) about them. (It will turn out that there are also other ways of comprehending those same tensions more fully, namely, art and religion. Their relation to and subordination to philosophy turns out to be one of the key disputes in the *Phenomenology*.) The "familiar" serves as our "intuitive grasp" of things (our settled convictions and our never fully self-conscious ways of understanding the background of meanings in which we move), and when pushed, we tend to treat these meanings as if they were unmovable first premises. Hegel's thesis: they are anything but unmovable first premises.

¶32. Hegel speaks of the "power of the negative"—this is one of the most often cited lines from the Preface. In general, the negative is that which we bring to bear to distinguish something from something else. Robert Brandom makes very good use of this to articulate the first three chapters of the book.[2] He argues that Hegel sees that in addition to formal negation (not-A), there is also a material negation (which he identifies with Hegel's "determinate negation"), what he calls "material incompatibility" (such as from "is red" one may infer to "is not green"). For Brandom, the fundamental unit of sense is a "judgment" (which for him is taking on a commitment), and thus to be conceptually "contentful" is to stand in relations of material incompatibility and compatibility. Not-A as a determinate negation is not just everything that is other than A. (A religious rebellion is not a prime number, not a cabbage, etc.) For Brandom, this logic reflects the way the world is. (If "red" materially implies "not green," that's because red things can't also be green.) But for Brandom, all this is just ordinary "inferring" and cleaning up whatever incompatibilities we run across as we survey our commitments. For Brandom, we can't adequately predict in advance (as the finite creatures we are) where we will run into such incompatible commitments, and when we do, we are logically committed to cleaning up the incompatibility.

In my view, this is not what Hegel is really after, although it is an important insight on Brandom's part, and he uses it skillfully to clean up various Hegelian puzzles. Hegel is interested in the "conceptual" or "metaphysical" disputes that seem to generate their opposites, where the kind of ordinary "cleaning up" we do is not appropriate or often seems beside the point. The various sides of such conceptual disputes generate each other, much as Kant thought the two sides of an antinomy were supposed to generate each other. Like Kant, Hegel thinks that the incompatibilities arise for these kinds of metaphysical-conceptual matters necessarily, and not just as a feature of our finite ignorance or our having unwittingly stumbled into a set of mutually contradictory claims. (One could make something like the same case for Wittgenstein, but that would be out of place here.) If "the understanding" focuses on the (sometimes reflective) application of concepts to data given by "intuition," then "reason" focuses on the kinds of concepts that seem to be a priori and not as a matter of generalizing from data. For Brandom, that amounts to saying that "reason" is a matter of drawing inferences (and that the "the understanding" can function only within the system of reason). (But think of Kant's discussion of beauty in the third *Critique*: "Beauty" behaves like a norm but can't be specified in terms of inferences. You can't lay down a rule for counting something as beautiful.) For Hegel, this kind of negativity is fluid. We are always explaining something in terms of something else, until we reach "self-consciousness," which is supposed to explain itself in understanding how it sets its own limits and is what it is in the process of defining itself in terms of reasons. Thought defines itself as setting its own limits, not having them imposed on it by an alien authority. In "making sense of making sense," thought is making sense of itself. It is the "difference that is no difference." It is self-negating.

The negative sets the bounds of something, the point at which it no longer is what it is. In the trivial sense, the stream becomes a river, a ragged mass of matter becomes a planet, etc. But what are the bounds of sense? When we make sense of making sense, are we reading those limits off of Platonic heaven as we observe it?[3] Or is thought (reason) setting its own bounds, as Kant suggests? If the latter, then thought is self-bounding, and if so, then it is "absolute negativity." The limits of sense are those where we encounter not a barrier (with something on the other side) but real limits (i.e., at the limit we start speaking non-sense). In Hegel's use, "negativity" usually marks some conception or shape of life's one-sidedness, its failure, etc., and its negativity is supposed to drive itself forward to something positive that emerges out of its failures.

¶33. The distinction between pure concepts as setting the bounds of sense and ordinary "concepts" (representations) as generalizations (or something like that) of ordinary experience appears again. Kant's categories, for example, cannot be justified as generalizations. Hegel says that "the former determinations have the I, the power of the negative, that is, pure actuality, as their substance and as the element of their existence." This is an oblique invocation of something like Kant's conception of the synthetic unity of apperception, the "I think" that must accompany all my representations, and the various categories (pure thoughts, forms of unity) that make it possible for the "I think" to do that.

¶34. The movement of the content (how one such a priori concept necessitates a new statement of itself or materially implies another concept) is structured so that earlier versions, at least in time, are seen as imperfect versions of the later concept, not just different ones. Hegel is here rejecting a widely held modern view: the existing public criteria in any specific period for possessing a concept and mastering it simply are the meaning of the concept. On Hegel's view, the Greek concept of, for example, the state is not simply different from our use (which it is) but is an imperfect, not fully developed concept of the state.

¶35. Hegel makes a point that he couldn't really expect his readers to understand. The *Phenomenology* is a *Wissenschaft* that is only the opening salvo in a more comprehensive *Wissenschaft*. But since Hegel hadn't yet published the other parts of the *Wissenschaft* (the first part of which was the *Science of Logic*, the first part of which only appeared five years later), no reader could really know what he was talking about.

¶36. We have a short description of what will be the science of the "experience" of consciousness (or of the "learning experience" of consciousness). Objectivity is the "negativity" of "knowing": knowing calibrates itself to objects that it takes to set its limits for itself. The objectivity, for example, at which astrophysics aims is set by the universe itself, and astrophysics measures itself in terms of that. But since all consciousness is (not necessarily self-reflective) self-consciousness (Kant's synthetic unity of apperception), the objectivity at which spirit aims is set by itself, and that makes it a moving target. As spirit determines itself (in terms of its *Gestaltung*, its "shape" or form), it takes on a different shape. As it takes on this different shape, it "returns to itself," having given itself this new form. The "form" of the social substance that is, say, early modern Europe upends itself as it comes to understand how unlivable it has become (as it comes to a fuller self-consciousness).

¶37. Hegel speaks of the inequality (*Ungleichheit*) of the substance with itself. This is a reinterpretation of Kant's idea that what is wrong with an action has to do with the contradictoriness of the maxim. For Hegel, it is not the maxim, but "the substance itself" (a form of social life) that is at odds with itself. The question: What is it for the substance to be in "inequality" with itself? (Equality with itself = *Sichselbstgleicheit*.) Here's one way of taking this: Hegel wants to shift Kant's idea of a maxim's being self-contradictory to the idea of a form of life (a "substance") being at odds with itself and therefore in a deep sense self-contradictory. The norms to which we hold ourselves and each other put some kind of irrational stress on us. The contradiction has to do not with the form of the maxim itself but with how it is held and made operative by those working within a form of life. The individual acts by actors in a shape of life *show* what is at work in the practice; they do not describe what is at work.

There is his view that such disparities (self-inequality) in the "substance" lead to breakdowns of historically specific forms of life, such that it becomes something else. Although there is one "substance" within all the different forms of life, namely, *Geist*, *Geist* nonetheless sets its own conditions such that it has to *make itself* the "substance" behind the ways it must appear in the concrete world. This does not exclude the view that in all these circumstances, *Geist* is limited by the material conditions under which it works.

On that view, the inequality of *Geist* with itself is the way in which a historically specific form of life is at odds with itself at the deepest level. It is at its basis a deeply irrational form of life. It also finds it hard to get at this since it is always expressing what is most deeply at work in itself, and the way in which it is at odds with itself is not immediately apparent but only comes into sight as the form of life works itself out in its development over time.

If *Geist* is indeed equivalent to self-conscious life, then self-conscious *Geist* is more explicitly self-conscious, and part of his view is that as self-conscious life becomes more explicitly conscious of itself, its internal contradictions become more difficult to navigate and to endure. So it seems, Hegel's phenomenological *Wissenschaft* will be the discursive articulation of what would otherwise only be the nondiscursive *showing* of what is at work in forms of life. This is the logic of the phenomenology he has written, which is itself "speculative philosophy," a way of comprehending how what at first seem to be mutually exclusive concepts or representations are in fact both essential components of a more organically unified whole.

¶38. Here we have the theme of why a preface to a book like this is not really possible (and here we are at ¶38 of the impossible preface). It's easy to sympathize with those who, on looking at the size of the book and density of its prose, would want to ask, say, one of us: So what has Hegel proved? And hope to get an answer like, "Hegel has proved that the true is just as much subject as it is substance" (at which they would ask, "And what does that mean?"). This can't be done, and it's worth pausing for a while, so Hegel says, to think about why it can't be done. The answer has to do with the "negative" and with the nature of what one is doing in philosophy.

¶39. Hegel says, "To be sure, we can know falsely." This is Hegel's "phenomenal" statement of knowledge (as something like warranted belief). Nowadays, we'd be inclined not to speak in this way, and contemporary philosophers like to say that one simply by definition cannot know falsely. After all, to know falsely is what? To know an object, the false? Hegel says: "For something to be known falsely means that knowledge is in inequality with its substance." If we "know falsely," we are asserting a warranted belief that X is the case, but X is not the case. Thus, we'd nowadays be more inclined to say that we therefore don't *know* that X is not the case. But Hegel says instead that we are asserting something on the basis of the warrants we have, which are embedded in the social space (the substance) of our subjectivity but which are false.

This is very similar to what has been called the disjunctivist approach to things such as perception: when I perceive falsely, I don't perceive something that isn't there, I simply fail to perceive.

¶40. Hegel distinguishes the kinds of ordinary truths we seek from the more convoluted ones we seem to be working with in philosophy.

¶41. We need reasons to justify what we say about things. Even when we are gathering facts about things in the study of history, we have to bring into play all kinds of evidentiary and reason-giving capacities.

¶42. Hegel seems to be noting that mathematical and geometrical proof is not purposive in the way that a *Wissenschaft* about *Geist* is. *Geist* develops, and we don't understand *Geist* unless we also understand the development and what the agents took themselves to be doing—not just what happened but what the actors in question took themselves to be doing and what they turned out really to be doing. That's not the case with the mathematical proofs. Hegel seems to be adopting a somewhat "intuitionist" conception of mathematics here (*avant la lettre*, so this is an anachronism to ascribe to him here). He seems to be saying that mathematics does not *analyze* a prior reality into its components. The truths are constructs (although necessary and a priori) out of some more basic rational capacity. The object of the proof is what it is outside of the proof. That's not the case with *Geist*.

¶43. The content in the geometrical proof is defective, Hegel says, by which he seems to mean that the kind of dissection that one does in old-fashioned Euclidean geometry is itself meaningless vis-à-vis the object being constructed unless there is a self-consciousness about what one is doing in constructing the proof—what he calls "the negativity of the content." Unless I do the proof—get out the straight edge, fix the compass, etc.—I can't be said to have a proof.

¶44. The theme of the lack of purposiveness in geometrical and mathematical proofs returns. In the kind of purposive accounts Hegel is proposing, there is something like, say, a capacity that has to actualize itself along a certain path. There is nothing corresponding to "actualization" in the geometrical proof. So if you want to prove Goldbach's conjecture—every even integer greater than two is the sum of two prime numbers—one needs to set out to find some things from which it will follow so that the conjecture is true (proven). There is no teleology to this, even if it turns out that there was only one way to do the proof. (Hegel never talks about Goldbach's conjecture, as far as I know. But he could have known it.) Hegel concludes from this that mathematical cognition, good as it is, is defective as a complete account of cognition since it has no place for such purposive accounts. (And as of this writing, Goldbach's conjecture is still just that—a conjecture.)

¶45. Here we have Hegel's reflection on why mathematics and geometry are not the proper models for the kind of philosophy he is proposing. In geometry, we get pi, thus an "infinite" that cannot be comprehended. But his point there, roughly, is that the concept of magnitude is the basic concept at work in mathematics, and magnitude is not equivalent to time, nor is it an idealization of time. Philosophy, as it were, concerns the foundations of mathematics, not with mathematical proofs.

¶46. Time and mathematics have traditionally been associated with each other, but time is special, so Hegel thinks. He says that "time is the existing concept itself," by which he means that in time itself we have something like the speculative unity of discreteness and continuity that is one of the hallmarks of speculative thought. Things are discrete, and things are continuous, but it would seem that they cannot be both. Time, however, is the unity of discreteness and continuity.

¶47. That "discreteness/continuity" metaphor (of the infinite) reappears again in Hegel's famous line that "the true is the bacchanalian revel (*Taumel*), where not a member is sober." There's another way of taking the idea of the *Taumel* (the revel). The Greek word for comedy (as in Aristophanes's comedies, about which Hegel later says nothing could be better) is that of a singing revel (a revel in odes). So maybe the truth isn't just a revel, but a kind of comedy. (See Aristophanes's *Thesmophoria*.)

¶48. Hegel throws down the gauntlet: philosophy is not best pursued by producing a theory, giving an argument, and then using it to refute one's opponents (i.e., the way we mostly do it nowadays). That raises the stakes considerably for him.

¶49. Just because one attempts to put philosophy into an approachable form and eschew the pomposity that sometimes comes along with it doesn't mean that we have to give up on rigor.

¶50. You will read all the time about Hegel's system as consisting of thesis-antithesis-synthesis. Here is Hegel's rather withering dismissal of such nonsubstantive formalisms as thesis-antithesis-synthesis.

¶51. Yet another slightly peevish swipe at the "nature-philosophers" and the Schellingians. They divide the world into triplicities, and once you have divided the world into three categories, you can always find something interesting to say about some of the things within those categories. Worse, they treat these arbitrary groupings as if they were explanatory, as if what was really at work in the natural world were these triplicities. Even worse still, they then say that what is really at work in these triplicities is the "absolute," like a monochromatic painting that is all white absorbing everything into itself.

¶52. Even what is best in philosophy can't avoid its views being taken up by others and put into a form that amounts to being flayed and having one's skin used as a backdrop for some fatuous use. Nonetheless, what is best there still sometimes shines through its frivolous use.

¶53. The real sense of the triadic scheme is this: the "content becomes an other to itself" (the bounds that determine the content, meaning, as what it is turn out to demand explication as not being some determinate other; the other of bird is not, e.g., triangle but its contrary, say, reptiles or mammals); it "takes this unfolding back into itself" (what it is to be this kind, or this law, or this inference is set by its relations of negation: it cannot be a reptile if it is a mammal); "it makes itself into a moment" (its meaning is now set by its place in a developing whole of such meanings).

The simple notion of judgment as subsuming something under a predicate already presupposes what it is subsuming as having a determinate content. Kant tried to come to terms with that by claiming that intuition had a priori content (space and time). Hegel argues elsewhere that this subjectivizes knowledge as dependent on our own intuitive apparatus. Space and time belong to the philosophy of nature as the way in which nature is a priori conceived as being divided into magnitudes and differences.

¶54. The proper way of understanding "being is thought": this might sound as if we infer from thought to being (or from the idea of something to its existing). The point is, however, that the gap between true thought and being isn't there. True thought doesn't stop short of being. If something is, it is intelligible to thought. (This is an ancient Greek notion.)

¶55. Hegel gives his own riff on explanations by substrata. Fine in their own way, he says. But such explanations eventually run up against a priori concepts—this was Kant's point—that are not themselves substrates of anything but are rather "kinds" that require a more logical treatment. What goes on in such a logic of kinds is a matter of the self-dissolution of judgments about the absolute (or, to put it another way, about the limits of sense). Thus, Hegel says of *nous*, the basic substrate for Anaxagoras, that it's not really a substrate at all but simply thought itself: "that it has its otherness in itself and that it is self-moving are contained in that *simplicity* of thinking itself, for this is the self-moving and self-distinguishing thought, the thought which is its own inwardness, which is the pure *concept*."

¶56. The "kind" of basic thing that something is in this "account of all accounts" has to do with its logical form, that is, the form in which the world shows itself as intelligible to thought. It is *logic* because it concerns itself with the principles of pure thought, not with empirical objects of investigation (as do the other sciences). If logic is the science of sense-making—nothing that contravenes logic makes any sense—then this kind of logic is an investigation of the way in which, ultimately, *Geist* makes sense of *Geist*.

¶57. This kind of developmental logic—of our actualization of the capacities of self-consciousness—is one in which form (logic, the science of pure thinking) and content (reference to possible objects) fuse. It will be the successor, so Hegel seems to think, to Kant's transcendental logic.

¶58. Hegel concedes that this may make people uneasy. It seems excessively abstract, and it requires careful attention to terms. It also requires that we pay attention to the limits of sense-making, since it is all too easy to think we are making sense when in fact we are merely saying things that make us think that what we want to be true is in fact true.

¶59. Hegel takes a shot at the kind of "above it all" or superironic stance that thinks that it is thereby really committed to nothing intrinsically except its own activity of committing itself. Hegel says of such a view that "it is the negative which catches no glimpse of the positive within itself." The negativity of self-consciousness—its not being completely absorbed in its object or activity but instead knowing that it is engaged in that activity—is there but that is all there is. "I can always step back from any commitment," says this person, and that leaves him/her with . . . nothing. There's just self-consciousness, I = I, empty.

¶60. Hegel brings up in an oblique way a Kantian issue. Pure thinking looks as if it's just pure logic (if p, then q; p; therefore q). In that case, all content has to be supplied externally to such thinking activity. The Kantian-Hegelian proposal is that there is a peculiar, ownmost content to such thought that is the subject of transcendental logic (Kant) or "phenomenology" or "dialectic" (Hegel). This can't be construed as an independent subject taking on attributes but as a subject that is what it is in developing itself into what it is ("not a motionless subject tranquilly supporting the accidents; rather, it is the self-moving concept which takes its determinations back into itself"). The world shows itself to such a subject, but how does the subject show itself to itself as having the world show itself to it?

¶61. The topic is the "speculative judgment." The key idea here is therefore that substance as substratum or as some kind of final subject at the end of the chain of justification would be indifferent to everything. As standing above all determination and issuing forth such determinations from itself, it would be itself indeterminate (the object of the monochromatic painting). But what is indifferent to everything but has no determination itself? Well, it's Nothing. Note too in ¶56 where Hegel identifies the speculative with the idea that reason sets its own tribunal (or as he puts it, that thought is self-moving). In his lectures on Aristotle, Hegel identifies the "speculative" with *theoria* (in Greek).

¶62. Note that Hegel thinks that we can be under the illusion that we are making sense when we make some of these kinds of "nature-philosophy" judgments. It is the kind of illusion that persists even when we know it's an illusion.

¶63. In speaking of the "philosophical proposition," Hegel might seem to be suggesting that it is somehow esoteric, beyond normal comprehension. That is far from the case. It is something having to do with the limits thought imposes on itself, which form the limits of sense, beyond which is . . . nonsense, nonthought.

¶64. Hegel warns us not to conflate clever argumentation with "speculative" (dialectical) practice. Hegel doesn't go much more into it in this paragraph, but I think what he's driving at is something like the following. The ordinary propositions of "clever argumentation" say something is or is not the case. When we get to the a priori level (that of our most basic concepts that lie at the roots of the basic forms of life), we are not doing the same kind of thing. We are trying to bring out what is at work in the form of life in propositional form and see if its developmental trajectory ends up in contradictions or irrationalities of a different sort. In the case of the "speculative" propositions, we have the idea (itself to be developed) that such and such a claim would not be intelligible without (some further successor claim) such that the two together shift the meaning slightly of the first proposition, and what looked contradictory turns out to be (at first) in order in this new shape. In the more ordinary case (e.g., the empirical cases), if we have a contradiction, we have to discard one of the sides or redefine it or something like that, but the idea that the meaning of the proposition is fixed and is intelligible on its own remains. An example of a speculative proposition in Hegel's sense thus might be something like: "The I is a We, and the We is an I." This sounds like it is saying that the singular is the plural, and the plural is the singular, which, put like that, to many ears sounds like nonsense. But Hegel's point is that these two concepts (first-person singular, first-person plural) only make sense when both are considered in terms of the whole to which they contribute sense and from which they draw their own sense.

¶65. Hegel expands on that theme. We are not simply adding up all our commitments, seeing which ones stand in contradiction to the others, and then taking the appropriate steps. Nothing wrong with that, as Hegel says: "non-speculative thinking also has its rights, which are valid but which are ignored in the speculative proposition." What we are to do is to see how these terms develop as they are shown in the practices that they shape (and how they in turn are shaped—that is, developed—by the actors acting in light of the practices): "this oppositional movement must be given expression." We are not called to exercise some esoteric capacity (e.g., "intellectual intuition"). But he does call on us to look at his conception of what "truth" truly is. In one form, it is simply stating what is the case. But, as the *Logic* will later make more clear, this operates in a different way once we are in the province of subjectivity (i.e., no longer looking at the logic of being or essence but that of "concept"), where we have the concept of something as its "standard," a kind of fact-stating evaluation of a living thing. That's why he says, " 'the true' is subject. As this subject, it is only the dialectical movement, this course of self-engendering, advancing, and then returning into itself." This is what a subject is, and it constitutes what it 'ought' to be, and in Hegel's usage, a living thing, a human agent, even a whole social practice, can fail to actualize its concept.

¶66. It would be easy (and many have done it) to think that Hegel really is recommending that we exercise some kind of esoteric capacity to grasp dialectic, so he says: "it is worth remembering that the dialectical movement likewise has propositions for its parts or elements." But he restates his point about dialectic again: "there is no kind of content that comes forward which behaves as an underlying subject." The subject of the book—*Geist*—is *not* a substrate underlying appearance. This is also a Kantian point: it would be wrong to think that from the "I think" we can infer to an underlying immaterial entity that supports all these thoughts.

¶67. Another obstacle to doing this kind of speculative philosophy is this: since people live and breathe in the social practices in which they have been brought up, and which they manifest in all their various acts, they often think that they already know these things in a good-enough way. What this shows, so Hegel says, is that philosophy must itself become a *Wissenschaft*, indeed, the science that all the other sciences need. It's of course a bit odd for Hegel to be claiming this, since Kant et al. had made philosophy into the kind of *Wissenschaft* that requires being taught in universities. Philosophy has to be "professionalized" in that sense. (Hegel thought this would be a good thing. It's not clear to me that we have to agree with him on that point.)

¶68. Hegel continues his tirade against those at the time who think of philosophy as kind of inspired thinking untethered by argument.

¶69. We have one more dismissal of the Romantic, inspiration-above-thinking mode of doing philosophy.

¶70. There is no "royal road" to *Wissenschaft*, no shortcut for those in the know. Those who think that they are on the "royal road" perhaps keep up on what's going on in philosophy by reading the reviews, maybe the prefaces to works, and some other things. Not so, says Hegel. If you don't get the development of the position, you don't really get the philosophy.

¶71. Hegel gives us a slightly gloomy and a little bit cynical prediction about how his work will be received. If the trends of the time really are as he describes them, then there's not much hope that people will take the time and trouble to figure out what he's saying. Still, you have to hope based on a practical faith that truth will prevail. You also have to hope that what seems as if it might just be your own little hobby-horse will turn out to have wider significance. And, once again, you have to hope that the "public" will be more open-minded than they are said to be by their self-appointed representatives in the world of journals.

¶72. The theme of revolutionary times comes up again in this closing section. The world is awash in the putative universality of the ideal of science and of the ideals of the French Revolution with its proclamations of the Rights of Man. There seem to be some great currents afloat, some great social forces at work, and the role of an individual author in this vast movement is bound to be small, even inconsequential. All you can do is do what you must, do it well, and hope for the best.

2

The Introduction

The Preface was written after Hegel had completed the *Phenomenology* (i.e., already completed his "voyage of discovery"). The Introduction was written as he was beginning the *Phenomenology*, when he still thought of the book as "Part One: The Science of the Experience of Consciousness." We are at the beginning of the voyage, and we've got an idea of what we will discover. (Do note again that experience in this sense is *Erfahrung*, as in the phrase "learn from experience," not in the sense of what is intimately undergone in the privacy of one's own heart.) The voyage begins, and even the author does not yet know it will end in a "phenomenology of spirit" rather than just a "science of the experience of consciousness."

¶73. It comes easily to us to think that in philosophy, we first have to ask for something like a "criterion of knowledge" that we can apply to various statements. If we had such a criterion, we could then know in advance whether something was even a candidate for being known. This stems from a kind of classical version of skepticism: how can I know that my representation of reality corresponds to reality itself?

However, behind that, the more general question at first seems to be: What is the line between thought and what thought is about? How is it drawn, who or what draws it?

Hegel wants to suggest (a little ironically) that the proper way to put it is:

Suppose that what we want to know if (and especially) the "absolute" (or the "unconditioned") is cut off from us such that we cannot know it.

Or suppose that the absolute cooperates with us (as in some of our own current talk about the world "making" something true, or "cooperating with us").

Perhaps knowledge (*Erkenntnis*, cognition) is an instrument, perhaps it is a medium. Does it make sense to speak of subtracting

Hegel's Phenomenology of Spirit. Terry Pinkard, Oxford University Press. © Oxford University Press 2023. DOI: 10.1093/oso/9780197663127.003.0002

whatever it is the instrument changes or that the medium distorts so that we end up with the thing itself? If we do, what are we left with? Nothing.

In any event:

To draw a line between thought and the world is to stand on both sides of the line.

This is of course reminiscent of Wittgenstein's "preface" to his *Tractatus*: "To set a limit to thought, we should have to find both sides of the limit thinkable (i.e., we should have to be able to think what cannot be thought)." (For the curious: there is no reason at all to think that Wittgenstein got any of that from Hegel.)

¶74. Hegel speaks of people in his time having a mistrust of *Wissenschaft*. This seems to be a mistrust of all philosophy that speaks of the "absolute."

But is the assertion of the primacy of the finite itself "infinite"? That is, is it a "boundless" assertion to say that the "whole" is a set of finite things? Where is the person standing who says, "The whole is finite" in order to be able to say that? Is he or she standing outside the world, a little like (some conceptions of) God?

Maybe this is all just wholly abstract, so the suspicion goes, with no consequences for anything significant. Thus, the mistrust.

But ought we mistrust the mistrust?

Such a procedure shares a certain picture of knowing as "representationalist" at its core. When we state something, so it seems, our statement (representation) might stop somewhere short of the fact. That supposedly is what happens with false statements. Why should we take that view, however "natural" it might seem to be? Hegel's view: when we say winter has arrived, if that is true, winter has arrived. The thought and the state of affairs are one. That is not the same thing as saying that the thing is identical to a psychological state of mind. It's that the thought, winter has arrived, is that winter has arrived, and winter has arrived.

We should not only ask: how do we truly judge of things? But also: how are things truly judged?

¶75. The absolute alone is true, and only the true is absolute.

Yet Hegel quite clearly thinks that something about this is wrongheaded. He says that, in fact, this just shows how little we understand what we are saying when we use these words. At this level of abstraction, we can easily be misled into thinking we have rock-solid arguments for one side or the other. Or that we think we are making sense when we are making little to no sense at all.

Maybe we can know (in some sense of "know") lots of things without knowing about the absolute. But is there a kind of internal push or teleology in reason itself that wishes to extend its knowledge to the unconditioned? Kant, for example, says that reason is pushed by itself to the "unconditioned." Part of the task Hegel sets for himself is to show that we are indeed so pushed, that it's the failure of our trying to do something else that necessitates our taking a more speculative stance. It's not that we start out asking, "What is the absolute?" and we at first fail to do so. It's that we start out asking something else (such as "What do I know with certainty?"), and it is in failing to make good on that question and failing to make good on what succeeds it that we realize that what we had been doing all along, although we could not have stated it that way at first, was looking for the absolute. What we were doing "in itself" (*an sich*) had not yet developed enough so that it could be "posited."

Note too how he says that although we might also think we already fully understand words like "cognition," "absolute," and so forth, it's not clear that we do. He's hinting at his more developed view that with regard to these basic concepts, we do not necessarily understand the full meaning just because we can master the public criteria for their use. Their meaning develops over time and over the course of inquiry.

¶76. What is *Wissenschaft*?

Note first that in Hegel's day *Wissenschaft* wasn't quite what we now call science. Theology, for example, was aspiring to be a *Wissenschaft*.

The alternatives to *Wissenschaft* might seem only to be mere appearances, but *Wissenschaft* itself is also an appearance. It's one of those things that cropped up in European culture (along with the divine right of kings, romanticism, opera, sonata form, etc.). These other modes that make the claim to *knowledge* are themselves appearances, finite, limited, maybe not really attuned to the better argument, but the same charge can be made against *Wissenschaft* itself. All of them seem to assume that one must arbitrarily start from somewhere. Hegel's point might be put in our terms as the claim that

Wissenschaft is only itself a "cultural form" alongside lots of others (religion, folk wisdom, etc.). In those cases, we have one form merely giving us an "assurance" that it, not science, is the truth. Hegel will argue that *Wissenschaft* is indeed an "appearance" in that sense, and that that does not vitiate it, once it is fairly well understood. Still, "science" has to vindicate itself beyond these others without just begging the question.

Is there "untrue" knowledge? (Is there something else that is not "cognition" that actually give us a better apprehension of the absolute? E.g., religion, art, mystical feeling?)

Is there an identity of something (the absolute?) which has various "guises" under which it appears (mystical feeling, religion, philosophy)? How does *Wissenschaft* establish itself without begging the question?

In the *Logic*, Hegel calls the pure concepts of metaphysics a *Schattenreich*, a realm of shadows. What's casting the shadows? (What's the light source?) One possible answer: the absolute.

It can't be that nonphilosophy "points to" philosophy (which would be the case if it is philosophy as a "discipline" that exclusively investigates the "presuppositions" of everything else, a conception at work in Fichte's *Wissenschaftslehre*). It's not that philosophy is the presupposition of all normal activity but that certain forms of normal activity cannot achieve the ends to which they are pushed to entertain without bringing in philosophy. (Besides, that would beg the question as to whether we are then just presupposing the truth of the experience whose presuppositions we are looking for.)

Thus, we must have an exposition-exhibition-showing (a *Darstellung*, which has these three meanings) of "phenomenal knowledge" (*erscheinende Wissen*, "appearing" knowledge).

But in doing so, as Richard Rorty used to say, are we then really only celebrating our own achievements and seeing the past as really just an earlier or failed version of ourselves?

¶77. It seems that as the *Darstellung* (exposition) of *erscheinende Wissen* (of knowledge as it appears) simply can't be the free, self-moving *Wissenschaft* in its own shape, its own gestalt. After all, in *Erscheinung* (appearance) things get moved around by other things, not completely by themselves. And it would then have to take the

Erscheinung for granted or "presuppose" it, which would undermine its claim to be a self-moving "science."

Or is the *Darstellung* that of the path of "natural consciousness" on its way to *Wissenschaft*?

What does "natural" mean here? One obvious sense is: lack of artifice, a sense of its being the "real way" to exist, as when we speak of leading a less artificial, more "natural" life.

More likely, though: it refers to the life of a self-conscious organism and the way such self-conscious organisms must conduct themselves. They are not, cannot, fully be aware of the whole context in which they are acting. They are acting in light of a background "attunement" that is more or less invisible to them. The question is whether we are just assuming that this path has a "natural," foreordained end and we are merely, as it were, listing its stops along the way.

Where do reasons run out? Wittgenstein: "I have reached bedrock, and my spade is turned. Then I am inclined to say: 'This is simply what I do.'"[1] And: "What people accept as justification shows how they think and live."[2]

A shape of self-conscious life (spirit) has its *Darstellung* (exposition) in looking at the justifications people take to be unavoidable within it. A "shape" shows itself in what people do, namely, giving justifications (among other things they do).

¶78. As natural consciousness *realizes its concept*, it finds it did not know what it thought it knew. It is not as if its path was preordained. It is that it keeps breaking down in such a way that it is logically required to take a different step, which will turn out to be the path to *Wissenschaft* without its having aimed at that.

There are at least two components to this: first, the concept's abstract meaning only becomes concrete when it is put into practice; we don't fully know what we mean until we see how our meanings work out in practice. Meaning depends on use, but meaning is not reducible to use.

The "concept" is what the thing is "in itself," and it realizes what it is in itself only over time. The concept "shows itself" in its uses, but its uses exhibit and develop the concept.

Here's one way to take "the in-itself," the *Ansich* (or *an sich* or *ansich*, as it is differently written in the book). When you grasp the concept of something "in itself," you have an idea of the trajectory along which that concept can develop.

First, natural consciousness is only "the concept" of knowledge. The "concept" must develop itself in history. Knowing what knowledge is in itself is getting a handle on the trajectory along which the concept can develop.

Second, the concept's self-realization is not that of a neat linear progress (a claim which is implicit but not fully stated in these paragraphs). Rather, it moves forward by continually breaking down and "losing" its truth.

But this suggests that it thus continually "loses" itself, as if it were false, which suggests that something else is true.

This puts us on a path of doubt, but which begins to look like a path of despair, where everything we try fails. (Hegel is making a play on two words there: *Zweifel*, doubt; *Verzweiflung*, despair.)

It is thereby a *self-consummating skepticism*—a skepticism that is so corrosive it undermines even the concept of skepticism itself. Skepticism turns out to be the negative of itself, and so it fails because it turns out to be one-sided.

One sense of negativity is that of content made intelligible only in terms of its contrastive relations with other content. The *Verstand* (the understanding) is content to occupy itself with such contrasts, and when it finds itself with incompatible commitments, it has to drop one or change the contrast. *Vernunft* (reason) is dialectical, understands that certain "negativities" (limitations, one-sided failures) are necessary and inevitable. They can't be just dropped. They have to be comprehended as having a place in the whole and dealt with as such.

¶79. To show that this skepticism is "self-consummating," we need to show that there is a necessary progression within its concept to the "truth." The various ways in which "consciousness" (and then "self-consciousness") takes itself to be itself form the progression in which there are various "stations" (or "way stations"—Hegel is using "stations" in the same sense as when one speaks of the stations of the cross), and all together they form "the path of despair."

As a way of taking itself breaks down at each "station," what consciousness finds, so it seems, is "nothingness," that is, the breakdown of "meaningfulness." (Not that all words all lose their meaning, but certain key terms as explications of the absolute lose their meaningfulness—it is the breakdown of intelligibility and the apparent breakdown of there being any point to the progression.)

This kind of loss of meaning and its replacement is *determinate negation*. It is determinate in that it is the "nothingness" of a particular form of life ("shape of consciousness"). It is the unintelligibility of *that* form, which as a form of life takes itself to be the unintelligibility of *all* forms.

Once again, it's helpful to turn to Wittgenstein's idea: "What people accept as justification shows how they think and live."[3] So what happens when how we think and live breaks down? When what we are doing doesn't make sense from our own perspective?

This is not the limited skepticism that refutes one thing and waits for the next to appear.

The general idea as announced in the last sentence: the breakdown of intelligibility is necessarily a new form of life that must live with the consequences of that breakdown. But there are new shapes, and there is a logic of sorts to the progression.

We get the idea, already there in a roundabout way in the Preface, of determinate negation. Not just the not-X, which is everything else but X, but determinate negation, such as: if this is indeed a lizard, then it is not a mammal, and not abstract negation, such as: if this is a lizard, it is not a prime number.

Hegel notes that skepticism, which throws everything into doubt, always pushes on toward the conclusion of a "nothing." Radical skepticism would be: you don't know anything; or, rephrased, you know nothing (presumably including the idea that you don't know that you know nothing). After all, determinateness has been thrown into the abyss—you don't know x, y, z—and it turns out that there is nothing that you do know. The object of knowledge is without determination— that is, nothing. But this nothing is always a "determinate nothing." It always starts from something like: well, we do know *this* (followed by: no, you don't). So it might be a skepticism that says: you don't know that God exists; of course, you do know there's a rock in the field. Next step: you do know you're seeing something, but you don't know there's a rock in the field (that's an unwarranted inference from sense data). It turns out that these kind of determinate skepticisms appear at various times in a kind of necessary progression, and such skepticism eventually swallows its own tail.

¶80. Where would such a progression end (if at all)? When concept corresponds to object, or when object corresponds to concept? Knowledge need not go beyond itself (i.e., no longer be "finite," determined by something else that is its limitation). Limits mark the point where violating it means you are no longer making sense. Limitations are like boundaries or fences; even if you cannot see what is on the other side, you know something is there.[4] As we noted earlier, Wittgenstein said in the Preface to his *Tractatus*: "To set a limit to thought, we should have to find both sides of the limit thinkable (i.e., we should have to be able to think what cannot be thought)." (Hegel would agree with Wittgenstein on that point, although their disagreements on other things would be large.)

The problem here runs deeper: a natural (self-conscious) life is logically forced by its nature to go beyond its limitations, which it initially takes as limits.

Hegel says: *consciousness suffers this violence at its own hands.* "Consciousness" is always tempted to conceal this from itself—tempted to place itself at the center of things as the "dissolving skeptical attitude." The break between consciousness (as absorption) and self-consciousness is itself a self-inflicted wound.

Hegel rather contemptuously dismisses the kind of ongoing skepticism that is the province of academic philosophy. (Rightly?) It is just an erudite form of vanity, the idea that one might be "quick on one's feet," always "good for a counterexample," etc. It is a manifestation of the desire for independence (being-for-itself), the desire to be the one setting the boundaries, or, if not, at least showing that there are no boundaries. (In other places, Hegel also lets on that he thinks this is a distinctively modern attitude and is therefore a "determinate negation" of its own.) Is the "desire for independence" just a psychological fact about people? (Hegel thinks it is a desire that arises because of the very nature of self-conscious life itself, but more on that later.) Does that desire, as a desire, easily turn into its opposite (a desire for dependence)? At the speculative level, it would seem that both are true: "We are independent" and "We are dependent."

¶81. It might seem that we have to presuppose a general standard to do this investigation.

We might call such a standard the *essence* of the matter, which would be itself the *an sich* (the "in itself," or what the matter is in itself). This illustrates one of the problems of a "phenomenology" in Hegel's sense. In other sciences, "phenomenology" shows how the independent theoretical structures or "standards" are manifested in appearance. But in the Hegelian version of phenomenology, those standards cannot be assumed independently of the way they show up in appearance.

No such standard in any non-question-begging way has yet been given.

¶82. In our knowing something, we have a consciousness of something that is taken to be independent of us and to which we relate our consciousness of it, such as in perceptual belief: we see the rose, which we take to be independent of our seeing it, and we relate that consciousness of it to the object. But when the object being studied is knowledge itself, what is the "in itself" (the *an sich*) of knowledge? It is "for us" in our examination of it, but aren't we already using it to assess it? Hegel says that he will first sidestep the issue since the issue so far is phenomenal knowledge (*erscheinende Wissen*), knowing in the world of appearance, so we don't have a whole lot to go on. Maybe—he entertains the thought—things just are as they appear to be.

¶83. One way out (to be rejected): there are our standards (lying in us), such as "our language," or "ordinary human standards" which, in some way, we are supposed not to be able to get around. But if we do separate our activities of knowing ("for us") and the thing itself (as existing in itself), then it seems that there might obviously be a gap between things as "we" must take them and things as they are "in themselves." Somehow we are standing in some third place, looking at (1) how "we must" think, given our natures, and (2) what the world is really like.

Note the "abstract determination" of knowing and truth: when we know a thing, it is the *thing* we know, not our representation of the thing. In the successful case of knowing, there is no gap to be bridged between knowing X and X itself. Yet we also distinguish our activity of knowing from the object known. How do we render those two consistent?

Knowing that you know is a difference that is no difference. Yet some think that we do distinguish knowing what knowledge is from ordinary knowing.

¶84. Knowing has its own standard within itself; thus it is comparing itself with itself.

The "in itself" of knowledge is the *true*, is the standard we seek. What is knowing in itself?

If knowledge = concept, and if essence (the true) = object, then we want to know: Does the concept correspond to the object? (Does our concept of knowledge correspond to what knowledge really is?)

On the other hand, if in itself, the essence of the object (the true) = the concept, then we want to know: Does the object correspond to the concept? That is, does "knowing" measure up to its own internal standard?

All of these moments (in itself, for us, for another, etc.) fall within the activity of knowing.

Note that large swathes of contemporary epistemology deny this move. They hold that there is indeed an "object" (namely, knowledge), and we must see if our account matches up with that independent object. For them, the test of this has to do with our considered beliefs (what we nowadays call our "intuitions" about whether we would be said to know X in such and such circumstances). Such intuitions serve some sort of function as the independent facts to which the concept (one's theory of knowledge) must correspond. Hegel thinks that the concept of knowledge has a kind of built-in normativity, so that it always makes sense to ask: Is this really knowledge? That is, does this claim to knowledge measure up to its concept, or must it change itself? Knowledge changes itself as it measures itself against its own standards. It has "negativity" built into itself. It always makes sense to ask, "But is this really knowledge?"

This is what Hegel means (at least initially) by the "object" changing as the investigation progresses. This is the "negativity" of the investigation. Something other than the knowledge claim itself limits the claim to knowledge. This is negativity as limitation, absolute negativity as self-limitation.

Note too the way Hegel speaks about our not having to limit ourselves to "our" way of knowing or "our" standards. This is his not so oblique reference to (and implicit rejection of) the Kantian idea that our logical forms of judgment are limited in content to the forms of "our" intuition.

¶85. Hegel speaks of a pure looking-on (*Zusehen*). So we are not adding anything ourselves to what we are investigating but merely, as it were, looking at how the activity of knowing measures itself against itself.

This might suggest (and indeed has to many people) that what is being described here is some kind of Platonic viewing of the eternal forms as they pass over into one another, as happens in Plato's *Theaetetus* and *Parmenides*.

If knowing fails to measure up to the standard it sets for itself, then it falls short of knowing (and thus isn't knowing at all). It knows that it does not know. What counts as knowledge thus changes. This is also part of traditional skeptical arguments: we must change our account of knowledge itself. (The reply to the skeptic is often to remake the concept of knowledge, make it contextual, etc., or something like that.)

Some readings of Hegel put a big stress on this pure *Zusehen*. It's as if Hegel were a kind of proto-Husserlian of sorts, just looking at ("describing") what happens in Platonic heaven (the "pure essentialities") and not doing anything itself. On their view, Hegel is simply reporting on what happens in Platonic heaven. (See ¶6.) For them, he's watching the Forms move among themselves. That seems both textually and philosophically wrong to me.

Note how Hegel ends with a quasi-Kantian note. The problem of the examination of knowledge is not that we have a determinate and fixed concept of knowledge and then go out to look at examples to see if they fall under the concept. Instead, we are examining the very terms by which we carry out the exam in the first place.

It gets more complicated. There is knowledge of the object, and knowledge of knowledge. Hegel's thesis: in all knowledge of the object, there is also a knowledge of the knowledge. This knowledge of the knowledge *shows itself* in the particular acts of cognition.

¶86. This is the dialectic. Knowing investigating "knowing" creates a new object—by which he means, I take it: for each claim that this is knowledge, it always makes sense to ask, yes, but is this really knowledge? There is always a potential gap, a negativity, at work.

Hegel's own distinct thesis: this is carried out by learning from experience. We look at all the attempts that knowing, in trying to give an account of itself, makes, and we learn from the failures of those attempts. Ultimately, this will lead to Hegel's own historical style of doing philosophy.

"Our" contribution is putting all these dialectical movements into an order (a progression).

So there is a being-in-itself of the object (our initial concept of it, which we take to be identical in content to the object itself, thought not stopping short of the fact). Each is the nullity of what came before it.

¶87. This progression happens behind the back of consciousness—that is, it is not a goal at which consciousness explicitly aims, even if what turns up in the progression turns out to be the goal that "consciousness" was really seeking, what its own inner teleology was pushing it toward. (Or this can be interpreted as the idea that *Geist* is a "thing-substance" directing the show from behind the curtain, using us for its own ends. I disagree with that interpretation. But perhaps you think it's right.)

¶88. The path to *Wissenschaft* is thus itself *Wissenschaft*, the *Wissenschaft* of the *Erfahrung* (experience, learning process) of consciousness: it is thus the science of what consciousness learns from experience (namely, the experience of having failed at securing what it had taken itself to be securing).

It is clear at the end of the *Phenomenology* that it is supposed to be preparing us for something like Hegel's next book, the *Science of Logic*. It might seem therefore that the *Phenomenology* (as starting out as the "science of the experience of consciousness") would not itself be a "science" but only perhaps a "ladder" to "science" or a kind of "not really philosophy" introduction to philosophy. But that's not what Hegel says here.

¶89. This *Erfahrung* ("learning from experience") must itself be a *system* of such experiences. The system would aim at the place where its appearance (*Erscheinung*) is "selfsame" or "is equal to" (*gleich wird*) the *essence*—where knowledge measures up to its own standards. Or rather: by testing itself against its own standards, it finds that it continually breaks down until, at the end, it measures up to the standards it sets for itself.

That point would be the genuine *Wissenschaft* of *Geist*, and it points toward absolute knowledge. (Or perhaps just is absolute knowledge itself?)

3

Sensuous Certainty, Perceiving, Force, and the Understanding

I. Sensuous Certainty, or the "This" and Meaning Something

¶90. We begin with the immediate, the certain. One of the things that emerges quickly is that we really aren't sure what "certainty" is. Is certainty equivalent to where asking for reasons runs out, where I conclude that this is "simply what I do"? Not really—one can run out of reasons and still not be certain that one is where one should be.

We look for some instance where we would initially be comfortable and settled with saying, "I know that." The initial position should also be free of concepts, since whatever conceptual description you give will open things up about whether you are already begging the question. We look for something we would know without having to know anything else.

¶91. Of what are we certain? If we just say, "It is" (while pointing something out), we haven't said much (other than: it's not nothing).

This would be what we were looking for. It's nonconceptual: it's just a pure act of pointing out. You just point at something: that one. You don't (supposedly) give it a conceptual characterization (through a predicate). You don't say what it is at all. You just say: that one.

¶92. Of course, this is only an example of many such sensuous certainties. It can be repeated. Where is the certainty? It seems as if "consciousness" could simply point at something—"that one"—and it would be in possession of knowledge. "Which one?" followed by "That one!" But of course it is "I" pointing out "that one," and to whom am I pointing it out? Is this a practice I could imagine myself playing all alone? After all, this act can be repeated indefinitely, so it is something

Hegel's Phenomenology of Spirit. Terry Pinkard, Oxford University Press. © Oxford University Press 2023.
DOI: 10.1093/oso/9780197663127.003.0003

like a practice. The "immediacy" at work here begins to look a bit odd, since it is a mediated immediacy.

¶93. The object makes our beliefs true, and it is independent and indifferent to our beliefs. That I am "certain" of it has to do with the "I," not with the object.

But what of the case when the object is knowledge? Is "knowledge" an independent essence that explains the difference between cases where we know and those where we don't know?

Maybe we should begin with no opposition at all. In particular, no subject/object opposition.

Or maybe we must always begin with some kind of fundamental opposition, such as Frege's distinction between "concept" and "object."

¶94. We have to look to see if sensuous certainty measures up to its own standard.

¶95. Take the use of an indexical (a term whose reference varies with the speaker): this is now, that is now, etc. Hegel calls it the "indifference" of the Now (the indeterminacy of reference). The same goes for "here," which can refer to any place (indexed to where I am when I say it).

¶96. The referents of "this," "here," and "now" depend on me. They are, as referents, "mediated." It seems that there is a "universal" at work here in what is supposed to be a singular, unmediated act of pointing out. When I say "now," it is night. When I later repeat the act, it is day. Already we have a "universal," a "norm" of sorts—a possible correspondence to many objects.

¶97. It's a "negative." It is what it is in its exclusion of its contraries. In taking ourselves to be engaged in a practice structured by sensuous certainty, we thus can't say what we mean in sensuous certainty. We mean the nonuniversal, the purely singular. What we say is something that is abstract and general.

¶98. But Hegel says that such indexicals are "mediated simplicity." Compare Bertrand Russell's attempt to locate logical simples which could only be named. A simple, so Russell argued, cannot be spelled out in a description. Hegel's reply would be: the use of these simples requires other knowledge, even if very bare and abstract. The simple is actually complex in order to be simple. Or as we can put it in a more metaphysical mode: given the mediation from our side, there are no logical simples in the world. There is nothing that can only be named and not described.

There is an obvious misreading of Hegel here that more than one person has made. The mistake is this: when Hegel says the "this" is a universal, he is claiming that it's a predicate; but "this" is not a predicate. Hegel's point is that its use has a normative component, something like a rule for its use that is embedded in a complex of other rules. If that's right, then the idea that we might have nonconceptual knowledge that is also noninferential has more stress put on it. In fact, the stress will be enough to cause it to collapse.

¶99. The essence (what is self-identical over qualitative changes) is "pure being," which is also supposed to have mediation and negation internal to it. What is "pure being"? The "It is"? If so, it's not so "pure" since we have to know a number of other things to be able to know that "it is."

¶100. What is the universal? What I mean by "this"? (Is this a private language, i.e., one that cannot in principle be communicated to somebody else?)

The universal here seems to be my seeing something and being certain of what I'm seeing.

But things seem to have reversed themselves here. What is the object of knowing seems to amount to "what I mean" in my mental act of grasping it.

¶101. Now, the obvious: in using indexicals like "this," "here," and "now," I assume a point of view on things, a self-location. So maybe the things I was pointing at aren't really there, but (so it seems, or here is the proposal) my referential act of pointing was still meaningful. ("Look, a robin!" "There's no robin there." "Oh, I was pointing to something else.")

¶102. The constant here is not the thing ("that one"), but the agent doing the pointing, the "I." When I say "I," I seem to be doing the same thing as when I say "this" (the reference varies with the speaker). Yet it seems different. And I cannot say what I mean when I say "I" except to insist by saying something like "me." If I say, "I am the one," I am already engaged in a complex mediated practice that involves much more than just my pointing to myself.

¶103. So what sensuous certainty is about is not "certainty about an object" but "certainty about my pointing and various objects." I know I was pointing out something, even if there's nothing there.

¶104. It seems that all that is going on is myself as a pure intuiting. This one, now, here, I—I just "see" it, intuit it. If I give it any more fleshing out, I have gone beyond sensuous certainty. It's as if I'm just a pure pointing—if that makes any sense at all. Even when I point to a tree, there may be no tree there. All I seem to be certain of is that I am pointing.

¶105. This use of indexicals should also be nonreflective. If I have to think about it—ask myself whether I'm really pointing at something— I'm already bringing in a lot of conceptual resources that I'm supposed to be able to do without. I'm "mediating" the immediacy, as Hegel would put it.

¶106. Suppose someone asks, "When?" and I say, "Now," and the person then asks, "The now right now or the now of a few seconds ago?" We see that something is going wrong. My immediate sensuous certainty of "now" ceases to be now as time marches on. So what is it that I'm immediately aware of?

¶107. We draw the conclusion: pointing out the "now" is not an act of pointing out a "logically simple" that cannot be described. Such seemingly nonconceptual knowledge is really a component of a "movement," as Hegel says. The "movement" seems to be something like an inferential movement: for me to be able to know this, I must also be knowing a host of other things. What we also have here is the relation between the discrete (as a series of independent "nows") and the continuous (the flow of "nows" with no gaps between them).

¶108. Here are the other things I have to know: the "here" is a "this" here, etc. All this foregrounds how the discrete and the continuous, which seem to be the negations of each other, are in fact both required if we are to comprehend how what seemed like the absolutely simple act of "pointing out" turned out not to be so absolutely simple.

¶109. In sensuous certainty, the object of which I'm certain takes normative priority. I'm either seeing a tree or not. It doesn't depend on me whether there is a tree. But what exactly is this normative priority? Even the animals don't give absolute normative priority to individual objects. They eat them. The normative "standing" of the objects depends on the animal's priorities, what the possibilities are for the kind of being it is. (Lettuce is food for rabbits, rabbits are food for foxes.) What counts as "this" has to do with priorities we have "now." What counts as "now" (this moment, this day) depends on other priorities we have. Are we led to think that maybe there's an absolute "this" or "now" at the bottom of the series, a ground-level logically simple moment of time that isn't itself temporal? But Hegel has, he thinks, shown us that this way of thinking about the discrete and the continuous is a nonstarter.

The idea that the whole can be determined by adding up independently discriminable, absolutely individual things (Russell's notion that the universe is more like a bucket of shot than a bowl of jelly) is not true. This isn't really an argument yet. Hegel gives the example of the Elysian mysteries as a way of "connecting" to the whole. There is a horizon of significance on which the kind of pointing out going on in sensuous certainty depends, but it itself does appear in the semantic field of sensuous certainty.

¶110. An Ineffable (what cannot be said in any way) could never serve as fodder for inference. It wouldn't be a "universal"; thus, it is untrue, and it can't be a "norm." From the standpoint of knowledge, the ineffable would be a nothing. No inference, hence no knowledge, would follow from it.

At the end of sensuous certainty, we start to get a sense of how the book is going to proceed. We start out with a certainty: I know what it is I am doing in the very doing of it. (This is characteristic of all action.) I know I am aware of this, here, now in the act of being aware of this, here, now. That's my certainty. What has collapsed is its truth. (The certainty hasn't gone away.) Its truth collapses because of the contradictions engendered, first of all, by this way in which "consciousness" takes a certain shape (what I know with certainty is what I point out, or that I'm pointing out, and what I'm pointing out is in any event ineffable), and, second, when it begins reflecting on what it's doing because of the contradictions it's bringing in on itself, destabilizing its own claim to truth. I'm certain I'm aware of this here now, I'm certain of it by virtue of doing it (say, pointing something out), but I can't be aware of this, here, now—or at least not like this. So what am I really doing? (Note: we are not asking, "What am I presupposing?" but rather, "What am I really doing?" Yes, I am pointing out some things, but what am I really doing when I do so?) In some ways, large parts of the book will be about the disconnect and reconnect of the issue, "Here's what I am doing (certainty)" and "What am I really doing (Truth)."

II. Perceiving, or the Thing and Illusion

¶111. The result of sensuous certainty: a purely meaning-free, or nonconceptual, act of pointing out does not *on its own* make sense. It needs a wider context of meaning for it to even *seem* like it was meaning-free in the first place. (Or to put it as Hegel would: the truth of immediate certainty is the universal.)

So what are we experiencing in sensuous certainty is the wider context.

What we are perceiving is not just a "this" but a "one." It's a simple (reminiscent of Bertrand Russell's arguments about how perception simply had to include such simples). It is "simple" in the sense that it cannot be further analyzed into components. This suggests that although sensuous certainty could not stand on its own merits, it is preserved in a wider context of something like "perceiving." The way in which sensuous certainty has broken down is "determinate negation": the way it fails shows that it was always a component of a specific wider context, in this case of "perceiving."

¶112. What we perceive are simples with instantiations of general properties (white, cubical, etc.). Each of these properties is "not" the other, and it excludes other such properties. (If red, then not green. If cubical, then not spherical.) Thus, Hegel says that only perceiving has negation in its essence. The perceptual object's simplicity is mediated by the way it is a "one" of many general properties.

¶113. X is a simple (a "here") with a bundle of general properties attached to it. The perceived X "also" is an a, b, c. (E.g., the cube here is also sugary, sweet, white, hard, etc.)

¶114. It is a "one" that is "also" white, cubical, etc. The "one" is distinct from these properties.

Nothing follows from the one's logical essence. That it is "one" thing does not imply anything further about it. The X might be white, might not be white. The "one" is therefore indeterminate, but the properties are determinate only in their excluding one another without implying each other. (E.g., that it's white does not imply that it is sweet.) The "one" is determinate only as a "here."

¶115. The perceptual object therefore is one thing as contrasted with other things, its properties are general (e.g., red, which can predicated of many different things), and these general properties do not imply each other. The "one" is just the medium in which all these general properties are located and individualized, and the "one" is their unity. With that, the description of the perceptual object is brought to its culmination. Or so it seems.

¶116. This looks like what we were trying to say in sensuous certainty but failing to say. The perceptual object makes the perception true or false, and our apprehension of the object, if it is a true apprehension, is relatively passive. If something goes wrong in the act of perceiving, there is not anything wrong in the object but in the act. E.g., "I thought I saw a cat, but there was no cat there." The perceiving subject is aware that his perception might be an illusion. The way to describe the illusory perception is to say that it was not really a perception. Illusory perception of the cat is not perception of something else (a "cat-seeming") but a failed or at least inadequate perception. The act of perceiving is failing to live up to its own internal standard, or, as Hegel says, it is not self-equal.

¶117. There is what we learn from experience ("no cat there") and what we take to be "for us." (Hegel thinks this is a classic wrong move in the dialectic of perceiving.) "I thought I saw a cat" and "No cat was there" look like they imply "I thought I saw something catlike, but there was no cat there." From that it looks as if we ought to infer further: the experience (for us) of seeing a cat when a cat is not there is identical to the experience of seeing a cat when the cat is there. Presto: the "curtain" of appearance, separating us from reality, springs up. We might be seeing "nothing" in itself (*an sich*), but we still say we're seeing "something." The "one" I thought I was seeing (the cat) is not the "one" I see, but what I see is a community of properties (what looks like a tail, green eyes, black coat, four legs, etc.). It looks like what I'm really seeing is a bundle of properties, none of which implies the other. I took those to imply the presence of the cat, but, although I was mistaken (no cat there), I was still seeing something. Consciousness, as Hegel puts it, seems to simply double back on itself, "return" into itself.

¶118. Consciousness means (or means to say) something, but what it meant isn't there. So consciousness "returns into itself" (also in ¶117). It marks itself off as something separate from appearance. It was, so it thought, "outside" of itself (as in its "natural consciousness," consciousness takes itself to be seeing things that exist independently of its awareness). It corrects itself (internally): "I wrongly inferred from my catlike experience to the proposition that there was a cat there."

¶119. So how things (the "ones" of perception) appear to me depends on the properties. Things aren't really red, they just seem that way to me. "We" or "I" is the universal medium of the properties. The properties of the "ones" are really features of "our" apparatus of sensing them.

¶120. Things as "ones" are distinct from each other. But how are they distinct? They are so through their (perceptible) properties. It is the one as the thing that is really white, cubical, etc. The thing thus must be conceived as the *Bestehen* (the subsistence, enduring reality) of all the various perceptible properties. The chemist John Dalton proposed that we think of things as "enclosing surfaces" of properties. Properties, he thought, attach to the "pores" of the thing. (Call this a bad early version of a physicalist-naturalist metaphysics.)

¶121. But we still need to distinguish the thing as it is on its own, and the thing as it is "for us" in perceiving.

¶122. In perceiving, the thing is supposed to be "the true." But likewise, we are the singular "ones" who take it to be true. The thing seems to us to be such and such, and we also take it (note that taking is an activity) as being such and such.

¶123. But when we make perceptual judgments, they are true when the thing is as we perceive it to be. It's the thing that makes the judgment true, not us or our way of talking. "We" seem to drop out of the relation. "The thing thereby is for itself and *also* for another": it is "for itself" in that it has an independence for us and is what it is on its own; but it also is "for us" as we perceive it. I, the perceiver, am one thing (reflected back into myself, distinguishing myself as one independent element in the relation), and the thing is also reflected back into itself.

¶124. Hegel has given us a picture of the world as found in perceiving that resembles Bertrand Russell's idea of the world as a bucket of shot. The world consists of ultimate "simples" (things) which have various properties. The world for this shape of consciousness would be the sum total of individual simple things that can be concatenated with other such simple things in terms of the properties of each. Each thing as a "simple" is what is on its own ("for itself") apart from all other things, but the world as a sum total of them is what it is only in contrasting these simples with each other, but this contrast is "unessential" and therefore contingent.

¶125. The "thing" thus is what it is apart from all its relation to other such "things," and it is what it is only in contrast to other things. Its relation to others is what makes it the simple "one" that it is. It is what it is apart from all others, but it is what it is only within the wider context in which such simples are supposedly perceived.

¶126. Hegel speaks here and in ¶125 of the thing's "perishing" through its essential property. If a thing is an ultimate simple that is what it is apart from all relations to others, and if the thing is also what it is only in certain relations to others, then the "thing" cannot be what it is.

¶127. The thing is thus the "negation of itself" in that it instances this contradiction in our conception of it. It is, necessarily, essentially contrasted with other simples, but that contrast is also unnecessary, unessential to it. That itself is a distinction without any basis to itself, a merely "verbal" distinction.

¶128. Hegel restates this opposition between the thing's "oneness" as having no essential relation to other "things" and its "oneness" as requiring its contrastive relation to others. But we can equally as well say that its being-for-itself is just as inessential to the thing as its contrastive relation to others is. The thing is what it is on its own no matter what other things are, and the thing is what it is only in the wider context. (Note that just as continuity and discreteness were both necessary to sensuous certainty, being-for-itself and being-for-others seem to be mutually exclusionary but also necessary to each other.)

¶129. The "thing" as a "one" is thus "sublated." That is, it is still around as a singular thing (a "one"), and it is still to be contrasted with others. It has thus been sublated (*aufgehoben*) in that it has been preserved while at the same time being canceled. (Hegel is happy to use an ordinary German word, *aufheben*, for this since it means both to cancel and to preserve.) We have a typical philosophical-metaphysical dilemma that prompts us to think: well, it can't be both, so it has to be one or the other. We are driven to reflection on this, and so for the first time, "Consciousness truly enters into the realm of the understanding." ("The understanding" [*Verstand*] here could also be equally well rendered as the "intellect," but following the tradition of translation, we leave it here as "the understanding.") We find ourselves reflectively struggling to make sense of what otherwise seems to be perfectly sensible. (Hegel will contrast "the understanding" in this sense with "reason," which grasps things that seem to be at odds with each other as making sense once they are located in the unities in which each plays a kind of actual, working role.) The thing as grasped, at least implicitly, by "reason" (although Hegel does not mention "reason" here) is a unity of being-for-itself and being-for-others, a purported "unconditioned absolute universality."

¶130. None of this works. The "universality" which was supposed to save the day in terms of making sense of what we're saying and doing turns out to be empty.

¶131. The lesson to be drawn: we think that by speaking of perceptual knowing in this way, we are making sense. ("What could be more obvious, could be deeper?" so we think.) But we are not really making sense when we draw out what it is that we are saying. It obvious that when I say, "Look, over there, the white cube," I'm saying something perfectly sensible, and so I am. When I start to ask how it is that something so banal could be true, and I pay attention to what I'm saying as I draw these conclusions out, I find I'm all of sudden just babbling. I'm dealing with abstractions that "the understanding" has invoked, and outside of the wider context in which those abstractions play a role, I find myself contradicting myself. If I am to make any sense of myself, I have to do one of two things: come up with the ultimate philosophical theory of perception that opts for one side of the contradiction and definitively disproves the other; or move on to the wider context in which this contradiction dissolves. Hegel's lesson: you'll never in an eternity come up with the definitive philosophical refutation of one side to the advantage of the other; the problem lies more deeply within perceptual language itself when it is isolated from its wider context in social practices. Time to move on.

III. Force and the Understanding; Appearance and the Supersensible World

The chapter on force and understanding is one of the most densely Hegelian of all the chapters in the book. It's crucial but on the first, second, and third readings also mostly baffling. Unsurprisingly, it remains a real bone of contention among Hegel interpreters.

¶132. "Perceiving" has disclosed that what is going on in perceptual knowledge is not an immediate intake of content but some kind of conceptual thought of the imperceptible in the content. We can think these things, but we can't "see" them or "hear" them. True judgments of perception require "thought."

If we think of the whole (the background) in terms of which the foregrounded thing with properties stands out, then that whole is the unconditioned. Hegel says that the unconditioned returns into itself, which means that it is now considered to be an independent something-or-other existing on its own (in some way or another). It is motionless simple essence, that is, it is the background substructure we use to explain what is going on in appearance. It's the "behind" in all such essence-explanations (Why does the blue tie look green in the shop? What caused the fire in the garage?) Appearance is in flux, essence stays stable and explains it.

To say that consciousness has not yet grasped its concept is to say that it still operates as if everything were a perceptual object. This leads "the understanding" to suppose that all forms of explanation will be in terms of substrates that explain appearances, which will lead to the substrate of all substrates that explains everything else: the final substrate, the essence of all that is and that (somehow) explains all that is turns out to be seen by "consciousness" as something existing on its own. Hegel says, without explaining much what he means, that "consciousness has not yet grasped its *concept* as *concept.*" That idea will be developed in this section: "consciousness" thinks it is trying to describe an independent object that is nonetheless not observable (perceivable), namely, the "unconditioned universal." This "conscious-ness" of course recognizes that it is starting to do theoretical work in all this, but it still takes itself to be responding to some object of some sort. What "consciousness" does not realize is that it is in fact responding to the way its own conceptual activity puts it in a position to grasp the whole conceptually that cannot be consistently construed along the lines of its focusing on an object akin to the perceptual object. It comes to this conclusion once it realizes it is dealing with "infinity," which cannot be surveyed except in thought.

¶133. This also gives us the concept not just of individual truths but of "the true." The true would be the ultimate explainer, the uncondi-tioned, what explains everything else.

¶134. So here's our basic picture: the unconditioned explains the conditions, but is not itself explained by anything else. It has a being for us (being for another), and it has an independent nature (a being for itself). So we have the makings of a proposal: explanation works in terms of this independence/dependence relation. The unconditioned can't be conditioned by anything else. We now look to see how this pro-posal fares once it's put into practice.

¶135. If taken on the model of a perceptual object, the "uncondi-tioned" also displays a gap between form and content. In perception, we have multiple general contents (sweet, square, cubical) and a "one" (the singular thing) of which they are properties. But perceptual things aren't self-standing, self-sufficient. They are what they are only in re-lation to other things. Maybe this perceptual model for the "uncondi-tioned" isn't the right one.

¶136. The form of things is for them to be singular things with gen-eral properties that come to be and pass away, and shift around or don't shift around depending on the circumstances.

What explains this is "force," namely that which what propagates the things and/or their properties. The things or the behavior of things is thus to be taken to be an *expression* of the force. Why did the leaf fall? Gravity. Why did gravity do that? That's what gravity does. The falling was the expression of gravity doing what it does.

The force is one, completely determinate as it is, and it expresses itself in the flux of appearance. It explains appearance, but, as the One, it is thrown back into itself. (I.e., it is what it is apart from its expression.) Gravity is what it is independent of the singular leaf's falling.

What is force in itself, apart from its expression? Is the force different from its expression?

Force, so it is now taken, has to be the "substance" of the differences: it is the unity as the substrate under the differences of appearance (now considered as the sum total of things and their properties).

But if force is One, how does it explain the difference of the differences? Force (as a theoretical, unobserved something) is one thing that supposedly explains a lot of different things.

As observed only in its expressions, it is the "inner" of things (the imperceptible substrate of appearance). It is something "posited" to explain things. As such, it emerges not as an object of any sort explaining things but as the "un-objective," the unperceived "inner" of the perceptual world. We don't see it—we only see its expressions—but we know it "has" to be there. Hegel's sense of "inner" here has to do with what you can see (the outer) and what you can't see (what is the inner of the outer).

¶137. We have an implicit reference to Kant's *Metaphysical Foundations of Natural Science*: insofar as there is matter, there must a priori be two forces of repulsion and attraction. If there were only one repelling force, everything would fly apart. If there were only one attracting force, everything would crash together into one big undifferentiated lump.

What solicits attraction? What solicits repulsion?

¶138. Something solicits the force to express itself. What? It can't be the things of appearance, for that would make the force into a "conditioned." So it must be another force. So if there are two forces, one solicits the other. What prompts something in appearance to get the force to express itself? Repulsion comes in because of the attractive powers of things; attraction comes in because of the repulsive power of things. If so, then appearance "must" (a priori) be the equilibrium of the two forces.

The One of force necessarily splits into two forces. Kant's attraction and repulsion are an example.

¶139. So what we get is a "play" of forces, all operating behind the scene, but directing everything in appearance.

¶140. The difference of form between these two forces (whatever they are) is that between soliciting and solicited (or active and passive, as Schelling, among others, put it). The difference in content would be that between force as the medium of the various matters and force as One. If force is One, then the independent elements of nature (in mechanical explanation) are what they are independent of the force even as it is force that moves them around.

¶141. There must therefore be two forces. The One force splits into two forces in which each is dependent on the other to make it actual (*wirklich*, in Hegel's special sense of being "what is really at work").

If there are two forces, then there must be some mediating point between them.

So let's say: the substance (explanatory substrate) of things is one that must divide itself into two. (This is pretty abstract, even for a metaphysical argument.)

Each force is what it is only in relation to the other force. (Attraction is only attraction in its relation to repulsion.)

As so abstract, force seems to be "force," that is, the concept of force. That seems to amount to the loss of force's reality (its *Realität*, not its *Wirklichkeit*—its actuality, its counting as what is really at work in any explanation of nature). Force becomes something more like a theoretical construct to explain the flux of experience.

The consciousness of a force in its phenomenal expression is thus the consciousness of the force as it is in its true essence. The force just is that "inner" that expresses itself (necessarily) in these ways.

The force(s) is (are) thus the object of "the understanding," not perception. As unobservable, they are grasped only in our intellectual grasp of them.

We conclude thus that only through "the understanding" do we get at the "inner" of things.

We postulate theoretical entities (nowadays gluons, genes, etc.) to explain why things behave as they do.

So we have what looks something like the elements of a syllogism: "the understanding" (or "consciousness") on one extreme, the inner on the other extreme, and appearance as the expression of the play of forces in the middle.

What we have then is that "the truth of force remains therefore only the *thought* of force," and we now have, as Hegel says, an idea of the unity of the "inner" world behind appearance as "*its concept as concept.*"

¶142. There is force as it is on its own, and there is force taken as the "inner" of things, which is (again) the concept as concept—not merely the concept of force as the ultimate explainer, the substance of all that is, but the concept of force taken explicitly as a concept that grasps the whole in ways that perception cannot. Perception as it were strives toward a totality that it cannot reach because of what it is. In coming to this realization about itself, "perceptual consciousness" comes to grasp that its success hangs on something like the "concept as a concept" since the totality at which perception aims can only be fully grasped in conceptual and not merely perceptual form.

¶143. "Consciousness" now draws a new conclusion about itself. The real essence at which it took itself to have been aiming is not something it can grasp immediately (noninferentially or without any conceptual intermediary). It turns therefore to the "play of forces" it posits as being there in order to mediate between itself and the nonperceptual "inner" of things as the other extreme, so what links "consciousness" and the "inner" is the "play of forces" it posits as necessarily being there (as the mediating middle). This play of forces can itself be perceived as the expression of forces. (Although we can't see the forces, we can see the helium balloon going up and the leaf falling, both of which are expressions of different forces at work in the world.) The world we see is thus a "semblance," a seeming-to-be of the "inner" of the world, and if we take all the semblances together, we get the concept of the world as not merely "seeming" but as "appearing." What results is that "consciousness" takes the "inner" of things to be the truth of the appearing world (it is what the appearing world really is), and it understands that this "inner" is not itself perceived but conceived, although it is still "not yet acquainted with the nature of the concept."

¶144. What we therefore have now is a "shape of consciousness" that distinguishes this-worldliness from an otherworldly beyond. We live in the world of appearance, as a kind of this-worldliness, but we (supposedly) know that its truth—what really explains it—is an otherworldly domain.

¶145. Having made that move, we now realize that the true object of our investigations will have to be the inference itself (the syllogism) from the consciousness of things to the positing of what things are in their truth (in the "inner" of the world).

¶146. Of course, this "inner," although it has to be there, is also empty (at least for this shape of consciousness). What the world is in itself, beyond our this-worldly capacities, is unknowable. Perhaps we should draw the conclusion that we must live in terms of the world of appearance (as "this-worldly" people) but keep reminding ourselves that it isn't true. Some people call that a concept of the holy. Hegel says it would be more like a daydream.

¶147. But the appearing world just *is* the supersensible world as it appears to us, even if its appearance has to be taken as false. The appearing world is not, as it were, a fake world. It is *the* world as it appears to us. It is the real appearance of the true, inner world. What we have is the world as sublated: the world, as all that is the case, is both canceled (the appearing world is not the true world) while being preserved (it is the real way in which the true world appears to us).

¶148. Our object of investigation is thus not so much the world as it is our intellectual grasp of the world, although this is not yet "posited" as such. What "consciousness" finds in this dialectic of explanation of the appearing world by an "inner" unobservable world is that all the appeal to forces just drops out as the basic explanation, and what one really has is a concept of the flux of the world as explained by the inner world, which is now regarded as a "simple." If we knew the "inner" of the world, we could explain why there are these forces and not others. The "inner" itself, though, remains beyond explanation; it is the unexplained explainer which is itself empty. Thus, what is present is an even more wildly abstract concept: the universal difference. We have the appearing world and the inner world, and the two are different. Just as earlier the discrete and the continuous looked like opposites but turned out to be required features of a more determinately structured whole, here the inner and the outer also look to be opposites, and the issue will be whether they too are required elements of a more determinate structure.

¶149. What is at stake is the "universal difference" between the inner (supersensible world) and the outer (the phenomenal world). The inner world is the flux of the appearing world in its essence. What is that essence? It is the universal difference of inner and outer as that of stable, unchanging laws (the laws of nature). The phenomenal world is in motion, but the inner world is not. The inner world is the realm of the laws that determine what is happening in the phenomenal world. The inner world is thus doing the work of explaining what is going on in the phenomenal world.

¶150. What happens when something in appearance fails to exhibit what the law governing it requires (as when something that is supposed to dissolve in water fails to dissolve)? One way is to come up with an ever more general law that will incorporate that difference into itself. That quickly leads to emptiness since the most general law that will cover everything will end up being something like "Stuff happens." The concept of a law, however, is still important. It says that not everything is contingent, a pure accident.

¶151. Hegel speaks of the universal law (of attraction) and all the determinate laws that nonetheless belong to experience. Here's an example that helps us see what Hegel is getting at. It thus still seems that we need to talk of a variety of forces. If we drop a cannonball and a leaf off the top of the tower of Pisa, one will accelerate faster in falling to the ground than the other. This in no way invalidates the law that F = ma. The leaf accelerates more slowly because of air, wind, the leaf's shape, etc. In other words, other forces interfere with the leaf's falling which are themselves powerless over the cannonball. The law, F = ma, has an internal necessity to itself. That necessity remains, but what actually happens involves an "other things being equal" clause, such as "this will happen unless . . . ," where the "unless" can be close to infinite in length.

¶152. Hegel speaks of something of great interest to people of his day, namely, the phenomena of positive and negative electricity. If electricity is to be regarded as a force, then it seems that it has to lie in the nature of electricity that it "double" itself into positive and negative charges. "The force *must* double itself in that way simply *because* it *must*." It is just the "nature" of electricity to do that. But what is the power of this "must"?

¶153. Hegel gives another example, this time involving gravitation, about the relation between laws and what actually happens in the application of a law to the appearing world. Newtonian-style laws take various elements, treat them as completely independent of each other, and go from there. The law relates things that are indifferent to each other. What we want, though, so he will go on to say later, is some idea of necessity, of why the world must take this and not that shape. We want to know not just what happens but what is doing the explanatory work in explaining what happens.

¶154. Here Hegel seems to be casting doubt on the idea that explanation consists in giving laws for things. We explain an event (e.g., lightning) by giving the "law of electricity." But in practice what we do is cite regularities of appearance. (This is the standard Humean account of laws as regularities.) When we get such a regularity, we claim that it explains the event (and this may be very helpful for predictions). But if we ask what explains the regularity, all we get is another statement of a regularity. What we want is some account of why this regularity holds.

¶155. It looks as if the laws we are proposing are mere restatements of appearance. Thus, the explanatory enterprise looks to be tautological. The attractive force of a body causes another body to be attracted to it. This looks like a difference that is no difference.

The law must be given a more determinate character.

¶156. We continue the attraction-repulsion scenario. The inner is not in flux, but the appearing world is. The inner is "at rest," it is what it is, it doesn't change. But the inner of things must divide itself into two forces: for example, attraction and repulsion. What is like (a body being attracted) becomes unlike (it also must be repelled). In fact, it looks (and people like Schelling were quick to grab onto this) as if the fundamental law governing the inner itself is that it must divide itself into like and unlike, positive and negative, etc. The inner One repels itself and attracts itself. It also has positive and negative electricity, magnetism, etc.

This looks like the very concept of explanation itself pushing us to this kind of substrate. This in turn pushes us to a law governing such a substrate that states the substrate has the positive and negative within itself. Voilà, it looks like we have found a deeper explanation for things than the physicists have—and all on the basis of a priori reasoning.

¶157. If the "inner world" behind the appearing world is to explain the appearing world, it will consist in a set of laws (stated as regularities among independent items) that are said to explain the phenomenal world, and the "inner" world will supposedly explain why the regularities of the appearing world are as they are. The proposal so far: the inner One contains positive and negative in itself, and it expresses that positive and negative in various regularities in nature.

Now we get one of the weirdest and the hardest things to explain in the *Phenomenology*: the inverted world. It's not a topic to which Hegel ever returns. Commentators have pulled their hair out trying to make sense of it.

Here's one way to go at it.

We have been pushed to the idea that there is a final substrate of all the world, whose very nature is to repel itself from itself. Call the substrate S. Now, we ask, why must S repel itself from itself? We could just say, sorry, we don't know, that's just the way things are. But reason cannot be satisfied with that. It is natural to think that there must be a G that explains why S is the way it is. There is no reason at all not to think that the law of self-repulsion holds for G too, and that S's self-repulsion is the result of G's nature. It's just what G's do. G in one of its modes causes S to take on one of its modes. S's attraction is caused by G's repulsion, G's attraction causes S's repulsion.

¶158. With that in place, we can make the following assertions: in the inverted world, sweet will be sour, black will be white, etc.

Yikes. How did we get here? Well, we started out with a meaning-free reference to objects in sensuous certainty. We could just transparently "take" objects to be this, here, now. That didn't work.

Or we could get at things with a purely referring gesture that takes them to be, although within a set of descriptions (e.g., the thing with many properties). That too didn't work.

So maybe we are referring to things that we can't see, so that we only have a priori descriptions of those things (or of one Thing), and those things explain what it is we really do see and why they are what they are and behave the way they do.

If so, then a skeptical worry: even the whole world might be actually inverted on us, such that everything that appears up is really down, left is really right, green is really red, sweet is really sour, just is really un-just, and so forth.

The phrase the "inverted world" (*die verkehrte Welt*) was a well-known trope in Hegel's time. In England, it was known as the topsy-turvy world, or the world turned upside down. Popular in Europe was a whole series of woodcuts illustrating it. In them, children teach the teachers, rabbits hunt the hunters, and (of course) women order men around. (The inverted world as an inverted globe also appears in Brueghel's painting illustrating Netherland proverbs.)

¶159. We thus have a law that is not the statement of a regularity but something more like a necessity—like becomes unlike, etc. There is the phenomenal world, and there is the inverted (topsy-turvy) world. Both are real.

¶160. What we get out of this is "infinity." At first, this infinity looks like what Hegel will later call the "bad infinity." The image is that of a straight line that extends out to . . . infinity. If you follow the line out to the end, you will never get there. The image of the "good infinite" will be that of the circle: if you start your journey on the circle, you will eventually come back to the same point, and if you do this infinitely many times, you will still traverse the same points. Where we now are in the book has us moving back and forth between the world of appearance and the supersensible (unobservable) "inner" world that explains the world of appearance. It looked like we had to opt for one or the other— accept that the appearing world is real and the supersensible world is false or accept the appearing world as false and the inner world as true. Actually, we need both as "moments" of a whole that at first seems to be at odds with itself. But we are not there yet.

¶161. We have several models now to think of this "infinity." We can think of it as one concept with "difference" within itself (the inner needs the outer, the outer needs the inner; neither is what it is except in this contrastive relationship). Or we can think of it as something always already "estranged" (*Entzweite*, broken in two) in itself. Or we can think of the unity of these poles (positive/negative; inner/outer, etc.) as something that is primary and see the "difference" as no difference, that is, as not involving any fundamental tension within itself.

¶162. Hegel makes his point that this concept of infinity applies to the whole world. When we try to conceive of the world as a whole, we continually find ourselves confronted by a series of such oppositions that in turn give rise to large swathes of philosophical problems. We fall into an illusion of sorts when we treat all the elements (or "moments") as if they were separate things to be additively joined to each other. As Hegel said in the preface, "The true is the whole," and this holds here.

¶163. There are two absolutely key Hegelian principles announced in this section. First, there is the principle of the dialectic: "Infinity, or this absolute restlessness of pure self-movement which is such that whatever is determined in any manner, for example, as being, is instead the opposite of this determinateness." Dialectic has to do with what seem like unsurmountable oppositions or dualisms that at first seem to force a choice on us: this one *or* that one (e.g., freedom *or* determinism). Dialectic is supposed to show us how to hold onto both without simply contradicting ourselves and without letting the tension between both slip away.

Second, there is the introduction of the really central Hegelian concept, that of self-consciousness: "As infinity is finally an object for consciousness, and consciousness is aware of it *as what it is*, so is consciousness *self-consciousness*." When we try to look at the world as a whole in order to explain the world of appearance, we have to ask ourselves where we are standing when we do that. It might look as if it were impossible, since to view the world as a whole we would have to be standing outside of the world. We might think of that as the God's-eye point of view, but it is not our point of view. The other way to think of it is that we as limited, finite, partial creatures can self-consciously form a conception of ourselves as taking such a view, and the task of dialectic will be to show that this opposition—between my own embodied, partial point of view and the point of view of looking at the world as a whole—are not in fact hard and fast oppositions that demand a choice of one or the other (as sometimes what is called the "point of view of man" and the "point of view of God" are often said to be). Infinity appears to consciousness only in thought, not in perception.

¶164. This speculative unity of what seem to be opposing concepts is paradigmatic of self-consciousness itself. Hegel says: "Consciousness is *for itself*, it is a *distinguishing of what is not distinct*, or it is *self-consciousness. I distinguish myself from myself*, and *in doing so, what is immediately for me is this: What is distinguished is not distinguished*." Self-consciousness is thus not that of two things, as "consciousness" is. In consciousness, there are two items: my consciousness of the object and the object itself. It looks at first as if self-consciousness would be the same thing, but it is not. There is "I" aware of "me," so that "*what is distinguished is not distinguished.*" Self-consciousness is the "truth" of consciousness in that all consciousness is also self-consciousness, not as a separate reflective act—as if in seeing a dog, I also had to stop and think, "I am seeing a dog"—but as one complex act. It might look as if there were two acts—my consciousness of X and my consciousness of my consciousness of X—but what seems like two is really only one (act). My consciousness of peeling the potato is an awareness that I am peeling a potato. This is the puzzling (at least at first sight) aspect of self-consciousness.

¶165. We now see retrospectively why we had these difficulties with "consciousness." The "standpoint of consciousness," as Hegel calls this, suggests the picture that behind the appearing world is a true world. However, now it seems that the curtain of appearance has been lifted so that we see that there never was a curtain of appearance. There are simply people—subjects, agents—making statements and constructing theories about appearance, and all of this is going on in appearance itself. What seemed like a syllogism of sorts linking one extreme (consciousness) with another extreme (the inner world gained by reflection) via the world of appearance has vanished since all the terms have merged. If there ever was a curtain, we're the ones who put it up, and now we're the ones who take it down.

The key to all this is, of course, "self-consciousness," and so Hegel closes with: "It likewise turns out that the cognition of *what consciousness knows while knowing itself* requires still further circumstances. The exposition of those circumstances lies in what follows."

4

Self-Consciousness and
Self-Sufficiency
Mastery and Servitude

It is worth noting that this chapter on self-consciousness is in two parts as indicated by Hegel's table of contents: the first part has to do with the attempt by self-consciousness to show itself as a *self-sufficient* (or independent) self-consciousness; the second part has to do with the *freedom* of self-consciousness. That of course makes us wonder: what does Hegel take the relation to be between *independence* (*self-sufficiency*) and *freedom*?

¶166. Hegel gives us a recap of the move from chapters 1–3 on "consciousness" to the move to self-consciousness. Finally, we have an object of knowing that is more explicitly to be appraised in terms of how it measures up to its concept, not in terms of how the concept measures up to the object. The being-in-itself of self-consciousness (its *Ansichsein*) is also its being for an other (namely, itself). Self-consciousness is "other" to itself with a "difference that is no difference." This looks like a pure, transparent self-presence. But it will turn out not to be.

¶167. Two things to note: (1) This doesn't "do away" with the appearing world. The appearing world is not an illusion, nor is it the neo-Cartesian claim that we are certain of ourselves or our own mental states but not of the world itself. (2) Instead, as Hegel says, we are in the "realm of truth."

Hegel now says: this self-consciousness is "desire." And "This unity must become essential to self-consciousness." What is this? Why is the unity not already essential?

First, there is the matter of translation. Hegel says self-consciousness is "desire *überhaupt*." That little phrase can be translated as "desire,

Hegel's Phenomenology of Spirit. Terry Pinkard, Oxford University Press. © Oxford University Press 2023.
DOI: 10.1093/oso/9780197663127.003.0004

period (nothing else)" or as "desire in general." I take it to be desire, period (or "full stop," as other dialects would have it). Why? For Hegel, desire is a feeling of a *lack* in an organism, and this feeling of a lack typically impels it to an activity to ameliorate that lack. In desire, the organism is thrown out of unity with itself; it needs something other than itself or its current state. At first, the object that disturbs self-consciousness is, Hegel says, life itself (itself as a living being). As a living being, it must take in other stuff in order for it to "be" at all. The self-conscious animal is not only desiring but aware of what reasons underpin those desires, even though it can also be mistaken about those reasons. The phrase "This unity must become essential to self-consciousness" indicates that self-consciousness has an inherent lack that is more than just lack of food, sleep, or such. Self-consciousness is inherently out of balance with itself. What that is will be the topic for the next several paragraphs.

¶168. Hunger, sleep, disease, etc.: self-consciousness doesn't set those terms for itself, even though it can intelligently alter its behavior vis-à-vis those things. More importantly, it can decide what these things are to mean for it. From that vantage point, life seems to be external to the internality of self-consciousness and the goals of self-sufficiency it sets itself. (Or external to the only barely articulated goal of being the "truth.") A truly self-sufficient life, Aristotle says, would lack nothing; it would be analogous to a city that need bring in nothing from the outside. So what is "internal," what is "external" to self-consciousness? The strict opposition between "internal" and "external" is one of those distinctions Hegel is seeking to relativize.

Self-consciousness is the "unity" of life as it projects itself forward in light of its past and its present. Life, apart from self-consciousness, has the structure of "lacking" something (sleep, food, a mate, etc.), but life is not "for itself" in the way that self-consciousness is. For self-consciousness, what it truly desires is potentially up for grabs. Self-consciousness "immediately marks its object with the character of the negative" in the sense that it distinguishes itself from any particular project or lack. In doing so, self-consciousness is led to thinking of itself as independent, self-sufficient, as it sets its own terms of engagement with the world. It will now learn just what that amounts to.

¶169. Since self-conscious life is now the object of investigation, Hegel gives a short and fanciful characterization of life itself. (He will return to it in more detail later the book.) His characterization turns on several metaphors: it is fluid while being stable, motionless while in motion, etc. Two things stand out: first, life itself as a process precipitates (another metaphor) the various species out of itself. (Exactly how it does that, Hegel has no idea.) Second, all the various organs of a living thing are independent but also are what they are only in terms of their function with reference to the whole animal or plant.

¶170. The unity of a living thing displays the kind of unity in difference that Hegel claims emerged out of the considerations in "Force and the Understanding." The organs are each different, but each plays a functional role in the living thing. The "infinite system" of the system of life "estranges" itself into various species and genera.

¶171. Life becomes a process of living things coming to be and passing away. Life takes on a "motionless" feature when we see it as something like the tree of life (with all the branches having their distinct species, etc.). (Hegel was obviously not in a position to have anything like the Darwinian theory of evolution. He only had the idea that different species emerge from the overall process of life itself and were not individually created by some divinity.) Individual plants and animals act as if they were independent, stable shapes, but they meet, procreate, and pass away in the process. When he says, "The fluid element is itself only the *abstraction* of essence, or it is only *actual* as a shape," he means that the life process on earth is the essence of living things, but that is only the abstract essence (as "life in general"). For life to become really something at work in the world ("actual," *wirklich*), it has to become an individual living thing meeting up with other individual things.

¶172. The individual animal acts in the terms of its species (what counts for it as food, as a mate, etc.). But the animal is not aware of the universal (the norm) by which it acts. Rather, it acts only in terms of singular things (desires for this particular food, for a mate in this individual, etc.). A non-self-conscious living thing cannot genuinely distinguish the general from the singular.

¶173. Self-consciousness, however, is aware of its genus *as a* genus, aware of itself as member of the genus, yet different from it.

Self-consciousness is a "life" for which the genus exists as genus. (Other ways of putting this might be Heideggerian: we are the beings for whom our being is an issue. Or perhaps in terms of Charles Taylor's phrase, "Man is a self-interpreting animal.") What our genus is *an sich* (in itself)—what its trajectory of development must be—must itself be set and achieved by us, but as it is achieved, it shifts its shape. We become what we are, but that shifts. Or, as we might put it, self-consciousness is consciousness of the *form* of life in which we are participants (the *an sich* of our life). This idea of self-consciousness as "form" will reappear over and over again in the book.

¶174. The simple "I" is the "universal," and is the difference that is no difference (i.e., self-consciousness, the self as differentiating itself from itself while maintaining that there is no difference between "I" and "me"). The (seemingly) independent moments of self-conscious life are what they are only in terms of the whole (self-conscious life itself). Unlike the ordinary animal, which pounces on things to capture and eat them, the self-conscious animal is aware of what it is doing. If he finds fruit ripe for the picking, he is aware of picking it as the kind of thing "we" self-conscious animals do. "I" do what is appropriate for what "we" do.

¶175. If self-consciousness is to be the truth, then it must seek a satisfaction that it cannot find in "life" itself. Why not in life itself? The idea is that it needs its authority to do the appropriate thing to be confirmed. The ordinary object of desire cannot do that. (The animal can run away from me or confront me to defend itself. It cannot question my authority to do so.) For my self-sufficiency (independence) to be confirmed as true, I need an object that can "effect the negation of itself" within itself. This "object" of consciousness has to be something that can linguistically communicate to me that I have the authority to do what it is I am doing. The only "object" that can do this is another self-consciousness. I need the other to confirm or bestow an authority on me—an "independence" somewhat akin to sovereignty. If I am truly independent, I will be authorized to give orders, but nobody else may give me orders. Whatever normative independence I have must come from an other confirming it. I cannot bestow that authority on myself.

Thus, "*Self-consciousness attains its satisfaction only in another self-consciousness.*"

¶176. This is what is necessary to complete the concept of self-consciousness. First, there is the unity of self-consciousness, the identification of the object of self-consciousness (me) with the subject of self-consciousness (I). With that, we see that the subject-object model of self-consciousness is itself annulled. There are not two acts of consciousness involved, an awareness of an I, and an I being aware of that I. There is only one act. Second, this unity of consciousness is empty and requires filling (requires mediation), which it does by attending to what it lacks (the desire for what would fill it out). Third, there is the doubling of self-consciousness in which (as we saw in ¶175) there must another self-consciousness available to authenticate my own claims to what I am doing. It is only when all three aspects are present that the "certainty" that is there in self-consciousness becomes a "truth": the certainty is the idea that in acting (or believing), I must be aware of what I am doing for it to count as an action at all, and for me to authenticate that I am doing what I take myself to be doing, I need authentication from an other (another self-consciousness).

First, the "I" seems like the object of consciousness ("the first immediate object"). But this is absolute mediation. Self-consciousness as absorbed in its object (or its action) is otherwise empty and is full only of the object. I am not explicitly thinking of, say, moving my body when I'm chopping vegetables; I am focused simply on chopping vegetables. But the objects of such self-consciousness, where I am aware of what I'm doing (e.g., chopping vegetables) as opposed to doing something else, are also "other," independent. In the doubling of self-consciousness, I am aware of the Other as him/herself being aware of him/herself as something other than me. Both of us are aware of the other's active stance in this regard.

¶177. There are several statements here on which much, much commentary has been written. This is an absolutely key paragraph.

A self-consciousness *is* only for a self-consciousness. Hegel's point is that the idea that we are all self-enclosed self-aware beings breaks down under its own weight. We are the self-conscious beings we are only in our relations with other such self-conscious beings. This is a conceptual, metaphysical point, not the bromide that we all need to be raised in a society, learn a language, etc.

But Hegel says that only here is it really the case that it is the unity of itself in its otherness (its *Anderssein*). Note: it's not that the boundary between self and other is erased, only that self and other have this type of peculiar unity, which is not the unity of two "things" standing side by side (like two rocks or two patches of color). Here we introduce the idea of the second person. There is *one* thought with *two* subjects: I/ You; You/I. Later (¶671) he will describe this as the existence of the I extended into *two-ness* (*Zweiheit*, i.e., expressed as the second person).

The concept of spirit, the absolute substance, which in the complete freedom and self-sufficiency of its opposition is the unity of that: I that is We, We that is I. Note the first-person singular and plural here. The idea that there is a genuine "We" here is one of the key issues. The paragraph seems to be saying that there can be a group action that is self-conscious as a group. (It would be an apperceptive first-person plural.) Many people would want to say the opposite: there are no groups that are self-conscious, there are only individual self-conscious agents who coordinate their actions and fictively assign what thereby gets done to a fictive "group" agent.

Hegel doesn't explicitly use the language of first person, second person, etc. here. That approach comes about (I think) first with Wittgenstein in the *Blue and Brown Books* over the issue of whether "I" is a referring term. But it can help us to use this to figure out what he's saying. The second person is signaled in: "A self-consciousness is for a self-consciousness. Only thereby is there in fact self-consciousness, for it is only therein that the unity of itself in its otherness comes to be for it. . . . The concept *of spirit* is thereby present for us." We get to Spirit (I, We) only through the second person (one thought, two agents). As I've put it elsewhere, in such a case, each thinks of the other as an *immediate second person* to its *first-personal reference*. It is in my first-person grasping of "you" as *your thinking second-personally* of "me" that "*you*" *grasp "me" second-personally*, and it is thinking within that complex thought that we comprehend ourselves thereby as plural, as what Hegel calls "The I that is a We, and a We that is an I," which he identifies as *Geist* itself.

This is the turning point: we leave the colorful semblance (*Scheine*) of sensuous this-sidedness and the empty night of the supersensible beyond, and step into the spiritual daylight of the present. We move away from empiricism and away from at least one strain of Kantianism. Fine, but where are going?

A. Self-Sufficiency and Non-Self-Sufficiency of Self-Consciousness; Mastery and Servitude

¶178. Part of the issue has to do with the obviously finite status of embodied agents.

Robert Pippin takes self-consciousness to be an avowal of commitments—that is, where I exercise authority and thus only exist as an *Anerkanntes*, as one who is recognized. (I have real authority only if I am recognized as having authority.) But where is the independent argument for that claim?

Why is self-consciousness doubled?

One reading: Hegel is endorsing the "intersubjectivity" thesis, that all subjectivity is essentially a precipitate out of intersubjectivity. But is that true? It's hard to square with other elements of the text.

Hegel's view seems to be: my own claim-making activity is licensed not exclusively by me but by something authoritative outside of me. At first, that "authoritative outside of me" looked to be the objects of "consciousness" in chapters 1–3. But now we see that it can only be another self-conscious subject. The subject is *Selbständige* (self-sufficient), but also *Anerkanntes* (recognized). It is both extremes within a unity. That unity is that of self-conscious life in general. If I am self-sufficient, I need nothing else, but I am that putative self-sufficient being only by having another subject authorize my activity. This is a form of self-sufficiency within dependence, which at first sounds contradictory. To authorize myself independently would be like pinning a medal on myself, by "recognizing myself," but I can't do this.

I need the other; otherwise I have a bad contradiction or a paradox.

It seems to belong to something like the same family to which Wittgenstein's "private language argument" belongs. There can be no pure self-authorization that only I can make.

It is at this point that something like the possibility of self-deception makes its appearance. In my self-certainty, I know what it is that I am doing. But another can challenge that. ("You say you're just trying to be helpful. Actually, you're just trying to be the center of attention.") My self-certainty can be "truth" only if there is an appropriate match between what I take myself to be doing and what others take me to be doing. And even that match can itself be a matter of mutual deception and self-deception. When one starts reflecting on that possibility, a sense of metaphysical vertigo starts to set in: Where do we stop the regress so that I really do know what I'm doing? It might seem as if self-deception only involved an individual agent somehow being wrong about an internal mental state of his own. Hegel's idea is that the "truth" of what you take yourself to be doing is not a matter of describing private, internal mental states, but of what you and others together take yourself to be doing.

I am not a mind simply looking out from within at others. I am a body reflecting on itself, which means reflecting on its being known by others.

¶179. In recognition, self-consciousness "loses" itself, in that its status is determined by the recognition it receives from an other. At first, it sees itself as the essence which demands recognition from the other. In seeing my own authority in my self-consciousness as resting on the recognition by an other, my self-consciousness is "outside" of (or external to) myself.

I count as knowing only if my knowing is known (authorized) by an other *who has the authority* to do this.

I see the other who is doing this not as having the real authority to withdraw recognition from me but as giving me the recognition I take myself to have deserved. Hegel says: "It also does not see the other as the essence but rather sees *itself* in the *other*." I see myself from the other's point of view as having or not having the authority I claim with "self-certainty" to have on my own.

¶180. If the first self-conscious being has its status only as being recognized, then, so it seems, for it to be an agent on its own (for itself, *für sich*)—for its self-certainty to match up with the status given it by the other—it must sublate that status of having a status only in recognition by an other. Since its status only exists in the eyes of the other, in sublating, transforming the other, it sublates itself.

It knows itself only in being known by an other. But the other must have the authority to entitle it to do that. Thus, there seems to be an insoluble problem. This suggests: maybe we have to "presuppose" something outside of ourselves that does authorize us. But what would that be? And why wouldn't it be subject to the same problems?

¶181. If I claim with any self-certainty to occupy a certain status, then I am assuming that the other is freely concurring with my claim. How could he do otherwise? But for the other to be freely concurring, the other has to have a certain independent authority to do so. It seems that implicitly I am demanding that the other recognize me no matter what, but for the other to do that, the other has to have this independent status himself. I am both denying his independence (in claiming that he has no real choice but to recognize me) and affirming his independence (I "set the other free again").

¶182. Each of us, I and the other, necessarily does this. Each starts with the assumption that its project to claim a *Selbständigkeit* (self-sufficiency, independence) that is not dependent on recognition from the other, or at least is such that it demands recognition from the other but takes itself not to require extending such recognition to the other.

¶183. Each is doing something with regard to himself which is identical with what the other is doing with regard to himself, and this kind of self-direction on the part of each is also directed at the other. (This basically restates the point made in ¶182.)

¶184. Each is the mediating middle of the other. Each would have a self-sufficiency only in being recognized by the other agent as self-sufficient. Hegel says, "It is for consciousness that it immediately *is* and *is not* an other consciousness," which is one way of expressing the idea that each agent takes himself to be self-sufficient but also realizes that he is self-sufficient only by being recognized by the other, and in doing so, he comes to realize that he is as he takes himself to be, but that amounts to being what he is only in the eyes of an other.

Hegel notes that this is like "the play of forces": each is both the soliciting and the solicited (so to speak).

¶185. We thus have the "pure concept" (not the empirical concept) of recognition, the doubling, *Verdoppelung*, of self-consciousness in its unity. (Hegel is not denying the empirical concept in all its psychological complexity. He is merely drawing attention to the pure concept.)

But now we are to look at it in terms of how it appears to self-consciousness itself, how these two living agents will have to see it, at least at first.

The mediating middle (which is each of them) breaks into extremes. At first, one is recognized, the other merely recognizes. The master demands recognition from the slave but refuses to recognize the slave; the slave recognizes the master (as master) but does not get recognition from the master in return.

¶186. Each is *Fürsichsein* (being-for-itself). But each is also one object among many. Each takes itself to have certain entitlements that stand outside of questioning (each is certain of himself), but each takes the other not to be entitled to anything particular (each is not certain of the other).

But this certainty has no truth, since it ultimately comes from recognition from the other. (Rather, it is the contradiction: I am a full rational agent on my own; I am entitled, I entitle others; and I am only so entitled in being recognized by others; my entitlements come from others.)

For his certainty to have truth, he would have to be a subject who does not require recognition from others. But he can't have that. So what he needs is for the other subject basically to entitle him to something like the claim: I don't need you, but you need me.

¶187. The agent must show himself as the negation of his objectness. His being one object among many is a limit, and he wishes to show that there is some way in which he goes beyond that limit.

Each stakes his own life. He can set principles for himself for which he demands recognition (he can claim a status for himself for which he demands recognition).

He could be a "legal person" without having done so (he could have a legally defined status), but he could not be self-sufficient (he couldn't have a status that he sets for himself or that he "just has" as the self-sufficient agent he takes himself to be).

Each wants his certainty as self-sufficient to be a truth, wants the other who recognizes him to acknowledge this truth and recognize him as the self-sufficient agent he claims to be.

Note that this isn't intended as a piece of normal psychology: Hegel isn't saying that some people indulge in these massive ego-trips, or that some people love to dominate others, etc. (all of which may be true). It's a conceptual point about subjectivity in general. It may indeed have psychological consequences, but that's not the point here.

¶188. A struggle to the death over this matter isn't solved by one of them dying. The dead other cannot do any recognizing. If what matters most to me is your recognition of me, killing you will not satisfy that.

¶189. If life is as crucial to agency as self-consciousness, there is a possible reason to submit. Each at first stakes an unconditional claim to recognition from the other, but one of them reverses himself and makes the claim less than unconditional. At first he says that recognition is worth life itself and then changes that to recognition is important but not worth dying for. One of them thus becomes *Herr* (the lord, master), and the other who submits becomes the *Knecht* (vassal, bondsman, slave). There arises a world of masters and those whose existence is to serve the masters. Those in servitude become treated like any other "thing": there to serve the needs and interests of the master.

The simple I is "absolute mediation": the subject is spontaneous; the I is only in taking itself (and being taken) to be an I. This "simple I" is self-conscious life itself, a "we."

Another way of looking at this movement is to see it as exhibiting the fragility of a shared life. At first, they are together in recognizing that this what "we" creatures do (e.g., gathering fruit). Each as an individual makes these kinds of claims and takes himself to speak with the authority of the whole (of humanity, as it were): *we* are the kind of creatures who gather fruit. Since the authority of the whole takes precedence over other claims, when the break comes (each claiming to speak in the name of humanity itself but together making incompatible claims), there is no way out except for a kind of struggle over who really has the authority on the ground.

¶190. The *Herr* relates to things through the vassal or the slave. The *Herr* consumes (relates to things as objects of his desire), whereas the *Knecht* produces. Production and consumption part ways. (This mirrors a kind of feudalistic world, where some produce so that others may simply consume.)

¶191. The other (*Knecht*) posits itself in the *Herr*'s consciousness as inessential, as a possibly superfluous thing in (1) his processing of things (fabricating, cooking, cleaning, etc.) and (2) in the *Knecht's* dependence on a determinate existence (that of the *Herr*).

The *Knecht*, Hegel says, can't achieve absolute negation. The absolute negation would be the successful claim to be fully self-sufficient. The master thinks (wrongly) that he has this. He needs the vassal only in the same way he needs other things (food, a nice bed, good shelter, etc.). The vassal or slave is just a tool for getting those things. The *Knecht*, of course, is also a self-conscious life, but the norms of the world are not set by him. The *Herr* sets the rules as a kind of sovereign life—he can command, but no *Knecht* can command him—and the *Knecht* has no option except to obey. The *Knecht* must therefore reduce himself in his own eyes to what the *Herr* takes him to be. Or, as Hegel puts it, "What the second self-consciousness does is the first's own doing, for what the servant does is really the master's doing." The *Herr* says: you are nothing, you are but a tool, and the servant says, yes, I am nothing but a tool. This is a form of reciprocal recognition, but it is one-sided, unequal.

¶192. This brings about a conceptual reversal. The truth of the *Herr* is the *Knecht*. In the *Knecht's* recognition of the idea that he is but a tool, he confirms the self-certainty of the master that he commands but cannot be commanded. The *Herr* is thus utterly dependent on the *Knecht's* acquiescence. This is the "truth": what the concept turns out to be (the object as corresponding to its concept). People are masters only in being recognized as masters. They are masters only through the acquiescence of the servants (secured by violence on the part of the masters). But there is the twist: the masters remain entitled masters in principle (as opposed to keeping themselves in power by force and fear alone) only by relying on the continued recognition by the slaves. They in fact are who they are only be way of their dependency on the slaves.

¶193. As Hegel's account takes this new turn—"The *truth* of the self-sufficient consciousness is thus the *servile consciousness*"—the master ends up dependent on the slave, and his vaunted self-sufficiency begins to crack open. The slave, who had taken on (or rather had been forced to take on) the master's view of him as a tool now realizes that he is more than a tool. It is his recognition of the master as master that makes the master a master. The slave is prompted to his own "return into himself," to come to see his own agency at work in the process, and it is he who will fashion a true self-sufficiency. He may lack autonomy, but he certainly has agency.

¶194. It is the *Knecht* (the servant or bondsman) who has experienced the true nature of self-conscious life. He "felt the fear of death, the absolute master." This brought on the vertigo we had seen earlier in the account, but this sense of vertigo goes even deeper. The *Knecht* had experienced the floor falling out from under him— "all that was fixed within it had been shaken loose"—and thus the *Knecht*, not the master, had experienced the true essence of self-conscious life: to find oneself (as Heidegger famously said) "thrown" into a world not of your making, both absorbed and alienated in that world around you and projecting forward to an end that is certain, death. Self-conscious life is thus "absolute negativity, *pure being-for-itself.*" Negativity enters the world through self-conscious life. The world on its own is just a concatenation of facts. Self-consciousness in representing the world to itself (as in "Perception" or in "Force and Understanding") represents possibilities (that, for example, that tree might not have grown there) which are negations of what is (the tree grows over there). Negation, negativity, is the essence of self-conscious life, and death is the idea of oneself no longer existing: a possibility which will become a necessity. In grasping this existential truth about itself, the servant (*Knecht*) comes to understand that in working on things for the master, he is in fact acquiring his own sense of what counts and does not count. His self-consciousness is no longer completely commanded by the master.

¶195. If the *Herr* gets his desires satisfied through the slave's work, he finds that this kind of satisfaction lacks *Bestehen* (subsistence, stability). The *Knecht*'s work, on the other hand, is, as Hegel puts it, hemmed-in desire. It is the life of production that looks beyond consumption. Productive work educates and acculturates.

The producing, laboring consciousness comes to an intuition of itself as self-sufficient. (Note: it is an "intuition," not a fully elaborated conceptual account—we might rephrase it as a "glimpse" or a "view" of itself as self-sufficient without the *Knecht* necessarily being able to articulate the details. Or we could say: it is a nondiscursive grasp that the whole in which he/she exists is false, even if he/she can't quite yet articulate its falsity.)

¶196. One of the timeless complaints by masters about their slaves is that the slave is intrinsically lazy or is perhaps too stubborn to get things done the right way. Actually, this represents the way in which slaves craftily subvert the wishes of the master. As Hegel puts it, the *Knecht* in his stubbornness or obstinacy (*Eigensinn*) acquires a mind of his own (*eigne Sinn*). This is freedom which remains within servitude since it consists merely in defiance of the existing order. The "stubborn" slave resists his/her servitude, but doesn't necessarily challenge the status of slavery per se. (The ancient world had many examples of freed slaves who immediately went out and purchased slaves of their own.)

5

Freedom

Stoicism, Skepticism, Unhappy Consciousness

B. Freedom of Self-Consciousness: Stoicism, Skepticism, and the Unhappy Consciousness

So where are we? Mired in the aftermath of mastery and servitude.

We started by seeing if there was some way we could just get around the "meaning" question by suggesting that we could do well enough (self-sufficiently) with a meaning-free reference by indexicals like "this," "here," "now," "I."

That didn't work.

We found we were really engaged not just in pointing things out but in perceiving.

That too didn't fully work.

We found that in perceiving, we were also invoking more than just perceptual objects. We were also relying on the background conditions of laws and regularities, and that landed us in a real mess. It turned out that we weren't just conscious of things, we were also self-conscious about the "horizon" in which things show up for us.

We thus turned to self-consciousness as a way in which life became aware of itself *as* life (or, rather the genus, self-conscious life, aware of itself as the genus it is by being conscious of itself). We found that self-consciousness in fact was not just another extension of consciousness-of-objects but something with a different logical form.

What followed from that? Self-consciousness requires another self-consciousness for its truth, but it turned out that didn't imply just how they needed each other. One way of solving the puzzle was that of mastery and servitude.

That really didn't work.

Hegel's Phenomenology of Spirit. Terry Pinkard, Oxford University Press. © Oxford University Press 2023.
DOI: 10.1093/oso/9780197663127.003.0005

So where do we find ourselves now? (Note: not "What must I add to the account?" or "Is it time to change the subject?" but "What have I ended up doing?") Since the project of self-sufficiency has failed in its initial phase of mastery and servitude, the project changes into something slightly different, namely, self-sufficiency pursued as freedom, in particular, as freedom of thought taken to be a form of self-mastery available to everyone.

¶197. The servant has become the self-sufficient consciousness by virtue of having the self-sufficiency in the object. In ¶195, the laboring consciousness came to the intuition (*Anschauung*), that is, the not fully discursively articulated view of *self-sufficient existence as himself.* The conclusion for him to draw was that he needs no other criteria for thinking than his own, even if (subdued by force) he remains a servant. This provokes his inertness as servant to give way to a conception of himself as self-moving but self-moving only in thought. Although I may be in chains, he thinks, I remain free in thought.

The "*pure abstraction*" *of the I* is now taken to be the essence for self-sufficient consciousness, to be what is really at work in the world. Note the abstraction from out of the body to thinking of simple self-conscious self-relation (self-conscious being for itself). This is where we begin to tie ourselves in knots in yet another way and are led into mind-body and soul-body dualisms. Thus, the "*pure abstraction*" *of the I* sees its difference from others not as an objective matter (not merely as one body distinct from others) but as a subjective matter (i.e., an abstraction, the concept of a pure self-relation itself not, so it seems, essentially related to embodiment).

The two moments (pure self-relation and relation through the body) "fall away" from each other, seem to become "undone." The unity in which they are "moments" comes to seem like only an additive unity consisting of "parts."

"I know myself only as being known by others" seems to give way to: I really only know myself alone.

But since self-consciousness is always form-consciousness—self-consciousness is consciousness of the form of life to which I belong—my self-consciousness is always of the form "self-knowledge as known by others." I know myself by manifesting myself through the concept (subject, agent) which is a form I share with others and can only authenticate with others.

The idea is that as the moments fall apart from each other, we seek to have our being-for-itself in an immediate unity with our being-in-itself, or more colloquially put: we seek to have the "pure" self-relation become identical with what "we" really are (in this case, it would be "thinking beings"), what the trajectory for own development is to be.

Yet although this figure of self-consciousness has this concept of itself, it has not yet developed this concept. Hegel's thesis will be: the development of this concept will be "working it out" or putting it into practice (*ausführen*). But that has not yet been shown. This is not an *analysis* of the concept but a *development* of it (of what it is *in itself, an sich*, what its trajectory of development is).

Thus, the "I" is not yet "genuinely self-differentiated." Its distinctions seem to "happen" to it instead of being developed out of it (or so it seems to itself). It is not yet a *gleichbleibendes Ich* (literally "same-remaining I," but better rendered as "self-consistent I").

This is not to say that from the point of view of the servile consciousness, this is the way things lucidly appear. The servile consciousness seems to itself to be a culturally shaped thing (one of the many *gebildete Dinge*), but it also sees the master as existing on his own (being for itself). It sees itself and the master as "consciousness," that is, as occupying a subject-object divide. (Me here, you there.) (Hegel speaks here of *Bildung* in its classical, nineteenth-century form as incorporating education, culture, formation of character, and thus the ability to make good judgments.)

The new form of self-consciousness is in its own eyes "essence as infinity." That is:

Now it is *freedom*, and not self-sufficiency, that is the determining conception of self-consciousness. And freedom seems to mean so far: free thinking, bound to nothing but itself and thus "infinite." The master may be forcing me to do stuff for him, but he can't force me to think x, y, z. (Here Hegel refers to subjectivity "moving in concepts and not *Vorstellungen*," "ideas" or representations.) Pure thinking has no boundaries other than those set by reason itself, so reason is here the "infinite."

Thus, in thought, one's actions are not entirely dictated from outside oneself (as is the case when the slave acts in the world according to the dictates of the master) but in terms of one's dictating things to oneself. I am *bei mir selbst* (at one with myself, alone with myself). In pure thinking, I am self-moving, not being moved by something exterior to me.

The experience and the idea of freedom emerge out of the failures of self-sufficiency in the practical world. Both the slave and the master fail at sustaining the projects of mastery and servitude.

This is supposed to start the development of working out the idea that "the truth must be comprehended not merely as *substance* but also equally as *subject.*" Self-sufficient thought would have its conditions within itself and not have to go outside of itself or beyond itself to vouch for itself. It should thus be the principle that allows us to organize our other thoughts such that the whole becomes intelligible. Thus, self-sufficient thought either really is Aristotelian happiness or flourishing, *eudaimonia* (as distinct from what Aristotle thought) or is the Hegelian replacement for (or successor to) Aristotelian *eudaimonia*. In any event, Aristotle didn't seem to think that slaves could genuinely flourish.

¶198. This will be true freedom, but here freedom is still just abstract, consisting of a denial of dependency as the "essence." On this conception, what counts for self-consciousness is pure thinking, where what I do aspires to be independent of all determination from exteriority.

Hegel identifies this with ancient doctrines of Stoicism, and he also claims that this conception has not yet formulated the true view of freedom within dependency.

¶199. *Eigensinn* (stubbornness, obstinacy) is the freedom found within servitude. It is a kind of inflexibility. One does what one does because of who one is, and one is inflexible about that. It is a way of stopping the infinite regress of reasons with a simple: this is what I do.

Hegel tells us that Stoicism made perfect sense at a certain period in history when the ancient world was descending into crisis, fragmentation, and increasing irrelevance. It was, Hegel claims, a universal form of the world spirit (the *Weltgeist*) in a time of universal fear and servitude (*Knechtschaft*) coupled with universal level of high culture

(*Bildung*). ("Universal" at least in the Mediterranean world—the world of the high cultural achievements of Greece and Rome mixing with and depending on the widespread exploitation of slaves.) Hegel's interpretive thesis: the practices that embody the distinct statuses of master and servant (or slave) are pushed into a conception of themselves as pure self-relation in response to the failure of mastery and servitude to make sense of itself. Stoicism is thus also an intelligible response to the existential issues facing agency in any period of fear, servitude, and a high level of cultural education.

The activity at stake is that of being free from dependence (*Abhängigkeit*, not *Unselbständigkeit*, dependence, not un-self-sufficiency) on how things happen to be. But since of course we are dependent on the world and each other, it must be independence in thought we are talking about.

¶200. As aspiring to self-sufficiency, this "essence" of self-consciousness is not the abstract "I," the formal "I" that is free when it thinks, nor is its essence something else (like a master) outside of itself. It is the I that in its *Anderssein* (Otherness, being-other) has returned into itself and has transformed this otherness into its thought of it. It takes this to be freedom, even freedom from its natural life, but, as Hegel puts it, it is not "living freedom," but only the thought of freedom. This condemns it to emptiness, however edifying its claims to free thought and reason may seem to be.

¶201. It has not grasped itself as *absolute negation*. The line between inner and outer is still presupposed, and only the inner is given authority. It is, though, the idea that thinking draws its own boundaries, sets its own limits, or that, as Kant put it, reason is its own tribunal. (If so, it would be "absolute" and not relative negation.) Instead, it is an "incomplete negation of otherness" in the sense that it cannot really achieve the full self-determination to which it aspires. What it thinks remains dependent on content from outside the pure form of thinking itself.

¶202. Skepticism is the stoic freedom of thought actualized, and as the actualization of stoicism, it is the truth of stoicism. Stoics, if they push their thought to its conclusion, will thus become skeptics.

¶203. Skepticism highlights the nature of the dialectic. The kinds of basic concepts that are at work in dialectic look like they generate contradictions within themselves (or "antinomies," as Kant called them). Those contradictions create a set of problems that demand a resolution (or otherwise, as Kant also said, we would have the "euthanasia" of reason). The problems that skepticism generates come from taking ordinary concepts, making them into abstractions, and pushing them to such extremes.

¶204. This dialectical movement of generating contradictions (a "negative" movement) seems to skepticism to be part of the nature of things, not just a way it treats them. Self-conscious skepticism knows implicitly that it is doing this, but it somehow forgets it. Self-conscious skepticism, in becoming aware of its own freedom to pursue this line of thought, in effect thinks of itself as the point which is stable and unmoving while everything else is falling away. Yet self-conscious skepticism has no determinate content to itself. It is instead doubting and "negating" all these other (determinate) things about which it is thinking. Self-conscious skepticism is the empty thought (but of itself as stable and unmoving) of the non-empty (and in flux) things of the world.

¶205. Skepticism establishes itself as the essence that is selfsame, self-consistent in all its semblances (*sichselbstgleich*). In that light, the self-conscious skeptic as a thinking *individual* claims a *universal* authority. But where exactly is the skeptic standing when he draws that line? No other act of seeing, hearing, thinking can be authoritative against itself. The skeptical self-consciousness is the determinacy that also has no real determinacy but whose guises, semblances, do have determinacy, and it is supposed to explain them. The skeptic, like so many shapes of consciousness examined up to this point, also experiences a kind of metaphysical vertigo, a feeling of the floor dropping out from under him, for it is a "perpetually self-creating disorder." The skeptic insists he is a contingent, singular individual, but he claims to speak for the whole, for all humanity. This is his freedom, which ultimately does not make sense, although it is easy to see the motives for becoming such a skeptic.

¶206. If the Stoic is an individual who claims to be self-sufficient in the freedom of thought, and the skeptic is an individual thinker claiming universal authority as a merely contingent individual, and neither of these works because, as they put the ideas into practice, their internal contradictions come to the fore, then a new shape of self-conscious life grows out of these two failures as a way of bringing them both together. The skeptic, Hegel says, is a kind of repetition in a new form of the relation between mastery and servitude: "The doubling, which was previously distributed between two singular individuals, the master and the servant, is thereby brought back into one singular individual." The skeptic is the "master" speaking with the authority of the whole (claiming to speak for all humanity) while at the same time holding himself to have no such authority (as a "servant").

The name of this new shape is called the "unhappy consciousness" (similar to what Kierkegaard would later call "despair.") Why is it unhappy? Because it cannot actualize itself, since it is contradictory. It is thus estranged from itself (*entzweit*, split in two).

¶207. It seems to come to a unity with itself, but it then falls apart again. As estranged from itself, it is always at odds with itself, and this metaphysical lack of equilibrium is painful. It consists of a contingent point of view (the individual) and a God's-eye point of view (the view of the world as a whole, to which it aspires but which it cannot as a contingent individual have). It believes that the whole is intelligible (that its world ultimately makes sense), but it cannot make sense of it. At best it sees through a glass darkly, but it believes that one day, as in a twinkling, all will be made known unto itself and all will be clear. In this world, though, things remain unclear. Strikingly, Hegel says of this doubling that it is a correct view of the concept of *Geist* as an I that is a We, and a We that is an I. It is just that in this form, it cannot achieve the unity it needs between the two. It aspires to this unity but despairs of ever achieving it since achieving it would be to overcome this deep contradiction within itself, and surpassing it seems to be metaphysically ruled out.

¶208. If the truth about the world (which it seeks) is only available to the God's-eye view, then it must take itself as the skeptic does: it is the unessential element in the relation between the world as a whole and the world seen only as the individual contingently finds it. Hegel now calls the God's-eye view that of "the unchangeable" versus "the changeable" as the singular individual's point of view. This opposition is rock bottom for this shape of consciousness and is the source of the unhappiness it experiences with life.

¶209. If the truth (the essence) is the unchangeable, and we take ourselves as needing to measure up to the concept (that the object— ourselves as self-conscious beings—should correspond to the concept), then contingent life must seem (at least on reflection) worthless. It perhaps is a mere passage into a better time, a Pilgrim's Progress. One seeks to cast it aside, but this individuality keeps reappearing.

¶210. Hegel here seems to be alluding to a kind of nondiscursive, mystical take on the issues contained in this kind of self-opposition. (Although Hegel does not explicitly tell us this, it does seem that he is talking about the passage from the slave societies of the ancient Greco-Roman world—a shape of consciousness bound up with the dialectic of mastery and servitude—to the early medieval Christian and then later feudal societies after the collapse of the western Roman Empire.) Here we see the kind of Neoplatonism that informed much of early Christianity as the way in which "the unchangeable" comes to incarnate itself in singular human life (the logos became flesh, as the Gospel of St. John has it), and the singular life (the "changeable") comes to see its truth in uniting itself spiritually with "the unchangeable." The unhappy consciousness thus comes to see itself united with the unchangeable, and instead of being unhappy, it experiences a kind of joy.

¶211. This forms a learning experience for this shape of consciousness. It finds its unity in that of the universal and the singular (the unchangeable and the changeable), but it finds that it must attribute that to the unchangeable itself. This seems like a reconciliation, but the way that this reconciliation comes about turns out itself to have the same problems of estrangement that led to the reconciliation in the first place.

¶212. The unchangeable has the gestalt, the shape, of an individual as something that has merely happened, as an event in time. The unchangeable (the One) seems as distant as ever. (Hegel says: "The hope of coming to be at one with it must remain a hope, which is to say, it must remain without fulfillment, without ever being present.") The individual who embodies this full reconciliation appears, dies, and thus seems distant. (This seems to be Hegel's redescription in more logical-metaphysical terms of the passage in early Christianity from Jesus's mission to his death and the founding of the church in his name.)

¶213. The desire (the feeling of a lack) to unite with the unchangeable has two parts: first, the unchangeable is shapeless (a metaphysical something-or-other that cannot be specified, a Neoplatonist "One"); then, second, it becomes shaped (it acquires a determinacy in the shape of the Jewish and then the Christian God).

¶214. There are three phases of the way this aspiration to be united with the unchangeable proceeds: (1) pure consciousness, not consciousness of this or that but of a sense of being "one" with the unchangeable—this is too abstract ultimately to make much sense, and it is even more abstract than "sensuous-certainty"; (2) the individual who goes to work on the real world; (3) consciousness of its being-for-itself, its *Fürsichsein*, its self-relation.

¶215. As "pure consciousness," it takes itself to be aware of the One without any further determination. It is just "one" with the "One."

This is of course "pure thought," that is, an orientation within the whole which cannot be given in intuition.

¶216. This kind of pure consciousness is formally rather much like the stoicism and skepticism that earlier had been overtaken by the "unhappy consciousness." It aims at the unity of the thought of universality and the thought of the irreducible singularity (or individuality) of the thinker, but it does not get there.

¶217. This aspiration does not succeed—its aspiration to pure thought remains impure—but it is on the way to thought, and although it is not really "thought" (*Denken* or *Gedachtes*), it is, nonetheless, devotion (*Andacht*). The pure heart feels itself painfully estranged, but it remains conceptually-emotionally committed to the aspiration to unity with the One. Hegel makes a veiled reference to the Crusades (which he always saw as a fairly insane endeavor) and its wanting to be in possession of Christ's grave—as if the empty grave could somehow fulfill the aspiration to oneness.

¶218. The "heart" or "mind" (*Gemüt*) takes an inward turn, feels itself as an actual individual (as the being who is really at work in the world), and it thereby seeks to authenticate itself in work and desire. However, although it acquires a self-feeling as a kind of self-assurance (*Selbstgefühl*), it ends up simply authenticating its own estrangement.

¶219. This estrangement takes on a slightly different character. The actuality on which this estranged individual works is no longer in itself a nullity; it is an actuality that has broken in two:

On the one hand it is a nullity, but on the other hand it is also a sanctified world, a shape of the unchangeable, and thus it takes on universality.

¶220. In this estranged world, the consciousness of self-feeling as self-authentication acquires an assurance about itself. However, it also still feels its own nullity vis-à-vis the One, and thus it finds that any kind of enjoyment in the actual world seems to happen for it only in that the unchangeable gives up its unchangeable gestalt and gives itself over to him for enjoyment. The unchangeable (for the Christians, God) provides a world that can be put to use and makes a gift of talents and such so that the estranged consciousness may make use of the world.

¶221. The this-worldly consciousness and the otherworldly unchangeable now line up. However, in projecting its activities into an otherworldly domain (God-given resources exploited by God-given talents), the this-worldly consciousness fails to authenticate itself.

¶222. Since the unchangeable has practiced a kind of self-abnegation and taken on the shape of the singular consciousness—the Christian overtones here are impossible to miss even though Hegel is presenting this as if it were only the development of a certain kind of logic of self-conception—the singular consciousness also practices a kind of self-abnegation and "gives thanks" to the unchangeable. In doing so, it seems to be renouncing its prior claims to self-sufficiency, but this is only a semblance of self-abnegation. In practice, the singular consciousness (the flesh-and-blood individual) is still absorbed in its labor and consumption. The unity between the universal (the unchangeable) and the singular (the acting individual person) fractures again. What we have is once again "only the doubled reflection into both extremes." (God and man are still not fully reconciled.)

¶223. This practice of self-abnegation (giving thanks, etc.) in fact marks off the "inner" realm of subjectivity even more prominently. The individual, in the practices of giving himself over to the "unchangeable," also produces a "return into himself" from out of those practices.

¶224. Yet the conception of itself as a nullity in the presence of what really counts (the unchangeable) remains. What are we supposed to make of this? It looks like it is repeating in a different idiom the relation between servant and master (the *Herr*, the lord).

¶225. By its own concept, its life functions (its animality) are to it matters that do not relate to its true nature (its in-itself). It feels itself polluted. They betray the individual's lack of unity with the truly spiritual. Those functions now appear as the "enemy" of the practices of pure self-abnegation. (It is not hard to see what Hegel is talking about under the guise of this logic of shape of consciousness. This is a reference to the rules governing celibacy and the like in the early church.)

¶226. As it thinks of the negation of its actual life in favor of the world to come, it also affirms its own powers.

¶227. The unity between universal and singular (God and man in this shape) is an object of aspiration, but it continually undoes itself. It takes on the form of a syllogism—an inference—in which one term (existing individual people) is brought together with another term (the unchangeable) via some mediating term. This "term" is another conscious being who mediates between the unchangeable (God) and the singular changeable (people). (It's obvious, even though Hegel doesn't say it, that this mediator is a priest. Hegel is trying to argue that this role for priests in the early church was not some accident of history but the result of following out a certain kind of logic about how to accomplish the aspired unification.)

¶228. Hegel makes reference to pre-Reformation Christianity and the place of the priesthood in it. The unhappy consciousness turns its will over to the mediator (priest), and thus its actions cease to be its own. Nonetheless, since it is actively turning its will over to the mediator, its own activity is not completely negated. Even fastings and mortifications retain something of an active will.

¶229. Turning one's will over to the mediator means giving up the consciousness of both its inner and outer freedom, and it deprives itself of comprehending its own self-relation (*Fürsichsein*) in the real world (*Wirklichkeit*). It thus empties itself of all its own content and makes itself more thinglike (obeying rules given from outside itself without having to reflect on any of them). However, it never gives up nor can it fully give up a sense of its own agency. These are things it *does*. Nonetheless, the unhappy consciousness preserves the external (goods) for itself, and the inner is in its consciousness of its decisions.

¶230. As all this has developed, what has really been going on—what is the "in itself," the trajectory of development of all this activity—is the growing sense of the affirmation of the unhappy consciousness of its own freedom and authority. All of this surrendering one's own will to that of another is not exactly that of the servant giving way to the master but that of a singular individual coming to adopt a viewpoint on his own will that considers its authority to derive from its aspiration to universality. The will of the mediator (the priest) is not merely that of another individual imposing his own views on the unhappy consciousness but is that of a claim to universality, to the God's-eye point of view as embodied in an individual. Now the idea of being open to a principle, of acting "in light of" a universal norm and not merely an ethic of tradition, comes to be shaped out of this way of responding to the mediator. Incipiently this is an appeal not to a priesthood but to reason itself, although one is not yet there.

6

Reason

First Part

¶231. We have before us the supposition generated as a result of stoicism, skepticism, and the unhappy consciousness that individual consciousness is *in itself* the absolute essence. The "idea" behind this is that the world (or the form of the world) is not something "beyond" and otherworldly but is already there and open to us. When Hegel says that the unhappy consciousness has posited individuality in its full development, as the negative of itself, he means that, whereas formerly, the in-itself was, as he puts it, the otherworldly beyond, now it is to be found in "singular individual consciousness" itself. The individual by utilizing his own rational resources can in principle grasp and understand the form of the world. Rather than seeing the absolute essence of the world as something like an object—the negative of consciousness, what is "beyond" consciousness—the negative is that of self-consciousness positing itself as different from itself but yet identical with itself.

¶232. The negative relation to otherness becomes positive since the otherness is just itself. This is because the result of the "unhappy consciousness" was the realization that "self-consciousness is reason," and thus it becomes "idealism," which Hegel takes here to be the conviction that reason is capable on its own of grasping the true form of the world. Thus, reason takes itself to be "all reality," which means that things can be explained without reference to an otherworldly beyond. (It is worth noting that this is *not* the thesis that everything is mental or is a mental construct out of experience, which is sometimes what "idealism" is taken to mean.)

¶233. For those who have not read Kant, Fichte, or Schelling (Hegel's immediate predecessors in the development of German idealism), much of what he says here will be more than just a bit obscure.

Hegel's Phenomenology of Spirit. Terry Pinkard, Oxford University Press. © Oxford University Press 2023.
DOI: 10.1093/oso/9780197663127.003.0006

It was Fichte who summed up his version of idealism in the formula, "I = I." Fichte thought that the basic a priori structure of a fully "scientific" philosophical theory could be generated by looking solely at the a priori conditions of self-consciousness. Nothing has any meaning unless it is posited by self-consciousness, which for Fichte was equivalent to saying nothing makes sense that goes beyond the requirements of reason itself. (The idea that making sense of things required a mostly incomprehensible otherworldly beyond was what made the "unhappy consciousness" unhappy.) The force of the formula "I = I" is the idea that it is not a tautology (as is "A = A"). The "I" has to differentiate itself from itself and actively preserve the identity. This "I" is therefore not just a something alongside others, not just one object among many. Rather, it is conscious of *Nichtsein*, the nonbeing, of all "otherness." But it has forgotten the path it took to get there, and, as Hegel says, for those without some knowledge of this path (from sensuous certainty to the unhappy consciousness), "This assertion is incomprehensible."

Here is a way to think of this. Fichte tried to pose the issue of what Kant called the "synthetic unity of apperception." This involves a single complex thought: thinking of the multiplicity as a multiplicity, which requires a single complex subject to think it. Thus, the claim: "I that thinks X" is identical to the "I that thinks Y" is a synthetic proposition and not analytic; thus, I = I looks like a disguised synthetic judgment, or, as Kant had put it, the analytic unity of consciousness is possible only under the presupposition of a synthetic unity.

Fichte, then Schelling, tried out the idea that concepts are not inherently empty but have content in their relation to other concepts. Fichte went further and argued that I = I was such that it could not be understood except in relation to a Not-I, but that one did not have to go outside of the inferential structure to get there.

What we had taken to be authoritative for us was something other to us setting the terms for us (ultimately the otherworldly beyond). Fichtean idealism says, no, the subject does that all by him/herself. He/she sets her own terms. If the "other" of any type sets the terms, it's only because we have authorized it to do so. The "other" cannot authorize itself.

¶234. This assumption (that we set the terms of what the world means, and not the other way round) is the starting point of such idealism. But the idealism that begins with this is just a mere assurance that this can be done. It takes itself to be articulating an immediate certainty—I am I—and to be drawing conclusions from that alone. What might seem equally certain—that there is an "other" to my thought that plays a role in how I truly think—is in fact something that reason as self-consciousness shows to be the case. Hegel now adds the proviso: the relation to otherness will depend "on just which stage it [self-consciousness as reason] finds itself occupying vis-à-vis how the world-spirit is becoming conscious of itself." This will turn out to be a central claim of the *Phenomenology*, but here it is simply put forward as if it were clear what that might mean. Roughly, the thesis is something like this: what we take to be our relation to "otherness"—or more generally to other people and to the world as a whole—will take different forms depending on the development of humanity's ("the world spirit's") view of itself and the world, and, so Hegel thinks, this development will have a progressive element such that as history progresses we will be able to see how we are getting better at comprehending that relation to otherness.

As idealism first states its viewpoint, idealism's thesis seems incomprehensible. Why in the world would one believe that the form of the world is completely available to finite little hominids like us?

¶235. Hegel tells us that reason is aware of itself as being all reality: there is no otherworldly beyond that reason cannot in principle understand, even if there is lots of contingency in everyday life. But at the point at which we've arrived, "the in-itself" (what the world is really like) is only the pure abstraction of reality. It's as if "reality" as the "in-itself" is something like an great white light, indeterminate on its own, which we otherwise arbitrarily carve up. A lot of what Hegel says here depends on knowing what had transpired between Kant's *Critique of Pure Reason* in 1781 and Schelling's early 1800s development of the "Identity" philosophy. Since it seems like the people in Jena were talking about it all the time, Hegel obviously felt he could just gesture toward it and readers would get what he was saying.

This assumption won't work for most people who are not presently living in 1790s Jena. Here is a partial background. In that period in Jena, philosophical discussion centered on the rapid development of Kant's philosophy with its conception of knowledge as resting on nonconceptual intuitions of space and time held together (and thus conceptualized) by the unity of self-consciousness and the denial that we could even in principle know what the world was like in itself apart from the conditions under which we could experience it. In the 1790s, Fichte daringly rejected Kant's doctrine of the unknowable thing-in-itself, declaring it to be a nonthought, a "pipe dream," and suggested that one could derive all the a priori categories Kant had done from the requirements of self-consciousness alone (from the "I = I"). Famously at the time, Fichte argued that the "I" by its nature had to "posit" something that was different from itself (the "Not-I") and thought that by a kind of thesis-antithesis-synthesis logic he could derive all the a priori categories there were to be found. Within a very short time frame, Schelling had taken Fichte's idea of the "I" and expanded it into a Spinoza-inspired conception of a kind of cosmic "I" that was "positing" the natural world as well as other self-conscious thinkers. (Schelling tended to identify that expanded "I" with God.)

Here we find Hegel referring to the "simple category." If Aristotle had said that the most general and highest category of all that is real is that of substance and accident, the Jena makeover of that would substitute the "I" for "substance" as the highest and simplest category. Hegel says that would amount to saying that "self-consciousness and being are *the same* essence," which is perhaps a key way of describing the overall view of Jena 1790s philosophy. All the important differences in the world should follow from consideration of what is necessary for this self-consciousness to be. (And so Hegel says that on this view, self-consciousness has difference within itself, but is itself *sich selbst gleich*—selfsame, self-consistent—in this otherness.) But Hegel notes a skepticism about whether this approach has succeeded in doing what it claims needs to be done.

¶236. There is supposed to be one category, out of which emerge a plurality of distinctions. If Fichte and Schelling are right, then the "I" (or Kant's "synthetic unity of apperception") is "the category." The other categories (substance, causality, etc.) are species of this one category. Kant at least tried to provide a pure schema for this, to show us how to go from the forms of judgment to the a priori intuitions of space and time to produce the categories and then to apply them (for which we need a "schema").

¶237. Pure consciousness proceeds in a twofold mode: (1) a restless mode in which it grasps the other and sublates ("transforms") it; (2) a mode at rest (motionless), the object as the movement of all the distinctions being posited. Or, to put it differently, on the one hand, it looks as if the "I" is active, doing all the work; and on the other hand, it looks as if all the action is going on in the object itself and we are simply observing, as it were, all that happening.

¶238. What this amounts to, so Hegel claims, is something like the following picture. There is the "pure category," and it is either waiting for something to be given to it (which it then "sublates"), or it is just observing the essence of what is going on. This amounts to an "empty idealism," which becomes an "absolute empiricism," since all content comes via some kind of "alien impact" produced by the other. Thus it also becomes skepticism.

¶239. This kind of idealism fails. It becomes empiricism or skepticism. It is led to this because it asserts the abstract concept of reason as "the true." At best, it ends up with an idea of itself as infinitely striving to do something that is always out of its reach.

A. Observing Reason

¶240. Formerly, "consciousness" just perceived. But now it observes and generalizes. In doing so, reason seeks its own infinity, its own normative "boundlessness." In doing so, it seeks to have the whole world in view, not merely to perceive this or that.

¶241. Reason aspires to bring everything into its domain so that there is nothing that remains outside of rational inquiry.

¶242. Observing reason wants to learn, it says to itself, not about itself but about the essence of things. It takes the unity of self-consciousness, reason, and the world as immediate (without any tinge of skepticism about whether "reason" is up to the task). There emerges a gap between what this shape of consciousness takes itself to be doing and what it is really doing (which we, with the help of our narrator, see). Reason thinks it is just observing what happens and piling up statements of regularities (such as "Event of type A is always followed by event of type B"). What "observing reason" is really looking for is what is actual, that is, what is really doing the work in all these appearances. It wants the concepts of things—their essence or nature—that explains why the regularities hold, which is not itself just another regularity.

¶243. The project: turn the methods of "observing reason" onto nature, then onto self-conscious life itself, then onto itself.

a. Observation of Nature

¶244. It doesn't merely observe; it determines what is to count as an important observation. This is what is meant by saying that the perceived thing should have the significance of a universal, such as a universal law.

¶245. Nature is rich in various things. Some of them can be rendered into statements of regularities, some not. Likewise, classifying things into species and genera can take many forms. Nature is rather blotchy in this regard. To know what we are observing, we must go deeper and seek the essence of things, see what is really doing the work when we try to describe and explain nature.

¶246. For there to be genuine explanation, we require a distinction between essence and inessential, that is, a conceptual and not a purely observational distinction. We must know what the semblances are semblances *of.* We aren't perceiving simply individual things. To know them, we must classify them and so on. So the issue has to do with us (our cognizing) and the things themselves.

¶247. The problem of classification: in nature, there always seem to be items which don't neatly fit into the classificatory schemes. If we are looking for the essence of things in terms of simply classifying them, we find ourselves confronted by the vast array in which nature, as it were, refuses to cooperate with us. These classificatory schemes seem to be more our way of seeing things than nature's way of doing things.

¶248. Merely cataloging distinguishing "marks" (claws, milk production, two-chambered hearts) does not necessarily explain. What we need is a concept that explains these marks. (And, of course, this will drive Hegel into the claim that what we seek in observing nature— the essence of things, what is really at work, cannot itself be an object of observation, although observation can tell us what exactly it is doing. But that will come later.)

¶249. If the law does not have its truth in such a concept, then it is not a law but only something contingent. (It is at best a regularity.) Reason seeks necessity in its laws.

¶250. Hegel refers to the Baconian inference by analogy as a mode of induction; but an inductive study of induction shows that such inferences rarely do the work they are supposed to do.

The stone falls because of its "essence," what it is in and for itself. We wish not merely to show that stones fall (even according to a formula) but to explain why stones fall (what is at work in the appearances in which dropped stones fall).

The law must "show itself" in experience and be conceptual (be an ideal series, a system of ordering).

Here is an example of such a progressive generalization of laws: glass and resin electricity become positive and negative electricity. The latter is no longer bound up with the manifold of *things*.

¶251. In looking for a law as a regularity, the observing consciousness is actually seeking an explanation of why the regularity holds in the first place. Observing consciousness seeks the natures of those things and their relations to each other—what he calls here "the concept" or what we might just as well call the "deeper conceptual relations" among the components of the law. These deeper conceptual relations are the "pure conditions of the law." As "pure," these conceptual relations delineate a demarcated totality, a kind of sphere of inquiry concerning the natural powers at work in that sphere (where the sphere may be that of matter in motion, or that of classifying animals, and so on). The individual things in that sphere only really exist in terms of their place in that limited sphere (for example, acids and bases only exist in terms of the sphere of inquiry demarcating the proper area of chemical investigation). It is the powers that are at work in that sphere that do the actual explanatory work, but observing reason nonetheless initially follows its instinct and instead of seeing these spheres as conceptual paradigms for further investigation, tries to turn them into material things which are themselves held together by further regularities.

¶252. Hegel is drawing on a book of his times: F. A. C. Gren, *Grundriß der Naturlehre*, 1801, in which Gren distinguishes heat-matter, light-matter, oxygen as different matters meshed together, electrical-matter, magnetic-matter, and storm-matter.[1] "Matter" in that sense is never observed; it is a conceptual posit. It also seems to be a rather empty concept.

¶253. The pure law—as the concept of the essences at work in nature—freed from sensuous being is the truth of the experimenting consciousness.

¶254. The organic offers a special set of problems for observation. All organic descriptions are functional in that they make reference to the ends served (and to how the whole organism functions). This is a prime example, so Hegel is arguing, of why genuine explanation in natural science is not merely gathering regularities but coming up with a concept of what is really at work in a certain domain of nature.

¶255. So are there such "laws" having to do with regularities in organic nature? Hegel refers without mentioning it to a book written in 1804: the "laws" discovered by Treviranus (1804) *Biologie, oder Philosophie der lebenden Natur für Naturforscher und Ärtzte.* There are always exceptions, and Treviranus notes the "great influence" that produces what regularities there are. As Hegel notes, "the great influence" is as empty an explanation as could be. The organic realm especially contains so many exceptions to all the general "laws" that the biologists of his day claimed to find.

¶256. The organism has itself as its end: it is a *Selbstzweck,* an end in itself. The organism achieves itself in its self-feeling (*Selbstgefühl*). To "observing consciousness" this all smacks of "external teleology" (as if organisms had been intelligently designed to serve the purposes of the fabricator). The teleology of which Hegel is speaking comes from Kant's concept of inner and not external teleology. Inner teleology has to do with the way in which particular organs of an animal or plant are what they are in serving the survival and reproduction of the organism.

(In the lectures on the history of philosophy, Hegel credits Francis Bacon with abandoning external teleology, but he reiterates the idea that Kant has reintroduced inner teleology into the understanding of life.)

¶257. Hegel here reiterates his idea that in explaining nature, we are looking for essences, for the kinds of things that are really at work in natural science, and only secondarily (although importantly) looking for the empirical regularities that are explained by the essences. The end or purpose of an organism is such an explanation, and the purpose is both the result (we understand the organism when we understand how its components are ordered with regard to its sustaining itself and thus we arrive at the purpose at the end of the inquiry), but this purpose is the "first" in that it has explanatory priority.

¶258. The structure of self-consciousness is fundamentally similar to that of organic life. It has a purpose intrinsic to itself, but in the "shape of consciousness" that is "observing reason," it is not clear to itself what this intrinsic purpose is. In fact, it seems to observing reason that its purpose has to come to it from outside (just as external teleologists think that the purposes of life itself have to come from a creator who designs them with those purposes in mind—what Hegel calls another "understanding," i.e., intellect, *Verstand*). When Hegel says that the concept of something is outside itself, he is making the point that it has its purpose external to it, like the components of a watch, for example. The watch doesn't sustain itself or reproduce itself.

¶259. Although "life" (the organic) is not a concept fundamentally constructed from induction (or abstraction), the "instinct" of reason (Francis Bacon–style observing reason) is to treat it as such, to see its own concept as falling outside of itself, to intuit it as a thing requiring an external maker. To the instinct of reason, the organism sustaining itself is nonpurposive on its own. Whatever purpose there is to the organism comes from somewhere else. The instinct of reason inclines it toward seeing organisms as machines.

¶260. Yet observing reason (following its "instinct") cannot see organisms as purposive, even as purposive as machines. A watch has a purpose given to it by people. The organism, on the other hand, just seems to do things. Self-conscious agents may have their purposes before them, but (to the "instinct of reason") organisms don't entertain purposes. They just act according to their instincts (according to the mechanical laws that govern them). The (Kantian) idea of an inner purpose throws that view into question.

¶261. Observing reason follows out its own nature and thus cannot grasp the organism in terms of the purposiveness inherent to the concept of life itself.

¶262. So how do "purposes" and things fit together according to observing reason? We postulate an "inner" to the organism and link it to the "outer" (its behavior, etc.). We now have what looks like a (spurious) "law" of organic life: "*The outer is the expression of the inner.*"

¶263. This law is not the same as the laws discussed in the mechanical conception of nature, where each side of the law is a "thing" which is identifiable independently of the other thing. Thus, with regard to some kinds of organism, we might look for the law which finds one kind of thing (e.g., an inner psychological state, such as hunger) to be related to another kind of thing (an animal eating a plant to satiate its hunger). The so-called law will be that certain kinds of "inner" states (hunger) will typically be lined up with certain kinds of "outer" behavior (eating). The organism itself is the unity of these two independent "things." (Hegel is making reference to the views of some contemporary biologists and philosophers who were being discussed in Jena.)

¶264. So what is the relation between the two? It can't be just that hunger results in eating and not some other type of behavior. What shape (gestalt) do the inner and outer have to have?

¶265. Hegel makes reference to a biologist-philosopher C. F. Kielmeyer (who taught at Tübingen University, although after Hegel's time there). Kielmeyer postulated three basic organic properties: sensibility, irritability, reproduction, each of which would have its own proper expression in the "outer."

¶266. Each of these three "organic properties" is a way of articulating the idea of an organism that is its own end (i.e., of the Kantian idea of inner purposiveness).

¶267. These three properties become expressed in different organic systems (muscles, nerves, etc.) corresponding to the different purposes served.

¶268. These organic laws would, first of all, govern identifiable parts of an organic shape/gestalt and, second, involve the "universal fluid determinateness" that pervades the whole system, that is, would be the parts they are only by way of the working of the whole system.

¶269. Hegel makes reference to an "Idea" in the sense that Schelling used the term. (Hegel would later adopt the term himself for a slightly different purpose.) His point is that people like Kielmeyer and Schelling thought that all such observation had to begin with an intellectual intuition of the whole of such organic life. For Schelling, a structure counts as organic in which every part is present in the Idea of the organism as a whole (and Schelling also thought that the universe as a whole had to be comprehended as organic in that sense). Comprehension of the Idea, however, is not something which observing reason can do since the Idea cannot be empirically observed.

¶270. Each of these parts of an organism would also be treated as an observable *thing*. But some things aren't really things at all, such as "universal fluidity" (i.e., the life process as a whole). Hegel muses a bit on how Kielmeyer's three functions (sensibility, irritability, reproduction) do not function completely independently of each other. Nor does the Kielmeyer conception of each of these functions having to have the same magnitude work. Instead, each should be thought of as a "moment" (Hegel's term for such wholes where the parts are all present in our conception of the whole).

¶271. Hegel takes up Kielmeyer's idea about the relations of magnitude among these various functions and basically argues that there is nothing to the laws he claims to have found.

¶272. What has a qualitative basis in conceptualizing organic life (such as the difference between irritability and sensibility) falls away in Kielmeyer's biology, which talks of these as if they were things varying in magnitude with each other.

¶273. The Kielmeyer conception (also taken over in key parts by Schelling) finally falls apart.

¶274. All of this is supposed to be a priori, to follow from the very concept of an organism. But does this work?

¶275. This way of regarding the organism fails in its aspirations to give an a priori concept of the organism. Instead we get a picture of the organism as a heap of separate parts instead of being itself already a unity that governs its parts. Its parts have to be taken, as we might put it, as parts of an *organic* process and have no organic meaning outside of that kind of process.

¶276. Hegel speaks of a fluid movement here, which is the process of organic life. This kind of process is not that of a heap of individual "things." Hegel notes of the anatomy of a dead organism, "As those kinds of parts, they have in fact ceased *to be*, for they cease to be processes." To grasp something as a process of breathing or of nutrition, we have to supply an account of the organic process as distinct and having an end.

¶277. Such laws of inner/outer fail to meet the criteria of being laws; the parts of the law aren't identifiable independently of each other but are moments of a concept; and one can't break down the internal teleology of the organic into those kinds of separate things. One instead needs the concept of fluidity, of the life process as a whole.

¶278. To keep the inner and the outer completely separate (purpose and parts of the organism) is to lose the conception of the organic. Hegel blames this on "representational thought," by which he means here "additive thought." Rather than an additive conception of the organism, we need a more holistic, "conceptual" understanding of the organism.

¶279. The relations between perceiving and "the understanding" that were previously treated in the first chapter of the book help here. "The understanding" is additive, but where the object of investigation is the organic, we cannot simply add organs and functions onto one another. We must look at the way the "transitions" in the organism take place as it develops itself.

¶280. In the Kielmeyer/Schelling conception, the idea of an organic law is supposedly preserved by looking at the organism as self-contained, as reflected into itself. If we do so, then all conceptual necessity is lost.

¶281. Seeing the elements of organic life as independent things bound together by mechanical laws and put into quantitative form means abandoning the concept of the organic as one where the Idea of the whole is present in all of the parts.

¶282. This Kielmeyerian conception is really just a matter of playing with words. In it, we lose all sense of the "inner."

¶283. If the inner is not the proper object for observation of its laws, what of the outer?

¶284. The outer is the layout, the shape of the organic creature. Its "other" as part of its contrastive concept would be inorganic nature. Organic life, though, is being-for-itself, self-relation as opposed to having its determinateness dependent entirely on others.

¶285. As things have taken shape here, the extreme terms of the quasi-syllogism here would be:

> There would be the being-for-itself of life as turned against inorganic nature (consuming it, using it) and life's being reflected into itself (as having the shape of life itself and of its actively sustaining itself).
>
> The outer (being in itself) would be the concept of the organism as a physical object.
>
> The middle term would be the actual organic creature itself as mediating the physicality of its existence in the world with its own internal purposiveness.

But this doesn't really help much. It describes the life process as a whole (what marks the living from the nonliving), but it does nothing to say how different life-forms take shape. (The Kielmeyer idea of magnitudes of sensibility and irritability going up and down is unable to do that which it is intended to do.) Life takes many different forms: "It is a matter of indifference to this stream of life what sorts of mills it drives." In this view, the organic life-form becomes the empty One to be filled out by all the different species of living things.

It seems therefore that for the Kielmeyer-Schelling view to hold, it would have to make it an ordered relational system and put into the form of a mathematical law. That would look like this:

> Extreme terms: (1) indeterminate life; (2) middle term: number; (3) actual life.

Hegel clearly thinks this is practically amounts to a reductio, but it was indeed a leading view held in his time.

¶286. On that view of the inner/outer relation of organic life, each of the terms would also have its own inner/outer relation. Hegel once again rejects the idea that a mathematical law concerning the nature of life will work: "For number is just that entirely dead and indifferent motionless determinateness within which all movement and relation is extinguished. It has burned the bridge leading to the life of impulses, to various ways of life, and to whatever other sensuous existence there is." The concept of life is a qualitative, not a quantitative concept.

¶287. To grasp life, we must understand it in terms of its self-relation. Living things relate to the world by relating it to themselves.

¶288. Hegel introduces the idea of specific gravity, a concept near and dear to Schelling and later others as well. It has to do with the relative density of a piece of matter, and Schelling wanted to use it to explain a number of different phenomena. In particular, in this usage, it refers to how decomposable something is. The specific gravity of something, as its "inner," will thus be expressed in various ways by its "outer" (such as hardness, color, and so on).

¶289. The specific gravity of something is supposed to be its density (its being-for-itself, what it is independent of its relations to others). It is thus the "unity *brought to rest*," that is, as being one thing that just is what it is. This unity also conditions its cohesion, which has to do with the relation of the thing to others. (Schelling thought that magnetism was a prime expression of cohesion.) It is thus the "simple inner" of a thing, which is supposed to conserve itself in all its relations, but such being-for-itself really can only be what it is in relation to others, so "that intensity without the extension of relations is a vacuous abstraction." If nothing else, it would not account for the self-movement of organic life (as conserving itself, reproducing itself, etc.) since it would itself be inert. Hegel insinuates that none of this (a kind of summation of various arguments being made in the *Naturphilosophie* of Hegel's day) makes much sense.

¶290. Hegel is making further reference to research in *Naturphilosophie* of his time in which there is an attempt to construct series based on magnitudes on this or that scale to explain various processes in nature that would add up to a view of the unity of nature as an organic whole. The use of "number" in these contexts makes the unity of nature into an additive rather than an organic whole. This way of proceeding, Hegel concludes, represents the way in which many of these speculative natural philosophers are at odds with what they aspire to be doing.

¶291. This additive way of combining the inner with the outer misses the fundamental character of the organic, which is to be a unity of elements that are different from each other (as are kidneys and livers) but where each is a functional part of the whole organism (so that what counts as a kidney has to do with the functional role it plays in the organism). The organism is not its liver, but its liver is an essential part (or "moment") of the organism.

¶292. The actuality of the individual organic creature makes reference to the organic universal (the genus) and the determinate organic universal (the species). Organisms are what they are as belonging to their species, and the species is what it is in terms of the individuals that make it up. The unity (species) and diversity (individual organisms) are one whole.

¶293. Thus, discarding all the stuff about magnitudes of this or that, we come up with something like the syllogism of life:

The first extreme term is universal life as universal (genus).

The second term is the same life as an individual (a universal individual, e.g., "the" whale).

The middle term would be composed of both species and genuine individuality: this whale.

¶294. More on the idea of "number" being the mediating middle. But what of the diversity of species and the way in which new ones emerge and old ones vanish? (Hegel doesn't answer this with a theory of evolution along Darwinian lines.) Ultimately, the whole process of speciation out of the universal life process is patchy. The "universal individual" (earth) as the site in which this occurs does not produce a clear and seamless movement.

¶295. There is no conceptual sequence of living forms. One species doesn't follow from another as a matter of logic.

However, things are different when it comes to consciousness. There the syllogism seems to be made up out of the following: the extreme terms are those of (1) the universal spirit (self-conscious life in general) and (2) individuality (i.e., individual people); (3) the middle term is the system of shapes of consciousness (such as are being discussed in the *Phenomenology* itself).

Suppose the syllogism of organic shaping (*Gestaltung*) were the following: the extreme terms of inner universality and universal individuality, with the middle term as that of species/actual individuality. All of this would lead to a movement and expression of universality and self-systematizing in which the middle term for consciousness itself would thus be:

> The system of the settled shapes of consciousness, the life of spirit organizing itself into a whole, whose objective existence is *world history*, which is a history of how self-conscious life has come to think of itself.

Organic nature has no history in that sense. From "life" (its universal), it descends immediately and contingently into existence. The whole is not for itself as a whole, that is, nature is not conscious of itself, nature aims at nothing, nature is not organizing itself in terms of an end appropriate to "nature as a whole." "Life" does not conceptually imply amoeba or robins or us. It's just the way things shake out.

This raises the question Hegel later tries to answer: How about history as the history of shapes of consciousness? Does it have any way of marking conceptual progress? (We know that the answer will be 'yes'.)

¶296. Reason comes to an intuition of itself only in entertaining the idea of a universal individual (the planet earth) as a system only in the broad sense that such life is not just "life" but "life on earth."

¶297. But reason can be led astray by this. An idle interest in such opinionating (*Meinung*) leads it to all sorts of odd ideas about the world as a whole.

b. Observation of Self-Consciousness in Its Purity and in Its Relation to External Actuality: Logical and Psychological Laws

¶298. The reflective observation of nature shows that there is a conceptual unity to inorganic nature as an additive collection of things according to, as Hegel puts it, "laws, whose moments are things which at the same time behave as abstractions" (or in other words, as mathematically expressed laws, such as in Newtonian physics). Organic nature, on the other hand, displays a more unified form of the natural. The species and the individual are different but are not to be conceived as different "things." The concept of the organic has to do with where the whole is present in all of the parts. This "free concept" makes its most paradigmatic appearance in the way Hegel concludes the paragraph: "This free concept, whose universality has that developed singularity just as absolutely within itself, is found by observation only in the concept existing as the concept itself, or in self-consciousness." It is only in self-consciousness that we have the full unity of the universal and the singular individual itself. The self-conscious individual manifests the universal—for example, a language—in his action, and the universal—the language—shows itself in the individual (e.g., in particular speech acts). In some ways, the rest of the *Phenomenology* is an elaboration of what that final sentence of the paragraph implies.

¶299. Observation turns back around onto itself and makes its own observing activity the object of observation. This marks, although Hegel doesn't speak of it here, one of the great turning points in modern philosophy. Rather than go immediately to the things themselves, philosophers from Descartes to Hume start to think in more general terms about what it is to know things at all and what the limits of knowledge would be. This leads to the apotheosis of Kant as bringing this movement to fruition.

When observation decides to observe observational activity itself, it follows the instinct of reason and searches for the laws of thought. At first, that takes the shape of looking not for the normative laws of thought but for the ways in thought naturally and necessarily takes shape as a natural event. It is thus at first a fully naturalist and psychological approach.

¶300. This approach, while suggested by the "instinct of reason," only confuses the place thoughts have in our practices (their "movement") with their being "at rest," as entertained outside of the wider context (the practices) in which they have their content. This contradicts the unity of self-consciousness, which is not a unity of independent things but of meanings.

The problem is not that thoughts construed this way lack content but that they lack form, that is, any conception of how they relate to each other as meanings and not merely as something like individual psychological states linked to other individual psychological states. To know that something is red is to know that it is not green, and that is an inference, not a statement about how a subject cannot have red and green thoughts in the same spot. To understand meaning, we need to have "speculative philosophy," which grasps singular meaning holistically, as "the whole of the thinking movement, or knowing itself."

¶301. The problem is that observing reason is an exemplification of thought in terms of meanings linked to each other in webs of inference and belief, but observing reason can be led to seeing it as a fixed set of things, as when one is describing somebody's views from the outside or third-person point of view (e.g., "Friedrich believes X, Y, Z").

¶302. This raises the issue: What is psychology? The first answer: it is the way in which spirit (self-conscious life) conducts itself vis-à-vis "the various modes of its actuality as an *only found otherness.*" It finds certain facts about itself (its ethos, its sedimented beliefs, etc.), but in part it is also "self-active" vis-à-vis these facts so that it can select which of them it will take up. The agent manifests shared norms but is always a singular individual with his or her own distinctive style of manifesting those norms which show themselves in his behavior.

¶303. Observational psychology can discover all kinds of facts about people's psychology. But it also has to understand that these all fall under the unity of self-consciousness, and the issue of consistency or inconsistency among all these "facts" comes to the fore.

¶304. Observational psychology wants to discover laws of thought (following the "instinct of reason") that govern all individuals. But it also can catalog the way in which individuals differ from each other (one wants more to do X, another wants more to avoid doing X). None of this is particularly interesting, so Hegel seems to say. What it needs is to find "individuality's law," why specific individuals do such and such things with an apparent necessity.

¶305. The object of investigation would be an individual and all the facts about him and his natural context.

¶306. Of course the effect that circumstances have on individuals depends on the individuals themselves. Thus, the individual can subvert the streams of influence impinging on him and take them in other directions.

A more fully self-conscious awareness of being in a certain state (say, of having an intention to do X) can change the context of that state.

¶307. To speak of psychological necessity (in terms of the laws of thought) is thus empty or relatively empty. The individual always has the capability of transforming the influences working on him.

¶308. There seem to be no such laws since there is no way of necessarily relating the independent components of the law (situation and individual). The individual and his world are not like the independent elements of a natural law.

c. Observation of the Relation of Self-Consciousness to Its Immediate Actuality: Physiognomy and Phrenology

¶309. Since there is no law relating the world and the individual, it seems that if observation is to find any laws, they must be those that govern the individual himself.

¶310. The individual has a being-for-itself; thus, it seems he must have an *original determinate being*, something he is prior to his choices. (This is a very *Verstand*, "the understanding," way of looking at the matter. It assumes that there must be a first origin in the string of events.)

The individual must be seen as bodily. But to the extent that the individual is what he has done, the body (not done by him) must be an expression of what he has done, a sign, a way of putting his original determinate nature into practice. So we have the old law: the outer is the expression of the inner.

¶311. The inner of the individual (psychology) is supposedly expressed in various bodily organs: gestures, facial gestures, etc.

But this relation of inner and outer is troublesome.

It seems on the one hand that the outer fully expresses the inner with nothing left over—this would be an early form of behaviorism.

On the other hand, it seems that the outer (being in public space) detaches itself from the inner and can take on meanings that the inner did not intend to express. (One can, for example, become an object of public derision without ever having intended to do so.)

Psychology totters between these two extremes.

It seems that on this view, what we really do is *will* to set our bodies in motion, or *try* to set our bodies in motion, or *manipulate* something to set it in motion. What happens after that is up to nature.

¶312. What would be the organ of such expression of the inner in the outer? The inner is an activity, and the outer (the mouth, the hand, etc.) is the vehicle by which the inner is expressed. This expression seems to be too much or too little. Too much if the expression exhausts all that is inner; too little if what is expressed is taken up by others and twisted to mean something other than the inner had willed.

¶313. But what if the "external shape" of the outer is neither an organ (mouth, eye, etc.) nor an act? What would be the relation between the two? Perhaps the "outer" is a "sign" of the inner. Is the link that of convention? A way in which an otherwise "dead" sign is animated by the inner, determinate sense to acquire a meaning?

¶314. In a deeply ironic tone, Hegel entertains an artificial sympathy for physiognomy. In seeking explanations, random combinations of things will not help. However, physiognomy realizes that it is seeking the explanation for why certain observable regularities do occur. Astrology and the like are pseudo-sciences and have no account of why their supposed regularities hold. Physiognomy, on the other hand, has a clear sense of what kinds of laws are being sought. They are the laws having a deep conceptual connection among the components of the law, and physiognomy has found that kind of connection with the opposition between the (unobservable) inner of subjectivity and the (observable) outer of deeds and actions.

¶315. Hegel continues by displaying an artificial sympathy for the so-called "science" of palm reading and why it should lead to physiognomy as a superior explanation. If the fate of the person is what the trajectory of his "in itself" (the concept of him) points towards, and the hand is the paradigm way in which the individual (as what he is "in itself") brings himself to external appearance and actuality, then since the explanation is supposed to proceed from the internal "powers" of the individual (as what he is "in itself"), the palm will surely manifest that deeper power in some clarificatory way.

¶316. The idea that an organ is the explanation of action supposes that we need an account of action as an external relation between two independent "things": an inner thing and an outer thing. Just as the action is the result of the workings of the inner (so the actual doing would be "current" within the inner organ), the deed (what was done) is something that is public (and is external to the inner), and the deed is still supposed to link in some non-accidental (i.e., conceptual) way to the inner. The link has to do with the way the voice and the handwriting would be the external manifestations of the inner.

¶317. Still adopting his stance of artificial sympathy with this position, Hegel concludes that the outward expression of the inner (in the action) must be the individual's inner thinking of how to link his inner state with his outward state. In saying, "I shall close the window," the individual must be thinking of his inner state, figuring out how to express it in outer motion, forming the expression, and then by using his voice, putting that inner thought into the outer, public space.

¶318. In observing the "outer," subjectivity "reflects itself back" to the "inner." One can think of it in something like the following way. From a third-person perspective, one might observe a person saying something and then ask if what she said really expressed what she was thinking. One "posits" an inner state that is supposed to be expressed in the outer behavior. Hegel notes that, so it's said, one can just see, for example, by the facial expression whether a person is serious (whether his "inner" lines up with his "outer"). But then it seems that the "inner" and the "outer" are just two things which may or may not actually correlate with each other.

The problem with introducing that kind of self-knowledge into the picture is that it means that people can indulge in tactical and strategic behavior, altering their behavior in light of what they take the other person to believe about them. The reflectedness-into-self empowers the speaker to be at odds with his "outer" expressions.

But it also means that the formation of an intention is often something that goes on in the action itself. To have an intention is not so much to inspect a psychological state within oneself and describe it but the more practical effort to look for the reasons you have for acting. If so, that changes the picture.

¶319. From the individual's point of view, his reflection-into-self is expressed in his works and not as features of his physiognomy. Physiognomy operates on the assumption that there is an opposition between the practical and the theoretical, but that the distinction itself is a practical distinction. What is sort of valid in physiognomy's approach is that individuality actualizes itself in action and makes it into who the agent is. The individual can express himself in his actions, but he can make an inward turn and look on his own actions from, as it were, the outside. Observing reason is thus led to the picture that has the truth of subjectivity lying in the determinate inner "intention" irrespective of how it is expressed in the "outer."

¶320. Physiognomy claims that it studies not what it is to *be* a thief, but to know what it means to have the *capacity* (or disposition) to be a thief, and it finds this in things like a "flat brow." Thieves look like thieves.

¶321. This just boils down to unfounded opinion, empty supposition. It has the same status as the person who says: it always rains when we have our fair. Or when I hang out the wash. It's hardly a "science."

¶322. The true being of a person is now said to be what he does. Self-conscious individuality seems to be infinitely determined and infinitely determinable, and it also seems that deliberation on this might go on infinitely. To know a person's "inner" (intention, plan, etc.), we have to know the "outer" (what she does, etc.), and then we have to do the whole thing over again, as when we say that we can't be sure of what the person meant by uttering the sentence "X" unless we know what she was intending to say, and we can't know what she was intending to say unless we know what is meant by "X." This would be a "bad infinite." But in the deed, the bad infinite is put aside (or so it seems); the deed is just this or that, it has a meaning. It was "murder, theft, beneficence," and we see who the person is in both his "inner" and "outer" modes.

The individual is what the deed is. Not just something meant to be, intended, but what the person has become. This isn't spirit, *Geist*, but what the person *is* is expressed in the deed. This opens up the individual to ways in which his whole being can become inverted.

¶323. Psychology sees the inner and outer as counterparts. Physiognomy claims to see the outer as the expression of the inner, like language, making the invisible visible.

¶324. To the extent that in all these views the inner and the outer are seen as two independent things that are to be linked in some kind of law, we must be looking for a causal connection between them.

¶325. It follows: if spirit is to be the cause of bodily movements, it itself must also be bodily. If a bodily movement occurs because, for example, I am trying to move my arms, then the trying itself has to be a physical, bodily thing. What would be that organ?

¶326. The answer to the implicit question of ¶325 immediately suggests itself: the brain or the nervous system as a whole. That in turn suggests: self-consciousness *is* just the brain and spinal cord itself. And that in turn suggests: we should think of spirit (one extreme term) needing a middle term (the brain, the spinal cord) to enter into bodily movement. Spirit might be willing, but it needs the brain to take that "willing" and transmit it into the movement of arms and legs.

¶327. Brains, physiognomy, spinal cords: spirit is none of these, not because it's made of a different stuff, but because its existence is the meaning (and moments) of what it does—thinking, meaning, understanding—that are involved with each other in logical and semantic ways, not necessarily causal ways.

¶328. It's natural to think of the "head" as the location of spirit. Now, there are many reasons (once one has gone down this road) to think of the skull as the repository of spirit. But it's just wrong to think of the skull as an organ of spirit. But maybe (not really) we can hold onto the idea that the brain is the "living head," the center of minded, spiritual activity.

¶329. Since we had the picture that action involves a spiritual element (an act of will, a trying, etc.) which is linked to bodily movement by some middle term (here the brain), it's now natural to think that maybe the brain (as the organ of spirit) can push against the skull and thus shape it in ways that are somehow appropriate to the action being willed. This would illustrate a causal connection between spirit and skull, mediated by the brain pushing out against the skull in ways that happen to shape it so that we could infer back from the bumps on the skull to the various intentions, tryings, and the like that caused them.

¶330. The exact causal relationship seems rather puzzling. (It's worth noting Hegel's poker-faced irony here.)

¶331. The brain has the significance it does because it is brought under the category of the subject, being-for-itself and *In-sich-sein* (inwardly turned into itself). It relates to the skull bone.

¶332. The stance of poker-faced irony continues. What is the nature of this relation and what can we learn from it?

¶333. It's odd, isn't it? The skull bone does nothing—there are no murders committed by skulls—it says nothing, and it isn't even a sign of anything.

¶334. We might entertain the thought that perhaps all our thinking activities each have to have their own particular space in the brain where they go on. But what of the skull?

¶335. What is going on in phrenology? How are the bumps on the skull supposed to be related to actions? To emotional states?

¶336. It is not enough to relate two things (bumps, actions); there must be some notion that these things *can* be related, some "inner possibility" of relation.

¶337. Resorting to dispositions (or propensities) here doesn't explain much, and for all that, it has little lawlike character when it is brought to bear on self-conscious life.

¶338. Maybe the bumps on the skull can be related to just about anything at all. In other words, maybe (note the irony) there is nothing of substance going on in phrenology.

¶339. For the phrenologist, what is really supposed to be at work here? It can't be as he says it is. The very idea that what you think and intend is set by the structure of one's bones is, to say the least, outlandish.

¶340. It's clear that the "instinct of reason" which motivates it to look for causal laws everywhere would still reject phrenology. What is interesting about phrenology in all its craziness is the way it moves in the space of thought that sees the relation between spirit and its expressions as that between self-conscious individuality and that of "things" such that self-conscious individuality itself becomes conceived as reified, thinglike. It is at this point that observing reason has to reverse itself.

Do note here a sample of Hegel's Jena "genteel" anti-Semitism; he also speaks of *Entäußerung*, "self-relinquishing," *kenosis*. Hegel's anti-Semitism got much weaker later in Berlin, most likely under the influence of Eduard Gans. But genteel anti-Semitism is still anti-Semitism, and "genteel" adds nothing justify it.

¶341. Hegel gives us here a nice recapitulation of where his argument has gone so far. Observing reason in its study of inorganic nature quickly moves to abstractions and to laws governing relations in nature. What is supposed to be at work in nature are these laws. But what explains why the laws hold is some "inner" of nature (or so the proponents of *Naturphilosophie* have argued), and that "inner" becomes an empty "One" of nature—that is, nature itself understood as an organism and inorganic nature as fashioned in terms of what that "organism" requires. The One is thus the concept of nature as a whole, and it is supposed to be doing the explanatory work in the study of nature. It is because of its laws that the laws of inorganic nature are what they are. Organic nature involves inner purposiveness (the functional purposiveness of organisms), but this purposiveness is read off it by another being, self-conscious life itself, for which the purposes exist *as* purposes.

¶342. Observing reason turns to the process of thinking and tries to find the laws of thought. It is finally driven to the study of language, and it tries to find the laws of that.

It is in stating and articulating purposes that the being-for-itself of freedom emerges. To be in a state of indecision, for example, is to be in a state of not knowing what reasons are preponderant.

¶343. Observing reason turns away even from language and looks to establish laws of thought as causal relations. It sees spirit's expressions as mere "things," inert objects, and it thus sees spirit itself as something inert, thinglike. This reaches its absurd conclusion in phrenology, for which "The being of spirit is a bone."

¶344. The unhappy consciousness emptied itself of its self-sufficiency, made its being-for-itself into a thing. But this thing is to itself as a self-conscious entity, an organism undertaking certain commitment. It is the Category, the "I," Kant's transcendental unity of apperception. Consciousness becomes conceived as reason itself, and, as reason, it becomes at first observing reason, which reaches the "infinite judgment"—an unconditional, unbounded metaphysical judgment—"that the self is a thing."

Observing consciousness is the "shape" in which the category presents itself to itself as a thing.

But seeing itself as such a thing, and as self-consciousness (assuming a position in social space, undertaking commitments, taking on and acknowledging responsibilities), it wishes to "engender itself," that is, see itself as the kind of thing that does just that.

Self-consciousness isn't just a matter of special access to psychological facts. It has to do with agency, with the idea of rational authority, the ability to decide what to do based on what is the best reason to do it.

¶345. This brings us back to the idea already explored and rejected, that there could be nonconceptual "observation." This is more like self-deception than anything else, and the proponent of nonconceptual observation can thus in all sincerity declare something outlandish, such as "Consciousness is a bone."

¶346. This is where we are led when consciousness views itself as a thing, and this is what the approach that takes "representational thought" (*Vorstellung*) as its paradigm leads toward.

Reason, though, estranges itself into itself and its opposite (norms and things, ought and is). As "representational thought," *Vorstellung*, it holds the two separate; as concept, that is, as conceptual thought, it unites them.

7

Reason

Second Part

B. The Actualization of Rational Self-Consciousness through Itself

¶347. In "Reason," self-consciousness has the thought that it is "all reality," that nothing in principle exceeds reason's grip—not even the
basic articles of faith. However, following its "instinct for reason," it
directs itself onto the observational study of nature (successfully but
not without metaphysical baggage), and it finds that it is pushed into
seeing things from the point of view of representational thought and
thus seeing itself as a thing to be "observed" in the way it observes natural things. Nature has a formal structure (externality, etc. plus the
purposive structure of organic life), and it is easy to see why we would
think that formal structure applies to us too (since we're part of nature).

So is it reverting to the picture we found in "Consciousness" to be
"the True"? But it has already run into trouble with this when it comes
to organisms.

Again, the interpretive hypothesis we're maintaining here: the difference between *Verstand/Vorstellung* ("the understanding" / representational thinking) and *Vernunft/Begriff* (reason/concept) has to do
with that between ordinary inquiry and thought and metaphysical-
conceptual inquiry and thought. In "the understanding," when we run
into contradictions we know we have to clean things up: deny one of
the sides, or rephrase it so it isn't there. However, the paradoxes that
philosophy-metaphysics brings in its wake don't lend themselves to
that way of dealing with certain kinds of contradictions. They have to
treated differently, and this is Hegel's basic metaphilosophical point.
Some, like Wittgenstein, think that what seem like intractable puzzles

Hegel's Phenomenology of Spirit. Terry Pinkard, Oxford University Press. © Oxford University Press 2023.
DOI: 10.1093/oso/9780197663127.003.0007

reaching contradictory results are the outcome of our putting ordinary language under too much stress. Hegel has a slightly different view.

Geist (as species) doubles itself in that each individual self-consciousness is a self-consciousness only in having others recognize it as self-consciousness. *Geist*, self-conscious life, *exists* only as broken up into individual agents recognizing each other. Each is the self-sufficient member of the species only in such recognition. This will be a problem that will be one of the issues requiring us to move from "Reason" to "*Geist*" after this section.

After the travails it has put itself through, reason is no longer the *immediate* certainty of being all reality. That immediacy is gone. It must now, as it were, work for this certainty. Reason becomes skeptical of itself. Each consciousness is certain that it is recognized by the other; but each regards other and itself also as a thing.

¶348. Hegel notes how observing reason has repeated the movement of "Consciousness."

There is also a second repetition of what goes on in "Self-Consciousness": *Geist* passes from *self-sufficiency* to *freedom*. So it should follow a similar logic that got us from mastery and servitude to Stoicism, etc.

But there is a potential spanner in the works. Modern individualism enters the picture.

We can't be immediately sure that nature will yield itself to human investigation, we must work for it; and we can't be sure others will recognize us as having individual authority, we must work for it, that is, demand recognition from others, and we do this by giving and demanding reasons; thus, active reason raises itself to the universal: not just *my* reasons, but Reason.

What are the "stations" (like those of the cross) along the way to demanding that others recognize us (and their demanding we recognize them)? Just "giving and asking for reasons" (the slogan of the pragmatist Hegelians) won't be enough.

The "True" here is this picture: self-conscious beings related to other self-conscious beings with the mediation of Reason. But here this is construed individualistically: each person connects to Reason on her own. It's a kind of view of relation to others as being rather "game-like," not in the sense of play but in the sense of strategic interaction.

¶349. Hegel tells us that now we start with the "concept" of a recognized self-consciousness. In doing this, he is signaling that whereas before we had a rather intuitive notion of self-consciousness, now we have developed the concept of self-consciousness to such a degree that we can look at the development of this concept with greater attention. The *Phenomenology* is thus now more clearly a self-aware philosophical (i.e., conceptual) investigation of self-consciousness. But this is still the concept "for us," not necessarily for the "shapes of consciousness" themselves. (They may still be conceptually unclear about what they are doing.)

What would a "certainty" of such recognition look like? It would be *Sittlichkeit*, ethical life. For his own purposes, Hegel distinguishes between morality and ethical life (*Moralität* and *Sittlichkeit*), even though he admits that in ordinary German, they mean more or less the same thing (as do "morality" and "ethics" in English). "Ethical life" is the canonical translation nowadays of *Sittlichkeit*, and it's a fairly good translation since it emphasizes the "life" part. What it doesn't get, though, is the *Sitte*, the "customs," part. I think a better translation would be "moral ethos" (although I stuck with "ethical life" in my own translation of the *Phenomenology*). It is the way that the moral views of a way of life become embodied and reshaped in the practices, habits and traditions of a particular form of life (or what we nowadays rather loosely call a "culture"). For morality (as a set of universal rules and duties) to be real (actual, *wirklich*) in a way of life, it must be given a more particular shape and become more anchored in the habits, customs and dispositions of people, and it becomes that in a moral ethos. What is actual (what is really at work in such a life) are those individuals, and in *Sittlichkeit* those individuals are a common sense of authority and judgment. (This is how Hegel viewed archaic Greece and the polis.) Individuals have a sense of how their life is supposed to go as a whole, what they are supposed to do at various stages in their life, and what it would take to live a successful life (that is, one lived in terms that are objectively good) and, in the Greek case, each shares with the others a commitment to that moral ethos.

But how does "individualism" play out in ethical life?

Sittlichkeit is "the absolute spiritual *unity* of the essence of those individuals in their self-sufficient *actuality*." Notice how it speaks of the *unity* of agents that also emphasizes the concomitant *disunity* (self-sufficiency) of those agents.

It forms a "universal self-consciousness": this is a term that Kant uses in the first *Critique* to describe the conditions of a self-consciousness that is related to objective reality in terms of objective rules (the categories).

In this introductory section, Hegel is getting ahead of himself. He is characterizing the archaic Greek world, which he doesn't get around to treating until the *Spirit* chapter. He thus is telegraphing, as it were, where he thinks this dialectical development will lead. This section is thus more like a conclusion of a line of argument rather than its beginning.

¶350. Think of the "life of a people" as a social imaginary (to use Benedict Anderson's well-known term). Each is who he/she is as a member of the whole. They are thus "dissolved" within it in that each is who she/he is only as a member of this "life of a people." However, they likewise see the whole as something they build, individually and collectively, so they are not really "dissolved" in it but maintain their own self-sufficiency. This is part of Hegel's idea of a "speculative" proposition. What looks like something for which one has to take a side (dissolved / not dissolved) turns out to be something with a kind of deeper unity to itself.

We have the apparent paradox of mutual dependencies: only in the free recognition that I am dependent on the whole am I a self-sufficient individual—that is, only in certain (appropriately structured) dependencies am I independent. This paradox-at-first-glance turns out in the dialectic not to be a paradox at all.

¶351. Pure individual doings and impulses of individuals relate to the needs they have as natural creatures (drinking, eating, etc.). But even these events have a social content. What each does is the universal skillfulness (*Geschicklichkeit*) and *Sitte* (ethos) of all. The work of one for his needs is also a satisfaction of the needs of others, and he achieves the satisfaction of his own only through the work of others. The individual thus unconsciously (that is, without having to reflect on it) brings forth a universal work. For this reason, the individual gives himself up to the universal (the social whole), which in turn sustains him. This universal essence is only the expression of the individuality itself (which is a semblance of true self-sufficient individuality), and in that community, I intuit—I just see—without having to have any theory that they are for-themselves this same self-sufficient being that I am. I see myself as you, and I see you as me. There is a deep, shared identity.

¶352. Reason is actualized in a free people; but in ¶354 Hegel says that by necessity it can't last. A free people would be one in which each acts according to the law of his/her own nature. Each would have his/her place, its requirements, and all would find that place "their own." This account will turn out to presuppose that "our place" is itself rational, that it makes sense to be in that place. Thus, if the ethos of such a people is relative to that people themselves, then the wise men of antiquity had it right: "*Wisdom and virtue consist in living in conformity with the ethos of one's people.*"

¶353. This shows us where we should be headed (to a full moral ethos, *Sittlichkeit*). This is the goal that would, if it were to come about, achieve the logic of the aspirations that have already made their appearance in the book. However, that idea of living in conformity with the ethos of one's people would not show that we are in fact headed there. It is one thing to say of the teleology of reason that it hasn't yet arrived at ethical life and another thing to say that it once had it but has since moved away from it. More or less that means: we can see the archaic Greeks as having gotten it right and ourselves as falling away from them and thereby failing in our own modern individualism; or it could be that we are moving toward a modern *Sittlichkeit* but haven't quite gotten there yet.

¶354. The first possibility: *it moves away from it.* A free people in such *Sittlichkeit* is the concept of a free people in-itself. In-itself, the concept is not yet fully developed, and as the concept does develop, the practical reality of such *Sittlichkeit* falls apart, and this falling apart of *Sittlichkeit* is not only not accidental but necessarily comes about. Hegel doesn't say that the people of *Sittlichkeit* (i.e., the archaic Greeks) are completely absorbed in the common life and have no life apart from it. In fact, they are individuals participating in it, but their full consciousness of their individuality hadn't developed out of its *an sich*, in-itself character. They don't know yet that their way of living out this *Sittlichkeit* contains the seeds within itself of their coming to be totally opposed to this *Sittlichkeit*. The "in-itself" of their concept puts them on a trajectory that is bound to shatter their ideal.

Once a "higher" form of self-consciousness about this *Sittlichkeit* appears, it realizes the limitations of such a form of life—in Wittgenstein's sense that what people accept as justification shows how they think and live: once another form of justification enters, the whole cannot hold together.

¶355. The *thought* of individuality dissolves ethical life. In original *Sittlichkeit*, the individual is at one with the "ethical substance" (the whole array of institutions, norms, expectations, dispositions, habits, etc. of a form of life). There is the assertion—here only intimated—that the individual as claiming a special status for him/herself must arise out of the confines of this moral ethos, and when the individual succeeds in doing so, that moral ethos (or ethical "life") can no longer survive. This is the trajectory of the thought of individuality as it develops, and it will culminate much later in the book with the individual appeal to conscience. In the original moral ethos, the requirements of my position are not chosen by me. In more modern times, though, I have to consult my conscience about whether such claims are, for me, real.

¶356. *It has not yet arrived at it.* The trajectory for this development has been set, but Spirit *makes* it in such a way such that to the individual himself, it seems to him that he *discovers* it as something new and unprecedented.

"The individual" is not yet a real social fact, just an "inner essence," an aspiration trying to make itself real. Those striving for such individuality (as a modern status) must therefore seek to create the conditions under which they can indeed be recognized as such a free-floating individual by other such free-floating individuals. (Hegel says that it seeks to double itself, to create its opposing image and to become conscious of its unity with the objective essence.) But for this to have any practical reality (or motivational force), it can't be seen as a matter of creation (not as simply something made up) but of "finding," "discovering" the status of us all being such "individuals." This kind of unity with others (where you and I both recognize each other as such free-floating "individuals") would, so it seems, be happiness itself, and so the individuals of modern life go off in the pursuit of happiness. They will later on that same path declare the pursuit itself to be a right.

We are developing this conception of rational self-conscious individuality from its undeveloped "in-itself" up to the achievement promised in ¶177: "the experience of what spirit is, this absolute substance which constitutes the unity of its oppositions in their complete freedom and self-sufficiency, namely, in the oppositions of the various self-consciousnesses existing for themselves: The *I* that is *we* and the *we* that is *I*." We will also be leaving behind a whole way of looking at all these issues themselves, as Hegel tells us a good bit later, when he says that we will be moving away from looking at "shapes of consciousness" and instead looking for "shapes of a world."

¶357. We have what at first looks like an odd conclusion. *Sittlichkeit* is the truth of all that has come before in the book. But this "truth" is something that we already had in archaic Greece, and we lost it. How? Why?

This shape of consciousness aspires to *Sittlichkeit*, and, coming to recognize that as its true aspiration, its efforts are the beginning of its ethical (as distinct from its moral) life. So as things will turn out, it will not attempt to recreate the *Sittlichkeit* it has lost (ancient Greek life) but will concern itself with the emergence of self-consciousness of the ethical substance, not indeed as *Sittlichkeit* but as *morality*, a higher "shape of consciousness." As things have been presented thus far in the book, this takes the shape of the individual coming to comprehend his/her self-relation (her *für-sich-sein*, being-for-itself) in a different sense than has so far been the case. Where we are is the point at which the individual is still understanding himself as maintaining self-sufficiency in opposition to sociality, of being an "I" only as opposed to a "We" (and thus failing to comprehend himself fully as *Geist*, self-conscious life in its true form). We conclude with the idea that the movement from now on is not that of the individual emerging in his full individuality by relinquishing his former moral ethos but that of the individual gradually "resocializing" himself. Hegel concludes with a line that sums up his line of argument perfectly: "However, while our time lies closer to the form those moments take when they appear after consciousness has forsaken its ethical life (and when, in searching for that ethical life, it repeats those forms), those moments may be better represented in the expressions of those ways in which it is search of ethical life." Modern life, so Hegel seems to be saying, finds itself in cycle of repetition of its failures: it tries one thing, fails, tries another and fails, then repeats the first one again (and fails).

¶358. This begins with the idea that the agent's status as self-conscious life entitles him to see his own pursuits as the essence of self-conscious life. The agent thus sets out to actualize itself as an individual in the full sense. It steps out of the traditions surrounding it and makes an attempt to see itself as engaged in its ownmost personal pursuits as authorized by the whole (or as its authorizing itself to speak in the name of the whole).

¶359. This will take three forms in which each fails, and in which each provokes its successor to take on the form it does, which in turn fails. Modern life, Hegel seems to say, finds itself in an odd loop of sorts in which it keeps repeating these failures. Part of this is dialectical: each shape of consciousness to be examined here is prompted to actualize itself insofar as it is seen to be the only truly rational response to the failures of the other.

In all these cases, it tries to actualize itself as an entitled individual in the pursuit of its own ends.

At first, it takes itself in its abstraction as a being-for-itself and seeks to see itself (intuit itself) in an other as such an entitled individual.

In the second case, it identifies its ends as authoritative for the whole. It does not substitute its own particular ends for the voice of the whole but rather sees itself as speaking authoritatively for the whole.

In its third form, it seeks to sacrifice itself for the universal and thus sees itself as a paragon of virtue.

a. Pleasure and Necessity

¶360. One sees oneself as an individual, but not yet actualized. One needs recognition. One must *become* the individual one is in oneself, *an sich*. One "develops" one's concept of what or who one really is by seeking to develop one's concept of one's own calling. To drive this point home, Hegel misquotes some lines from an early version of Goethe's *Faust*, which suggests naturally enough that this shape of consciousness is illustrated best by the figure of Faust. (Goethe has it that Faust perishes by necessity even if he hadn't given himself over to the devil. Hegel has Faust perishing because he has given himself over to the devil.)

¶361. One can't just wait for happiness to come as a gift, that is, as a matter of luck; one has to go in pursuit of it. Since what one needs for one's own happiness is recognition from the right kind of others, one goes in pursuit of such recognition. For such an individual, the world as he finds it is fruit ripe for the picking. Hegel introduces a twist to the account here. The actual model for the section is not only Faust but equally as much the figure of Mozart's Don Giovanni (who in *Don Giovanni* even sings an aria praising *libertà*. Hegel first saw a production of the opera in Frankfurt in 1797 and was very moved by it.) Both the Faust and the Don Juan legends sprang up at the same time in the Renaissance (in the 1500s). They are "moral tales" about going beyond the bounds set by nature or God—which involve forbidden knowledge (Faust) and carnal pleasure (Don Juan). Thus, both legends, as two sides of the same coin, provide grist for Hegel's mill.

¶362. We have the other as an object of pleasure, but this is not just "desire" (as it was in the dialectic of mastery and servitude). The individualizing agent wants to be self-sufficient and in that sense be the "master." This leads to stage-managed recognition: Don Giovanni's mad pursuit of seduction. He can only be a "self" by manipulating the recognition of others such that he gets them to freely recognize him without their being aware of his manipulation. Earlier the master had not tried to manipulate the slave but had simply demanded (with the credible threat of force) the self-imposed subordination of the one who becomes the *Knecht* (the vassal, servant, slave). Here the agent seeks the consent of the other by manufacturing the consent. Faust does this with Gretchen by getting Mephistopheles to use his dark magic to assist him in his seduction and betrayal of her.

¶363. The problem with stage-managed recognition is that it is stage managed. It is not real. Once the staging becomes clear, it's over. The Don Juan / Faust characters live within a contradiction.

How does Giovanni stage-manage his recognition? He typically sings in D major. When the woman he is trying to seduce sings in a different key, he changes, so she will think: "We are singing the same way!"

Like Faust, Giovanni sees the world as an open field for the satisfactions of his own desires (his own lacks). The other agent is to be his mirror, a means to his own fulfillment, and each is only a means. The actualization Giovanni seeks is thus what Hegel would call a "bad infinite": it is Don Giovanni's model of "one after the other." (This is made explicit in the "Madamina" aria sung by his servant and enabler, Leporello.)

¶364. The Giovanni character declares himself to be an *Eins* (a "One") outside of all the other social conditions. A kind of "I don't need you, but you (at least some of you) need me." We are all to celebrate *libertà*, but I'm the only one who is really free, although my freedom demands that you recognize me as free and that you do it freely.

The purpose belonged to being-for-itself, *Fürsichsein*, the particular kind of self-relation practiced by Giovanni: I am who I am by doing what it is I need to do to be the *Eins* (the "One") that I am. But I haven't succeeded. All the other characters are hunting me down for my misdeeds, even though I never *coerced* anybody. I just seduced them and lied to them. They are all prisoners of convention, whereas I am free of all convention. That the others are hunting me down only shows that my type of self-relation is not yet free but only, so Giovanni has to think, free in its not fully developed state of freedom (in its being-in-itself, *Ansichsein*).

¶365. How can Giovanni comprehend this? His situation passes over from the lively individual plucking the world's fruit into something like the lifeless necessity embodied in the statue of the man he killed (the Commendatore) coming to look for him. (The statue is lifeless yet oddly alive in its demand that Giovanni repent.)

It was his own doing that led to this (his essence is his necessity), but it seems everything has gone wrong, turned topsy-turvy, inverted. Once the master of manipulation, now he's being hunted, and he becomes a riddle to himself.

(This leaves open the question of whether Hegel has given us a convincing interpretation of the opera. Giovanni's fate has been treated differently by different directors.)

¶366. In this paragraph, we seem to pivot from Giovanni back to Faust. Giovanni isn't alien to himself but defiant in the face of the Commendatore. Faust, on the other hand, finds that all the power he has amassed has turned out only for the worse. Faust is simply baffled (at least in Part I). Faust can't save Gretchen. Giovanni on the other hand is defiant and refuses to deny his "essence." Accepting who he is, he is in his own eyes not "alien" to himself but, as being hunted by the others and as confronted by the Commendatore's vivified statue, as baffled and increasingly tending to violence, he is alien to himself. We would imagine Giovanni simply exclaiming that he is the only free one, everyone should be like him, and the world should be a different place. But not everyone wants to be like him, even if all the characters in the final quintet seem to miss him.

The logic of the contingent events surrounding the character subject it to an alien necessity. Faust cannot save Gretchen, and Don Giovanni finds himself condemned to some sort of hell.

b. The Law of the Heart and the Madness of Self-Conceit

¶367. The individual of pleasure and necessity comes to experience its essence as the "universal," which it sees as cold necessity and fate. However, if it takes the "universal" to be what it essentially, inherently, is, then it becomes the law of the heart.

The failed individual of pleasure and necessity turns into the individual who demands of all that they follow his dictates to become individuals (and thus become truly free).

The individual's being-for-itself now claims universality. Formerly, it just claimed a validity for itself as doing what the whole (*Geist* as self-conscious life) demands of any free person. Now it demands that the world change to accommodate its inner law.

The "law" is within it. That individual, acting on the law of his nature, not only demands the world acknowledge that law but also that all individuals acknowledge it as the law of their own nature. I am free in following a law of my own nature. You must become free and follow the law of your nature, which is the law of my nature. Be like me. I speak with the authority of the whole. I do not claim to be speaking as the finite creature I am. I speak with the voice of reason, which resides in my own "heart."

¶368. This "law of the heart" is the purpose that animates such an individual. To the question "Why are you doing that?" his answer is: I speak not just for myself but for all people.

¶369. That not everyone sees this can only mean that, for the agent embodying the "law of the heart," the world as he finds it is in contradiction with itself.

¶370. This "shape" doesn't have the carelessness or recklessness (the *Leichtsinn*) of the previous "shape." Rather than simply asserting itself (as Giovanni did) as "being an individual" and trying to seduce others into recognizing him (or resorting to force when they do not), he displays the earnestness of a person engaged in higher ends. He is, after all, not merely asserting himself but asserting the rights of humanity. What he is as an individual and what is necessary for others to be such individuals (and thus to realize themselves) are fused. Necessity and individuality are one: the law of the heart. The previously undeveloped being-in-itself of self-conscious life is now developed into a self-relation, a being-for-itself that takes its own single individuality to be normative for all others. Giovanni and Faust wished to be individuals that stood out and apart from the collective and thus gained their standing because of that opposition. The agent of the "law of the heart" thinks that as an individual, he is expressing the standard for the collective, as what the collective really is.

¶371. The problem is that other hearts (plural) are not in agreement. (Even if they were, they would soon fall out of agreement.) The world as we find it therefore must be a bad place in which others either are prevented from achieving their true essence or have been too corrupted to do it.

¶372. But suppose the individual embodying the "law of the heart" succeeds. His law becomes the law of the land. Hegel says that as soon as it's actualized, it thereby ceases to be the law of the heart. It's now the universal power, a form of *Sein* (of being, of what is the case). But as the universal power, it is indifferent to this individual heart, and thus the individual heart can't find it as its own. That's the point of its being the law of the *heart*. It is no longer the individual speaking in the name of reason. It is institutionalized reason addressing the individual as to what is expected of him.

¶373. The individual in his self-relation (being-for-itself) takes himself to be the law—a kind of "everybody be me." But if he/she is successful, then there is still the problem that only the heart of one individual has its actuality in its deed, which expresses his own self-relation or his pleasure. He can't take pleasure in others' acts even if he thinks it's necessary that they do as he does. The result is that the others don't find their "heart" in his acts.

¶374. There's a way out, a kind of view that "we should all be acting in terms of a law of our own nature." (All hearts are really one heart.) But that's not possible when this mode of self-relation is in place. It's incumbent on all individuals to be the kind of individual for which I (the law of the heart) have carved the path. (Rousseau said in his *Confessions*, when God made me, he broke the mold. Except that the law of the heart would have said instead: everybody should be me.)

¶375. The character embodying the law of the heart realizes that other hearts have different views. If their views are as good as his, then the necessity for him being him is not really necessity. This ends up in a form of madness: the world should be such that I can be me, and in fact I call on all hearts to be me. But all hearts, being the individuals they are, must take my call to be the "hearts" they are as an opposition to them. I am the essence, but it's clear others think I'm not. The reality of things is that all are called to be me, but the reality of things is that all are called not to be me.

¶376. The law of the heart goes off the rails. What is nonessential is declared to be essential and so on.

¶377. Hegel notes how the heart's throbbing for the welfare of humanity passes over into the essenceless-ness of a kind of crazed self-conceit. The individual professing the law of the heart goes into a fury of self-hate and hatred of others. If I'm the law, how could others fail to acknowledge that? Hegel notes the role of conspiracy theories for this type of self-conceit: he gives the example of Holbach and others who claim that the populace has been massively deceived by an elite (fanatical priests in league with despots, etc.) who have tricked them into being something other than they should be. The world has been turned upside down by this elite. The real topsy-turvy figure, though, is not the supposed and mythical elite, but the "law of the heart individual" who is hellbent on exposing the whole mess and overturning everything so that everybody can finally be their true individual selves, which is for them to be me. The madness of the "law of the heart" is reinforced because it is convinced that it and it alone is being *rational*.

¶378. It gets worse. The conspiracy theorists see that others don't buy their version. Why? They are either in on the conspiracy or are radically deceived.

¶379. The struggle for recognition takes on a new shape. It's that the "universal order" is thus the universal war of all against all. But, cynically seen by the law of the heart, that's just "the way of the world," each is in it for himself, the essence-less play of the establishment of individualities and their *Auflösung*, dissolution. Some are up, others are down, everybody's in it for themselves.

¶380. This pushes the law of the heart into a new shape. The individual still knows that he/she is the universal law. It's just that others don't see it, and they can't see it because, given their own corrupted "hearts," the true universal law cannot show up for them. So what we have is two sides of the coin. On one side: the universal order, the self-relation of restless individuality (everybody is in it for themselves). On the other side: an "essence at rest," an innerness, which isn't yet actual but can become actual only by the sublation, the *Aufhebung* of individuality. Perhaps what I, as the law of the heart, am required to do is simply do it myself and become the knight of virtue in a corrupt world. Others may scorn me or think I'm nuts, but it's they who are crazy and who really deserve the scorn. Virtue in this sense is the willingness to sacrifice individuality for the sake of the universal, so that it now knows individuality as the inverted and inverting element in the world. True individuals are virtuous individuals. Everybody else is just a single sheep in the flock. The knight of virtue must show them the way.

c. Virtue and the Way of the World

¶381. Hegel's summarizes the logic of the three sections:

The first shape of consciousness: active reason was self-consciousness as pure individuality, over and against empty universality. (It was modeled on Don Giovanni and Faust, the great "disrupters.")

The second shape of consciousness: active reason was both parts of the opposition; this form of life had the universal law *and* individuality in its shape.

Now we have the third shape of consciousness: for virtue, the law is the essential; individuality is what is to be sublated (the *Aufzuhebende*, what needs to be "transformed").

True discipline is the sacrificing of the whole personality as a way of authenticating that it's an individual who is not immersed in his individuality (unlike "the way of the world" against which it sees itself as struggling). The "way of the world" is the opposite of virtue; in it, individuality makes itself the essence; it's the inversion, the *Verkehrung* of the universal. (The "way of the world" is like Kant's idea of radical evil as the propensity to make self-love instead of the moral law into the test of one's maxims.)

¶382. The "way of the world" is thus that of both preceding movements, out of which the shape of "the knight of virtue" has arisen. If Giovanni and Faust were in pursuit of their own happiness through the manipulation of others to recognize them as the free spirits they took themselves to be, and if the "law of the heart" belonged to a self-involved moralizer who took himself to embody fully the voice of the social whole, virtue seeks to sublate them and thereby to realize itself. The two earlier shapes of consciousness understood themselves to be great disrupters of the existing order in their efforts to realize themselves, and virtue, like them, also wishes to be a great disrupter, in its case of the false order it takes them to have instituted.

¶383. These shapes are taken in terms of the purpose that animates them (what they are trying to accomplish?). The purpose (end, *Zweck*) of virtue is to invert the inverted way of the world, to bring forth its true essence. The inverted world is full of people pursuing their own narrow interests instead of trying to actualize their essence (which is to be fully *individuals*). It's thus topsy-turvy from the way the world in its essence is (according to the knight of virtue).

For this shape of consciousness, the true essence of the world is, unfortunately, the undeveloped in-itself—the concept and the trajectory it sets—of the way of the world. Or, to put it another way, the true essence of the world is not yet actual. Note the contrast (essential to these kind of essence explanations) between the semblances (*Scheine*) of the world in its appearance and the true essence of the world, that is, the explainer behind the series of semblances that explains their unity.

The way of the world and the knight of virtue "go to battle" with each other. The (metaphorical) weapons are the very essence of the battlers themselves.

¶384. This mode of explaining individuality-as-virtue must take the semblance (*Schein*) of the world to be untrue. The "inner" of the way of the world is really in accordance with true virtue. It thus predicts that the way of the world can't succeed. The way of the world, it says, is at war with reality (or human nature).

¶385. So what is "the good"? It consists of the (nature-granted or God-given) talents, powers, abilities that we humans possess to discern the universal good. When correctly used, those powers lead us to virtue. But the way of the world misuses them. (This is also reminiscent of Kant's idea of radical evil: self-love inverts the law that reason gives us. The resolve and courage of the assassin are not the virtues they are in a person who truly follows the moral law.) That means those powers are thus passive instruments. They can used for good or bad.

¶386. The knight of virtue is really only shadow-boxing (literally, mirror-fencing), which he can't take seriously since he believes that the good is the really real so that it accomplishes itself, as existing in and for itself. The good, he says, is not up to him, it is a feature of reality, and the way of the world is doomed just because it clashes with reality.

The knight doesn't wager the good, Hegel says (the good is not at stake); rather he battles for it. But that good is actually only the talents he has (that is, the universal that is void of individuality), which are supposed to be sustained and actualized in the struggle.

But the universal is the undeveloped in-itself, and its actualization means that it exists at the same time for an other. The knight of virtue sees the good as something independent of him such that, although that good actualizes itself, he himself must actualize it, and the good really exists only when he actualizes it, when it has being-for-another.

¶387. In response, the way of the world in effect says: don't be so prissy. To the way of the world, the essence of the world isn't the undeveloped in-itself the knight of virtue takes it to be, it's individuality itself that is the essence. It says to the knight: look, Mr. or Ms. Virtue, that's just the way of the world. The way of the world's principle is the negative so it can wager and bear the loss of everything. Both of them accept that the world has an "in-itself"—accept that, in itself, the world offers certain determinate possibilities for self-development—but each differs as to what that is.

In the eyes of the way of the world, virtue is like a cloak one throws off as needed. If the individual needs to pretend to be virtuous and self-sacrificing to get his way, he will act the part of virtue, and when he doesn't need that, he can toss the cloak aside. The knight can't do this and still be the knight.

¶388. Whereas the way of the world can attack the knight from all different perspectives (but which all boil down to "That's the way the world goes, kid"), the knight can't do that. He can't be as manipulative or as callous. The way of the world can set traps for the knight. The knight can't set traps for it, but can remain secure in the conviction that the way of the world will fail. (The skillful liar may succeed in the short run, the knight thinks, but eventually its lies will catch up to it, and it will fail.)

¶389. Thus virtue is conquered by the way of the world because the knight of virtue's purpose is the abstract, nonactual essence, and its activities and deeds exist only in words. The actual (the real) is what is essentially for an other. The real world is full of real people with real dispositions, habits, acculturations, fears, etc. The knight of virtue rests his case on the distinction between the in-itself (the concept of what the world really is in itself on its trajectory to full development) and Being (*Sein*, what is), but that distinction has no truth to it. To speak of virtue, we must begin with people as they are (formed, acculturated, embodied, etc.) and see what virtue would be for those people. What is possible *for them*? But we can never base our conception of virtue solely on what people do. That would be to confuse the concept as the in-itself with the concept as developed (posited and as in and for itself). The knight of virtue is just as much a creature of modern individuality as are the other great disrupters of modern life.

¶390. The way of the world wins not because one reality has beaten out another. The knight of virtue rested his case on an empty conception at the start. His shape is built out of empty words and edifying discourse that builds nothing. Hegel makes it more or less clear he's speaking of the modern neo-Stoics who attempted to resurrect a Stoic virtue in an age when new forms of association and commerce were threatening the old order of things. (Hegel doesn't mention Bernard Mandeville, but he would have been one well-known illustration of this.) The older conceptions of virtue rested on a form of *Sittlichkeit* which gave it reality. What we have is talk, talk, talk of virtue without paying any attention to the social reality in which virtue can become real.

¶391. Hegel says that what the knight learns is that the way of the world is not nearly as bad as it looked, that maybe all this "individuality" stuff has more going for it than he thought. The knight of virtue loses out, and he thereby turns out to be a comic figure trying to resurrect ancient virtue in a modern context—a kind of Don Quixote of the modern moral world.

¶392. This might sound like the cynic's way out, but, so it turns out, the way of the world is also conquered by its own means. The individuality of the way of the world thinks it is only acting on the basis of its own personal utility, but it's better than it thinks. It's actually living in a newly established system whose in-itself is a "universal doing." Older hierarchies are being challenged, new networks of relations are being set up, and a new prosperity seems to be underway.

From the standpoint of the knight of virtue, it looks like there is an intelligible form of the world (in which there are objective goods or "laws" and there are distinct individuals who are called upon but not forced to act in terms of those laws). However, the way of the world, having "individuality" as its key principle, in principle seems to have no form to it and instead to be just churning chaos. However, this chaos turns out to have its own laws, so perhaps it does have a form to itself—only not the form that the knight of virtue thought it had.

Instead, the world is not viewed as corrupted by any kind of conspiracy but as having a course to itself that is inimical to ancient virtue. Nonetheless, the knight still thinks it can only be redeemed by the display of virtuous, heroic individuals such as himself.

Or can it? It is useful to think of two other Mozart operas Hegel would have known about. One would be the "way of the world" found in Mozart / da Ponte's *Cosi fan tutte*. The other would have to do with how the way of the world also can be led to reconciliation: that would be Mozart / da Ponte's *La nozze di Figaro*.

¶393. The strivings of individuality are an end in itself. The use of its powers is what animates what would otherwise be a dead in-itself. However, the real undeveloped in-itself is not the abstract universal but is the present and the actuality of the processes of individuality.

C. Individuality Is (to Itself) Real in and for Itself

The end of "virtue and the way of the world" marks a change in the direction of the *Phenomenology*. In fact, it is where the "science of the experience of consciousness" ceases and the "Phenomenology of Spirit" almost begins. Eckart Förster has argued (convincingly in my opinion, although not in everyone's) that Hegel originally intended to have "virtue and the way of the world" as the penultimate chapter of the book, to be followed by a short chapter called "C: Science." This also fits the interpretation that sees all that comes after "Self-Consciousness" as section B, such that all that comes after that and before the final chapter, "Absolute Knowing," is a development of the theme of self-consciousness and not chapters with fully independent themes of their own. Förster argues that while in the process of writing the *Phenomenology* Hegel came, under the influence of Goethe's "Metamorphosis of Plants," to understand that his version of the "development of the concept" was best seen as historical and therefore not just a matter of "consciousness" but also of the more general category of *Geist*, or "self-conscious life" as we have been interpreting it here. The printer had already printed the pages of the book when Hegel must have told him that it actually was going to be much longer so that the printer would have to destroy some pages already printed (at no small cost). The dispute between Hegel and the printer almost caused the whole project to be scuttled, but it was saved at the last minute.[1] This section, "Individuality, Which, to Itself, Is Real in and for Itself," was written after Hegel changed his mind about the book and was to serve as the transition to a new and separate section on "spirit" instead of having "virtue and the way of the world" wrapping up the discussion.

In this section, Hegel sketches out the lineaments of his idea of the development of the "concept" of self-consciousness. We begin with the concept as "in-itself," that is, not developed. Those who are acting and thinking in terms of an undeveloped concept cannot foresee what will happen when that concept is put into practice in the actual world and forced into its development such that those acting in terms of it come to see where it logically leads. The "science of the experience of consciousness" seems to end with the idea that we move from the idea that we must *become* "individuals"—in a world where this becoming of individuality requires these individuals to be disrupters of a world in which "individuality" has no stable and recognized place—to the idea that we *already are* "individuals" and no disruption is needed. To the question "Do we develop the concepts, or do the concepts develop themselves?" Hegel's answer seems to be: both, and necessarily so. The concepts seem to have a logical life of their own, but without our taking them up and putting them into practice in various ways, they would be dead and would go nowhere.

Hegel's point about individuality which in its own eyes is already real (and does not have to "become" real) is a characterization of our time, and is a development of the concept that has also forgotten where it came from. To use Hegelian terms, it is heavily mediated, but it has forgotten the mediation and now takes itself as a unarguable starting point, to be what seems to be an "immediacy."

¶394. Self-consciousness now grasps the concept of itself that up until now was only "our" concept of it. That is, "we" (the readers guided by our narrator, Hegel himself, who has already climbed the ladder to the absolute and has now come back down to guide us on this path) had an understanding of self-conscious life that mostly escaped the "shapes of consciousness" which were under discussion. "We" saw their true aspirations, but they did not (or not entirely.) Now the shape of consciousness present before us (*Geist* in one of its semblances) has as its concept of the in-itself of self-conscious life the same concept that we (at least at this point) also have. It now takes its purpose (the final end of self-conscious life) to be the self-moving permeation of the universal (talents, powers, and abilities) and individuality. The previous ends have been sublated ("transformed") and now seem to be only chimeras. The "category as such" is now the object being studied: negative self-consciousness existing for itself—that is, self-consciousness setting its own "identity" (its limits, its "negative") in terms of itself distinguishing itself in its social space (that is, in its recognition by others) and in terms of understanding its relation to and limitation by receptivity-sensibility. More colloquially: in determining, say, my inhabiting a position in social space (as a postman, an accountant, a factory worker, etc.), I find that I have requirements thrust on me that are "for me" only in my actively taking them up. Truth and certainty, so it seems, are no longer separated: what has a grip on me (truth) is also something I myself have a grip on (certainty). It is not alien to me. Or to put it another way: in "certainty" I know what I am doing (working as a postman, a waiter, a teacher, etc.) in the very doing of it. To use Elizabeth Anscombe's terms: I know this nonobservationally and noninferentially. But this may have no "truth"—perhaps the status comes to be something for which there is no good reason or evidence. (E.g., one might believe oneself to be a faith healer but then come to believe that there are no such things as faith healers. You had a certainty about what you were doing—chanting, burning incense—but now you see it had no truth.)

This gives a new purpose for this character (this semblance of *Geist*): the exhibition and expression of individuality is now as an end in and for itself. I do not need to become an individual but need to (learn how to best) express myself as an individual.

¶395. The account with its previous shapes is now closed. It now just seems that individuality is real (actual), and it's a fact, something that must be taken into account and which cannot be discounted or itself "sublated." There is no going back.

If that is true, then one might entertain the thought that individuals do not require recognition from others to be such individuals. Indeed, the illusion might well arise for these individuals that they are what they are independent of any recognition by others.

¶396. As Hegel puts it, this new "shape" goes out freshly from itself, without concern about others. It takes itself to be real without having to require recognition. Thus, to be an individual, it doesn't need the recognition offered in the "pleasure and necessity" chapter, the "law of the heart," or "virtue and the way of the world." It just is what it is. Hegel remarks that individuality is actuality in its own self. It looks like a movement of a circle spinning in the void, playing a game solely with itself. When it acts, what it does changes nothing fundamentally about what it means: its expression is supposed to be the pure translation from the not-seen (my innerness) to the seen (my being-for-others).

a. The Spiritual Kingdom of Animals and Deception (or Betrayal), or the *Sache Selbst*

The very title of the chapter gets Hegel scholars twisted into knots about how to render *die Sache selbst*. There simply is no good one-to-one English translation. A *Sache* can be a thing, a fact, a matter of concern, a cause. You can also say (as we do in English), "That's not my thing" (*nicht meine Sache*). We might try the "nitty-gritty." Or we could try: "the crux of the matter." We could also call it "what is of substantial importance," or "what really matters," or "the thing that really matters." Just about every Hegel scholar has his or her own favorite, some of which appear on the above list, some not.

¶397. We have in itself real individuality, again singular and determinate. It (thinks it) knows it is "absolute reality" (that is, it takes itself to be capable in principle of knowing exactly what "Reason" requires of it without having to consult anybody or anything else), but its reality is really just the abstract universal, only the empty thought of the category of "self-consciousness."

¶398. Individuality is thus at first posited here as simple being-in-itself, *Ansichsein*, whose internal development is complete or nearly complete. From that the inference is made that such individuality is an "originally determinate nature": originally determinate nature, that is, *an sich*; the individual is who he/she is; he/she is originally *determinate* (negative, distinguished from others), and as a quality (as a kind of fact about themselves), by which they are distinguished from other such individuals. They are not indeterminate; there is something distinctive about them. If so, then we have a completed "self relating to self," the relation to others is *aufgehoben* (sublated, transformed). Whatever your relation to others is (your being-for-others), you are what you are (that is your being-in-itself, your *Ansichsein*).

Hegel calls this a transparent universal element, individuality free and equal to itself (or "self-consistent"), developing its differences unhindered by its being-for-others. Or, as he rather ironically puts it, the originally determinate nature is a pure reciprocity with itself in its actualization. What you ultimately "are" is not subject to relations to others. Other things about you may be relational, but not this fundamental identity.

¶399. The purpose or final end of this originally determinate nature is just having its nature itself. As such, it is existing, even if it is not yet doing anything. Moreover, this determinateness isn't a limitation that the doing would want to go beyond. (Why would you even want to do something against your real nature?) Rather, it is a *limit* (it defines you), but not a *limitation* (something you could see yourself as going beyond).

¶400. Acting involves the difference between the purpose (something that is not yet existent but which we plan to bring about) and the representation of doing it (as in "I do X in order to Y"). Second, although actual action may involve something like bodily motion, the representation of the means-end relation is, Hegel says, "motionless"—the difference between my actually doing X and my representation, "I am to do X in order to Y." Third, there is the difference between something being my purpose, and my representation of it from a more objective viewpoint—not so much "I will do X in order to Y" as "If one is to Y, one should X." So where does the "original determinate nature" fit into this? What is the difference between *my* willing a purpose and "somebody in general" willing the same purpose? Is there a difference except in the person being referred to?

¶401. Where does the agent's "original determinate nature" fit into this picture? At first it looks like it doesn't. There are particular purposes—such as "I am thirsty, so I'll have a glass of water"—and there are purposes that fit into some skill or talent I might have—such as "I'll transcribe this violin sonata for the piano"—but that does not necessarily indicate anything about my "original determinate nature" (any number of people can adequately transcribe violin parts for piano). Hegel notes: this peculiar coloring, this tinting of *Geist* (as an ability, a talent, etc.) exists as the only content of the end itself. I just have different purposes and different talents which I exercise from time to time. However, my individuality is supposed to express itself in these actions, but how is that supposed to take place? It looks like it's just supposed to be the straightforward translation of the inner into the outer. However, it cannot be so simple: consciousness must bind itself to this norm and not let itself be led astray by random thoughts. Nor is the original determinate nature something known only internally by the agent. It too must be developed out of its in-itself. If so, then the agent only really knows who he is (his original determinate nature) after he has developed it in action. So where to begin the action? I could start with a conception of who I am (my original determinate nature) and develop it in action; or I could start with the development in action in order to figure out who I really am. It seems I am caught in a circle: I can't really act until I know my original determinate nature, and I can't know my original determinate nature until I've acted. But of course I have to act without having solved that problem. And the idea that my original determinate nature is something like a fact internal to me is belied by the necessity of my having to develop it. Hegel says that my original determinate nature "only has the semblance of that of a *being*," that is, of something factual and already fully present.

¶402. The argument shifts to the expression of the original determinate nature in its "works" (like a book, a piece of music, a craft project, etc.). It's a matter of interpretation how broadly one takes the concept of "work" to be here. Is the result of any action one's "work"? For those who take this chapter to be "the" crucial expression of Hegel's philosophy of action (a major theme in some contemporary interpretations), then "work" will be taken to be whatever it is the action does. A "work" is just the "deed" and not anything necessarily as determinate as a book or a craft project. (It might be something as ephemeral as a spoken insult.)

In any event, the work is a determinate something or another, which differentiates it (it is its negativity) from other works just as one's own original determinate nature differentiates you from other individuals. Hegel canvasses some views on how this might develop. One person can perhaps forcefully express his/herself while another has trouble: the former would be said to have a "stronger" will or a "richer" nature. (The person is better at it or has more to express.) Consciousness is the "universal" as opposed to the determinateness of the *Werk*. The *Werk* is what the agent means it to be (as expression). If the work can be more and less forcefully expressive, then this prompts a new question: How *well* does the work express the original determinate nature? How *good* is the work, period? This is part of the background to the idea of aptitude: an individual may have a great aptitude that only gets inadequately expressed in his/her work.

There is a problem: the work may well forcefully express one's nature, but if one is very shallow, then there's just not that much to express. So the "well" and "good" issues can't be just "more or less." But since all we have is expression—a self-presenting, a putting on view (a *Darstellen*—which is like exhibiting oneself on stage or like a picture in a gallery), one couldn't say what would be good or bad there. If all that is at stake is individual expression, then what would be called a bad work is really the individual life of a determinate nature that has actualized itself in the work. To call the work bad would be to go beyond its expressing the individuality behind it and would be based, well, on who knows what? Nor can it be the more or less difference of strength of will. Insofar as it is expression that we're after, then the original nature alone is the in-itself, the *an sich*, the standard for judging the work. (So some might say that A is really smart whereas B is merely clever, even though A's work so far has not been as good as B's—still it's A's "smartness" that is supposed to be what is at stake.)

¶403. If the expression of some inner fact in an outer work is all that is at issue, then there can be exaltation or lament. People just express who they are, and that's that. The inner fact and the outer work stand in a unity as comprising who the person is. Any semblance of an opposition between the inner and the outer would be just that: an empty semblance.

¶404. Hegel says that the work is the reality that consciousness gives itself and that in the work, consciousness has *for it* what it is in itself, *an sich*, as universal consciousness. (Hegel speaks here of *Realität* and not *Wirklichkeit*, namely, the existence of something that may or may not be in its genuinely developed state or really be what is in force here.) Hegel asks: Does this shape's experience confirm this? But note: this is not asking for the usual empirical confirmation when we ask questions of that form. It's Hegelian, dialectical *Erfahrung* of which he's speaking. It is more like asking: If we try to live this out, do we end up not making sense of ourselves?

The real question is whether the individual ("consciousness") finds its works to be expressive of its original determinate nature. Once it has expressed itself, its "work" confronts others who are equally capable of making that work into their own work as they interpret the expressions others make, and there is no necessary hierarchy that establishes who gets the last word. If in fact my work "is" me (as the making outer of what is my inner), and what that work means depends just as much on others as it does on me, the whole affair collapses. If my work is me, and what my work amounts to is up to everybody else, then who I am (as my original determinate nature) is not really a fact about me but is up for grabs depending on who is doing the interpreting.

¶405. Clearly this is not going to work out. What we have is an opposition of sorts between being and doing. We got here by looking at how one's concept develops (or develops itself) in becoming actual. Here we seem to have an opposition between being and doing—is what you are because of what you do, or is what you do because of what you are? It seems like the "developmental" idea could be applied to that opposition or to any of the related components of the opposition.

¶406. The concept of a "work" here contains a ground level contradiction. What I am (my original determinate nature) is a kind of fact about me, but that fact depends on whether others or I take it to be a fact (which means it is not a fact but something more like a conjecture). Luck also enters the picture.

¶407. That all the elements of action are in a kind of flux means that the "vanishing" of each element as fixed and immovable has itself vanished as the fixedness and immovability itself vanishes as a condition of what it would mean for an "original determinate nature" to express itself in action.

¶408. Hegel says that "the *true work* is only that unity of *being and doing*, of *willing* and *accomplishing*." The action is not absorbed into the deed, nor is it absorbed into the willing of the deed, nor is it absorbed fully into a statement of the actor's "being" (his original determinate nature). This is the true "concept of individuality that is real in itself" as involving all of these things.

¶409. What this shows is that the crux of the matter (the *Sache*, or the *Sache selbst*) is not any one of these elements as isolated from the others or as having a deeper explanatory role to play but the holistic relation of all of them.

¶410. We thus arrive at (something closer to) the true concept of self-consciousness, in which self-consciousness arrives at "a consciousness of its substance." What is at issue here—the *Sache selbst*, the crux of the matter, what really counts—is the whole context of the sociality of self-conscious life, and once again we see that what look like a series of oppositions, in terms of which one thinks one has to choose one over the others as "what really matters," turn out to be more like basic tensions instead of oppositions, all of which are held together in a certain kind of holistic way. In particular, what looks like a new opposition comes on the scene. Is spirit as the sociality of self-conscious life what explains individuality, or is it individuality that additively builds up the idea of spirit? It is, of course, both. The tension between individual and society will not go away, but it will, however, lose its contradictory character when we come to understand that both are necessary and that there are more and there are less satisfactory ways to integrate that tension. As things stand at this point in the book, the tension is real, and it is not clear just how this tension or contradiction is to be handled.

¶411. We might call a consciousness honest if it doesn't deceive itself or others as to what really counts. In this case, this looks like one in which this interpenetration of substance (as habit, institution, practices, and so forth) and subject is comprehended and affirmed. This is also, according to Hegel, a form of idealism (and it's clear he doesn't mean anything like a complete mind-dependence of the physical world). This idealism grasps how these seemingly ground-level oppositions and contradictions are in fact necessary for a properly conceptual comprehension of a world of self-conscious lives. The honest consciousness acknowledges that all of its doings are social, and that its sociality is also dependent on the ways in which individuality is recognized and acknowledged. But how really honest is this "honest" consciousness? Or does this grasp of the interpenetration of substance and subject open up a new way of deceiving oneself?

¶412. One way for such an "honest" consciousness to proceed is to acknowledge that individuality and sociality are two sides of the same coin and therefore to congratulate oneself on just about anything that happens. If the person does nothing, it's because he didn't want to do anything, and that is just as much part of the show as anything else. If he does something, he can take credit for any good that comes out of it because that is also part of the show. Good luck simply means he's been living right.

¶413. The honesty of this character (this shape of consciousness) is that it doesn't bring all its thoughts together. The problem with such sincerity and honesty is that one can be sincere about something and still be deceived about what one is doing or why one is doing it.

¶414. The truth of this honesty is that it isn't as honest as it at first seems to be. The person claims to be interested in what really matters, full stop, but also only with what really matters only to her. She can excuse herself with not attending to things with the dismissal, "That's not my thing (not my *Sache*)."

¶415. The key sentence (or part of the sentence) for this paragraph is this: "*The whole* is the self-moving permeation of individuality and the universal. However, because this whole for consciousness is present only as the *simple* essence and thereby as the abstraction of *the crux of the matter*, its moments, as separated moments, fall outside of the whole and thus come undone from each other." It's making the point that invoking the truth of substance and subject being equally crucial is here still too abstract. The spiritual kingdom of animals is the illustration of this in the deceiving/deceived mode. If the whole is conceived abstractly as an additive collection of individuals each expressing himself (with the aim being honest or sincere), so that in doing what "we" do (as the "species" here), each individual "I" in expressing his own original determinate nature honestly is expressing his true individuality and doing what the "we" in fact does, then this conception of honesty does not provide any real content to what people do except that they honestly express their individuality. These individuals are expressing the "spiritual" form of their collective life (what "we" do) in a way that animals express the form of their species. The lion roars, the robin chirps, the dog barks. It is ultimately an ossified form of self-consciousness that also opens itself up to both deception of others—as in the old joke that sincerity is the greatest thing, so if you can fake that you've got it made (variously attributed to George Burns or Groucho Marx)—and self-deception.

¶416. Hegel gives a more descriptive account of what he has in mind here, not so much developing a new thought as illustrating the dialectic of this form of the world. The individual acts to carry out some plan or interest, makes it into a *Sache*, that is, something of substantial importance. His action is for-another. Others claim to take him at his word, and they jump in. But as soon as they join in, he points out that he was just interested in doing his own thing, not their thing. They feel deceived. Worse, it seems that if the other praises what he's done, it's just to show off the other's own big-heartedness and thus is not honest. Yet at the same time, each continues to say that her only interest is "her own thing," but they all keep bringing things to the light of day for-others, thereby showing that it's not just a personal concern. There is what is of substantial importance to me, what is of substantial importance to us, and the flip-flopping from one to the other in this highly individualized "spiritual" (self-conscious) kingdom of animals (acting in light of what "they" typically do) continues.

¶417. Hegel returns to the idea of mutual deception and self-deception to open the paragraph. What does this show? It is supposed to illustrate that what is showing itself here is neither a pure interest (or a disinterested interest) in the thing of substantial importance (*Sache selbst*), nor is it just a pure act of self-expression good in itself. It is an interest in individuality (expression) that takes its cue from what is of substantial importance for "us" (the *Sache selbst*). That is, it is a way of individually existing that takes its cue from the form of life in which it finds itself. And it takes its form of life to be the articulation of "Reason" itself, not just tradition or the way we just "happen" to do things. But it didn't realize that this was what it was doing and, acting on the basis of a purely individualist model of this, it breaks down. What showed itself turned out to be at odds with how we were taking what showed itself.

Thus the question: Does this shape of consciousness succeed in what it is trying to do, namely, to motivate dialectically the introduction of *Geist* instead of just "Reason"? How one numbers the table of contents makes a difference here. Is this AA Reason on the way to BB *Geist*, which is on the way to CC Religion? (So the book's structure is: consciousness, self-consciousness, and Reason, whereas *Geist* and Religion are then subheadings of Self-Consciousness?) Or is it C Reason, a new section, which has *Geist* as a subheading? Or are Reason and *Geist* each new sections, not subheadings of anything?

It reveals that this world, as we (in Jena?) found it, doesn't make sense in the terms in which it has to state itself, and its senselessness shows in how it plays out. The idea that it rests on levels of deception and self-deception shows this. What is the "essence" here? It could be the interest on the part of each individual in acting on his/her interests. It could be the *Sache selbst*, "what is substantial importance." Or you might draw a slightly different conclusion and say: well, in Jena people are focused on what really matters and all of them see themselves as "in" the movement of working that out. It's both the "doing" and the *Sache selbst* together. The impossibility of making sense of this form of the world means that the real form that has emerged has to be articulated. Hegel says, "Rather, it is an essence whose *being* is the *doing* of *singular* individuals and of all individuals, and whose doing exists immediately *for others*, or it is a *fact (a substantial item, the import of something)* and is only a fact insofar as it is the *doing of each* and *all*, the essence that is the essence of all essence, that is *spiritual essence*." What is "at stake" in all this is all the moments at once: individual subjects expressing themselves, each confronting and relating to the other, having to do with what matters to each individually and to all together, in other words, *Geist*. All the moments are thus what they are (have their "determinateness") as moments of something that characterizes the whole, this shape of self-conscious life, and the whole functions only in terms of what its parts do. When he says that this is the "simple category," he means that whereas until now (in the "Reason" chapter at least) the "category" was self-conscious reason (this was the "character" whose development we had been tracing), now it is *Geist* itself. *Geist* doesn't exist separately from the individuals who make it up, but what it is it is as distinguished from the members in the way that all species of animals are distinguished from the individual members of the species. There is "the antelope," but to determine what "the antelope" does, we must look at antelopes and see what in fact they do. There is "*Geist*," but to determine what it is, we must look to see what "self-conscious lives" do. The "form" of self-conscious life is thus not without the content that specifies what it is this species does. But the judgment is "generic," not that all self-conscious people do this. It's more of a norm-fact with two sides: universal and singular act, each of which *shows itself* in the other and is not a matter of subsumption under a universal rule.

So this is what reason requires: it is to be the way in which *Geist shows itself* in individual actions. Until this point, the "we" in the "Reason" chapter has been oddly impersonal. It is just the structure of thinking that individuals happen to share as each sets his own ends, a background of attunement equally available to all. The unity of subjects is loose, abstract, mostly external (negative) in its character. As we move from Reason to *Geist*, the unity becomes stronger, but it has to preserve the disunity (the negativity) of the agents if it is to be a genuine *Aufhebung* of what we have developed in the "Reason" chapter.

The summary of the "Reason" chapter would go like this: we thought that we were simply aware of singular things, then revised that to speak of awareness of singular things as against a background of regularities and hypothesized forces. That moved us to self-consciousness. At first, that seemed only to imply that what explains what I do is what we (as self-conscious lives do) typically do. Our species ("we") manifests itself, shows itself in what each of us does. The problem was that such a view didn't have a place for conflict in it, and that was resolved in the relations of mastery and servitude. (What "we" typically do is serve or be served, and the two are exclusive.) The lesson we drew from that was to focus on individual freedom (stoicism, skepticism, etc.) as having to do entirely with our own self-relation abstracted out of our relation to others. What "we" do has little to do with what I (can) do when I exercise my freedom of thought. That itself didn't work, and, by way of the unhappy consciousness, we arrived at the thought that what was manifesting itself in our individual actions was cosmic Reason itself (not just a species-specific trait, not just my own isolated reflection, and so on). But that was relatively empty. We then treated reason in *Verstand* terms ("the understanding"), seeing it as the discovery of regularities, laws, and the like, but that fell apart when we brought it back to ourselves, and we have thus ended up (via Faust, Don Juan, self-conceited moralists, self-deceived virtue-followers, and the still individualistic self-deceived spiritual kingdom of animals) with the idea that Reason is the manifestation of *Geist*. But we aren't quite there yet. Does Reason have to give way to a view of itself as the manifestation of *Geist* as it develops in world history? The next two short sections try to argue that it must see the deeper "essence" of itself as *Geist*. By the time Reason finishes the argument, it will see that looking for the "deeper essence" was the wrong way to go in the first place, although we will be able to comprehend why it was both wrong but nonetheless necessary to do so only at the end of the book.

b. Law-Giving Reason

¶418. We begin with a restatement of what *Geist* is: the spiritual essence is in its simple being pure consciousness and *this* self-consciousness. (Universal and singular: *Geist* is the species that exists only as the individuals who populate it are aware of it. The universal is manifested in the singular, the singular *is* the universal as manifested.) The idea of a fact of "original determinate nature" as setting the boundaries of practical sense is now sublated (as it was stated, it was false; reformulated in the wider context of self-conscious life, it has a bit of truth to itself). Hegel calls it "absolute being," which here means that among all the species, only that of self-conscious life is capable of giving reasons *as* reasons to itself. It is absolute in the order of this kind of explanation of explanations, not absolute in the sense of everything else being dependent on it for its existence. The in-itself, the *an sich*, is now the "category" as "pure self-consciousness," which has all the moments we have seen up until now. It is the only "unconditioned" element of this procession. We thought the unconditioned was (again, as a summary) just what could be pointed out, or maybe what was just perceived, or maybe the whole set of forces posited by the understanding, or maybe the way in which some fail to legitimately claim authority over others, or maybe just the free, stoical, skeptical self-conscious individual, or maybe some abstract otherworldly "One," or maybe just our capacity to observe, rationalize, and thereby learn to control nature, or maybe a kind of Faustian–Don Juan self-assertion, maybe the heartthrob for humanity, or maybe the self-sacrificing virtuous individual. The "unconditioned" is manifested, but one-sidedly, in all of those, but none were the unconditioned itself. The form of the world is thus rather complex: self-conscious creatures who perceive a nature independent of them but which seems to be potentially intelligible to them, and whose lives are socially and historically indexed and who are essentially problems to themselves in trying to make sense of how all of this fits together.

¶419. This unconditioned divides itself into social spheres that embody unconditional laws (rules of conduct). The authority of the whole transmits itself into the authority of the moments, into these social spheres. (This is not the picture of a master principle, a very general rule of sorts, being applied to different cases.) This is the *Sache selbst*—what is of substantial importance to "us"—brought to fruition. It is individuality orienting itself, where its "reasons" are what matters to *us*, are of import to us, given our possibilities. (Put even more generally: what can matter to a life given that life's possibilities.) Its "reasons" now are taken to be embodied in social rules, matters both "inside" and "outside." With that, we have now the concept of the "absolute *Sache*" as *sittliche*, ethical substance. *Geist* is not a substrate underlying appearance (a substance) which explains all the varying semblances of things, but is what it is by appearing in the lives and actions of the self-conscious agents that make it up. We explain *Geist* not by looking for the underlying causes or substrates but by looking at what agents do, how they appraise the doings of themselves and each other, how they justify themselves to themselves and others, and we see that each "I" does what it does in terms of what "We" do, and what "We" do is a matter of how each of us does things. We can and should call this the "substance" of *Geist*, but only with the caveat that the substance isn't itself matter or force but something more like social space, the tissue of our flesh and blood lives as self-conscious lives.

The next point is that this ethical substance divides itself up into various "estates"—groupings of people in terms of hierarchies and tasks appropriate to each such estate—that each promulgate or embody the norms (as "determinate laws") that set requirements for the individual members of those estates to lead their lives, and, despite the apparent diversity of such requirements, the ethical substance is supposed to remain as the unity of these various estates.

Hegel now makes a series of statements for which he gives no argument (at least here, although he will expand on all of these points later).

From the standpoint of "consciousness" (but not necessarily from the standpoint of spirit), these requirements seem to be absolute, to be just the way things are. Consciousness is *bei sich* in, or at one with, or on its own with, itself in this substance. "*Bei sich*" is how Hegel always characterizes freedom.

¶420. Each position in an estate specifies a requirement for the person in that position. That requirement has to appear as absolute. As such, one can't ask of its origins or the entitlements that come with it. ("Who made you master?" is not a proper question.) This is the form of the world in which this (as yet unnamed) form of life tries to make sense of itself. Hegel is getting ahead of himself here, thinking of the next chapter he has decided he has to write. He is describing what the concept of ethical life (or moral ethos, *Sittlichkeit*) is "in itself" before it has had a chance to develop itself.

¶421. Where these determinate laws are present, a person with a healthy capacity for rationality will be able to see what he is required to do in a variety of different contexts.

¶422. This shape of *Geist* is reason itself in its concrete form. It is not just reason in the sense of formal rules, but the way in which institutions, practices, and individuals embody rationality in all its different uses. The "determinate laws" that govern the practical lives of individuals are also "immediate," in a way analogous to the way sensuous certainty took itself to have an immediate (or noninferential) knowledge of the objects of its awareness. (It thought it could know those objects without having to know anything else.) But what exactly is the putative immediacy of ethical laws? They would have to be such that you would just know without having to know anything else that, at least where you live, "Thou shalt not X," for example. (In this paragraph, Hegel is still talking obliquely of ancient Greek life without saying so, but doing it in an abstract fashion that makes it sound like more of a general thought experiment than about anything in particular.)

¶423. Now the discussion veers off. Suddenly Hegel seems to be talking even more obliquely about Kantianism and Fichteanism and not about archaic Greece. Is it really a matter of pure practical reason alone to make those kind of claims? (Of course not.) But let's try it out. "Everybody should tell the truth." Then there comes a host of qualifications. This command requires a modification with an "unless" clause or "all things being equal" clause. The problem with those "unless" clauses is that they add up to infinity very quickly. Pure practical reason thus cannot be action-guiding in those circumstances. If you have to take into account the virtual infinity of things in the "unless" clauses before acting, you will never act.

¶424. "*Love thy neighbor as thyself.*" Again, out trot the modifications that prompt an "unless" clause. It tells me what I ought to do, all things being equal, what to do unless, of course, this or that. "All things" will come close to "infinity." "Love your neighbor, unless . . ." It may be that what we mean is that the state should exercise a beneficence toward its citizens and provide a floor for their well-being. That turns it into a command issued by the state and not merely an ethical norm. Besides, commands often require much interpretation that pure reason cannot provide. "Clean up this room!" So what counts as "this room," what counts as "clean"? Who has the authority to say when the job has been done? Whatever the answer, it isn't pure practical reason alone (detached from "life") that is doing the work. Some grip on socially indexed explanations, given understandings of who has authority, etc., are in play. "Being" (*Sein*) is at stake as much as is "ought."

¶425. Each of these ethical requirements stated in the terms of formal universalization is inadequate to the nature of an "ethical sub-stance." For those living within an ethical substance, they have to be able to know when to help, whom to help, what the exceptions are, how to distinguish the need to make trade-offs from that of determining the right mix of different goods and so on. The temptation to look for an "absolute content"—something like a list of the various unconditional imperatives we might assume are to be there in ethical life as legislation (law-giving)—lies within the way "the understanding" tries to grasp "ethical life" in terms of a purely individualist comprehension of the relation between the "I" and the "We." Given that there is no such "absolute content"—an ethical imperative that can be specified without all the "unless" clauses—the only appeal left is that of formal universality, and that delivers nothing.

¶426. So taken away from the context of life, all that pure practical reason tells us is "be rational." That is formal universality, since we are being commanded to do what all rational beings would do. Reason requires you to do what reason requires, which is the "pure form of universality." This is no more than a mere tautology, Hegel sniffs. Kantians erupt at this passage, saying it's unfair to Kant. Maybe it is, but Hegel's point is that the appeal to pure practical reason outside of the wider context of life leads to these results. Anybody appealing to reason abstracted from the conditions of life is going to fall prey to Hegel's objection here.

¶427. Hegel puts forth a proposal: maybe ethical essence is only a "standard" for judging content and does not on its own generate the content. You've still got to figure out what's salient, but "ethical essence" will then tell you if it's permissible, required, or forbidden. This sounds like a second way of taking Kant's categorical imperative as a *procedure* for testing proposed laws and not as practical reason as actually giving the laws.

c. Reason as Testing Laws

¶428. The universality of ethical substance is thus (perhaps) only formal. This is what the *Sache selbst* seems to have turned out to be. What is of substantial importance is not what specific maxims you actually have (there are lots of those) but whether they can pass the universalization test.

¶429. We have another disputed Hegelian counterexample having to do with property. "Return borrowed property" is binding only if you already have the institution or social practice of property. Kantians especially object that this begs the question, or that it ignores the way the procedural interpretation actually works. Hegel's point is twofold: (1) Kantians will end up smuggling back in value claims into the test. (2) You will still end up with "unless" or "all things considered" or "everything else being equal" clauses, which makes it useless as a practical guide unless you bring in either background understandings of "moral salience," that is, "ethical essence," or some version of "practical identity," that is, something like "ethical substance." If you do that, you will need an account of why this set of moral saliences or that particular practical identity is not just factually "ours" but why we should think of it as "rational." In other words, you'll need to make the move from "Reason" to "Spirit."

¶430. This repeats the points just made but with a very slightly different twist. To characterize something as "property" suggests that it might have a simple definition but without the wider context of its stability, its use, its place in networks of reciprocal recognition, and so on, we cannot make sense of the norms that are supposed to govern it.

¶431. The inference to be drawn: "That both law-giving and law-testing have shown themselves to be null and void means that both, when taken individually and in isolation, are only *moments* of the ethical consciousness which never ceases to be in movement." If it's in movement, we need an account of where the movement is going, if anywhere.

¶432. If both of the moments—law-giving and law-testing—that are supposed to be the fleshing out and fulfillment of the spiritual, *geistige* essence are actually determinations of the *Sache selbst* (the thing that matters), that is, what is of substantial importance in rational life, then they are forms of the shape of consciousness called "honesty," which, as we have already seen, thinks that it is dealing with a straightforward "thing" (*Sache*) without any full awareness of the background conditions that are at work in such "honesty."

¶433. This honesty is necessary if the laws are to count as the essence of consciousness. We need an account not just of the rationality of the laws but of the kinds of character or subjectivity that is bound up with these laws. But if subjectivity can just throw everything into question, where do we stand? If it really is all relative, don't we end up with despotism, the arbitrary rule of somebody or group simply declaring law and demanding obedience?

¶434. This sets the stage to make the move to (Greek) *Sittlichkeit*. Spiritual, *geistige* substance is actual substance, so that these modes don't count individually but only as *aufgehobene*, sublated, and the unity (the substance) in which they are just moments is also the self of consciousness. Universality (as general ethical principles and social norms) and individuality (the "self") are in a unity instead of an opposition or a merely formal contrast.

¶435. In both forms (legislation and law-testing) these moments are in a negative relation to the real spiritual essence. The principles in their universality do not depend on the individual's legislating them. Their legitimacy has to come from the will of all or of reason itself, not the will answering only to the whims of individual choice. Nonetheless, the authority of these moral laws is not that of a master commanding a hapless subject, nor is it some "other" in which one has faith. They are embodied in the life of the people themselves. Hegel says, "Through the *universality* of its *own self*, ethical *self-consciousness* is *immediately* at one with the essence."

¶436. That places us in the position of making the full passage to *Geist*. Spiritual essence is for self-consciousness the *an sich seiende* law, the law existing in itself, working out its internal trajectory. As immediacy, that is, as something that simply seems to be there, these moral laws look like eternal law, as something that has simply been around forever. As Antigone says, from the archaic Greek point of view, these laws are eternal and who knows their source?

8

Spirit

¶437. How has *Geist* (or, rather our concept of *Geist*) come to be? We started with a picture of "the True" as the "consciousness of objects." This was "the basic picture of mind and world" in terms of which we were to think about everything else. That turned out to be self-undermining since it required reflective judgments that could not rely simply on that model alone but had to include a conception of our access to objects. Thus, we had "self-consciousness," which Hegel now calls "the category" (indicating how he takes "self-consciousness" to be *the* fundamental term in Kantian and Fichtean philosophy). "The category" is the most basic determination of what we are thinking when we are thinking about the world as we find it. In Aristotle's *Categories*, we are told everything is either substance or accident. In the *Phenomenology*, we are told that the true is just as much subject as it is substance. We are now in a better position to make better sense of that claim. In doing so, we could phrase it in terms different from Hegel's own usage but which, I think, equally express what he is after. Each thinks of the other as an immediate second person to its first-personal reference. It is in my first-person grasping of "you" as your thinking second-personally of "me" that "you" grasp "me" second-personally, and it is thinking within that complex thought that we comprehend ourselves thereby as plural, as what Hegel calls "The I that is a We, and a We that is an I." In such thoughts, in the actualized state of such self-knowledge, we do not swallow, as it were, the other person simply into our own viewpoint, nor do we see the other in the more simple terms of "what I would think if I were you," but rather, as Hegel puts it, remaining to see the "other as other" while remaining at one with ourselves.

Those who deny Hegel's statement in ¶177—"A self-consciousness is for a self-consciousness"—ultimately have to fall back on some kind of counterfactual, idealized pictures of subjects: what the ideal

Hegel's Phenomenology of Spirit. Terry Pinkard, Oxford University Press. © Oxford University Press 2023. DOI: 10.1093/oso/9780197663127.003.0008

subject, all alone, monologically would say. But Hegel thinks, no, we have to look at the (social, communicative) practices of subjects as they really happen—in real recognition, not idealized recognition. Hegel says: "Reason is, to itself, conscious of itself as its world and of the world as itself." This is supposedly our takeaway from the spiritual kingdom of animals and both law-giving (legislative) and law-testing reason. "To itself": it is not just "for us" (for us, the readers, led by our informed guide, Hegel). Now it also seems that way to itself.

¶438. Rather than giving a set of independent arguments, Hegel here gives us more of a kind of "looking backward" and a "looking forward" at where we've been and where we're going. Ethical substance is what is actual (what is really at work here, what serves to explain things) and the living background to this world of subjects and objects. It is the whole set of practices, institutions, and the like that forms the developing in-itself, the *an sich* of self-consciousness. (This *an sich* of consciousness turns out to be a plurality of self-consciousnesses.) It's a social space in a material environment. It is the "We" that is also an "I" along with a "You" and a "Them." To my mind, the classic mistake in Hegel interpretation lies in the inference from the unity of *Geist* and its explanatory place to the claim that *Geist* must therefore be a "substance-thing" of some sort (a cosmic spirit).

¶439. *Geist* is now said to be the absolute real essence supporting itself. It is not merely a semblance of something deeper that would be doing the real explaining. It's real, and the only thing that supports it is itself. In that context, it makes sense to speak of an ethos (a *Sitte*), but what supports such an ethos are the various entitlements, commitments, habits, customs, etc. of the people living within it. Hegel notes that all the previous shapes of consciousness we have looked at are abstractions from it. At the end of the spiritual kingdom of animals what we have been looking at has been shown (so he thinks) to be the penultimate stage of a series of shapes of self-conscious life.

This is *Geist* as it is experienced in the lives of those subjects who constitute it. But "*for us*" *Geist*'s reflection into itself is "posited"—that is, it has been made an explicit object of examination (in this case, "for us" and not necessarily "for itself"). Various aspects of spirit can be fully in force without being so posited. When they are in force in that way, they just appear as background necessity, just the way the world is, as the necessary features of the world as we found it. It is in that sense ("for us") that it was consciousness, self-consciousness, and reason.

So rather than have the basic picture as that of individual, self-conscious subjects each possessing the capacity to connect with capital-*R* Reason (or as each having all the resources it needs within itself to be rational) and, within that monadic picture, to connect with other agents through rational rules (like a strategic game), we are always already sharing content with other agents. The practice (*Geist*) shows itself through the acts and mode of self-consciousness which in turn make up *Geist* itself. This is the "organic" model that has replaced (or rather: sublated) our original monological "consciousness of objects" model and has extended (or rather: sublated) the picture of a monadic self-consciousness confronting another monadic self-consciousness.

¶440. *Geist*: insofar as it is immediate truth, it is the ethical life of a people. *Sittlichkeit*: it has to be an immediate truth; the first principles of engaged and situated practical reason reside there and are immediately known, such that rational deliberation can proceed from them. Our deliberations themselves can of course be "restless," but these background principles are the unmoved movers of our deliberations. Hegel says that "it is the individual who is a world" in the sense that such a world shows itself in the individual acts that produce and sustain it. But since he says *Geist* must break up the "beautiful" ethical life, he is signaling ("looking forward to") the point that although *Geist* can seem to itself to have the solidity of a natural order, it also breaks down, shifts, and its old commitments fade away into new commitments. We have already seen something a bit like this in the "Reason" chapter, but now Hegel goes full throttle with this idea.

What's crucial for *Sittlichkeit*: judgments about statuses in "ethical life" are fact-stating (this is what we do, customs, mores, ethos), and they are evaluative (here is a way in which life goes best, flourishes). They have the same logical structure as species statements: corals do best (flourish) in water temperatures of X degrees.

Hegel might seem to be what is nowadays called a "constitutivist" (although the term is a very loose fit for him). Roughly, "constitutivism" claims that some norms or principles are internal to rational agency such that the norm specifies what rational agency is and also measures singular agents as exemplars of their own kind. Some norms will be said to be unconditionally valid because they are internal to our agency.

If Hegel's views are versions of "constitutivism," then we ask, "What for Hegel is constitutive of agency?" and we come up provisionally with this short list:

1. Self-consciousness (Kantian element of Hegel's thought).
2. Self-consciousness as social and recognitive.
3. Self-conscious agency is a form of *life* (the Aristotelian moment in Hegel's thought) with the norms appropriate to that life.
4. Agency is always "second nature" which is then folded into the Aristotelian moment. Second nature consists in habits and dispositions to act in terms of specific ideals and norms of a social order that are not constitutive of what it is to be a human being in general but of what it is to be, for example, an ancient Greek, or even more specifically, for example, of an ancient Greek aristocrat or an ancient Greek slave.
5. Hegel also distinguishes the different *Gestalten*, shapes of *Geist*: they are genuine actualities (*eigentliche Wirklichkeiten*), shapes of a world, as he says, instead of just shapes of consciousness. (This makes sense once we have moved decisively away from the monadic conception of consciousness and self-consciousness into the deeply social conception of *Geist*.)

¶441. In this "forward looking" section, Hegel tells us where things will go, and we see that it looks a lot like a schematic overview of European history from Greece to Rome and then on to early modern and revolutionary Europe. (This has puzzled more than a few readers.) The account sketched here is that after the downfall of "true spirit" (at home with itself in the natural and social world, the world of archaic Greece), *Geist* suffers an estrangement from itself (an *Entzweiung*). It takes it that it is both distinct from the natural world and yet part of it. It's an independent "subject" in a world full of other independent "subjects." Out of the failure of being at home with ourselves, we develop a sense of our "standing back" and endorsing, refusing or somehow just failing to endorse the input of the world (natural and social) around us. The late "Hellenic" Greek world and the Roman world are the first actualizations of that idea.

¶442. Ultimately, we end up in absolute spirit (about which Hegel doesn't tell us much here). "Absolute" spirit will be self-conscious life reflecting on what it is to be self-conscious life, period. It will have three ways of doing this: art, religion, and philosophy. (However, in the *Phenomenology*, art is not yet specified as distinct from the others but appears only insofar as it is connected with religion. That's an important point, but more on that later.)

A. True Spirit: Ethical Life

¶443. Spirit in its simple truth is consciousness: the true spirit is self-conscious life that knows where it stands and what it has to do, but as "consciousness" it takes its spiritual (*geistig*) being to consist of an awareness of objects distinct from it. This singularizes the universal, and as the tensions among those "objects" rises, it tends to drive its moments apart. To us, as we think about things in our self-conscious lives, we run into problems with thinking about the absolute, the unconditioned, which lead us to think that these moments of the "whole" are really separate distinct items. (That is the standpoint of "consciousness.")

What nonetheless leads to the separation of *Geist* into substance and consciousness are the actions of the individual members of the form of life. Self-consciousness is the mediating middle of substance (the totality of natural and social life) and individual consciousness, that is, between the universal essence and individuals.

¶444. This presents a synopsis of the movement to come: how the true spirit (the one really in accord with itself) will fall apart because of its own doing. This form of social life internally provokes the establishment of a form of individuality that ultimately undoes the world that gave birth to it. Part of the peculiarity of what follows is that although it is abundantly clear that Hegel is speaking of ancient Greece, Hegel never mentions "Greece" but instead focuses on the logic of that kind of constellation of norms, habits and ethos.

a. The Ethical World, the Human and Divine Law,
Man and Woman

¶445. Similarly to the way sensuous certainty moves to perception, ethical life moves from unity to the multiplicity of ethical relations. This is an idea that in acting (in "true spirit"), we just "see" what is to be done. But there are lots of different ethical relations, and this view ends up amalgamating the multiplicity of relations into two groups: the two-fold of universality and singularity (as in perception). Universal laws (or at least laws of my group which are taken to be the fabric of the ethical world and thus the laws for everybody) and the laws governing a particular subgroup (warriors, mothers, judges, sons, artisans, farmers, and so on).

¶446. The singularity of a particular person has the signifi-cance of self-consciousness, period, not that of an individual con-tingent consciousness. Ethical "substance" is thus absolute—in the sense of self-founding—*Geist* realized in the multiplicity of existing consciousnesses. We have a *Gemeinwesen* (a polity, commonwealth, or, literally, a common essence or being), and we relate *ethically* to people as bearing a status within that *Gemeinwesen* (such as police, cousin, ad-ministrator, clerk, etc.). We can relate to them nonethically in all kinds of other, nonethical ways ("I don't like the administrator," "I think the clerk has a good sense of humor," etc.). As actual substance, the ethical substance is a *Volk* (a people sharing a way of life), and as actual indi-vidual consciousness, the particular person is a citizen (*Bürger*) of the people (*Volk*).

¶447. Human law is the "actuality conscious of itself" as *Sitte* (mores, ethos) and as the familiar law. The "immediate certainty" of these laws has to do with their functioning as first principles of prac-tical reason for the "citizens" of this way of life. Such citizens are "cer-tain" of these laws and norms. They don't ask, is this right? They *just know*, for example, that justice must be administered impartially, etc. Or they just know that of course a particular person was compelled by necessity to do such and such (e.g., because it was *his* child who was threatened, etc.).

In his later lectures, Hegel calls these principles the "unmoved movers" of action. They motivate and justify without calling for further justification or motivation for themselves. It is when they end up contradicting each other that they come into question, a situation that puts the *Gemeinwesen* (polity) at risk.

When the ethical substance is certain of itself as simple individuality, it is the government of such a "people." If the "people" are bound by certain ground-level commitments that seem to them to be *in-and-for-itself* elements of the fabric of the world, and they are moderately reflective about it, then they have a government that has clear boundaries (it governs them and not others). The government is in that case not something different from or other than the people. It is the people ruling themselves. (It is the ancient Greek polis.)

¶448. In this context, we also have a picture of divine law as standing over and against the human law: the state power has its opposition in the self-conscious doings of the actual substance, that is, in individual actors. The state confronts the individuals as a higher power than them, but it itself is subject to another power by virtue of the state's essence. For the ethical laws to appear as "eternal," they have to be the expression of the polity's own divinities.

¶449. If "ethical substance" appears to its participants as natural (as just the way things are, as "immediate existing substance," the world as we found it), then the paradigm case for this is the family. It is a natural formation and instills the proper habits and outlooks in its members. Each member has a set of "unconditional" duties. The family is the "natural" ethical *Gemeinwesen* (polity), but since it's a unit that has to preserve itself, its stance toward its own members (as in keeping with the Penates, the household gods) might come into conflict with those to the community at large. This is because self-conscious agents always potentially stand at one remove from their social space.

¶450. The ethical-as-existing-mores (the *sittliche*) is the in-itself universal (i.e., not necessarily fully developed in its complete trajectory), as that which all the other ethical relations really themselves are at their basis. The family is clearly centered around some very natural facts having to do with sex, gender, and the creation and rearing of children, and it also has its own lines of authority, and (for these Greeks), those would also seem to be natural and divine, part of the very fabric of the world. There should be no discrepancy there.

Thus, there is the truly universal, the *Gemeinwesen* (the polity, commonwealth) and then there are the individual self-conscious desires for riches and power. Since the *self-conscious end* is the individual, this can pull in different directions. The *Gemeinwesen* is thus put into the position of subjugating the family, of pulling individuals into a life of virtue, that is, life for the universal and not just for the good of their family. Otherwise there's no real *Sittlichkeit* (moral ethos) with its universalist aims.

In the family, though, the action that incorporates the whole existence of blood relatives has to do with the dead. They've been raised, Hegel says, to simple universality. (They've become the 'holy ancestors.') As the 'holy ancestors,' they are also normative for the living (and, in many versions of this view, may even enforce the norms by punishing us in some way when we deviate).

The *ethical as existing mores* relation in the family is neither sentimental nor that of love. One has a requirement to attend to the welfare of the children, independently of whether you like them. Likewise, the spouses have ethical requirements that are not per se matters of sentiment. Matters of inheritance and the like come into this.

Hegel claims here (it's sort of an argument) that one's grandparents don't cease to be the grandparents when they die. If they were due a certain amount of respect and deference in life, then they deserve that too in death, and on the logic of this way of life, no human law could ever change that. Even when the individual is a mere shadow (one of the "shades" in Greek mythology), she is still due something because she is your family member. You don't have those requirements vis-à-vis members of others' families. You would have a requirement to clean the graves of one's own family members but not those of others. Such a requirement is therefore an "ethical" (ethos, mores) requirement, not a "moral" requirement owed to all humanity. (So far, there's no "moral" requirement at all in play here; there are only "ethical" requirements.) The ethical requirement is also universal in the sense of: if you are a sister, you have an unconditional duty to perform the proper burial rites for your dead brother. On Hegel's view, the Greeks hover between: this is true for Athenians or Thebians but not for everybody (ethical); and this is the way all humanity should act (moral).

¶451. This paragraph reads like a long dithyramb on Greek burial culture. Nature gets transmuted into culture. The dead are taken to be part of a certain community. The dead acquire a meaning, that of the universality which is attained as pure being, death. (We owe the dead something. Do they any longer owe us anything?) Rituals are thus devised to make the dead into *Genossen*, "comrades," that is, into a fellowship of the living and the dead (of the *Gemeinwesen*, the community).

¶452. This duty constitutes the divine law, the positive ethical action vis-à-vis the individual. Although the human law has a people as a whole (a *Volk*) as its content, the divine law has the individual as the "abstract pure universal" (as a holy ancestor to be venerated) as its content.

¶453. The *Gemeinwesen* has its actual life in the government, in which it is individual as contrasted with other polities. It is actual *Geist* reflected into itself, taking the measure of itself.

1. It is divided into various "stations" or "offices" that carry their own responsibilities and duties with them. These "offices" relate to the whole of society in a way analogous to the way the organs of an animal relate to the whole of the animal. If the heart, lungs, liver, etc. all do their part, the animal is fine. If one part fails, then the animal becomes sick or dies. In the polity, if every member does what is required of him or her, then the whole will spontaneously harmonize.
2. Each "office" is filled with the people best suited for it. Nature and human activity collaborate to see to that.

¶454. War shakes things up. The polity reminds people of the fact of death and that the community endures even while individuals perish. As having its authority and continued existence depend on this consciousness of death (the ultimate lord and master), the polity and the government have their authority depend on the divine law, on the idea that the whole has a meaning and that individuals must meet their requirements vis-à-vis that whole. If individuals tend to drift away from the whole (and put their families or clans first), war brings them back into the whole. It reminds everyone that if the community is to have a continued existence, it must be able to defend itself, and that means that some will have to sacrifice. Pericles's funeral oration as recounted by Thucydides is the most spectacular example of this view, as he recounts all the glories and excellences of Athens in honoring the dead who have recently fallen in defense of Athens. (Actually, the great irony here is that Pericles's speech marks the beginning of the Peloponnesian wars in which Athens meets its downfall.)

¶455. Hegel describes the way he imagines that the prephilosophical Greeks took things. The divine law governs all the people, but, in particular, it governs the family and, even more particularly, governs the relation of man and wife: it involves a piety (ethical mores) that is mixed with both a natural relation (sex) and sentiment (the passions and feelings they have for each other). Parents meet each other as adults; they produce children, new actors in the world with their own being-for-itself.

Here and in several other places, Hegel likes to cite Aristotle's idea that parents love their children more than children love their parents. We educate the children to independence, which they assume, so the parents are sad in seeing their children leave the family, but they know this is the right thing to do, whereas the children in growing up and becoming independent are more than eager to set out on their own.

¶456. This is one of the most loaded paragraphs in all of Hegel's writings, given his strained and troubled relationship with his own sister and his own views on the proper relations between men and women (which for many contemporary readers will seem absurdly sexist).

Incest is just "felt" (intuited) to be absolutely off limits, so the relation of sexual desire cannot exist between brother and sister. (And the implication: if it is there, there is something "unnatural" in it in the sense of its violating some basic ethics-mores law.) Here is the logical-social problem: unlike her brother, the daughter cannot achieve a full self-relation in her parents. The norm for her is subordination to her father, followed by marriage, children, and subordination to a husband. It is not independence. For the brother, the norm involves the independence he will bring to the polis as a citizen. This is the "universal" for female relationships. In the polis, the brother meets other men as an equal. The sister will never get to do that.

The law of the family is that of the undeveloped in-itself as inner essence, inner feeling. The household deities of the family are its Penates. The ethos of the family and of *Sittlichkeit* in general for women is this: not this husband, not these children, but husband in general, children in general. That is your destiny. In the Greek family, the wife thus does not have a purely ethical life. The ethical aspect of her life is therefore also partly based on a natural destiny (as mother and wife). She is just the wife, whose recognition is not as the individual she is but as the "office" ("wife") she holds. (Not the "role" she plays—that is too theatrical a way of putting it.) On the other hand, the man-as-a-citizen can be recognized as the individual he is. He thus has the "right of desire" in family life, and he has freedom from such desire in public life. The wife has no such right. She must submit (sexually) to her husband, but not him to her. The only place where she can achieve the bare threads of such recognition of herself as an individual and not just an officeholder (the office of "wife") lies in the recognition she gets from her brother. Recognition, we remember, can only come about by your being recognized by somebody with the authority to recognize you. (This won't work with the parents, since the daughter is always unequal to her parents. The recognition is always skewed.) The loss of a brother is thus irreplaceable—even though in the position of mother and wife, a woman can have pleasure as something natural. This is an allusion to one of the most vexing passages in *Antigone*. When brought to answer for her deed, Antigone gives a largely incoherent and unconvincing argument to the effect that husbands can come and go, as can children (but you can always have another), but a brother—oh, irreplaceable! What is irreplaceable about it, so Hegel is arguing, is the recognition as an equal. Husbands are more like masters, women like vassals, so the kinds of recognition there are always off-center. Children don't have the authority to recognize. Other sisters don't have the authority (they are after all women too). Only brothers can have that. But Antigone's brothers are dead, so she must stage-manage the recognition from them if that is what she takes herself to require.

¶457. The family is a negative unity. It defines itself against others. The brother leaves the family and makes the transition to universality (i.e., the life of the polity and not the clan). The great bond of the little polity that is the family is broken.

¶458. The men (the brothers) step out of the family ruled by divine law and into the public realm of human law. They thereby leave the divine law of the family in the guardianship of the sister, who remains at home as guardian of the divine law.

Brother and sister thus get ethical significance. She must make sure the enclosed world of the family respects the traditional pieties about the divine invisibilities that govern the world as a whole, whereas the men concern themselves with the (larger) community as citizens.

When Hegel's mother died, Hegel and his brother went off to higher education, but Christiane, the sister, "decided" to stay at home and take care of their father. From what we know, she wanted a further education too, and by all accounts, she was as intelligent as (if not more so than) her famous brother. She was also very active and even took on some politically risky underground activities for dissenters against the ruling order. She also suffered in her adult life from various psychological problems (we're not sure what). When she did the normal thing and came to live with Hegel and wife after the birth of their first child, and Hegel went off on a short trip, he returned to find his sister and his wife at each other's throats. Christiane left, and Hegel and his sister never saw each other again, although there was some strained correspondence. She was also an old friend of one of Hegel's youthful girlfriends. When she learned of his death, she went to the river and drowned herself. Make of this what you will. It suggests that Hegel's interest in the "sister" here may also be partly autobiographical, but that is purely speculative.

We get the reappearance of the idea of an "original determinate nature" except that it does not have the determinate significance of the opposition (Hegel's term) between the sexes. Naturalness becomes ethical destiny.

¶459. Now we have a restatement of the view that the two laws depend on each other. Each seems to be a semblance of an underlying unity. The difference of the sexes still remains within the unity of the substance. Some people have taken Hegel to be developing the seeds of a conception of gender as differentiated from sex here. Rather than stopping short at the difference of the sexes, he seems to be saying that the difference only makes sense as a difference in a type of social order (substance). Although that idea is certainly nascent in Hegel's account here, if we see him as offering an account of gender equality, we are almost certainly giving him too much credit. He does clearly, how-ever, want to say that the biological difference on its own has no spir-itual, *geistig* content until it has been integrated into the "substance." For Hegel, there is the biological difference, what that *means* for self-conscious lives, and the two are distinguished. *We* might go on to de-lineate that as the reproductive capacity of sex versus the social lines of the distinctions of genders, but *Hegel* didn't go that far.

¶460. The chapter on Reason is said to have presented "substanceless" shapes of consciousness (or perhaps better put: shapes of consciousness not yet aware of their "substance"). We saw how the contradictions which culminated in the spiritual kingdom of animals provoked us to move to *Geist*.

¶461. Justice (at first) is taken to be the correct working of a quasi-natural ethical order. The need for a more reflective sense of justice arises only when the equilibrium is disturbed and must be put back into order. In a just world, each is in the correct position to keep the equilibrium of the whole steady. This is (at this stage of the argument) an "organic" conception. All the elements of the social world are like organs, and if each fulfills its role correctly, then the whole is healthy. If one of them fails to do so, equilibrium must be restored, and pun-ishment is the means by which this is done. (We might fairly ask: Why punishment? Why not a seminar on wrongdoing?) If it's human law at stake, the community must punish. If it's divine law, then the gods or the denizens of the underworld (such as the Erinyes, i.e., Furies) must carry out the punishment.

There is mention of Orestes and the Furies pursuing him. Orestes murders his mother (and her lover) because she has murdered his fa-ther, and she did this because he has sacrificed (murdered in another sense) their daughter, Iphigenia (and returned home from Troy with a mistress, Cassandra). Orestes is pursued by the Furies as a matter of cosmic equilibrium having to do with what should by nature happen to a son who murders his mother. It is unclear what Hegel is trying to say here, except that the justice that is finally achieved for Iphigenia and Orestes makes what is natural into something ethical-as-mores (into a "work"). All the members of the house of Atreus suffer under a curse, so it is not the polity that has wronged them. Even though the family suffers under a curse, this should give those Greeks no reason to doubt the justice of the polity or the cosmos. (It's worth noting that Hegel's reading of the plays has been heavily challenged.)

¶462. This introduces a theme crucial to Hegel's argument and one shared by many of his friends and, in a somewhat different way, by many of his entire generation (especially the early Romantics). It reappears in philosophy over and over again in Nietzsche, Heidegger, Arendt, MacIntyre, and so on. It is the idea of ancient Greek life prior to Socrates and the invention of philosophy as manifesting some kind of optimal condition for self-conscious life. When everything is going right in the polis, there is an equilibrium among all the parts. The basic opposition (divine and human law, difference of the sexes) is in fact harmonized. It comes back to itself "undefiled," each of the two elements calling forth the other. People such as Hölderlin will ask whether it can be recreated or reestablished and despair of it. Arendt points to it as the one place where freedom appears (and disappears, only to pop up again from time to time). If you read Marx a certain way, you see that his model of communism is that of Athens without the slaves and the oppression of women. In his lectures on the philosophy of history, Hegel also notes that this paragon in its true form only lasted sixty-seven years (not exactly an encouraging model). It is "true" when the facts of its life are adequate to the concept of its species-being: freedom and equality in mutual recognition.

But back to the family and sexual difference: the man unites universal spirit with the unconscious element of the divine law. Woman integrates divine law (the unconscious) with consciousness. The union of man and wife unites the two movements. Men test themselves by seeking glory and risking death, thus taking the equilibrium of the whole into the realm of natural events, whereas women seek to maintain the equilibrium of the whole by upholding the rights of the family in the polity. Each has his or her own ordained and "natural" place.

b. Ethical Action, Human and Divine Knowledge, Guilt and Fate

¶463. The problem with all of this is that the parts of the whole may be conceived as organs of the whole, but as self-conscious organs, they are not simply "organs." This much comes from the setup out of the *Sache selbst*. We saw the subjects there trying to make their individuality real (individuality first conceived as an aspiration, then as a metaphysical fact). Looking back from that (see ¶353), we can see that if the moves in "the law of the heart" and the *Sache selbst* are valid, then something like the *Sittlichkeit* as it's been portrayed so far can't last. "Individuality" will tear it apart, and a world of such individuals will not be compatible with such a world. But that is seen only by virtue of looking back. We should also ask another question. *Must* this form of *Sittlichkeit* fall apart on its own terms? How do things look from its point of view looking forward?

As yet, at this point in the development of the argument about true spirit (ancient Greece), the individual is not yet a singular individuality (*einzelne Individualität*), and the emergence of the "individual" with its own rights will turn the harmony of the oppositions of divine and human law into a straightforward opposition (or contradiction). Each side of the opposition now nullifies the other. This act of mutual nullification is seen as fate, something different from and ruling over both divine and human law.

¶464. Within this form of *Sittlichkeit*, "There is neither arbitrary choice nor is there struggle or indecision, as it has forsaken both giving the law and testing the law." This means that the people who are by the nature of things assigned to divine law or human law simply find themselves with that commitment and, in that commitment, find themselves with a character defined by it. Even if what exactly you are to do requires deliberation, the broad outlines of what you are to do do not— "Honor the divine laws," "Behave as a man (woman) is supposed to behave"—and the contours of what that requires are widely understood ("Don't cry"). But what to do when the requirements (duties) clash?

This isn't a clash of duty versus passion (a modern theme). Nor is it the comical expression of duty versus duty (which would only show an absolute inherently at odds with itself, which can be humorous). Comedy is about failures that fail to matter. Or it's about what we thought was crucially important turning out not to be. (Laughter is just about failure in general.) Typically comedy is about the failure of *Eigensinn*, obstinacy. Comedy reconciles us to the parts of our nature that refuse the rule of reason. (That's an essential part of the contingency of self-conscious life, something about which much philosophy typically has trouble saying anything at all.)

There can also be a darker nihilist comedy to the effect that nothing matters. But that's not in play here. So this isn't comedy.

¶465. In deciding for one or the other (divine or human law), ethical consciousness is *character*. One's character is defined by this basic option, and although one's character is not completely one's own choice, as self-conscious one must nonetheless commit oneself to what is in keeping with one's character. Thus, in the basic division, each sees right only on its own side. Antigone (divine law) sees Creon as unjustified "violence" (*Gewalttätigkeit*, maybe "outrage") and herself as in the right. Creon (human law) sees Antigone as obstinate (*Eigensinn*) and unacceptably disobedient.

¶466. The divine law is unconscious. Its laws are what they are, they don't change, we don't legislate them. They are eternal and are just there. Human laws are conscious: people (like Creon) make them, state them, and they are changeable. The ethical substance (the "essence") appears bearing the status of the unconditioned, the absolute. As such it cannot permit itself to be inverted. On this view of action, the agent does not act on a principle conceived as a distinguishable moment of thought; rather, the agent goes from principle to action directly. (It's not the sequence "from principle to psychological state to action"; but the simpler, more direct "from principle to action.") In the latter model, where is self-consciousness? When all goes right, the deed (the *Tat*, what results from a *Tun*, sometimes from *Handeln*), that is, what is done (distinct from the doing or the commitment to will-be-done), is recognized by all as the successful intention of a doing. (Antigone is performing burial rites; she's doing something. Antigone has performed the burial rites; there is a deed; Antigone demands recognition for having done the right thing, what was required of her.)

¶467. This is the way in which the ethical substance of Greek life is already at odds with itself, dividing itself into absolute duties that conflict with each other. Antigone takes only one side of this as her absolute duty (bury her brother). Her deed brings out the otherwise concealed and contradictory element of that common life.

Here the individual is thus the *form* that substance takes, but the substance supplies the *content*. In effect, the divine law (part of substance) proclaims: honor the members of the family, make sure the proper rites are performed. That's *content*. How are the proper rites done? By an appropriate family member. That's the *form* in which the divine law is carried out.

But unless Antigone is doing this self-consciously, her various doings (washing the body, sprinkling the oil, saying the words) don't amount to an action (performing the burial rites). And it must be that in this series of "an action being underway" she *knows* what is she is doing. So it can't be the simpler model: principle-directly-to-action. Aligned with ethical mores, *sittlich*, she is completely absorbed in her action, but she cannot be so absorbed that she doesn't know what she's doing. Still, there is not some extra mental state that leads us from the conclusion of a deliberation to the action. The conclusion of deliberation is acting. Antigone decides what she is to do, she argues with Ismene (her sister) about it, so she *knows* what she is doing. The action is now underway even if she doesn't do it until later in the day. As disobeying Creon, Antigone is also self-consciously separating herself from "ethical essence" since she *knows* that she is violating one of the basic laws of her community. In this way, Antigone's ethical consciousness puts the ethical whole to one side and focuses instead on her action's own rightness.

Antigone has, however, three unconditional duties: appropriately bury the brother, obey Creon, and not make up her own mind what her duties are. As Creon follows out his unconditional duty, he becomes a tyrant, and Antigone in her self-wrought doom and fanaticism becomes the heroine. Why? It is her demand for recognition as an equal. If her brothers are recognized as free and equal, why not she? Calling for her freedom and equality (as a member of the ruling family), Antigone in effect also becomes the voice of the excluded. In effect, she claims: If 'some are free', then why not me too? (That is the trajectory, the "in itself" of her decisions and her acts.)

¶468. Hegel gives a kind of descriptive account of what he takes the Greek view of this to be. The laws (and their respective deities) are bound up with each other; each calls the other forth. An injury to one brings the vengeance of the other into play. What this reveals to us is that our deeds and plans not only have unintended consequences, but that there is a kind of logic that makes matters into a fate such that what we do will not be seen to have the significance we intended. We cannot be in control of everything. Our deeds will have a kind of counterfinality. (Thucydides makes this into a theme of his history of the Peloponnesian wars. Hubris creates a kind of Nemesis for the Athenians.) Actuality has a hidden side. (Take the example of Oedipus: he doesn't *know* that he married his mother and killed his father; his *doings* are not his *action*, but they are his *deed* for which he is responsible.)

Hegel notes that the deed sets the unmoved into motion. Members of the audience at the performance of the tragedy of Antigone were being provoked into wondering if their form of life made sense. Its unassailable first principles were starting to look not so unassailable.

¶469. We can have our deeds ascribed to us without our knowing, without it being our action. But the situation is all the more pure if the doer knows the law, and Antigone's acceptance of her fate shows this: she deserves to be punished because she self-consciously violated the requirements of her position.

¶470. Antigone's and Creon's (and our, the audience's) recognition of this fate sublates the conflict. This throws us back to the very basis of *Sittlichkeit*, which is that of the certainty of right, that nothing counts but the right. The subject sets out with a determined character, but that character leads her to do wrong. What she is left with is not a real (actual) character (the firmness to do the right or accept punishment) but something like a (set of) dispositions, attitudes, a "cast of mind" (a *Gesinnung*). Because the ancient Greek individual is rooted in the deep structure of *Sittlichkeit*, the ancient Greek agent can have a *pathos*, a current of deep emotion that is enough to explain her doings.

Pathos is thus an emotion that endures and is enough to set a character as the character she is (revenge, ambition, courage, cunning, etc.). Moderns, so Hegel thinks, rarely have a pathos in this sense. We are too conflicted.

¶471. Since the Greek view of *Sittlichkeit* is that of a self-restoring actuality, in Greek tragedies there is a movement inexorably toward equilibrium. The two sides (the embodiments of human and divine law) are at odds, so restoring the whole means both sides must be punished. But this opposition actually destroys the whole. Both Antigone and Creon, as doing what they do self-consciously, become agents who are not completely absorbed into the "substance." The singular individual, a status incompatible with Greek *Sittlichkeit*, emerges, even if nobody can yet articulate it fully.

Absolute right is fulfilled in both sides going under.

Both, as essential, must meet their downfall. This is the logic of the situation, and it is, in Greek terms, fate.

¶472. The full contingency of nature in all of this shows up. The fact that the two brothers appear in a different birth order means that the polity, to preserve its unity, must honor one while punishing the other. There is also no room for negotiation on this point.

¶473. In doing so, the polity thus puts itself into opposition and struggle with the divine law, where even if it wins, it loses. The dead know how to find the tools for their revenge—in the tragedies (*Antigone*) and in the history (Thucydides). In the Greek view, the polity is brought down by these underground divinities, but in fact its own logic brings it down (as "we," guided by all-knowing narrator, more clearly see). In effect, human life, when it forgets its divine limits and basis, brings about its own demise. The tragedies show us (without fully conceptualizing it for us) that this form of life really makes no sense in the way it opposes divine and human law. It is this kind of failure that will lead the Greeks away from tragedy and into philosophy (from the world of Aeschylus and Sophocles to that of Socrates, Plato, and Aristotle). The beautiful nondiscursive world of Greek art-religion passes over into the alienated, split-up world of discursive philosophy.

¶474. Hegel says that in this *Vorstellung*—which can mean here both representation, the general *idea* we have of the Greeks, or this specific *performance* of the play—human law and divine law are embodied in individuals within the pathos of each. That pathos leads both Antigone and Creon into a kind of fanaticism. Hegel then says something that has kept commentators in business for a couple of centuries. The ancient Greek polis was made of up men confronting each other as equals in a democracy. That all rested on slavery and the subjugation of women. The women were assigned to the family, to the "private" sphere, out of public (i.e., political) view. This is a fundamental contradiction in Greek life and makes "the feminine—the polity's eternal irony" (Hegel's terms) into its enemy. What did he mean? Here's one way of taking it: by standing outside of the polity altogether but nonetheless playing an essential although somewhat denigrated role in ethical life, women were capable of seeing men's foibles that the men couldn't see. (They were thus the "eternal irony" of the polity.) The petty failures of the men strutting around and preening for each other, continually spurring each other on to violence and combat, were, for the women looking at them from the outside, more like matters of comedy. (On this, see two of Aristophanes's plays: *Lysistrata* and *Thesmophoriazusae*.) The "female" thus encourages the youth to turn the "solemn wisdom" of the elders into comedic matter. As the protector of the family, she is inclined to use her wiles to turn what is supposed to be debate over the common good into intrigue about how to further the family's fortunes. The polity in effect makes the feminine into its enemy. Hegel draws the conclusion that this is a disaster for the polity, and we are to take away from that the idea that women must be better integrated into *Sittlichkeit* instead of being treated like an alien principle. That might look like a call for women to join as equals in public life, but Hegel never ever goes even halfway to that point. For we moderns, he argues, the division into male-breadwinner / wife-mother–angel of the household is the proper division.

¶475. The Greek polity could only hold itself together by the idea that it is worth sacrificing one's very life for the survival of the polity. It is no surprise then that the Greek states spent a lot of time in warfare. In that situation, no matter how well you play it, your luck will eventually run out, and you will lose a war, and this eventually happened to Athens. In one of its defeats, its entire army was sold off as slaves by the Spartans. Eventually, Greek city-states collapsed into mutually quarreling and suspicious foes of each other—a *Volk* as an individuality is for-itself only as others are for-it; it makes itself independent of them, Hegel says—and as such became easy picking for the next great empire, Rome. The smallness of the city-states had been their glory, since it allowed the kind of face-to-face meeting that supported democracy. However, their proliferation, their glorification of warfare, and their constant battles against each other eventually made them unable to defend themselves from a larger, more powerful predator.

c. The State of Legality

¶476. We will run through this rather quickly, much as Hegel does. Hegel in effect gives a quick wave of the hand to the history of Rome, although in his later lectures in Berlin, Hegel was to devote much more attention to Roman life and politics. Here it's clear that Greece is his focus. Like others of his generation—but as one of the leading lights of it along with his roommates, Schelling and Hölderlin—he was tired of the endless invocation of Rome-as-home-to-Christendom in high culture and Hegel found the wonderfully named "Holy Roman Empire of the German Nation" to be a bit of a comedic piece. (Voltaire quipped: it was neither holy, nor Roman, nor an empire.) Hegel, Schelling and Hölderlin devised a subversive thesis: the defining beginning of European life was in fact not Christianity but pagan Greece.

So what is Rome? It's not city-states, it's an empire. The Greek city-states and *Sittlichkeit* dissolve and are sublated (canceled and preserved) in Rome (preserved in terms of cultural matters such as architecture, etc.). Or, as Hegel says, the universal unity into which the living, immediate unity of substance and individuality return is the *geistlose Gemeinwesen*, the spiritless polity. What holds it all together is not something living, substantial but a set of laws backed by the credible threat of force. It's a modus vivendi and not a piece of ethical life. Splintered into many people, it provides an equality in which all count as each, as *persons*. "Person" here is not the Strawsonian creature taking mental and physical predicates but something more like "legal status" or "officeholder" (or "placeholder" for a certain status). Now the agent is self-conscious not of itself as a participant in *Sittlichkeit* but of being a citizen or client of Rome.

¶477. The Roman citizen's substantiality is its being-recognized (*Anerkanntsein*). One's status as a Roman is no more than being legally recognized as a Roman and whatever follows from that. After that, whatever else is true about you is incidental. It's like a game, and you are supposed to play by the rules, and the players are its content, each of them being the *spröde* (aloof, prim, brittle, rough) unaccommodating "self."

¶478. We now have an account of what was earlier characterized as stoical self-consciousness. What Stoicism was in itself—in its not fully developed *concept* of the form of the world—is now the *actual* world. The principle of the state of Roman legality, the *Rechtzustand* is that of spiritless self-sufficiency. The "legal person" is free only in his thought, even when he fully acknowledged the force of Roman law. But, as we saw earlier, this type of being-for-itself only achieves the *thought* of self-sufficiency and not real self-sufficiency.

¶479. The *abstract* self-sufficiency of Stoicism is now actualized, put into practice, and the result is that it passes over into skeptical disarray and lots of twaddle about "the negative." In being actualized, this shape of *Geist* is the contradiction of self-sufficiency and non-self-sufficiency. The personal self-sufficiency embodied in Roman law is the same universal disarray and reciprocal dissolution. If, in skepticism, actuality has the negative value of mere semblance, *Schein*, then in Roman law, it has the positive value of 'mine,' as recognized, but both are the same abstract universal. If nothing counts essentially for me other than my recognized legal status, then there's not that much essential to being the Roman citizen. Thus, to call someone a "person" is thereby really an expression of contempt, *Verachtung*. It is to say that you are no more than a placeholder, an empty suit.

¶480. When the world is "atomized" in this way, so that there is nothing publicly essential about anybody, then everybody is just an empty "point" in the social space. Thus, in just a few sentences, Hegel passes over the vast complexity in the shift from the Roman republic to the empire by saying that in such an atomized world, the many "points" are collected together in the *Herr* (lord and master) of the world (i.e., Augustus). Hegel's version of Rome here is sort of a version of legal positivism, in which law is a command issued by a sovereign backed up by the credible threat of force. Other than that, there's nothing more to the validity of the law. For Romans, nothing would be deeper or higher—depending on which metaphor you want—than the emperor. He is just one individual, himself a legal person, who stands above and over and against all others. Actually, this lone self is in fact powerless, unactual. He is the monstrous self-consciousness that "knows itself" as (i.e., is certain in his belief that he is) an actual god, but he is in reality only a formal self, and hence his self-enjoyment slides off into debauchery. (This makes it sound as if all the emperors were like the Romans we've all seen in sword-and-sandal Hollywood movies.) Part of what is going on here is Hegel's stance in opposition to those who identify Rome with Christendom—as is he's saying, *this* is what you want to base European life on?

¶481. This lord and master of the world embodies and exercises a destructive power exercised over his subordinates. This happens when leaders atomize the public. The public becomes powerless and lonely.

¶482. This section and its arguments are all too short. The general idea is that the harshness and abstractness of Roman life provoked a stoical and skeptical inward turn. Public life became more or less insignificant, so people turned to more private pleasures and engagements (friendship, family, food, meditation, mystery religions). This created a new kind of *Geist* that was looking to unite, in a more coherent shape, the Roman person with this new form of inwardness. Rome initiates the formation of "subjective freedom" (private freedom) as a substitution for the public freedom of the Greeks. The new coherence to be brought to this turned out to be Christianity. But Hegel waits until the chapter titled "Religion" to spell out how that works.

9

Self-Alienated Spirit

In the dissolution of the ancient world (of "true spirit" and Roman "legality"), the key figure is Antigone. Antigone had been forced to make a choice among competing requirements where there was no real choice to be made (do the burial rites; obey Creon's order to abstain from the burial rites; don't make up your own mind where your requirements lie). There is also her passion to become free, which she can only do by being recognized as an equal, which requires her to stage-manage the recognition from her dead brother. In Antigone, we see the subject of the ancient world being thrown back on herself because (1) this is forced on her by the contradictions in which she finds herself; (2) the "public" subject (found in the *Sittlichkeit* anchored in the "substance") makes no sense since it is contradictory. The "public" self thus empties out into something more like the concept of a role-player, that is, into something vaguely theatrical. The Roman regime takes up that empty self and throws a legal cloak over it. To be a self is just to be an actor operating in terms of the rules. (It's to be an "officeholder.")

There is nothing essential with any real content for the "officeholder" self, just the private choices or the communal demands (be a Gaul, be a Jew, be a Teuton, etc.) which, within the Roman conception, are not essential to you. They are just the contingencies of where you come from, much like your height or hair color.

As the Roman world decays, this turns into the medieval European order where individual selves find themselves in various social situations which are not essentially congruent with them. A major part of the story here is being left out: Roman Christianity. Hegel will turn to that in the "Religion" chapter. (This is one of the places where he also probably began to think that he got the story right but slightly out of order.) That has a couple of elements. If the Roman world, as we saw, was essentially monadic—the relation to others is mediated entirely by a system of rules—then the Greek world was essentially

Hegel's Phenomenology of Spirit. Terry Pinkard, Oxford University Press. © Oxford University Press 2023. DOI: 10.1093/oso/9780197663127.003.0009

nonmonadic (at least for the males in the polis, the women and slaves being something else and very problematic), and its conventional, *monadic* legal rules were subordinate to the deeper nonmonadic relations of the polis; moreover, one's ties to the (monadic) laws were anchored in one's (nonmonadic) ties to the people. The new Christian world is a mélange at first of the monadic and the nonmonadic. God issues commandments (the monadic form), but he loves everyone and doesn't play favorites (nonmonadic form). So we have the emergence of a new conception: equality. We are all sons and daughters of God, so we have in principle a nonmonadic relation to each other. This is the form of the world for the post-Roman inhabitants. However, at first, there is no way for European life to combine these two, so European life seems to totter from one senseless shape of spirit to another without making any apparent progress. For Hegel in 1807, all the wealth of forms of late antiquity are interesting but not fundamentally important for the *phenomenology* of self-conscious life.

Self-conscious life in general and the self in particular become alienated (*entfremdet*), a key term Hegel helps to introduce into philosophy. The term itself is much older. Luther uses it in one place (Ephesians 4:18).[1] To be alienated is to have one's own being as other to oneself and thus to have a status that one cannot really inhabit (or one has great trouble inhabiting). Another form of alienation is to have a binding norm go dead on oneself—where the affective attachment to the norm goes dead but the feeling of its being required stays alive.

B. Spirit Alienated from Itself: Cultural Formation

¶483. The alienated self comes to be when the actual institutions which are *in force* and count as *valid*—where there is one German word for those two ideas: *Geltung*—are in opposition to whatever nonalienated self there is.

If the nonalienated selves are at each other's throats, then the substance will be alienated.

Self-consciousness does something to itself: it has an *Entäußerung* and an *Entwesung* of itself. *Entäußerung* is Luther's translation of the Greek *kenosis*, the "emptying" that God performs to become man.

More colloquially, it means "relinquishment." Hegel uses this heavily theologically freighted term to describe what Europeans will do to themselves on the way to the modern world. They "thin themselves out," "empty" themselves. There is also an *Entwesung*, literally a "disinfestation," but Hegel is also playing on the way the term literally looks like it means "de-essencing" (if there were such a word). So it's a thinning out and a moving away from the idea that self-conscious life has any kind of thick essential structure that carries genuine ethical import. Antigone didn't have the concepts for it, but she was on the way to such alienation.

Geist is this world and is itself alienated within it. The world is the negative of self-consciousness (what I am is not the way the world has me determined), and the labor of self-consciousness is to define itself negatively toward the world in order to affirm oneself. For example: the marginalized figure who defines herself *not* as the negative image, role, place, status she seems to have to be in the world as we find it, but as something affirmative and not of that particular world.

Note that the form of the world for the ancients included the idea that there was no getting around the "fact" of slavery. Some would simply have to serve others as their "property" since otherwise the economy wouldn't work. This was just the world as we found it, and there was no getting around it.

But what is the affirmative element here? Hegel seems to be claiming that at the outset, all Europeans are more or less in this position. Even the high and mighty have to say: yes, we are all equal in the eyes of God, but (the high and mighty add) God has also put me in charge, not you, even though he does not play favorites. Get used to it, that's the way things are.

Notice that it's *Geist* itself, not just individuals, that is alienated here. Self-conscious life knows itself to be free but also knows that it isn't free and perhaps can't even expect to be free, but may hope to be free.

¶484. The pure consciousness ("pure," which abstracts itself from its actuality, including almost all of its concrete commitments) is the alienated consciousness. I'm just "me," not all the things I supposedly also must be in this alienating world. I am none of those, so what am I? Something like merely an officeholder, a point in something like a chart.

The essence of things for the alienated consciousness has to be a *Jenseits*, an otherworldly "beyond." The existing world cannot lay claim to the universality it claims to have. In the beyond, we are all equal, but here, we're not. And there is no way (at least at first) to bring the two into line. The "beyond" is always beyond, that's just the way things are.

¶485. This is a form of spirit in *Entäußerung*, "emptying" or "relinquishing." It "empties" itself of what is considered to be essential to itself. Ultimately, it will be left with only a highly abstract version of itself as a "free rational agent," and the actual world as a contingent realm of the exercise of power (this-worldly, *diesseits*). The essential world is *jenseits*, the otherworldly beyond. In this world, for example, virtue and happiness are distinct, whereas in the postulated world beyond, the two are in accordance with each other, and it is the virtuous person who gets the reward. We then get a preview of where this is going. The French Revolution and the rights of man are going to be the logical outcome of this way of *Geist* trying to make sense of itself.

B. The World of Self-Alienated Spirit

¶486. What we draw from this is that we have a doubling of what is at issue. There is the world as I found it. And there is me, not in this world (as either a disinterested perspective on it or as a free but alienated marginalized figure), but nonetheless also part of the way this world is produced. As I see myself not as essentially in the world as I found it, I am in "pure" consciousness as if I were somehow standing outside of the world. This leads up to something Hegel calls "faith," which he distinguishes from religion.

a. Cultural Formation and Its Realm of Actuality

¶487. We have the spiritual essence infused with a self-consciousness that knows itself to be an *individual* (knows itself as *this* self-consciousness). The two—the spiritual essence and the individual—are thus at odds with each other.

As "this" self-consciousness, the agent confronts himself as just "thrown" into the world. He must therefore alienate himself from himself and the world around him if he is to fit into it. But he also has to learn to inhabit the world as he finds it. He does this by taking on the forms of the 'we-self.'

He is to make himself the "norm" by renouncing himself and in following the social norms thus claiming universal status for himself. In this way, "we" are all equal in that we are all equally alienated. So, as Hegel puts it, self-consciousness has reality only as it alienates itself and posits itself as universal. By submitting ourselves to the social standard set by "them" or by "society," we strive to become the universal (a person of the right type). We empty ourselves in order to become as one is supposed to be, and that has to do with what others think is "supposed to be."

¶488. Hegel tells us that "it is *cultural formation (Bildung)* through which the individual here has validity and actuality." The term *Bildung* is a key German term and is impossible to translate with one word: in Hegel's time, it was the idea of education (especially higher education), a process of forming oneself to be a cultured individual, acquiring an aptitude for good judgment (particularly in aesthetic matters), and so on. It was a cultural ideal. Hegel is here using it too in its sense of "self-formation." In the way he speaks of it here, this *Bildung* involves a push to social conformism. The individual is to strive as an ideal to make himself a "type." This is the concrete way in which the individual now seeks to realize his concept.

¶489. So Hegel says roughly that what appears in relation to the singular individual as his *Bildung* is the essential moment of substance (the social space) itself. What appears is self-consciousness making itself conform to its concept of itself to the extent its original nature permits it.

The "substance" here is a stand-in for a "form of life." It is the "subject" (as a plurality) actualizing itself as substance, as a collective form of life insisting on its members' conformity to a contingent ideal. The "substance" now seems more like a master issuing commands than it did as a way in which "We" and "I" were distinct but in harmony.

¶490. Having relinquished himself in his history from Roman legality to the eighteenth-century ideal of *Bildung*, the individual finds less and less of himself to be essential, to have "validity and actuality." The only essential content for emptied agency has either to come from nature (which is limited to what is necessary for life) or from society itself. To itself, the agent caught up in the way of life of this kind of self-formation thus feels the necessity to push himself toward social conformism. He has to alienate himself from whatever part of himself resists that push to conformism, and to the extent that he finds himself alienated from that social and self-induced push to conformism, he must alienate himself from that alienation and relinquish that part of himself too. He has to learn to want things because others want them, and those others must do the same thing. (It seems relatively clear that Hegel is describing the way a new class—what eventually came to be called by its French name, the bourgeoisie—is taking shape in European life.)

¶491. Hegel begins with a more logical and phenomenological description of what had become the way in which feudal, post-Roman Europe had emerged from its initial chaos and formulated itself most purely in French thought as the unity of three estates: the aristocracy, the ecclesiasticals, and the commoners, each serving a different function in the unity—I fight for you, I pray for you, I work for you. Post-Roman Europe was the "simple substance" in its "existing but still *unbegeistete* (unspirited, lacking spirit) moments." It was "unspirited" in that it had no sense of itself yet as a self-conscious unity, as a collective subject, but merely as parts of "Christendom." This unity breaks itself up into social estates in which the standards of each estate give the members the overall picture of what they are supposed to be educated to become. (Hegel speaks of *Masse*, which is not the modern "the masses" but, as the older Grimm's dictionary tells us, is something like the *Stände*, the estates themselves, of late medieval and early modern Europe.) As "Christendom," it had a sense of its unity, but as in-itself, undeveloped. It then split itself up into different polities but then also managed to come to a fuller understanding of itself as Christendom split into different polities with each structured by much the same understanding as the French division into the three estates or "orders" of social life.

¶492. The dialectic now concerns itself both with the terms in which these polities (and Europe in general) thought of themselves and how they actually took themselves to be, given the actuality of life on the ground. There is a sense of "the good" as that which holds the polities together as members of one Christian community. But there is also the sense that singular individuals make their own claims for themselves—the "bad." This threatens the unity of the whole such that it always seems to be in danger of dissolution, and it is a matter thus of such singular individuals to make the sacrifices necessary to hold the whole together.

¶493. Hegel makes a large historical leap from there to the early modern European contrast between state power and wealth. By the eighteenth century, people had begun to refer to the unity of the polity as that of the "state" rather than in terms of "serving the king." Hegel would have been aware of that, but he took "serving the king" simply to be the undeveloped in-itself concept of the state. In this movement, the state becomes "the universal," and although it is the result of collective activity, it becomes forgotten as being such a result and comes to be seen more as a natural part of the social landscape, as the basis for collective activity rather than its result. One of the major results of this newly conceptualized unity of the state is also the idea that the state as a subject of action can accumulate wealth for itself that is not merely the wealth of the ruling prince (as his own possession) but the wealth of the whole and available to each as part of his own consumption. With that arises a new idea best formulated by Adam Smith: the individual may take himself to be acting only for his own self-interest, but doing so actually benefits the whole. In Adam Smith's famous phrase, "He intends only his own gain; and he is in this, as in many other cases, led by an invisible hand to promote an end which was no part of his intention. Nor is it always the worse for the society that it was no part of it. By pursuing his own interest, he frequently promotes that of the society more effectually than when he really intends to promote it." (It is worth keeping in mind that this was still a relatively new idea when Hegel was writing this book.)

¶494. The individual thus finds the universal (the unity of himself and others) in two forms: in the state as a centralizing institution and in wealth, in which in the Smithian dispensation one's own self-interest also plays a universal unifying role. Now, instead of "self-consciousness is desire itself" (¶167), we have "*self-consciousness . . . is essentially judgment."* In this form of life, people are already living at a distance from their lives. (This is part of alienation and self-emptying.) They are making judgments about what is unconditional but doing so at a distance, and they are learning to live by abstractions ("the state," the "invisible hand," etc.). Between state power and wealth, this abstracted, emptied alienated individual can imagine himself as having a choice. (One or the other? Neither? Both?) If there are conflicts among them, the individual has to exercise "judgment" (which has no rules to follow but which can go better or worse). Central to that view is that the person of greater *Bildung* also has greater powers of judgment.

¶495. If the universal (the substance, the unity of the whole) itself necessarily embodies different and contradictory principles within itself, then the individual exercising good judgment has to find a way to navigate within those contradictions. To this self-consciousness, good is that object in which it finds itself, bad the object in which it cannot find itself. Good is its *Gleichheit*, equality to objective reality, bad its *Ungleichheit* (inequality) with it. If one sees the invisible hand as objective reality, one will see state power's interference with it as bad. If one sees state power and its exercise for the good of the whole as objective reality, one will see many movements of the invisible hand as bad. Which one counts as the true spiritual unity of the members of the polity thus depends on the considered judgment of the person of *Bildung*. Without the considered judgments of people of the proper formation, spirit as the unity of everyone would be powerless. But these individuals would not be what they are (as in-itself) without the unity of spirit. They (as embodying state power or wealth or both) are themselves developing only as exhibitions of the way in which an alienated spirit manifests itself through their actions. These two types become its main exemplars.

¶496. The consciousness existing in and for itself at first finds its simple essence in state power but not its individuality, and it thus finds itself subjugated into obedience. Its being-in-itself has to do with service to others via service to state power. What it finds is its in-itself (what it develops toward in terms of its concept) as existing in obedience to state power, but its being-for-itself is alienated. The individual takes an inward turn before this power, which becomes for him "the bad" as the reality of state power which is unequal to his own concept of what he is supposed to be. Taking wealth to be the good, he devotes himself to the enjoyment that comes with it, he supports a variety of artisans who cater to his needs, and he becomes beneficent (i.e., becomes a wealthy philanthropist). As such a philanthropist, he is (or so he takes it) to be on the developmental path to universal benevolence and beneficence. Spirit's unity, he thinks, is far better served by his philanthropic endeavors than by the state's exercising its powers. To be sure, his beneficence can at times go awry, but that's not the point.

¶497. The state, on the other hand, is the institution which claims to be the central point that organizes and thus makes real (or actual) the whole. The wealthy individual cannot make that claim. He is a transitory being, whereas the state endures. Instead of his being the embodiment of the universal, the state is the embodiment of the universal. "Good" and "bad" trade their referents.

¶498. Both are different shapes of consciousness and are different ways of exercising the considered judgment that the person of *Bildung* is supposed to make. If the good is the reality that is equal to the individual's concept of himself, then for one set of characters, state power is the good, whereas for the other set, wealth and beneficence as equal to his concept of himself are the good. In a way, each of the exemplars here takes himself to be expressing "the real world" in contrast to the other one. Since actual consciousness has both principles claiming to be binding for it, it chooses one of them (in its considered judgment) in terms of which it expresses "its" essence.

¶499. The noble-minded person gets around this quandary by generating an idea of himself as being genuinely in the service of the state—even Frederick the Great, an absolutist monarch, described himself as the first servant of the state. The noble-minded give the monarch the recognition the monarch seeks, and the rewards the monarch dispenses to them are met with appropriate gratitude. On this view, there is no (i.e., not supposed to be) contradiction between personal wealth and selfless service to the state.

¶500. Hegel now sketches the other side of this picture. The vulgar, "base" agent cannot see obedience to state power as its "substance," what motivates it. State power seems perfectly external to it, an interference with its own plan of life. Each side of this picture presents itself as the paradigm of agency, as that to which others ought to measure up (be equal to) and to which others of course fall short. The "base" merchant sees himself denigrated, sees the nobles as lesser than he but as having a higher social position. Not for nothing do these wealthy merchants have themselves ennobled when they get rich enough. They despise the wealthy and aristocratic, and they despise themselves for wanting to be aristocratic and wealthy.

¶501. The type of opposition that takes the form of "character" in the Greek world of Antigone has vanished, and a new opposition has taken its place. Instead of divine versus human law, we have state power versus wealth, with different characters embodying each. Each exercises "proper judgment" to decide where his basic commitments lie. On this view, we have the judging individual on one side, and these two essences as rather inert objects (or we might say "values"—Hegel calls them predicates that aren't yet subjects) among which choices have to be made or competing claims balanced in an all things considered judgment. We have the thoughts of the good and the bad (good is what sustains the polity, bad is what works against it), and the reality on the ground of the competing spheres of state power and wealth. As judgment becomes inference (we draw conclusions from these things), we come to see more reflectively that both moments of the opposition are necessary.

¶502. The "heroism of service": one alienates one's own ends in a noble sacrifice for the "universal." (This was expressed in the aristocratic cult of honor in the seventeenth century.)

¶503. The universal (state power as the vehicle of service to others) becomes merged with existence. As this paradigm takes over in thought, it makes itself actual. It is a version of what Hegel over and over again calls "spirit giving itself reality." A form of commitments, mindedness, institutionalizes itself, becomes ethical substance, that is, a kind of second nature (as habits, dispositions, expectations, etc.). In its sacrifice for the service to others, it acquires a new value: respect (*Achtung*) for itself and others in terms of their "honor" and their "dignity."

¶504. As the abstraction of the state replaces the individual monarch as the focus of loyalty, the "proud vassal" who once gave his allegiance to his overlord now gives it to the universal as an institution. The older idea of honor was bound up with specific ties to specific people, and that begins to crumble.

¶505. Hegel points rather obliquely to the in-between status at the time when loyalty to the prince was being replaced by loyalty to the state. The noble "counselor" who is to offer his considered judgment as advice offers it to the prince but does so in the spirit of offering it to the state. (In the passage from prince to state, one thinks of Louis XIV's—likely apocryphal—claim "I am the state" as encapsulating this.) In this transitional phase, there is not yet any real bureaucratic apparatus of state power and hence no real government, and hence no real "state power" (which is on the way to becoming real but at this stage is not fully realized). The individual prince gets conflicting advice from those supposedly exercising self-conscious judgment and thus finds himself powerless. The wise counselor who finds himself offering his considered judgment to a prince (who is perhaps too dull-witted to grasp it) is always ready to rebel and thus to exhibit disloyalty to the prince in the name of a higher loyalty of service to the state.

¶506. There is a contradiction at work in the form of life: the self-relation of the counselor (his being-for-itself) to the object of his actions, state power (as the universal, as normative for him). On the one hand, he can act for the good of the state but be condemned to death by a prince furious at his disloyalty to him. As Hegel puts it, this can count as genuine sacrifice but is "not one that returns back into consciousness," that is, it becomes a posthumous honor, not one the self-sacrificing individual gets to enjoy. What the person of judgment has to seek is a way of finessing this contradiction: preserve yourself and serve the state. Only when the person is willing to make that sacrifice can the object of his veneration, true state power, arise, but he should survive that sacrifice to bask in the honor of it all.

¶507. Hegel says that "this alienation takes place solely in *language*, which comes on the scene here in its distinctive significance." He then spends the rest of the section detailing in various metaphors how he understands the relation between language and *Geist*. This is one of several key passages where Hegel reflects on this relation, and is thus crucial for interpreting what Hegel means by *Geist* itself. Later, in ¶652, he says that "language is the existence (*Dasein*) of spirit," which at least seems to imply that without language, spirit would not exist. Here he elaborates. He says that "language is the *existence* of the pure self as the self," that in language the pure self is "*for others*. Otherwise, the *I* as this pure I *is* not *there*" (". . . is not there"—"ist . . . nicht da"—is a play on the German term for existence, *Dasein*, which looks as if its literal translation would be There-Being). In being a language user, the agent is both singular and universal. Language does not exist without speakers, but likewise speakers don't exist without a language. The language *shows itself* in the speakers, and the speakers each singularly *manifest* the language. This does not see language in the well-worn game analogy as a system of rules under which given acts of the speaker fall as instances or not, nor does it see language as any kind of foundation on which some other structures are built. Speakers give the language their own style, and the language takes its concrete shape from the speakers' exhibition of it. This tells us much about how to interpret Hegel's conception of *Geist*.

¶508. Hegel repeats some of the points made in the previous paragraph but sharpens them. First, spirit only comes into existence when its "moments"—the self-conscious agents who each on their own embody the universal norm of state power and/or wealth—are actual, and, second, when these agents take themselves to be expressing the actuality of (what is really at work in) this spirit—when the "pure consciousness" (roughly, their idea of themselves as ethically constrained by what their idea of the "essence" is) is not just thinking or dreaming of being these types ("state power" or "wealth") but is seen by them as what they really are. Hegel summarizes this: "In this way, spirit is the mediating middle which presupposes those extremes and is engendered through their existence." Spirit, the unity of its members, *shows itself* in their actions, and their actions *manifest* the spirit animating them.

¶509. One problem is that state power is supposed to be the universal (the unity of a collective life that binds us together and orients each individually), but it is at this point more of a singular institution exercising a power over individuals but not their spiritual unity. In speaking of exhibiting state power, the individual may be using the exalted language of honor and such, but it is just a singular institution that does not necessarily (and not actually) command that type of allegiance. The language used here is more of a mystification of the reality rather than its manifestation or exhibition.

¶510. This mystifying use of language eventually becomes more clear, and, as Hegel says, "The heroism of silent service becomes the *heroism* of *flattery*." The noble-minded man of honor comes to see that his "silent service" to the prince as better replaced by flattering the prince's self-regard. Sacrificing for the prince is not sacrificing for the universal. It is sacrificing one's own good for somebody else's without any kind of ethical backing for such a sacrifice.

So why sacrifice for the prince? If such a sacrifice for the prince's interest is to be legitimated, it must be because he is an "absolute monarch," he who legitimately gives commands but cannot be commanded by another, and whose legitimacy must therefore simply be accepted. The monarch becomes the "atom" that cannot communicate its own essence. Whatever authority he has must come from the courtiers now giving it to him, which they do by naming him the monarch (in expressions which address him as "Your Majesty" or the like). There is nothing left to do but tie your fate to his, flatter him, and hope he provides you with wealth or the means to get it.

¶511. This looks like it might just be a replay of the struggle for recognition that eventuated in mastery and servitude, but it's different because of the different histories of each. In this case, the flattering courtiers become who they are—in group counselors to state power—by flattering the monarch (who thinks, "I am the state"). The unity of the whole swallows up the differences of the agents (as being-for-itself) into one social whole now conceived (rather opaquely) as one self, one subject on its own. This self now strives for its own wealth—the wealth of the state being that of the collective wealth of all the state's members—which becomes distributed in the wealth of the courtiers. This all has its apex in the absolute monarch, and that means the unity of the whole is held together not by *Sittlichkeit* but by "contingency at the mercy of any stronger will." It is the unity of a house of cards.

¶512. To the extent that the noble person understands himself as serving the state, he sees himself as an equal to it and not as a mere subordinate of the prince. However, even as he disavows his own interests in pursuing the interests of the state, he is still pursuing his own (perhaps in the name of his own honor). In fact, in holding onto his own sense of personal honor (in the name of which he at first alienates himself vis-à-vis the state), he manifests his inequality to state power. He makes that decision, and the state has no legitimate claim to deny him. If the basic difference between the base consciousness (paradigmatically, that of the supposedly self-seeking merchant or bourgeois) and the noble consciousness was that the latter had the higher calling of putting his own interests aside in favor of the state's interests, then with this move, we see that the noble and the base are beginning to fuse together (both are inclined to seek their own interests ahead of those of the state), and with that fusion, the whole reason for there being of an estate of nobles itself begins to vanish.

¶513. State power was supposed to be the universal (the social unity which legitimately binds all together and which is supposed to command allegiance to itself), but it has become the inessential. The universal now becomes the idea of universal beneficence, the duty to do good to others. This can only be accomplished by means of wealth. Instead of state power as the universal, individual philanthropy becomes the universal. Those who receive it are supposed to be grateful. It is not that people have abandoned the idea that there is a kind of legitimate social unity that governs their actions but that this unity resides in the complex network of beneficence and corresponding gratitude.

¶514. Nor is it that state power has vanished. Rather, it is now seen as a possible means for the independent men of wealth to carry out their own plans. That means that the course of the development now takes the turn toward the unity of the social order having to do only with the creation of, consumption of, and protection of social wealth.

¶515. The noble's self-relation is that he (and only people like him) are selfless enough ("noble" enough) to wield state power. But as the noble now realizes that it is not really birth but wealth that makes the man, he too becomes alienated from his own self-image. He imagines himself as dedicated and selfless, but he is anything but (and now cannot be anything but). The general will has become that of making money, and it imposes itself on his own will as an alien will.

¶516. This form of agency is such that it can tell itself stories about how it is really pursuing the universal (the common good, the unity which legitimately binds society together) even when it is doing only one of the two opposing things that are supposed to embody universality. But at this point in the account, it finds that in actuality each person is dependent on all the others and on specific others for status (as a man of wealth). This leads to a sense of indignation since this kind of independence stands in a direct conflict with the self-image of a person independently pursuing the universal. Since all now is seen really to rest on the contingent approvals and disapprovals from others, all of the basis for this shape of spirit has fairly well crumbled.

¶517. This contradiction lies in the pure self itself (or, as we might put it, in the self-image of the agents at work here). However, as this pure self, it has one more move to make. (Hegel calls this its "absolute elasticity.") Its indignation at the fact that in actuality it depends on its reception by others becomes an indignation that others think they have the entitlement to make such a judgment of him. He "dismisses the dismissal" others have made of him.

¶518. As this works itself out, and as both the noble and the base have begun to fuse, the relations now shift to benefactor (typically a noble who can offer a social entrée for a non-noble that would otherwise be unobtainable) and client. Sharing the same abjectness, both are now in pursuit of a kind of social cachet. Wealth breeds not indignation at that state of affairs but instead arrogance. As Hegel puts it, it thinks it can acquire the other's whole self with a meal—that picking up the check gives it real entitlement to the other's full loyalty. That arrogance comes with an ignorance of the fact that all the normal constraints of social life are beginning to fray. The abyss is beginning to open. Like Marcel in Proust's novel, the subjects come to see that what one of them had taken to be the unfailing good taste of the aristocracy is really just a kind of bottomless triangular rotation. Ultimately, each sees nothing else than contingency in this bottomless depth, and the *Geist* that is supposed to hold the whole thing together turns out really to be just a *Geist*-forsaken superficiality.

¶519. The reality is, as Hegel stated earlier, that "the heroism of silent service becomes the *heroism* of *flattery*," and this is exhibited in the language now of a world in which the only glue is coming to be that of wealth. This world is now disrupted, and instead of a unity, there are only centers of social power, and the language of flattery is the language of this disruption. In effect, the kind of reciprocity which had earlier been the glue of this world has now become a kind of strategy game in which the status of the self is the "pure self," that is, the kind that is located in the middle of such strategy games. The language of flattery that is the mediating middle of this game is the being-in-itself of power—as getting people to do what you want. "Status power" is the goal of this development.

¶520. What is experienced is that all these moments have commerce with each other and each is the opposite of itself. This is the cultural formation (*Bildung*) that has taken shape, and it is a topsy-turvy world. If the actuality of the world is one thing, the way its members speak of it is another. There is still talk of nobility and baseness, of service to others and the like, but the reality is that of a set of strategic interactions of players seeking wealth and social cachet. The true spirit of this world is the kind of self-dissolving game it plays with itself.

¶521. The language that comes to show the reality of this world as it actually has taken shape is that of a universal deception of itself and others along with an emerging shamelessness to speak of this deception quite openly. This is captured in Diderot's *Rameau's Nephew*. (The book was translated by Goethe and published more or less as Hegel was writing the *Phenomenology*, so he is commenting on something he has just read or is in the process of reading as he is commenting on it.) There is the madness of the musician (Rameau's nephew)—it's hard to know what he is. He claims to be just "playing the game," giving the public what it wants. But he is acutely self-conscious that he is doing this. Is that true, or is he really the fool he makes himself out to be, or is he pretending to be a fool so people will not think he knows what's really going on? The interrogator (*Moi*, "me") is incensed by this but finds himself being taken in, so *Moi* has to ask himself if he himself is being duped by the nephew and whether *Moi* is really seeing things as they are. It's unclear if *Lui* ("him," the nephew) is the real hero of the story, the only really authentic character in the piece, or an immensely self-deceived fellow, or is just a foolish vehicle invented to investigate the foibles of society.

¶522. In the story, we have what seems to be the speech of this confusion and distraction that is nonetheless clear to itself. How can it be clear to itself if it is all so confused? Or is its clarity its knowledge of its own confusion? Or is this confusion part of its plan? Is it even clear that it is confused? It (*Lui*) speaks with the same words and turns of phrase as *Moi*.

¶523. *Moi*, who is so put off by the musician (*Lui*), thinks that this shows that the contemporary world is corrupt, that it has fallen away from its real essence and only needs to be brought back into conformity with it. *Moi's* call for restoration is, without knowing it, a call for undoing the whole show. What *Moi* doesn't see is that he's really calling for the dissolution of this entire picture.

In demanding the dissolution of this inverted world, *Moi* is demanding the dissolution (*Auflösung*) of this version of the world of *Bildung*. Collectively, this shape of consciousness is breaking down, and thus rather than "restore" itself, spirit—the I that is a We, the We that is an I—must come back round to itself and achieve a different shape of consciousness.

¶524. In a sense, spirit has already done this. The mockery of the fragmented consciousness leads to the idea that what we have is the vanity of its actuality noting itself for what it is: vanity. This has two foci: spirit noting that its actuality is broken and can't be simply restored; and spirit looking to another way of living a meaningful, self-conscious life. That will come, as we will see, in a form of emotionalist faith.

¶525. As this vanity of vanities becomes more clear to the participants, the self returns into itself to see where it stands in relation to this concatenation of the I and the We (spirit). In this return of the self into itself, it comes to the stance that the vanity of all things is also its own vanity—it advances to the brink of a kind of nihilism that isn't yet a full-throttle nihilism. It holds that everything people say and do is basically false, including what I say and do, but I'm better than all this because I know it's all false. Or as Hegel puts it, "What is meant and what is the purpose are separated from the truth. . . . Power and wealth are the highest ends of its efforts." Or as somebody else put it: everything that is solid melts into air. The only thing left to which a positive judgment could be attached is the pure I itself.

10

Faith, the Enlightenment, and the Truth of the Enlightenment

b. Faith and Pure Insight

¶526. We now see that the alienated "pure consciousness" is said to stand beyond the nonactual world of alienated spirit. Why is an alienated world nonactual? It exists, it is real in all the ordinary senses, but the alienated consciousness as the "pure self" takes it that it is *not* what is really in force in the world. Pure consciousness takes it that what is really running the show is something else.

What we have is a shape of spirit that is more or less contemporaneous with the later stages of the alienated spirit we just examined but which also proposes itself as that form's successor. The response of the alienated subject is to conclude that it is the world itself (or at least the social world) that is at odds with itself, not that it, the alienated subject, is at odds with itself. The true unity to be found is that within the subject's self-conscious life itself. This is neither stoicism repeating itself, nor the so-called virtuous consciousness that thought it was taking on the way of the world. Instead, it is consciousness of its own activity. It looks to itself and to something beyond itself to authenticate it. One way of finding that is through a kind of emotionalist faith.

¶527. As the successor to the alienated world of absolutist monarchs and the art of the Baroque, "religion" now enters *as faith* into the world of cultural formation, *Bildung*, but not yet in the way religion as religion is "in and for itself"—that is, not as it is both in its developmental shape and as it comprehends itself, not in its true form.

¶528. Since actuality—the world as the subjects in "spirit alienated from itself" find it—is contradictory to itself, the new form of subjectivity, pushed back into itself, looks for the unity of the world beyond the actual world and in opposition to it. It is thus a faith, not anything

Hegel's Phenomenology of Spirit. Terry Pinkard, Oxford University Press. © Oxford University Press 2023. DOI: 10.1093/oso/9780197663127.003.0010

like a sociological examination of the facts of this alienated world. When the substance of the world proves to be contradictory, people find their own consciousness to be substance-less. One version of this appeared earlier as the "unhappy consciousness." Now the consciousness that takes itself to be unmoored from its substance looks inward to where it can connect to a higher or deeper or more truthful unity on its own using only its own resources—resources not dependent on anything other than its own activity. This takes two forms. One is faith, which in a thinking manner connects to some type of supersensible world. That supersensible essence, Hegel notes, is "pure thinking" since only a self-conscious thinker could form the representation of a pure supersensible essence. The other is insight, which takes itself to free from prejudgment in confronting actuality. Hegel notes that "pure insight itself thus has at first no content," which is in fact its justifying conceit about itself. Without prejudice, it seeks to see into the essence of actuality. Formally viewed, faith and pure insight seem like very much the same thing.

¶529. We see both as alienated shapes of consciousness, also as a gestalt of self-conscious life as it finds the surrounding world to be untrue and seeks to connect its individual subjectivity to the Bigger Picture. This shape of self-conscious life has three aspects: (1) It itself is getting at the truth of things is outside of all relationships, which is another way of stating that each individual takes himself in principle to have all the necessary resources to discover these truths; each consciousness takes itself to exist "in and for itself" (to be fully developed in its concept of itself and to know it). (2) Each relates itself to the actual world as *opposed* to pure consciousness (to the consciousness of itself as capable of standing outside of all these relationships). (3) Each relates itself within pure consciousness to the other (faith to insight and vice versa).

¶530. Faith's absolute object is the real world raised into the universality of pure consciousness. Each individual has the capability on its own to grasp the pure essence (for the Christians, God), and, in the real world, the fellowship of others in the faith lacks the alienation that the world of *Bildung*, cultural formation, had. Hegel describes the members in this fellowship as "essences existing in and for themselves": each takes himself to be alone in immediate connection to the supersensible absolute essence, even when they stand in this fellow-ship with each other. They see themselves as at home in this part of their world, and it's only for us (readers guided by Hegel) that will see faith as remaining alienated. Faith, to itself (in its own eyes), neces-sarily disagrees. For itself, this shape is an "emotionalist" attempt to close the alienated gap.

¶531. Hegel tells us to look not at the content of faith but at the form. The form of the world for "faith" is the absolute essence. *We know* that it is spirit existing in-and-for-itself, the simple eternal substance of all these activities (the background socialities, practices, institutions, memorializations, etc. of self-conscious life). Just as "the sparrow" has no existence outside of the collection of individual sparrows but nonethe-less has a status that is not equivalent to the set of all existing sparrows, so does self-conscious life. In the realization of its concept (to be spirit), it passes over into being for another, and "self-conscious life" as a species becomes a set of individual mortals. "Self-conscious life," however, does not exist outside of this set of individual self-conscious lives.

¶532. The members of the fellowship take themselves to be "eternal spirits" whose existence is that of thinking of their unity with other such spirits. They are of this world and not of this world. Although they take themselves to be directly conscious of the abso-lute supersensible essence and not to be self-conscious, this is im-possible. If their consciousness were cut off from self-consciousness, their consciousness would then be one more thing alien to their self-consciousness.

A bit of background: Pietists talked of the "churches within churches" (the truly faithful as distinct from those members just going through the motions). Kant spoke of the invisible church as that of virtuous Kantian agents bound together by their respect for the moral law. When Hegel, Schelling, and Hölderlin were together at the Tübingen Seminary, they used "the invisible church" as a kind of code word for their emerging French-revolutionary stances (which they didn't exactly declare publicly at the time) . The invisible church is the church of the truly committed, but whether one is really committed or just going through the motions is "invisible" to others. However, although Hegel doesn't speak of the "in-visible church" here, something like this idea of the "invisible church" will make a reappearance at the very end of the "Spirit" chapter.

¶533. Each of the faithful sees himself in the world that is basically a world of vanity, which means it recognizes both its own vanity and its proclamation to be ready to right this world. Faith thus defines itself negatively against the vanity of that world. The faithful are not drawn to the cleverness of the courtly world, with all its ironic chatter about how wicked we all are. The faithful practice the obedience of service and praise, which in turn brings forth faith's consciousness of its unity with the in-and-for-itself existing essence. But this essence never appears. It is what is at the heart of appearance but is not itself visible in the real world. For this shape of spirit, the world of *appearance* is our shoddy, overly ironic wicked world. The *actual* world is that of the invisible church. The *concept* of the actual is thus the inner of the world (its essence, its core) which is all that is, and which works (*wirkt*, is actual), but which doesn't itself appear.

¶534. For pure insight, however, what counts is the concept it forms of the world, and for it that is what is actual. Both faith and insight take our shoddy-appearing world to be the appearance, maybe even a misleading semblance, of what the actual world is, but it takes a kind of individual reflective effort to get behind it to "see" the real thing behind it all. Faith is relatively unconcerned with "pure insight," but the reverse isn't true. "Pure insight" wants to turn its procedures of investigation onto faith itself, to see what faith is really about. (The Enlightenment, which will emerge from "pure insight," will in its French form come into conflict with religion in general and especially with the emotionalist type. In its German form, "Enlightenment" will not come into conflict with religion per se but only with the "superstitious" parts of it.)

¶535. Both faith and pure insight are investigating self-conscious life and what is essential to it. (That's what "we" know, as informed by our guide.) They don't necessarily know this. Faith is consciousness of the essence (God, the faithful would call it), but pure insight is self-consciousness of the essence (which is the thought of what is really there). Faith, that is, understands itself simply as directly aware of the "essence" (God), and its heart is filled with it. Pure insight, on the other hand, is more reflective about its consciousness of the essence.

¶536. Although pure insight sees itself as a contingent individual, it is intent on getting behind things to see what is really at work, and this constitutes its "pure" and not merely contingent purpose. As "pure," its purpose is to actualize pure insight universally. This is a bit like Kant's admonition in "What Is Enlightenment?" to learn to "think for yourself." The purity of pure insight's purpose has no particular goal as its content. It doesn't say, "Think X," but rather, "Think for yourself." What does it take for pure insight to work properly? For simplicity's sake, let's imagine the two choices are two heroes of the Enlightenment: Hume and Kant. Each has an idea of what following the course of reason would be. For both, pure insight is potentially the property of all self-consciousnesses. Thus, everything objective has the meaning of being-for-itself, of self-consciousness, or what would be clear to an unprejudiced insight. One can be an empiricist all the way, like Hume, or a transcendental metaphysician, like Kant. The important point is to approach things in a rational manner. Pure insight holds: this is a judgment that each of us must make for him- or herself. The result will be something we state in a third-person perspective from our own first-person perspective: "On the basis of the evidence, I hold that X is the case," where "I hold" starts heading for redundancy. Hegel says, twisting Kant's phrases on Enlightenment slightly: "This pure insight is thus the spirit that calls out to every consciousness: *Be for yourselves* what you all are *in yourselves—rational.*" It presents itself as the result of the development that the *Phenomenology* has sketched out so far.

II. The Enlightenment

¶537. Just as "faith" defines itself in terms of its rejection of the vanity of the actual world, pure insight ends up defining itself by its opposition to faith. What links them is their rejection of the actual world. Pure insight sees faith as one more element of the world as it finds it, but thinks faith is simply misguided thinking and is as much a part of a misguided actuality as a number of other things.

¶538. In the flux of the world of cultural formation, pure insight presents itself as a motionless consciousness: whereas everything else is in movement, it has a fixed place. The self-undermining, self-unraveling world of vanity is observed by this "motionless consciousness." This world of vanity, however, does have a good insight into itself and even a painful feeling about itself (that its world is broken, falling apart). Pure insight is at first just this witty ongoing self-accusation of vanity, but even when it comes on the scene as, say, a chronicler of this sorry situation, it is just gathering up what it finds and universalizing it.

¶539. This is pure insight's achievement. It differentiates itself from all the rest in that it brings it all together into a universal picture and makes it into an insight of all. It proclaims: here is what your world really amounts to—everybody is vain, everybody's a critic, everybody's ironic. In making that move, it in effect brings this world to its dissolution, its *Auflösung*. Particular wit becomes a paragon of a universal movement. We move, as it were, from Voltaire to the Voltaireans and to something even more general, to the Enlightenment. In French, they called it the *Lumières*. Germans had the "clarification," the *Aufklärung*. In English, it was often originally called the Illumination but became called the Enlightenment.

¶540. As it takes real shape, pure insight appears in its genuine activity in its conflict with faith. To make a short historiographical note: arguing over just what "the Enlightenment" was has become an industry unto itself. Historians such as Peter Gay argued that the dispute with religion was indeed the key to the Enlightenment. Ernst Cassirer, on the other hand, thought the antireligious activity was not so much the key as was the impulse to a rational and even scientific approach to things. Horkheimer and Adorno think they all missed the point, since the Enlightenment was, although unconsciously, in its very concept really all about domination (first of nature, then of each other). Hegel thinks that it has to do with actualizing a certain shape of self-conscious life, of bringing a certain line of development to a partial closure. Many historians nowadays argue that one should not speak of "the" Enlightenment but of "Enlightenments" in the plural.

a. The Struggle of the Enlightenment with Superstition

¶541. We now see that some earlier portions of the book have turned out in many ways to be earlier, not fully developed versions of pure insight. (They were pure insight "in itself.") All the moves that seek to comprehend consciousness as some kind of self-sufficient point in the world itself (itself not moving while everything around it does)—which is the "negative" conduct of consciousness—are really just various versions of pure insight that have not yet managed to self-consciously construe themselves as "pure insight." The truth of the matter will be that once it is understood as self-consciousness, all consciousness itself is in movement.

¶542. Pure insight knows faith as the opposite of reason and truth. It thus has to ask itself why the members of that shape of spirit would hold onto it, and they conclude that they must be laboring under an illusion so gripping that they can't see it for the illusion it is. One response for pure insight is to posit a vast conspiracy theory that "sees" through the ordinary goings-on. The people of "faith" (like so many others) are seen as hapless victims of priests, with their envious vanity, who are in league with despotism to keep the people in chains.

There were various versions of this kind of conspiracy theory afoot in the eighteenth century, the best known being the one made by the curé, Jean Meslier, who made many of the same charges and said he wished that "all the great ones of the earth, all the nobles, should be hanged and strangled with the guts of the priests." (This is sometimes wrongly attributed to Diderot.)

¶543. The Enlightenment as pure insight has three opponents: the deceiving priesthood, the despots, and the naive consciousness of the people of faith. Since pure insight's essence is (on its own account) that it is in-and-for-itself universal, its relation to faith has to do with what it has in common with it, since each is at least claiming to seek or to be in possession of a universal truth.

¶544. Pure insight's relation to the *unbefangene*—naive or unencumbered—consciousness of the absolute essence is that in itself, it is the same as itself, but its being-for-itself—its more explicit self-relation—denies this in-itself identity. It denies, that is, that both are on the same developmental path as it has taken shape.

Pure insight demands that faith account for itself in the terms of pure insight. If faith takes the bait, it enters into a game it cannot win. But then, according to pure insight, faith doesn't deserve to win.

¶545. Since both pure insight and faith take their subjectivities to be free from the messy world around them and to be in pursuit of the unencumbered truth (that is, the absolute), their communication is immediate, and they flow into one another. But faith is now starting

to lose the game. The communication of pure insight is a like a per-
fume in the air, like an infection circulating in the atmosphere. When
faith begins to fight the infection, it's too late, and it only makes it
worse. Hegel makes another telling reference to *Rameau's Nephew*: the
new idol sneaks in and takes its place on the fireplace mantel amid
the others, gradually moves the other idols to one side, then one day,
bash, crash, kaboom, the old idols have fallen, and the new serpent of
wisdom sheds its skin and appears in a new shape. The new idol drives
out the old idols. Diderot's little fable becomes the picture that Hegel
sees of one shape of self-conscious life displacing an older shape. It
happens at first gradually and then finally all of a sudden.

¶546. Hegel switches the metaphor from Diderot's tale of the idol
gradually pushing the other idols off the mantle to that of spirit's mute
"weaving." (There is perhaps an oblique reference there to the Greek
and Norse myths of the fates silently weaving the thread of humanity.)
It is not as if all of this is a fully self-conscious process. Nonetheless,
spirit is, we might say, "stitching itself together" without being clear
to itself what it's doing. Even though this process of stitching itself together follows a logical path, spirit's two sides at this point in the development take themselves to be the opposite of each other and create
quite a bit of noise in their opposition.

¶547. Pure insight begins defining itself negatively, that is, as "not
faith." Like faith, pure insight takes its subjectivity to have all the
capabilities it needs to aim itself at the truth. It also takes its intention—
to seek the truth free from any prejudgment—to be pure. There is a
possible misunderstanding here. The proponents of pure insight of
course accept the bromides that you have to be brought up in a family,
learn a language, absorb community standards, and so on, but when it
comes to exercising critical judgment, each must decide for him/her-
self. So how does pure insight conduct itself? Well, it has to be its own
critic: it is "is only the negative of itself." Hegel then claims that this will
compel it to turn it against itself, a process he fleshes out in the next
paragraph.

¶548. Pure insight recognizes no other basic standard outside of its
own standard. When pure insight as reason thus speaks of an other, it's
itself of which it speaks (in the Kantian sense that reason is its own tribunal and answers only to its own interrogations). This is the "absolute

category," and the subject must simply "see" that this is the correct way to go. That turns out to be the use of our rational capacities, to follow the *lumen naturale* (the light of nature) or to accept that which shows up in the light cast by the *lumen naturale*. (In Hegel's own time, some wished to replace talk about the *lumen naturale* with the idea of an "intellectual intuition" of the absolute. Hegel did not think of that as an improvement.)

¶549. The Enlightenment charges that for faith, "the absolute essence is brought forth by consciousness," which means that faith is just making this stuff up. It thinks it's talking about God, but it is really just talking about ideas it makes up.

Faith takes this to be a simple lie about itself: it claims that it just "sees" or "takes in" things by the divine light as much as Enlightenment just "sees" things as illuminated by the *lumen naturale* (the light of nature). Enlightenment trusts the light of nature, faith trusts the divine light. But for these emotionalist faiths (especially Pietists, but also evangelicals, Wesleyans, etc.), the "absolute essence" is not the abstract essence, something that is supposed to be completely beyond the faithful consciousness. It is, they take it, the spirit of the *Gemeine* (sometimes *Gemeinde*), that is, the "community of the faithful," which for "faith" is the true unity of "abstract essence" (that which casts the divine light) and self-consciousness itself. The earthly Pietist community took itself as undertaking the task of mirroring the "heavenly community" to come.

¶550. The Enlightenment charges that all of the commitments that faith undertakes are the result of the people being deceived by despots and faithless priests. Faith is unmoved by this for good reason. There are many ways in which one can be deceived (brass for gold, counterfeit coins for the real ones, etc.), but where one's "self-certainty" is at issue, deception is not really possible. One's self-certainty has to do with one's basic take on the world, which is a matter of spirit, the I that is We, the We that is I. That might be muddled and unclear even to oneself, but one cannot be deceived about it.

Hegel makes an offhanded reference to the 1780 prize essay for the Berlin Academy of Sciences instituted by Frederick the Great, although apparently spurred on by Jean Le Rond d'Alembert: Is it useful for the people to be deceived? (*Est-il utile au peuple d'être trompé?*) Hegel garbles it a bit, having it ask instead whether it is "permissible."

¶551. If this is how Enlightenment sees faith, how does faith see the Enlightenment?

This has three phases: (1) pure thinking as the absolute essence in-and-for-itself, (2) faith's relation to the ground of its faith, and (3) what it means for the outlook to be carried out in practice, and especially in a religious service.

¶552. Faith, like pure insight, takes itself to be oriented to disclosing the absolute essence, but it only acquires the empty form of such consciousness, that is, it remains at the merely formal stage of the unity of consciousness without any particular content flowing from that. As it were, it remains with the formal principle that if you open your heart to the absolute, it will be revealed. All content must come from outside that formal principle, and for this reason, faith sticks with the mode of *Vorstellung*, representational thought, to do that. It is empty, waiting for the divine light to fill it. On the other hand, pure insight is in the same position with the *lumen naturale*. Whereas pure insight seeks to be filled with the objects of sensuous certainty (as in the first chapter of the *Phenomenology*), faith seeks to be filled with the pure absolute. Pure insight takes its representation of sensuous objects to be the same as faith's representations, in statues and holy wafers, of the absolute, which makes faith seem all the more naive and credulous. But this is a mistake.

¶553. Pure insight takes what is eternal life for *Geist* and makes it into sensuous certainty. Faith finds this to be completely the opposite of what it takes itself to be doing in its services.

¶554. Second aspect: faith does not merely claim to be illuminated by the divine light, but it also claims to *know* this. It also claims to know it immediately (without having to know anything else). This is where Enlightenment jumps in. It claims faith has no basis to assert that it knows this. What it knows is merely something contingent (such as this or that stone statue). Nonetheless, Enlightenment also claims to know that this contingent knowing is indeed a knowing, and, as Hegel puts it, "The ground of knowing is the *knowing* universal," (which would be the *lumen naturale*), and Enlightenment's grasp of the *lumen naturale* (pure insight) is no more immediate than faith's supposed grasp of the absolute essence. Nonetheless, Enlightenment puts faith to the test: faith claims to have all these testimonies (from the Bible, early church fathers), but how reliable are they? However, faith does not or need not rely on such testimonies. It thinks it can know the absolute essence without having to know anything else. (It's a claim to immediate knowledge.) If faith starts looking for, say, historical evidence for itself, then it's become infected by Enlightenment and is giving up the claim to immediate knowledge.

¶555. Third aspect: in religious service, faith learns to sublate its own individuality, learns to measure itself by a divine standard and not just its own standard. Both it and Enlightenment practice a kind of asceticism, denying one's own natural point of view in favor of some kind of higher standard (the divine light or the light of nature). The proponents of Enlightenment make fun of faith's practices of fasting and the like—what Hume dismissed as the "monkish virtues"— but in indulging themselves in such things, the proponents of the Enlightenment only show that, in the eyes of faith, they have only the most impure of intentions.

¶556. Enlightenment finds the asceticism of faith to be silly. Why deny yourself meat on Friday? Why think you're better if you give all your worldly goods away? Enlightenment does not see its own asceticism as anything like such foolishness.

¶557. Enlightenment of course has a negative relation to itself in that it takes the standard by which it measures its claims to knowledge to be itself. It dedicates itself to the eradication of error, including its own. So what does it claim for itself? When all superstition is banned, what then? Since it grasps everything as contingent—as "representation," *Vorstellung*—the absolute essence becomes a vacuum, an X with no predicates. It contents itself instead with a wealth of finite, limited claims, but it can take no stance about the absolute.

¶558. We are now led to where this has been going all along: the Enlightenment is the triumph of empiricism or at least that expressed by sensuous certainty (the first chapter of the *Phenomenology*). Concepts are empty until filled in with content from experience. The most thought can do on its own is employ something like formal logic. Thus, consciousness is taken as sensuous certainty, meaning-something (*Meinung*), perhaps by acts of pure reference that have no further meaning. It is led back to this sensuous certainty by pure insight. In any event, this kind of empiricism is certain that it, the thinking subject of logical empiricism, exists, that there are other actual things outside of it, and that in its natural existence, it exists in and for itself and is stating the (well argued, so it thinks) truth.

¶559. The third moment consists in figuring out how Enlightenment sees its basic claims about limits and finitude to be related to its claim that this is an absolute claim to knowledge (or, as we might put it, it assumes the relation between the contingent individual who proclaims his finitude and limits to the light of nature which illuminates all for him to claim). This will lead Enlightenment as "pure insight" into the distinction between the way the world appears to us (being-for-an-other) and the way the world is in itself apart from all appearances to us.

¶560. If everything is "for another" (limited, finite), then one proposal would be to look at things in terms of how they relate to each other via the idea of usefulness. Once again, we have an opposition of sorts. Everything is up for use by everything else, and everything that is up for use also fights back to preserve itself and use others. (Hegel seems to be restricting this to the organic world, but he doesn't actually explicitly say so.) We are the self-conscious elements of that world, so we get to use things for our purposes (or so the argument goes). Everything else is or can be a means to our ends. Reason is a tool we use to get around in that world and to use things and to keep ourselves in check when we are dangerous to ourselves. Other things are there to serve and to please us. If they don't, they are "bad." Everything is a matter of strategic interaction.

¶561. Underlying this principle of utility are the ideas that singular things are what they are (in and for themselves), and they also are what they are in relation to others.

¶562. Enlightenment's idea of the absolute essence is thus that of the "supreme being." In the great hierarchy of beings, there is one being that reigns above all the others or is more real than anything else. (This is a vacuous concept.) The other idea—that religion is really only a matter of utility—is a horror for faith. In fact, to faith, the Enlightenment looks like shallowness itself, the inability to be open to the "higher."

¶563. Faith has the divine right of *Sichselbstgleichheit* (self-equality, self-sameness, measuring up to its concept) against Enlightenment. It measures itself by its openness to the divine light and takes no other measure seriously. Enlightenment, though, has the human right of self-consciousness, of *Ungleichheit* (inequality, un-sameness) even when it implicitly appeals to the light of nature. Human agents never simply are what they happen to be. Enlightenment is unequal to itself in that it is also its own greatest critic. Enlightenment has self-consciously the element of the negative within itself.

¶564. In its conflict with faith, Enlightenment brings no distinctive principles of its own but merely gathers up the principles that faith uses and points out what follows from the commitments faith takes itself to make (commitments about which faith "forgets" that they follow from its other commitments). Faith takes this as insulting, as a deliberate misunderstanding. However, Enlightenment has the upper hand in this.

¶565. The Enlightenment, Hegel says, is no more enlightened about itself than is faith. The Enlightenment is pure insight on the way to developing itself into conceptual knowledge, but it does not see this. In fact, both faith and pure insight share the idea that there is an absolute that lights up the world for each of them, and that they each think that individuals of pure insight or those of faith have all the resources already within themselves to see things according to the way they have been so lit up. In other words, they share the same picture of subjectivity relating to itself and the world, but they fill that picture out in very different ways. The appropriate concept of this would have to find a way to hold both of these aspects of the picture together while avoiding the either/or with which each operates.

¶566. This repeats some points made earlier. Enlightenment says that faith just creates fictions by positing various representations of the otherworldly beyond, whereas faith simply maintains that the otherworldly beyond is the essence of their consciousness, even if it is inscrutable.

¶567. Enlightenment points out to faith that its veneration of statues and the stories it tells about the celestial beings are just stories about spirits as if they were things. About this, Enlightenment is right. It itself, however, sees the actual world as bereft of spirit.

¶568. Faith, like Enlightenment, sees itself as contingent, but it sees itself as informed or illuminated by the divine light. Faith lives in the contradiction of "I can know nothing" and "The absolute essence shows me an eternal truth." The Enlightenment only recognizes contingent knowing and forgets that it's also making an absolute claim (about the way the light of nature illuminates things for reason). Hegel says that Enlightenment forgets that its absolute claim is one it also claims to know immediately.

¶569. Enlightenment says not merely that it's foolish to do penance, to fast, to give away one's worldly possessions, but it's also wrong to do so since it serves no purpose. The very idea that it does serve a purpose is another illusion. But faith does such things with the experience of making necessary sacrifices. It's felt as something simply required, not something serving any kind of utilitarian purpose.

¶570. The Enlightenment dismisses the utility of giving away possessions. Faith takes its doing so to be proof of its freeing itself from natural existence. Here too Enlightenment seems to have the upper hand.

¶571. Enlightenment dismisses faith's conception of the inner life, whereas Enlightenment has a conception of the inner life in terms of thinking but which is merely formal. To that, it adds that we are natural beings, so why be so prissy about natural drives? (Again, it's worth relating that to Hume's dismissal of what he calls the "monkish virtues.")

¶572. To the extent that Enlightenment insinuates itself into faith, it destroys the immediacy of knowledge of the absolute that is so crucial to faith. What Enlightenment actually does is undermine the dualism present in faith's outlook. Faith keeps, as it were, two sets of books, and it compartmentalizes them. On the one hand, it's awake to the material world, while on the other hand, when it comes to making sense of its attitudes to the absolute, it falls back asleep. Whenever faith tries to make sense of itself, Enlightenment points out how they are just taking worldly things and then fashioning a story about the heavens that copies them. There are worldly courts here, kings rule and judge with the help of councilors, and up above there's a court with a king-judge and lots of counselors willing to put in a good word for you (saints). In its practice, faith makes the infinite (the absolute) into something finite (a world of kings and councilors).

¶573. In losing the argument, faith gives up, loses its content, and becomes dull stupefaction. It just refuses to play the game anymore. It's empty, and it can't continue. It becomes instead *longing*, nostalgic. It becomes the same as Enlightenment: it becomes "consciousness of the relation between the finite existing in itself and a predicate-less, unknown and unknowable absolute." However, Enlightenment also has the stain of unsatisfied longing within itself. Like faith, Enlightenment is committed implicitly to a two-world metaphysics—the world of appearance and the empty world of the abstract essence that supposedly underlies appearance—and, so Hegel argues, as also implicitly committed to the resolution of that two-world view (or, as he puts it, "It will turn out that the stain is in itself already sublated").

b. The Truth of the Enlightenment

¶574. Consciousness has now become clear to itself. Pure insight that is developing itself (in itself) now moves toward actualizing itself in the way that it posits otherness within itself (which is a matter of seeing itself as self-critical—it posits itself as the standard to which it must answer without positing itself as an unmovable standard). This is "negative pure insight." Thinking distinguishes itself from itself as it assumes the role of critic and criticized, and this doesn't have a simple stopping point—it posits "a difference only through *the movement as a whole*." It alienates itself when it takes its own difference within itself (critic and criticized) to be some kind of difference among things, as if the critic were one thing and the criticized another. (This in effect is the truth of faith: it projects the absolute essence of thinking into an otherworldly beyond.)

¶575. This is a very compressed paragraph. Enlightenment falls into two camps about the absolute essence. One of them proves to be victorious since it more adequately incorporates the other into itself.

¶576. What are the two camps? In one camp, there is the view that the "pure essence" is really just "pure thinking," the thinking of those beings (or just "being" itself) that is beyond experience and explains it. This leads pure thinking back to some version of sensuous certainty and what develops out of that.

¶577. The other camp is the French materialist response. As we are led back to the objects of experience, we posit that behind those appearances is "pure matter" as the concept of what is left over when we abstract away from tasting, seeing, smelling, etc. This is "the absolute lacking all predicates."

¶578. These are different starting points for the same thing. One version of Enlightenment says that the absolute essence is the predicateless God; the other says it is matter. In this view, God, nature, and matter are all really the same type of concept. The difference among these concepts doesn't lie in the things themselves, the *Sache*, but in the starting points of these ways of taking what counts as the absolute. In any event, neither comes close to the concept at work in Cartesian metaphysics, which Hegel takes to be more or less the true view, that thought and being are in themselves the same, and that the thought of pure being is the same as pure abstraction. When Hegel says that "thought and being are in itself the same," he doesn't mean anything like the idea that one's psychological state of thinking about a stone is identical with the stone. He means that the content of the thought and the state of affairs are the same. "The stone is black" if and only if the stone is black. There's no metaphysical gap between the true statement and the world, and in true thought, thought does not stop short of the facts. More generally, Hegel is alluding to his own principle that will emerge in the very last section of the book, that there is no otherworldly beyond that thought cannot in principle comprehend. This is where the Cartesian *lumen naturale*, when it fully understands itself, will lead, but it will have to change its form to make sense of itself.

¶579. The "essence" is pure thinking, which is at once one and different (as is self-consciousness). It has to make differentiations within itself—different concepts—to get anywhere at all. (Hegel calls it "this simple motion rotating on its own axis.") However, actuality (what is really at work in the world) is, for pure insight, captured in the idea of utility, which now becomes the unity for which Enlightenment was seeking.

¶580. Pure insight, Hegel says, is the existing concept. It is not merely the concept of an otherworldly beyond or of the noumenal beyond of the world of appearance, but an embodied concept that now informs the psychology and actions of real people in whose lives it now is actualized. If that happens, then the world will become populated (at least to some extent) by enlightened people (Hume, Gibbon, Smith, Diderot, et al.). Remember, though, that at this time Kant said that although we live an age of enlightenment, we do not yet live in an enlightened age, and thus Enlightenment remains as the project of making itself real. For Enlightenment, utility is the completion of the actualization of pure insight, but this still rests on "representational thinking"—the standpoint of *Verstand*. As such, pure insight is not yet the comprehension of pure thinking but of pure thinking (as reason seeking a maximizing function) thinking about what seems to be its pure object—how to maximize utility. It is a metaphysics that does not understand itself as metaphysics. But it now asks itself: What does it take to produce more utility?

¶581. Hegel gives us an overview: the world of what we've called "cultural formation" (*Bildung*) is summed up in the ideal of the "vanity" of self-consciousness. As that view of the whole becomes more clear to itself, it transforms instead into the point of view of pure insight, the fixity of subjectivity seeing the world as illuminated by the light of nature.

Hegel speaks of three worlds. In the first, spirit's unity is thinned out and dispersed, and no real grasp of the whole is present. In the second, the whole comes gradually into view as something developing itself. The third is the idea of the whole as being articulated in terms of the rational principle of utility, of reason seeking to produce the most good.

With that, heaven is brought down to earth. We need no longer appeal to the otherworldly to critique our world since we now have all the tools we need in the concept of utility to critique it and to change it. If the philosophers have finally interpreted the world (in an enlightened fashion), then the point now is to change it.

11

Absolute Freedom and Terror

¶582. Hegel says that consciousness has found its concept—it now has a clearer comprehension of the path that self-consciousness is taking in its development. However, it has found its concept in the notion of utility, in the idea of something being of use, so that its concept finally seems to be fully established, and that it has perhaps reached the end of its self-development, while at the same time it also seems that all this is still a purpose, something it is still in the process of developing and, as purpose, trying to make real. The "utilitarian individual" is now taken as a statement of what self-conscious life really is and also what it is also trying to be. Utility is both a "predicate of the object"—it is other "things" that are useful or not—and it is not yet "the subject's immediate and sole *actuality*," not yet what is really at work in driving the subject's life and action. Emerging from the coming to be of pure insight, it is still the individual subjectivity whose content is to be filled by the *lumen naturale*. The world moves around the subject, but the subject remains fixed. Utility is the principle of unity that pure insight sought, but it is not yet the unity of being-for-itself—of the I that is a We and the We that is an I—that it was implicitly seeking.

¶583. It is now clear that the trajectory of spirit Hegel has been tracing is that of spirit's thinning itself out as it moves to Enlightenment, where as pure insight the subject is conceived as having no more intrinsic content than of a rational agent in general. (This has become the "concept" of subjectivity, which stands in stark contrast to the thickness of "true spirit" found in archaic Greek life and typified in *Antigone*.) Thus, Hegel says that now "consciousness as pure insight is not a singularly *individual* self which could be confronted by the object which would likewise have *its own* self. Rather, it is the pure concept, the gazing of the self into the self, absolutely seeing-*itself*-as-doubled." The social world of spirit is now, as far as its concept of itself goes, also fairly well atomized, but in this atomization, the self of pure insight becomes the

Hegel's Phenomenology of Spirit. Terry Pinkard, Oxford University Press. © Oxford University Press 2023. DOI: 10.1093/oso/9780197663127.003.0011

"universal self," that is, the norm of a rational agent maximizing utility, where the differences among individuals are ignored—where the universal self is not "confronted by the object which would likewise have *its own* self"—but is instead confronted by an otherwise identical rational self who is also oriented to maximizing not its own utility but that of utility in general.

¶584. Hegel opens with an assertion not usually made in connection with concepts of agency maximizing utility: "Thereby spirit as *absolute freedom* is now present." His point is that this thinned-out conception of agency now forms itself by its own logic into a "We" that is something like an individual rational subject itself. Spirit, it worth remembering, is an "I that is a We and a We that is an I." As we have seen, those two tend to pull apart from each other, and it is only "speculative," dialectical philosophy that can properly conceive how to hold them together. Now they are seen as identical with each other. What "I," as a rational agent in general, will is what "We" as the collection of such rational agents would will (which in both cases is that of maximizing utility). This is absolute freedom in contrast to nonabsolute freedom. In the case of nonabsolute freedom, there are normative boundaries to what one freely wills coming from something outside of agency itself. In absolute freedom, agency wills what is essential to its being an I that is a We and a We that is an I, and that is to follow the law of rationality in seeking to maximize utility. In doing so, in effect, every individual becomes lumped together into one big individual (the "We") without supposedly doing any violence to any individual since they are all willing the same thing ("undivided," as Hegel says), and it is "the will of all *singular individuals* as such." There are now no normative constraints on willing that are external to rational agency. The General Will forms itself.

¶585. This new unity of the I and the We is now the "undivided substance," that is, the new unity of the collective that has developed out of the older unities that have now faded away. It now places itself on the "throne of the world"—all the other unities of spirit are now at best only subsidiaries of this conception. Hegel makes a historical note in a logical guise: prior to this, the social whole divided itself into various social estates that had their own internal standards as to behavior, status, and the like. (The medieval triad of "I work for you, I fight for you,

I pray for you" is a paradigm.) These now appear as oppressive, and if they do not serve the needs of general utility, they are to be vacated. (This refers to a moment in the French Revolution when on the evening of August 4, 1789, the National Constituent Assembly abolished all the elements of the feudal order in one sweeping act of legislation.)

¶586. Still moving in a logical-historical mode, Hegel notes how, given this turn, even the principle of utility comes under fire. Why should utility be the final measure of rational action? "Utility" seems too conditional for such an absolute freedom. The divine light also vanishes in the face of absolute freedom's rise to preeminence. The traditional claims of religion thin out and vanish as the divine comes to be seen as nothing more than the "supreme being," and the "supreme being" also vanishes—like the exhalation of stale gas—and now there is nothing to ethically constrain absolute freedom except absolute freedom itself. Absolute freedom finds itself without anything to give it friction to develop a set of more substantive claims. The real opposition is now not that between reason as maximizing utility and reason as doing something else but between "*singular* and *universal* consciousness," that is, between the I and the We.

¶587. This new opposition reappears slightly as the universal will (that of all rational agents in general) makes itself into a singular individual. In the course of the French Revolution, key figures such as the Abbé Sieyès argued that this true singular individual is the nation itself, which, Sieyès argued, must be prior to everything. It is the source of all law since its sovereign will is the law itself, and it thus never needs anything but its own existence to be legal. This will is of course implemented itself by singular individuals whose self-conception is that of being a rational agent and who in making laws are "not making anything which is singular."

¶588. This new individual—the nation—give itself laws, and since like all forms of spirit it does not exist outside of the practices carried out by its members (just as the members have their "substance" in it), it must divide its activities in order to get things done. Hegel notes this was the basis for earlier divisions into social estates and the like. However, once individuals are apportioned to these various estates (or whatever other functional equivalent there would be), their "personality would mean a *determinate* personality, and it would in truth cease to be universal self-consciousness." They become individuals with their own more limited interests. However, individuals with this self-conception cannot see themselves as being represented by somebody else.

¶589. As soon as individuals acquire their own particular interests, it is inevitable that they will at some point not see the "universal work" of the nation as fitting in with what ought to be done. Yet to get things done, somebody or some group has to be in charge, and, so Hegel thinks, that will logically lead to one person. That means that others will be excluded, and this will lead, as Hegel will try to show, to what he calls "only the *negative doing* . . . only the *fury* of disappearing." This marks another turn in the French Revolution, where the Committee of Public Safety becomes the provisional government delegated to defend the state from enemies domestic and foreign. (That is its "negative" function of "defense.") The Reign of Terror sets in, and Robespierre becomes the head of the government. With him at the head, lots of other heads would roll and finally his own. Robespierre fell from power and was himself beheaded in 1794.

¶590. Hegel gives his phenomenology of Jacobin power here. (Robespierre was the head of the Jacobin faction.) The Jacobins put the unity of the state as their primary goal, and they did what they took to be necessary to defend that unity. They ended up being singular individuals who, on the basis of their virtue, laid claim to the authority to speak as the voice of the whole, the "nation" or "the Revolution" itself. In the logic of this state of affairs, this in turn led to a polarization of sorts. There is the calculating rationality of those who claim to speak for the whole, and there is the resistance of those who disagree. The voice of the whole now divides people up into those who oppose the nation and those who do not—a "wholly *unmediated* pure negation," as Hegel calls it. The defense of the nation requires that its enemies be expunged, be killed off. The Reign of Terror set about to accomplish this. But there seems to be a missing step here. Why *must* those who seek to defend the nation seek the death of the others? Why not just create some gulags where they have to perform, in effect, slave labor? Here Hegel seems to be appealing to the abstract logic of utility, although the text doesn't say that. The thinning out of subjectivity means that the people being excised are after all just the "unfulfilled empty dot

(*die unerfüllte Punkt*) of the absolutely free self," who, if they were consistent with their own status, would have to agree that this is an at least
prima facie plausible way of defending the state. The result: a series of
meaningless deaths, no more eventful than, as Hegel says, chopping a
head of cabbage. Absolute freedom, with nothing other to guide it as of
this point in the development, lacks the Kantian backstop of inviolable
human dignity, but Hegel does not make that point in the text here
(although something like that comes up in the next chapter). It is also
worth remembering that Hegel is not pushing a psychological thesis
here (say, to the effect that absolute power corrupts absolutely, or pure
freedom produces a deranged psyche for those in control, or that such
power results in cruelty and something toward which the powerful
are always tempted, or that a collective bloodlust sets in). Hegel's account here is supposed to be a phenomenological/logical one. (This is
one reason why in many of these historically oriented chapters, Hegel
speaks of it in the present tense, as if this were occurring, as it were,
outside of time according to the principles of dialectical logic.)

¶591. This means that the government necessarily becomes just another faction (namely, the faction who comes out on top). As a singular group, they are therefore partial, they do not speak with the
voice of the whole, and they must therefore also be overthrown so
that the real unity of the nation can be reasserted. In the new dispensation, legitimacy can only come from embodying the universal will.
The nonactual pure will, that of "pure intention," stands opposed to
the actual will posing as universal. In that context, being a suspicious
character—just being a suspect—becomes the same as being guilty.
(In 1805–6, when Hegel was still writing the *Phenomenology*, he was
also lecturing at Jena University on the nature of spirit, and near the
end of those lectures he argued that the rise of Robespierre and the
short-lived Terror instituted by the Committee of Public Safety was
due to the perceived threat by internal and especially external enemies.
These threats came from the allied German invasion of 1792, which
was repulsed, and the conservative Catholic reaction against the new
regime in the southwest. Once those threats ceased, Robespierre's grip
on power suddenly vanished, and he was deposed.)

¶592. Absolute freedom experiences itself as this "empty dot" in
terms of thinking of itself as just the exemplification of a rational agent

in general. This is its "abstract self-consciousness." Its reality turns out to be completely different. In merging the "I" and the "We," it finds itself as such an abstracted idea, becoming instead the "negative essence" as a universal will excising those other "abstract self-conscious" creatures it finds to be at odds with itself.

¶593. In the preceding paragraph, Hegel said that abstract self-consciousness erases, obliterates, *vertilgt*, all difference. As abstract self-conscious agents, full stop, we are all exactly the same. However, on Hegel's account, the concept of agency (as self-consciousness) should be treated as a "speculative" concept, one that on its surface seems to have two opposed, even contradictory, aspects. In the case of self-conscious agency, there is the singularity of the "I" and the universality of the "We." The difficulty of bringing those two together in a holistic manner is the problem which dialectical, speculative philosophy tries to resolve. "The understanding" (*Verstand*) attempts this by denying one side or the other. (Thus, it is driven to say that the "We" is just an additive sum of individual "I's" and nothing more; or that that there really are no singular "I's" but only empirical instances of some more general rule or structure.) To say that a "speculative" concept is "equal to itself" is to say that the apparent tensions in it have been overcome or resolved. In the case of abstract self-consciousness, this "equality with self" erases all difference since it claims that the universal will in the "We" is just the same universal will in the "I." However, the concept of *Geist*, spirit, in fact contains the negation in itself because the very concept of a "We," when properly developed, has to include a conception of singular individuals. The "We" *shows itself* in the singular "I's," and the singular "I's" *manifest* the "We." Abstract self-consciousness aims at complete "unity" (the Jacobin goal), pure equality with itself, but in the reality of its demands for unity, it fails to respect the differences among agents. As the Revolution progressed, on Hegel's account, the tensions between the I and the We re-emerged, and it became clear that the Jacobin conception of abstract unity had failed to resolve them. Thus, after the tumult of the Revolution and the fall of Robespierre, things calmed down, and the social order set about reconstituting itself into various groupings, but however much these groupings might resemble what had come before, they were now crucially different. The Revolution and the Terror gave them "the fear of their absolute lord and master—death," and so the Jacobin demand for unity above everything else vanished, but the people returned to their particular works, ambitions, and projects. It was no longer the feudal world with one's estate determined in advance for oneself but a world of individuals seeking their own paths. In this chapter, Hegel doesn't really develop that logic on its own, since his task here was the phenomenology of the experience of that logic as it actually took shape in people's lives.

¶594. Hegel raises the possibility that spirit might not progress beyond this point but simply fall back to somewhere it was before the Revolution. History might have turned out otherwise. In Hegel's day, this idea had a bite to it. The reactionaries really did want to turn the clock back: put the kings back on their thrones, reinstate the "good old days" when men were men and women knew it, etc. Hegel was saying in effect: even if you could turn the clock back, you'd just run through the same—same in essence, not in contingent details—series again. The dream of reaction has always been: wind the clock back, put the discredited authorities back in the saddle again. They do not realize that once their day is gone, it really is gone.

Turning back the clock was tried with almost no success in the short term after 1789, and, after the Napoleonic wars, with very little success in the long term after the Congress of Vienna concluded in 1815 (eight years after the publication of the *Phenomenology*). The explosion of the French Revolution revealed, Hegel says, something new and something old: for self-consciousness, "It consists in seeing its pure, simple actuality immediately disappear and pass away into empty nothingness." Self-conscious life confronted the "nothing," the fear of meaninglessness. Against this, the substitution of wealth for subjectivity, the chatter about "faith," etc. all pale: "All these determinations are lost in the loss that the self experiences in absolute freedom. Its negation is the meaningless death, the pure terror of the negative that has neither anything positive nor anything fulfilling in it." He adds: "It is the *universal will*, which in this, its final abstraction, has nothing positive and thus can give nothing in return for the sacrifice." The Terror had promised to save France and the Revolution. Were the sacrifices at the guillotine worth it? Hegel thought Europeans had at least learned a deep lesson from this experience.

¶595. Absolute freedom has thus had to balance the opposition of the universal and the singular will by comprehending that the opposition actually has to do with the *form* of self-consciousness. But for that to take shape, "absolute freedom" has to passes over from the self-destroying actuality of France (that is, the Revolution) into another country of self-conscious spirit—that is, the various German principalities. In this new country, absolute freedom is taken as the truth but not in terms of actual life on the ground. Instead, it takes shape in "thought" and not in politics. When this new thought puts itself into practice, we have a new shape before us: not the *ethical* life of ancient Greece but that of "*moral*" spirit.

German idealism and the French Revolution were paired from the outset. It's worth noting here that K. F. Reinhard—another character from the Tübingen Seminary attached to the University where Hegel, Schelling, and Hölderlin were students—argued to Sieyès in 1796 that Kant's 1795 *Perpetual Peace* would be of help in thinking through how the post-Terror revolutionary regime in France might think of its tasks. No less a personage than Wilhelm von Humboldt was charged in 1798 to lead a seminar in Paris on Kant's philosophy to the leading lights of the French government. (Kant was invited but declined.) Even Napoleon got into the game, although (unsurprisingly) he didn't like what Kant had to say. (Reinhard, by the way, was for a brief period the foreign minister of France, succeeding Talleyrand in that position.)

12

Spirit Certain of Itself

Morality

C. Spirit Certain of Itself: Morality

¶596. Hegel gives us a quick rundown of how we got here. As a result, it is now becoming clear (although it should have been clear all along) that the relation between the "I" and "We"—in other words, self-conscious life, *Geist*—is the major subject of the book, and we have been tracking its development as it is manifested in lived experience. What has now emerged in the move from abstract self-consciousness to moral spirit is that what is now at stake is not just wondering what we know but also the knowing itself. The opposition between self-certainty (what we take to be the unconditional components of the shape of spirit in which we live) and the object about which we are thinking has dissolved: our self-certainty is about our variable self-certainty. The backdrop of this is clearly Kant's epochal shift to a "critique" of pure reason rather than simply setting off to do a new metaphysics. Before we claim to know any metaphysical truths, we have to know just how far reason can go, that is, know what (if any) limits it has.

¶597. The "substance" that is the unity at stake now is just that of morality itself. That is, the unity of the "I" and the "We" is that of morality and of individuals acting in light of it. Following the demands of morality, the singular self-conscious agent now knows what he is to do, but not (as in the Greek case) as a result of the character and the habits he has developed in the thick world of the polis, but instead simply by reflecting on what morality requires of him. He knows immediately that morality is to tell him what he must absolutely do, and this knowledge is also absolutely mediated, since reasoning is discursive and inferential. This knowledge—morality is to guide me—is the

Hegel's Phenomenology of Spirit. Terry Pinkard, Oxford University Press. © Oxford University Press 2023.
DOI: 10.1093/oso/9780197663127.003.0012

new self-certainty, and there is nothing beyond itself (morality) that it needs to provide this guidance.

¶598. It might seem that morality can only tell me in thought what I ought to do, but it cannot actually motivate me to do it. In this new self-certainty, however, this is not the case. As Hegel notes, "Rather, the absolute essence is all *actuality*, and this actuality is only as knowing." Morality (or practical reason) is actual (*wirklich*) in Hegel's sense in that it is what is really at work in the world. As such, knowing that I am free makes me free. If I did not know this, I would not be free. In knowing what I ought to do, I am in fact (in actuality) motivated to do so. If I were not, morality (and practical reason) would not be actual, *wirklich*.

a. The Moral Worldview

Some prefatory remarks to this section: several of the sections under this heading are a bit perplexing for the following reason. Hegel seems to be talking about texts by Kant and Fichte, but he doesn't cite any texts, and moreover he treats Kant's and Fichte's view as the same view (all Kant and all Fichte scholars would have objections to this), and he invokes things like Kantian "postulates" which in his formulation are subtly different from the actual Kantian postulates. It is thus tempting to discuss these sections in terms of the ways they precisely mirror Kant and Fichte, how they precisely depart from Kant and Fichte, and so on. Interesting as that might be, that will not be the approach here, since that would require a book on its own to do justice to the comparison. Nonetheless, there will some passing reference to some more or less well known Kantian ideas along the way. Hegel is trying to articulate the phenomenology of the "moral worldview," with a secondary interest in how Kantian and Fichtean approaches give their own spin to what that moral worldview really is. Kantian and Fichtean views are treated in terms of how they give expression to the logic of the moral worldview as an expression of a new shape of self-conscious life. (It's also the case that Hegel's discussion isn't restricted only to Kantian and Fichtean views, but that too will be skipped over here.)

¶599. The absolute essence for self-consciousness at this stage is that of duty. This is not alien to consciousness. It is not experienced as a command from a deity or imposed by a natural law. It comes from "pure" consciousness itself (that is, it does not arise through particular desires or feelings). "Duty" is thus not really an object for consciousness at all. It is what *shows* itself in self-conscious life as determining how we are to deliberate, and we *manifest* it or exhibit it when we go about deliberating. We can deliberate or act well or badly, but this kind of practical self-consciousness in the service of duty sets all the terms itself for such deliberation and action. Self-consciousness, as consciousness, does indeed have objects, but none of these objects can determine the shape of this kind of duty. The actuality of these objects is thus of no meaning for "duty" insofar as duty belongs to self-consciousness, not to the objects of the natural world. We thus have this picture: a natural world of which we are aware and which is indifferent to morality, and morality itself, which is absolute and emerges from the fate of absolute freedom.

¶600. This constitutes the moral worldview (as distinct from the ethical life of the ancients, or the alienated life of cultural formation). From this moral point of view, nature is indifferent to duty. At best, it can make it hard or easy to do one's duty, but it cannot set our duties for us. For the ancients, there was a human nature that could be developed into a character with its corresponding dispositions and habits, but in the new, moral worldview, that position is no longer tenable, and this is no accident. This new picture of nature on one side and self-consciousness on the other has the moral worldview as its *Bestimmung* (its fate, determination, or purpose). It is also only that of a worldview, not yet a fully practical shape of spirit.

¶601. As the absolute essence, duty commands, and we are motivated by it. But sometimes nature makes this hard, and sometimes nature makes it easier to do our duty. Sometimes the nonmoral achieve their happiness in doing something that would bring pain or dissatisfaction to the moral consciousness, and moral consciousness feels aggrieved at the injustice of this.

¶602. Moral consciousness cannot, however, simply renounce its pursuit of happiness. If the moral worldview were that of divine commandments, that might not be the case, but this is the moral worldview that emerges out of the tumult of the Revolution and the concept of absolute freedom. The singular agent has an absolute purpose, expressed as duty, which follows from his freedom. In actualizing that purpose, the agent would actualize the way his "concept" is supposed to develop, and in doing so, the agent would become who he is supposed to be. Duty fulfilled thus plays two roles: it is the realization of a moral action, and it is the realization of a singular agent's "concept." The singularity of the agent (as distinct from his status as a rational agent in general, which was supposed to exhaust his status of agency in the prior stage of "absolute freedom") is a natural feature of him, as a "singular" person occupying space and carving out a distinctive path in time for himself. Since the concept of the moral worldview sees morality as not merely imagined—not just a fanciful thought-thing—but as really being at work in the world, it cannot be the case in this worldview that nature would make this impossible. This worldview must therefore "postulate" some kind of harmony between morality and nature. This "postulate" is a theoretical claim that cannot itself be demonstrated but which must be postulated as true if morality is to be genuinely actual (*wirklich*). Hegel notes that this doesn't look like a conceptual necessity—a matter of one concept requiring another concept—but a postulate to the effect that the world must in fact be this way if this worldview is true. This "lies in the concept of morality itself, whose true content is the *unity* of *pure* and *singular* consciousness" and which therefore calls for such a postulate to believe that it is more than just a "view"—that it is also true.

¶603. Hegel teases out this worldview—this picture, as we could call it, of the world—to show that it involves not just one postulate but "a whole sphere of postulates." In this picture, there is first of all consciousness in its moral stance experiencing a natural world that seems to be indifferent to morality. This consciousness is embodied and is therefore part of that natural world. The agent's natural aspect comes with its own set of purposes and willings that are potentially at odds with its pure consciousness of morality. Pure consciousness and natural consciousness seem to be opposed, but they are in fact components of a single agent (*"One consciousness"*), and the unity of the agent is a matter of pure thinking (the a priori idea of the unity of self-consciousness). Indeed, actual morality has to have that opposition of thought (pure duty) and sensibility (inclination, passion, desire, etc.) in it. Without the opposition of thought and sensibility (of pure duty and embodied passions), there would be no morality. Instead, we'd just all be disembodied angels automatically doing what the moral law required. If our passions pulled us strongly enough in the opposite direction, then the unity of pure and sensible consciousness which the moral worldview demands would fall apart. So we get a second postulate. It must be the case that our sensibility can conform to our duty (at least closely enough). Like the first postulate, it says: if my picture of the world is true, then the world must operate in this or that manner. If at some infinitely distant point, all our desires were brought into conformity with our morality, then as far as the moral worldview is concerned, there would no longer be a moral problem or even morality itself. We would simply always do the right thing because it would always be what we wanted to do. This has to be posited as an infinite task, never to be achieved. Hegel suggests that the idea of an infinite task which is never to be fulfilled (like all matters dealing with the infinite) comes with a set of problems and contradictions that more or less rule out our thinking about the infinity of this task very deeply.

¶604. We have two postulates: first, the harmony between nature and morality is to be a harmony concerning the "in itself"—the developmental trajectory—of the conceptual structure of the moral worldview. The second is about self-consciousness, being-for-itself, how we subjectively encounter and actualize the moral law: we experience it as a command that is distinct from our sensible desires but which we strive to bring together, which is itself an infinite task at which we never succeed.

What binds these two final ends together: actual acting. We act morally or immorally, and in doing so, we actualize the moral worldview, the picture we had of how nature and morality fit together.

¶605. In the moral worldview, we confront a variety of moral cases, and pure duty is supposed to tell us what to do. There should be one pure law which is above reproach and is thus holy (e.g., for Kantians, the categorical imperative). The variety of situations, however, seem to lead to a variety of different duties and as far as the moral worldview is concerned should be derivable in some sense from the one holy duty. This leads to two problems. First, there will be many alleged duties that will be thought by some to follow somehow from the one holy duty and to be sanctified by it. Since much other detail (a lot of it empirical) has to be brought into play to make those judgments, none of those duties will, however, really count themselves as holy—as in and of itself beyond reproach, as fully sanctified—in the way that the holy duty counts. For example, Kant himself thought that drunkenness and gluttony were morally ruled out. He also thought that homosexuality was morally ruled out. In fact, all use of sexual relations that were not possibly procreative were ruled out. He also thought that unlike men, women cannot be active citizens of the body politic, and suicide was absolutely ruled out. There are few dedicated Kantians today who would subscribe to that list, although almost all of them would think that the categorical imperative had something like a holy status. We can grant that Kant, like all the rest of us, is not an infallible interpreter of what his own proposal for the holy principle of morality (the categorical imperative) legitimates and does not. Hegel's point here though is that this picture—the moral worldview—leads to the distinction of the holy principle and the contested cases that somehow fall under it. To that, he adds yet another complication. What sanctifies the holy principle itself? Could we be as wrong about that as we often are wrong about what follows from it?

¶606. We have another postulate: there is another consciousness that sanctifies those duties as duties. It cannot just be "my" consciousness, which is too fallible. What would that "other" consciousness be? Well, it looks like it would have to be what "my" consciousness would will under certain counterfactual conditions. Not me, but the "ideal" me—"me" as knowing the requirements of pure practical reason—would perhaps be the sole judge with any authority here. That "ideal" me would be represented as "a lord and ruler of the world who generates the harmony of morality and happiness and at the same time sanctifies duties as a *plurality* of duties." What I have reason to will is what a fully wise and virtuous person would will. We can all argue about whether something like Kant's particular strictures are right or wrong, but (in the moral worldview), we are doing that against the counterfactual background of what a truly wise, rational, and epistemically supercompetent agent would will.

¶607. Of course, in actual action, it's me as this individual who acts. I act for my reasons, which may or may not be the ones I would choose under ideal conditions. So I ask myself: What's really my duty here? The answer is the same as above: the pure duty I would have willed under ideal conditions, that is, the one legislated by the postulated pure and holy legislator of duty, which is an ideal unity of the "I" and the "We."

¶608. Actual consciousness is thus always incomplete, unperfected. Moral duty is pure, it is necessary (i.e., unconditional). As the contingent, finite being I am, I can never be sure if even my deepest convictions are right, and thus none of them can stand beyond possible reproach. I can strive to do the best I can—and that includes coming up with a Kantian or Fichtean philosophy of morality—but none of that can carry the same authority as that of the holy, moral duty. Unlike what was postulated earlier, the moral agent cannot expect to achieve any happiness in doing what he takes to be his duty. Instead, he must depend on grace (i.e., luck) to provide it. This too seems to follow from the moral worldview.

¶609. The perfection of moral consciousness would be that of pure duty always being fulfilled in the right way. But moral consciousness is imperfect in its makeup. Therefore in a morally correct and adequate world, happiness would be distributed according to desert (i.e., according to virtue), and virtue is always at least a bit, if not a lot, lacking in real people and the real world.

¶610. This more or less completes the conceptual development of the phenomenology of the moral worldview. In both, the element of pure duty and actuality (what is really at work in the world) are at least in theory (or in the very concept of the "moral worldview") in a unity. Each is a "moment" (an inseparable component) of a whole, which would be that of this new shape of spirit. It is no longer a world of moral ethos (as in Greece), nor the alienated early modern European world where noble souls staked everything on a value such as honor, but a world of rational individuals, each concerned with cognizing and doing their duty. (How to make sense of that will be the task set for themselves by the moral philosophers of this new shape.) We have a sense of ourselves in the natural world as not really suited to do our duty, and we have a sense that nonetheless we are called upon to do it, and that anything less would undermine our status as agents operating in a social world itself shaped by the failures of "absolute freedom" and its aftermath.

¶611. If that is the concept of the moral worldview, how does it now play out in the phenomenology of the moral worldview? The individual answering to the call of duty does not need and thus probably does not have any deeply philosophical concept of how this all hangs together. All he need know is that he has what seem to be unconditional duties (as the "pure essence"), that these duties are all knowable, and that he also has a duty to think seriously about them (even though he may get some of them wrong). This is all captured in representational thinking: "Out there" (in some appropriately vague sense) is a "pure essence" (the realm of moral duty) which can't be denied, and there are some facts about the world (abstractly put as issues of human sensibility and desire), which clash often enough with pure duty, but by and large the whole thing hangs together.

¶612. By this stage, the individual agent knows that there is an actual (efficacious, really at work) moral consciousness. This agent now (at least thinks he) knows that this is the actual final end (purpose) of the world itself: the harmony between morality and the real world (the actual world, the world understood in terms of what is really at work in it). We have of course not achieved that final end, but we are each and all enjoined to try to bring it about. This final end exists (it's real, it moves us to do things), but it also isn't real and remains only a projection of our thought, even though as such it continues to move us.

¶613. This final end is both real and irreal (as a projected end given to us in reflection). What we get out of that is yet another proposition about the moral worldview. On the one hand, we end up saying (¶611) that the whole picture hangs together: pure duty is perfectly real, and it sometimes clashes with what we otherwise want, but that clash does not make morality (as articulated in the moral worldview) into a fiction. Yet we also end up saying that the harmony between nature and morality is something we are to bring about, that where we are right now is a state where we have not achieved the requisite harmony. If genuine morality consists in doing our pure duty, and that duty includes achieving the harmony between nature and morality, then we also end up saying: "There is *no moral actuality*."

¶614. The moral self is one self. Its "in itself"—the developmental trajectory of its concept—has it bringing these two aspects of itself together in one unity. This can be represented as a kind of "not here in the natural world" harmony of duty and nature that ought to exist but does not yet exist. The moral agent has an unconditional duty to strive to bring about this final end, even though he knows that he cannot succeed, and he also cannot believe that this is impossible at least in the sense that he also must believe he could make progress in the task.

¶615. It seems that when one is living within the moral worldview, the unity of the components is supposed to be like the unity of all things to do with *Geist*: there are two elements that look to be exclusive of the other, but in fact each is necessary to the whole of which they are "moments." The "I" and the "We" are paradigmatic for that. However, in the case of the moral worldview, its unity is a matter not of speculative, dialectical conceptuality but of representational thinking in which each is seen as a freestanding component of something like an additive unity (analogous to the way in which one might be tempted to say that there really is no "We" but only a heap of singular "I's").

b. Dissemblance, Playacting

The preceding gave us the worldview and how it works itself out in terms of its own internal logic. Now we proceed to look at what happens when this gets translated into practice.

¶616. In the moral worldview, consciousness has an estranged encounter with morality. First, it encounters pure duty as its own creation, not in the form of a divine command or just some fact that imposes itself on us from without. Second, it does not encounter it as something it simply makes up but as something whose validity is somehow "external to itself." On the one hand, duty is something it creates and on the other hand something it discovers.

¶617. The moral worldview is the elaboration of this fundamental contradiction. (Hegel loosely refers to what Kant says in the first *Critique* about the impossibility of the cosmological proof of God's existence: "I have stated that in this cosmological argument there lies hidden a whole nest of dialectical assumptions, which the transcendental critique can easily detect and destroy.") In practice, the reaction to this is to move from one side to the other either without noticing the contradiction or actively dissembling about it. One way to make that palatable is to represent each side of the contradiction (creation and discovery) as some kind of freestanding thing over and against the other such that each is at odds with the other. Seeing it that way allows the agent to avoid contradicting himself instead by simply switching sides.

¶618. Let's go back to the first postulate: the harmony of nature and morality. This has to be only a statement about the "in itself" of the concept since it is not real (not actual) in the current world. It can't be actual because it is a contradiction. However, the acting consciousness presumes that it's real since it seeks to actualize its purposes, and in achieving its moral purpose, the agent is gratified—he did what he set out to do. Therefore, at least in this case, nature and morality are harmonized, and the acting agent cannot thereby be fully serious about the harmony as a mere "postulate."

¶619. But there's an objection: this can't be taken as a serious problem since the example concerns a one-off action in which no disharmony of morality and nature occurs. The point is supposed to be a larger one about "the whole world." However, the example concerns the realization of a pure duty in the natural world, and since the person's absolute duty was to realize such-and-such in the natural world (not lying, helping another, etc.), he has succeeded in carrying out this final end of the world. So maybe the point is that it isn't pure duty at stake but something lesser (what he wanted to do at that point given his upbringing and character). From the standpoint, as it were, of nature, this latter possibility looks like what is really the case. The moral worldview seems to have this tension built into it since it includes the ideas that moral action is indeed possible, that moral action is done out of the motive of pure duty (the explanation of somebody's doing the right thing is that it was done because it was right, not for some other ulterior end), and that no naturalistic account of action has a place for pure duty within itself. Is the way out of this tension that "the moral law should become the natural law"?

¶620. Maybe we say this: that the moral law should become the natural law would be the "highest good." If so, then once again we would have a lack of seriousness about morality. If the moral law and the natural law are the same, then there is no "morality" in the sense essential to the moral worldview since "morality" supposes for its practice that there be something (nature) which is its negative and against which it defines itself. (This is the is/ought dichotomy so basic to much modern moral philosophy.) One might still maintain the distinction between acting out of the motive of duty and acting out of more natural motives (approbation by others, sympathy, etc.), but if the moral law and the natural law were identical, there would be nothing to it, so we would have to say that "moral action is superfluous."

¶621. The moral worldview proceeds from the idea that the "substance" of *Geist* is that of morality itself. It is what holds the "I" and the "We" together. Like the other unities we have seen, it too ends up holding together two aspects that look to be at odds with each other, the "is" and the "ought." As a worldview (and not yet a philosophy), when put into practice, it moves around in this tension without ever resolving it.

¶622. One way of dealing with such contradictions is to dissemble about them, to deny that one is in fact contradicting oneself and instead insist that one is merely doing different things in different contexts. Put into practice as a real shape of *Geist*, the moral worldview is driven to such dissembling. According to the first of its postulates (the harmony between nature and morality), it understands itself as moral when it confronts the experience of duty as that which cannot be assimilated to any natural drive ("It confronts a *nature which is opposed* to it"). In its second postulate (the possible conformity of one's sensible inclinations to one's moral duties), it experiences once again a compulsion of duty that cannot be assimilated to any natural compulsion. Yet when the moral agent acts, he acts as a "self-conscious sensibility" in which one's empirical sensibilities are the mediators between the self-consciousness of pure duty and the actual natural world. (Not for nothing do some philosophers feel the need to postulate that it is the experience of "pure" duty that therefore produces an "empirical" feeling of some sorts—such as that of "respect"—in order for us to be motivated to do our pure duty.) In fact, by taking all the ways these tensions keep popping up and we keep putting them off into an infinite (i.e., in principle never to be completed) task, the consciousness operating within the moral worldview also finds itself again dissembling about what it is about.

¶623. We are at best always stuck somewhere in the in-between-station of noncompletion of the highest good. The moral worldview takes it that it has an infinite task ahead of itself in which it postulates that it is capable of making progress. However, since the progress it is supposed to be making is that of decreasing the distance between pure duty and inclination, its goal at infinity would be that of zero distance. We would be getting more moral by lessening the distance. But this idea of imputing quantitative measures in the moral world is out of place. There aren't really lots of duties, there is only one pure duty, and likewise one pure virtue and one pure morality. Besides, if the goal is infinitely distant, then no matter how much you've traveled, you will still have an infinite distance to go.

¶624. The moral worldview is not really serious about moral completion since that occurs at infinity, that is, never. We are really concerned with that so-called intermediate stage. We know that we can't be expected to be moral drudges, doing our duty all the time with no gratification attached to it, but we also know that gratification can't come as a matter of desert, for none of us can ever be worthy of it. We thus hope for happiness as a matter of grace—hope, with no demand, no expectation. But if that happiness is that for which it is hoping, is it really serious about the pure duty it has been espousing? Isn't it really happiness it wants and despairs of ever getting?

¶625. It's a commonplace that in the real world, things often go badly for the moral person but well for the bad person—except that as the pursuit of the highest good is infinite (so that its task can never be completed), exactly how are we making such finite judgments about an infinite series? Since morality is thus always incomplete, unperfected, what sense is there in characterizing something as immoral? It would be immoral if somebody acted contrary to his pure duty, but until we get a perfected morality, what reason do we have for saying that a person has acted contrary to his pure duty? We can't know his motives—we can't even know of our own motives whether they were pure, that is, not simply inclinations—so we can't say that he wasn't acting out of duty. Here Hegel then suddenly goes a little Nietzschean *avant la lettre*: maybe all this moralizing about duty and happiness is itself the expression not of, say, transcendental freedom but instead of some unappealing psychologies, such that when somebody says that somebody ought not to have happiness coming to her, perhaps he is only expressing a sense of envy (or ressentiment?) giving itself the cover of morality. Besides, the real context in which one worries about the apportioning of happiness is that good friends wish it for each other.

¶626. Given the strictures of the moral worldview, it's tempting for those living within it to draw the conclusion that an action done out of anything but the purest sense of duty would be disqualified as being moral—only acting out of pure duty counts—and thus, not being really moral, it would have to be immoral. However, that seems to suppose that we know what our own motives really are (which we don't know) and thus we have to postulate an ideal, holy moral lawgiver (perhaps God, perhaps an idealized version of our own self) to make sense of this. The judgment about whether we are acting purely would have to lie not in our own actual consciousness but in the (idealized) consciousness of an other. This is only another case of dissemblance. Nothing counts as holy or pure except that which self-consciousness legislates for itself as holy or pure (in the terms set by the moral worldview with its background of absolute freedom). The idea that we should think in terms of our actual moral consciousness as measured against some other moral consciousness (my idealized self, the impartial observer, the holy lawgiver) is really just a dissembling about what the moral worldview commits itself to.

¶627. We run through the idea once again that morality consists in a series of counterfactual judgments: what the holy consciousness (or my idealized self, the ideal observer, etc.) *would* will in x, y, z conditions, where, however sensibility tempts it, it refuses or goes along with it. This holy consciousness is capable of determining all the particular duties one might have in a way that one cannot do for oneself. This seems to be an unmovable commitment for the moral worldview.

¶628. The reality of the moral life is that it has to deal with duty and with the inclinations to do otherwise. The "other moral consciousness" (the idealized model) has no real struggle. The addict struggling with a sense of duty and a powerful desire taking him in some other direction is indeed in a struggle. His idealized self, though, has no real struggle, since his ideal self would see his duty and do it. It is sublimely above the struggle, but it still defines itself negatively against such a struggle. This is dissembling, playacting.

¶629. Once these contradictions come to the fore, the moral consciousness of the moral worldview has to retreat into itself. When too many things have to be taken into account, the moral worldview ceases to be practical, action guiding.

¶630. The moral cases that confound us are the concretion of many moral relations, like an object of perception (a thing of many qualities). Taking the easy ones out of consideration, each moral case is "thick" with these complexities. This makes concrete morality look rather impure, since all these empirical niceties have to go into the considered judgment of what is required of this, here, now. Morality is real; we have to do things in the real world, and we have to act. We are to do our best given that we can't know exactly what the fully ideal counterfactual version of ourselves who has full knowledge of all the particulars would derive from his/her pure duty. In the actual world, the morality of the moral worldview is experienced as having quite a bit of content. As it becomes more reflective about itself, it becomes something like the "pure duty" of which we have been speaking, and it becomes empty of content. (This is a gap in the assumed worldview that the moral philosophers will try to close in their theories.)

¶631. Thus, in essence, the moral worldview is not a coherent whole but rather a syncretism of the contradictions engendered by itself. The moral worldview is instead a hodgepodge of various ideas that can be practical and action guiding only by a kind of playacting that pretends as if it were a coherent whole and keeps all the elements apart from each other as if they were freestanding building blocks rather than moments of a conceptual whole. Once it suspects it is doing this, it cannot but think of itself as engaged in hypocrisy. It claims the high ground of pure duty, but acknowledges that it acts out of some other motive.

13

Beautiful Souls

¶632. We begin with a review of the antinomies of the moral world-view. They all lead to a view in which there is another moral self-consciousness that sets the standards for or functions as the ideal of the real, acting self-consciousness (or gives it advice or something like that). This operates in the domain of representational thinking (*Vorstellung*) where we represent the domain of morality as that of a holy lawgiver or an idealized self, as something (even fiction) "in addition to" our representation of ourselves as moral agents in a natural world.

¶633. What emerges as the truth of the moral worldview—what is the projected endpoint of the development of the concept—is the self of *conscience*. Hegel gets to this point by reviewing the way he has gotten to this point. Spirit—as the I that is a We, and a We that is an I—forms itself into a shape of life within which the tensions inherent in what look like concepts at odds with each other are kept in unity. Each previous stage was the truth of the earlier stage in that each stage of *Geist* turned out to be what the earlier stage had pushed itself into once it began to comprehend what was at stake for it. (The next stage is not just different but is the "determinate negation" of the earlier one.) In facing its contradictions, the self of ethical life (Greece) gradually dissolves, falls apart, and what grows out of it is not another shape of ethical life but a more aggressively organized empire glued together by legality and the credible threat of force that takes over many of the virtues and ethical life of what preceded it but hollows them out. In that shape of life, the ethical self becomes instead the legal self, the "person," who exists only in being recognized as a "person," as a node in the legal order. That itself falls apart and in the wake of its dissolution there emerges the alienated shape of self-conscious life, which finally develops its self-conception into absolute freedom and the Terror. In such an alienated life, everything social seems to be in flux, collapsing,

Hegel's Phenomenology of Spirit. Terry Pinkard, Oxford University Press. © Oxford University Press 2023. DOI: 10.1093/oso/9780197663127.003.0013

shifting, changing, and the self, the self-conscious subject, contracts into a "point" which takes itself to remain fixed as all swirls around it. The truth of this shape of life is that of the "moral world view," the conception of the unity of self-conscious life as lying in a moral vision of how these otherwise alienated but absolutely free subjects can be together. Trying to put together the moral worldview as consisting of an indifferent, deterministic nature with free, self-legislating subjectivity leads to a kind of unending game of dissemblance about what the moral subject is actually doing. It is the growing awareness of the necessity of dissemblance that brings in its wake a unity of spirit that is simply that of "conscience." The unity of individuals in a social whole (a "We") is now taken to consist in a collection of agents each answering authentically and truthfully to their own individual consciences about what the "morality" of the moral worldview demands.

¶634. The idea of conscience is that of an agent making a kind of practical commitment to unifying the various tensions of the moral worldview without falling into syncretism or outright contradiction. To the extent that the moral agent simply takes it on himself to do the right thing because it is right, and consults his conscience about it (weighing all the reasons, being honest with himself, and so on), then the agent has acted out of duty. The appeal to individual conscience brings all those things together in a practical choice. In making the choice, the subject becomes the concrete moral subject that doesn't give itself an empty standard but a real one. In making the choice and acting, it is in its immediate unity actualizing moral essence. Conscience thus seems to be a kind of self-bootstrapping action: it makes its choice by acting, and in making its choice, it chooses the principle by which it will have acted.

¶635. So we begin with a kind of standard opening gambit in discussions about moral judgment. A case is before us. We suppose that the case is as it appears to the knowing subject. (It's not the mere semblance of some other deeper case or essence.) We assume that the case has some complexity to it. The case itself contains a variety of empirical matters, but these have salience only in light of the agent's purpose and what he knows about the whole situation. ("The case only is *in itself* in the way it is in this knowing.") Consciousness self-bootstraps its way into having done something. ("Acting as actualization is thereby the pure form of willing.") This acting doesn't require an intermediate step between the purpose and the act. (There's no need to posit a "desire" or "inclination" to get the agent to spring into action.) Nor does consciousness need to break up the case into a variety of duties as if each one were a separate "thing" of some sort (e.g., a self-subsistent value). Rather, each is what it is only within the whole of action. If there seems to be a conflict of duties, it is not that one is obligated to do A *and* obligated to do not-A, so that one must either choose blindly or else see which one "outweighs" the other. On this picture, conscience is the negative "One" or is the absolute self that erases these different moral substances as so-called prima facie duties. They are all but moments of a whole, not independent things. It deliberates and then knows the concrete right and does it.

¶636. That looks like it solves the problem of self-explication of the moral life of conscience: no more flittering back and forth among all the metaphysical alternatives. Conscience has to act, does its very best at judging, and then acts. What more can one demand?

¶637. In the appeal to conscience, the problems attendant on the moral worldview dissolve. There is no pure duty, only the duties I have here and now in this situation in the actual world. This is, moreover, not arbitrary action. Conscience takes into account the pure duty that is the linchpin of the moral worldview, but it sees that the complex situation within which it finds itself calls for a choice in figuring out what its real concrete duty is. For conscience to work like this, it must take the essence of this shape of spirit to be its own immediate certainty of itself. In a world of complex duties, it must see what is salient and what is not in the choice to be made. But there is a twist: What does this "self-certainty" look like from the "standpoint of consciousness"? That standpoint is that of the opposition of subject and object, or, to use the other Hegelian trope, that between *Vorstellung* (representation) and *Begriff* (concept). Representational thought is additive. It analyzes and breaks up affairs into their components and then sees those components as freestanding elements to be added up to constitute the whole which is analyzed. Conceptual thinking is holistic: each component only has the meaning that it has within a whole—change the whole and you change the meaning; change the meaning and you change the whole. From the "standpoint of consciousness," therefore, the form of moral action is just one's own conviction about what is to be done, and the content is one's own singular individuality which is brought to bear in undertaking the action.

¶638. Moral consciousness of the moral worldview grasped itself as the essence of action, as what the action really is in terms of the developmental trajectory of its concept, but "conscience" grasps itself in its own self-relation (its being-for-itself) as the standard by which judgments and actions are to be made. The contradictions and tensions in the moral worldview between the subject willing universal law (as "pure duty") and the actual, empirical self as driven by inclinations, desires, needs, and wants now just dissolve. In this picture, the agent of "conscience" knows what counts and doesn't count; he has a comprehensive and holistic grasp of what in the case before him is salient and not salient; he sees clearly what he ought to do, and this is enough to motivate him to act on the conviction he has thereby formed.

¶639. The spirit that holds this together is that of equal agents held together by a common commitment on the part of each to act from conscience—that is, to know the good, to develop the capacities to see what is salient in a complex situation, and then to act on that conviction. This is what the moral worldview somewhat incorrectly called one's "pure duty," but here the "pure" and the singularly concrete have fused. Echoing Jesus's comment in Mark 2:23, "The Sabbath was made for man, not man for the Sabbath," Hegel says of this shape, "The law now exists for the sake of the self and not the other way around, not the self existing for the sake of the law." This "knowing," as Hegel puts it, is now the "in itself," that is, the trajectory in which the concept of the agent of "conscience" will have as its endpoint his expressing the complete equality between himself and his concept. As an expression of the unity of spirit, it is now very much a collection of independent individuals living together as moral agents possessing deep convictions. In other words, the self-relation (or being-for-itself) of the agent of conscience is a unity of being-for-others. Each "I" is a person of conviction who also exists in this unity with others, and this forms the "We" that unites each of them.

¶640. In the moral worldview, the "We" was conceived like that of a set of independent monads each internally following the same (moral) law but without having to communicate with each other and where any communication would in any event have no necessary effect on the content of the (moral) law. However, as "conscience," the relation is not that between those kinds of monads but that of individuals with their convictions seeking to have their status as individuals-of-conviction recognized. In the moral worldview, there is the nonactual "pure duty" and the actual world of people with desires, inclinations, needs and the like (and the problem was keeping these two elements in one unity). In "conscience," the substance that keeps the whole together is just this being-for-others, a community of individuals consulting their consciences on how to act but also desirous of recognition by others of this. When Luther utters his famous retort in 1521, "Hier stehe ich. Ich kann nicht anders" ("Here I stand, I cannot do otherwise"), he is stating a conviction but also demanding or requesting that his conviction be recognized (in the sense of *anerkennen*, the "recognition" that we saw in the dialectic of mastery and servitude). He is an actuality in Hegel's sense, not an abstract ideal. The conviction is the essence of the action. (Somebody merely feigning conviction would make his act into a falsity.) Moreover, the conscientious actor (such as the example of Luther) is not asserting an idiosyncratic claim but manifesting a universal moral truth. Still, this way of manifesting a commitment amounts to a "meaning [that] is only that of a vacuous essentiality as such."

¶641. Hegel stops to compare this with what he has said earlier. One should keep in mind that Hegel changed his mind about what book he writing as he was writing it. It stopped being *The Science of the Experience of Consciousness* and became instead the *Phenomenology of Spirit*. The "spiritual kingdom of animals" was the piece he wrote to provide the transition from the original book on "consciousness" into the *Phenomenology* it became. (Or, rather, Hegel realized that he had been writing a *Phenomenology of Spirit* all along, but it was only at that point that he realized that's what he was doing.) In the "spiritual kingdom," the agents realize that "individuality" is the concept under which they are now working. This concept is now fully being-for-itself in that it does not merely implicitly characterize what is actually at work in their world but does so as they are now fully self-conscious about it. It is also being-in-itself since it seems to capture the trajectory in which they were developing their self-conceptions (and which

also seems to have reached its completion in this self-conscious appro-
priation of the status of "individuality" on their part). They thought
that an adequate unity of the "I" and the "We" was that constituted by
such individuals, each in pursuit of what really mattered, but it turned
out not only that the "I" and the "We" were not adequately unified in
that particular conception of the *Sache selbst*, but also that the pursuit
of the *Sache selbst* (as what was really of substantial importance) was
not a purely individual effort but a collective enterprise, a feature of
Geist and not just a "shape of consciousness." With that in mind, the
book took on a new focus. If the pursuit of the *Sache selbst*, what really
matters, was what was at issue, then what shape did this collective enterprise take, and was there any logic to it? The answer is that, yes, there
was a logic to it—it wasn't just a scattershot enterprise—and that it had
(up until this point in the book) taken the shape that the *Sache selbst*
was the substantiality of Greek life, the alienated form in European
life after the collapse of the western Roman empire, the status of absolute freedom in the Revolution, and now both the moral worldview
and agency as structured by conviction. The logic that is manifesting
itself—without actually discursively saying yet what it is—is the speculative logic of wholes whose basic elements seem to be in some kind
of tension with each other that threaten to turn into self-undermining
contradictions but which can ultimately be properly integrated with
each other.

¶642. These tensions that appear in any such totality or whole
of *Geist* also appear in "conscience." Although it is practical, "conscience" conducts itself in terms of its being a "knower." It takes everything into consideration, but it also knows that it doesn't know
everything that should be taken into consideration. It knows it
must do the right, and the "universality" involved has to do with its
knowing this and how it relates to the actual case in front of it. Of
course, each case is complex, and investigating and reflecting on each
case piles up new considerations. The conscientious subject knows
its knowledge to be incomplete—"It knows that its pretense of conscientiously weighing all the circumstances is an empty matter." Yet,
as acting from deep conviction, "Its incomplete knowing, because it
is *its own* knowing, counts for it as sufficiently complete knowing." It
has to go on what it has.

¶643. The abstract idea of "pure duty" which is central to the moral worldview here becomes the concrete self-conscious "I," which is now the "in itself" of *Geist* (the trajectory on which *Geist*'s concept of itself has been moving). Since conscience has to act on its own conviction, it is "absolute negativity" (absolutely nothing counts for it as determining its content except itself). But since it is the concrete self-conscious "I" that is doing the determining of what is to be done, we are back to the idea that our own desires, wants, and inclinations are driving the action.

¶644. Hegel here argues that, as it has been developed, "conviction" is as empty as "pure duty" was and that just about anything can be attached to it. From "conviction," nothing concrete conceptually follows unless something else is given, and in this case, that means something coming from the acting subject's own idiosyncratic take on himself and the world.

¶645. Every action in this context will bear the "flaw [stain] of determinateness." If moral action were a matter of pure (i.e., nonempirical) practical reason alone, then "pure knowing" would not be burdened with this stain. In the actual world, all action is burdened with it. To be sure, pure duty and pure knowing claim to take the particularities of the case into account, but when they do, the older oppositions of, for example, duty versus inclination reappear even though they were supposed to have been shuffled off. There are also too many ways for casuistical reasoning to enter. To that end, Hegel gives an example of what today would be called "effective altruism": do well so you can do good. The idea that one should insightfully balance all the competing or conflicting duties also falls aside since the concept of conscience and conscientious behavior rules out such contingent calculations. The agent of conscience eschews such calculations and does the right thing because it is right.

¶646. Because of his singularity, the conscientious agent inserts content into duty (where "duty" is universal being-in-itself), and it finds this content in its natural individuality. This in turn gives singular content the moral force of duty itself. However, this means that in the force of its self-certainty as carrying out moral duty itself, it assumes the majesty (as Hegel somewhat sarcastically puts it) of absolute autarky to loosen and to bind vis-à-vis all duty. As possessing such autarky, the conscientious self has shifted the concepts at work here: the conscientious self is now the in-itself, the basic concept developing its trajectory as what is really at work in this shape of spirit.

¶647. As acting, the self becomes being-for-others. He is one individual (possessing "immediacy, or being"), one among many. Each (supposedly) recognizes the others as such conscientious individuals.

¶648. Each agent is taken to be equal to himself (in the sense that there is no discrepancy between himself and what he thinks he is supposed to develop into). Each member of the moral community recognizes all the others as such conscientious agents (at least in terms of their concept). Some agents may fall short or fail to live up to their concept (their socially grounded picture of themselves), but that is not supposed to cast any doubt on the status of conscientious agency. However, an inequality appears. The "universal consciousness" is that which has the status to confer or withhold recognition, and in principle each (conscientious) member manifests this universal consciousness in his acts of recognition. But the idea that in his concept of himself he is free from any determinate duty means that the dissemblance, which was one of the irremediable tensions of the moral worldview, returns again. He claims to be subject to the full force of moral obligation, yet he also claims he has a kind of autarky that frees him from it.

¶649. Of course, what this means is that all the members of this moral community share equally in this autarky. Moreover, none can know whether the others are feigning conscientiousness. If pressed, each can explain himself or come to a judgment about the others. But it does seem that if by "evil," we mean somebody free from all moral obligation and thus free to do what it is she wishes, then given the autarky of each, each must regard the other as evil and make an exception for herself if in her heart she knows that others are in fact not feigning conscientiousness. She cannot know this about others, but she does know that others (like herself) have this kind of autarky.

¶650. What is known to the actor is his inner conviction. Once one has acted, one has a deed, and one is no longer the determining factor. Actuality, in the sense of both other people and the natural world, takes over. What is supposed to be recognized (*das Anerkannte*) is not the deed itself and all its manifold consequences but what the agent knew and whether she was acting out of conviction.

¶651. What is recognized is not just another thing in the world. It's the self of conscience, and this is what is anchoring the scheme. The effect of the action might be something to regret or celebrate, but there is no basis for regretting, for example, that one has done one's duty according to one's conscience. Importantly, it is not just that "agency" in general comes into focus but that "the self enters into existence *as a self*," with all the particularities of what makes a self into a self.

¶652. Hegel says: "Here again we see *language* as the existence of spirit." (That isn't quite true—in ¶507, he said something very similar but not exactly the same thing.) It is a clear statement that *Geist* does not preexist the linguistic community. We become the selves we are in and through the medium of language, within which we give recognition to others and receive it from them. (This kind of knowledge of other wills is the "universal self-consciousness" of which Kant spoke in the first *Critique*, §16 of the "transcendental deduction.") We are selves only through self-consciousness (Fichte's formula of I = I), and we are specific selves (the concrete self) in this recognition, in our second-person awareness of each other (see ¶177). The recognitive relation is essentially also a communicative relation, and it is only in language that self-consciousness becomes actual.

¶653. Hegel speaks of how the content and the differing uses of language show up here. It's not the inverted, inverting language of the disrupted self of *Bildung*—not the language of the alienated cleverness of the court. Nor is it the language of *sittliche Geist*, which Hegel here says is law as simple command, followed by a lament, which is really just bemoaning necessity itself. (He clearly seems to be thinking about Greek tragedy, *Antigone* in particular, where the "law" is the divine law that demands Antigone's punishment for her wrongful acts—because we suffer, we know we have erred, she says). Likewise, it's not the language of the moral worldview, which remains rather mute, since it exists entirely in innerness (or at least it takes itself to be). That view is self-defeating since a purely inner language of your own that only you understood would be, well, nothing at all. The language of conscience, however, is not so obviously caught up in those difficulties. It is essentially a second-person address explaining your justification to an other, who (on this picture) is ready as a matter of principle to recognize its authority. It is a "Here I stand, I cannot do otherwise" that is supposed to be given recognition by others as a statement of your conviction. This language of conviction and of deep consultation within one's own innerness is supposed to be the "middle," the medium, Hegel says, between self-sufficient and recognized self-conscious subjects. It supposedly shows itself in their individual statements about their convictions, and they manifest it in their ways of stating their own convictions.

¶654. The question as to whether the assurance that it acts out of conviction about its duty is really true makes no sense for conscience in this picture. That would suppose that there is a gap between the singular self and the universal self. However, since what motivates the singular self is just that which the singular self "sees" as justified, that gap cannot open (according to this picture of things).

¶655. The paragraph is basically a rather sarcastic comment on what Hegel thinks the truth of the matter is. Such a self-described conscientious agent is taking his inner conviction to be manifesting the divine voice itself. He is more: he is divine creativity itself manifesting itself to the world. He conducts a "worship-service within himself." (In the next paragraph, that becomes a "solitary worship service.") These folks also claim the title of moral genius. Kant had spoken in the *Critique of Judgment* of artistic geniuses, who create works of beauty for which no rule can be stated. The artistic genius doesn't follow the rules of, say, classical style but creates something new, which in turn can become a rule for future artists, who in turn will break the rules and now play the role of exemplars of the new rule which they embody. The self-described moral geniuses think of themselves in that way.

¶656. This "solitary worship service" is also the worship service of a religious community: that of the social world whose "substance" (what concretely holds it together) is that of each of its members following their own conscience, declaring it to each other and being given recognition for it. Hegel says of it in a fully ironic tone: "The spirit and the substance of their bond is thus the reciprocal assurance of both their mutual conscientiousness and their good intentions; it is the rejoicing over this reciprocal purity, the refreshment received from the glory of knowing, declaring, fostering and cherishing such excellence." In acting, the agent does what he does, declares it to be his conviction, and thus promotes that conviction into the universal norm for all. It knows that the right is a matter of abstract consciousness (knowing an abstract ideal), but it nonetheless identifies that with its own singular choice. (It knows that simply what it says or what it wants does not make something right, but it also in effect collapses the distinction between the two.) It in effect claims there to be a difference between its own singularity and what is right and then collapses the difference into no difference. It is in effect claiming that its own singular voice is really the voice of all right-thinking people.

¶657. In this phenomenology, we now see another way of concretely, even existentially, grappling with the "speculative," dialectical problem of a shape of life that seems to be determined by two (or more) competing terms that threaten to be mutually exclusive and to bring the shape into an unsustainable incoherence. Dialectical thinking takes such "speculative" problems to be tamed when the terms are shown to be equally essential to the working of a certain whole (and thus to stand together in a unity rather than stand apart in a dualism). When they cannot be so tamed, they take the whole down with themselves. The idea of "conscience" takes the extremes of the moral worldview ("pure duty without exception" and the natural agent driven by his own desires, wants, needs, fantasies, etc.) and seeks to abolish the dualism by the appeal to the singular agent taking his conscience and thus his genuine conviction of the rightness of an action to be the way the universal and the singular are genuinely reconciled. On that view, the singular agent guided by his own conviction *is* the existing unity that was sought. But what we end up with is not a reconciled unity but a shape of consciousness that is condemned to abstraction, to having no real substance, a shape that has refined itself to a purity that is the poorest shape of all. This makes this kind of absolute self-consciousness into absolute untruth.

¶658. Since it collapses into abstractions refined into an unlivable purity, this shape not only finds itself burdened with all the dualisms it thought it had resolved but also lives with them as intensified. It is left hearing only the echo of its own voice, and it is like the fading sounds of a church bell after its last ring. Faced with this, it cannot act at all since all action, it fears, would irreversibly stain its inner purity. It becomes a "beautiful soul," someone whose inner purity is so beautiful, no expression could adequately manifest it but whose beauty should nonetheless be celebrated.

It makes sense to ask about whom Hegel is actually speaking. Scholars diverge on this point. Lots of people before Hegel praised the idea of the beautiful soul, so it could be many of them. Among the prime candidates of his own day are some of the members of the Jena early Romantics, whom Hegel did not particularly like and some of whom seemed to detest him. J. F. Fries, a contemporary at Jena whose lifetime antipathy to Hegel was matched by Hegel's lifetime antipathy in return, would also be an obvious candidate.[1]

¶659. In the preceding paragraph, Hegel says that such a life dies out like an ember. Here he says it just evaporates. It takes itself to singularly incorporate the universal consciousness of "pure duty" into itself, but it also thereby radically distinguishes itself from all others. Once one has sealed off subjectivity from the world into a rather rigid inner/outer difference, then in this self-congratulatory little social circle, all may celebrate their own purity (the "pure self"), but the ends of these "pure selves" can only be those of "natural individuality," that is, just those they happen to have as a result of who they are in their social, psychological, and natural makeup. The emptiness of the identity of the self—as a kind of pure thinking—can only be filled with contingent empirical content. Once this becomes clear to the members of the community of beautiful souls, it also becomes clear just how great the opposition among the members can be.

¶660. Even in the self-conception of a singular beautiful soul, an inequality between its own self-certainty (what it takes to be the bedrock commitments of its shape of life) and its emerging concept of itself (or its "in itself") comes to the fore. There are two elements in tension with each other in this conception: pure duty and singular agency. To the agent who adheres strongly to his concept as having the universal (pure duty) count as bedrock, the singular beautiful soul can only be evil (as free of all general moral constraint), whereas to the singular beautiful soul, the (moralistic) agent adhering to pure duty is simply a hypocrite.

¶661. One side thus commits itself to the unconditional obligation of showing that the singular consciousness really is evil, whereas the other side commits itself to the unconditional obligation to unmask the hypocrisy of the former. They turn their moral fury on each other. If hypocrisy is the compliment that vice pays to virtue, then the hypocrite (so the charge goes) is even worse because he lets his inwardness be twisted by the outer expectations of others. Subjecting himself to the judgments of others, he is making himself into a thing with no claim on its own to any rights.

¶662. We imagine the accusations flying back and forth. Each is firmly convinced of his own rectitude. One is accused of radical evil, but he stiffly maintains that in following his inner conviction, he is exactly living up to his concept of what he is supposed to be. (He is "equal" to his concept.) As for the one who is accused of hypocrisy, he stiffly maintains (we are to suppose) that he is only pointing out (as he must) the radical evil of the other one. But when the universal consciousness confesses (in the sense of admitting) that he too is following (conscientiously) his own conviction as the singular person, he is confessing (by implication) that he too is evil.

¶663. What all the accusatory judgments against each other do is basically to legitimize both sides. The "universal consciousness" claims that in its actions, it is only manifesting the universally recognized morality behind all such moral judgments, but it is showing that this is in fact not recognized by everyone and thus by implication refuting itself.

¶664. What we see, Hegel says, is the beginning, the way into dissolving this opposition. The consciousness that accuses the other of evil isn't really himself acting but instead judging. This judgmental agent claims that he does not fall into the opposition of singular versus universal (which is what he accuses the "evil" consciousness of), but he does this by only *thinking* of the universal, not in terms of acting by it, and in thinking it, he comes to the conclusion that the first consciousness is "evil." In this way, he preserves the purity of his beautiful soul, and (so Hegel sarcastically says), "instead of proving its uprightness in action, proves it by means of speaking about its splendid dispositions." One of them acts, the other speaks (judging the first agent to be impure, "evil").

¶665. The basic problem here is that both sides continue to operate with the opposition of universality (as pure duty) and singularity (as the real, existing individual) and are trying out an experiment in living that seeks to overcome the opposition. What is actually at work in both of these stances is that one cannot separate the universal from the singular, although they are clearly distinguishable from each other. Hegel explains the old saying that no man is a hero to his valet by noting that the valet is just that: a valet, a servant, somebody who sees the hero up close in his singularity. Because he is so close, he cannot take the larger view. Proximity makes it all too easy to see some self-interested motive in all action.

¶666. The base (*niederträchtig*) character here is the judgmental consciousness who insists on keeping separate the universal aspect of the action from the more singular interest the acting agent has and explains the universal in terms of the singular. In keeping them separate, the judging consciousness by implication places himself on a higher plane and holds his judgmental chatter to be more real than the action taken by agent whom he accuses of being "evil." The agent being accused sees this in him, sees that he is placing his own singularity in the place of the "universal" (or putting himself and his faultfinding into the position of being the very embodiment of the universal itself) and, in seeing this, realizes that the person is not different from himself and is in some ways the flip side of the coin. He makes this clear by a confession of sorts that he is the same as the one accusing him, that both are manifestations of an underlying spirit, and his very act of stating this is what makes the spirit exist in individuals ("He does this because language is the *existence* of spirit as the immediate self").

¶667. This confession (*gestehen*) is also an avowal (*Eingeständnis*). The acting consciousness does this, declares it, expects the other to follow suit, but the other forcefully rejects this and becomes the hard heart. Here Hegel is bringing to the fore the Kantian claim that in acting from pure duty, neither I nor anybody else can know what my real motive was, since the pure motive on the basis of duty (pure practical reason causing me to act) can make no full appearance in the phenomenal world. As "pure actors" we are invisible not only to each other but also to ourselves. Note too that the paragraph starts with "Ich bin's," "I'm the one." (I think this has to do with a biblical passage, but not everybody agrees. See Isaiah 47:10. [In the King James Version, it goes like this: "For thou hast trusted in thy wickedness; thou hast said, 'None seeth me.' Thy wisdom and thy knowledge, it hath perverted thee; and thou hast said in thine heart, 'I am, and none else besides me.'"] In Luther's rendering, for those who want to know the German: "Denn du hast dich auf deine Bosheit verlassen, da du dachtest: Man sieht mich nicht! Deine Weisheit und Kunst hat dich verleitet, daß du sprachst in deinem Herzen: *Ich bin's, und sonst keine!*") The confessing subject in effect says: yes, the evil you accuse me of, that's me. The other rejects this and becomes the "hard heart," the heart of stone, who thinks of himself as special, as "none seeth me." It's just me. I have a beautiful soul, I don't have to acknowledge my own radical evil (at least not in that way). It becomes noncommunicative; it is addressed, and becoming stiff-necked about it, it refuses to respond. Hegel uses a theologically inflected language to characterize this: the hard heart is forsaken by spirit (*geistverlassene*). (He doesn't say: forsaken by God.) But spirit (self-conscious life) is the master, *Meister* of all (not the *Herr*, the "master" of the master/slave relation. It's the "master" as in the phrase "master craftsman").

¶668. The hard heart is the flip side of the acting consciousness that confesses. The hard heart, though, won't let go. Its own sense of its own purity is such that if it did avow it, it would confess to lacking this purity and thus to its own unity of self. If it clings to this purity, Hegel says, it will go mad, and (or maybe "or") it will waste away in a kind of tubercular fashion. (This may or may not be a reference to the poet known as Novalis.) So the beautiful soul dies like a glowing ember, fades away like a bell that has already been rung, evaporates, or gradually just dies out as a tubercular victim does. All that's pretty harsh. (Tubercular patients don't contract the disease because of their insistence on their moral purity.) How is there is any conceptual necessity to this? Or has Hegel lapsed into a kind of semiliterary narrative about such characters? Here's one way of approaching it. The beautiful souls basically take the speciation of self-conscious life to go all the way down to the individual, singular self-consciousness. But in doing so, and in separating themselves off so strongly from the community, they lose thereby the full nature of the second-person address, and they are thus only able to hear their own echo. Like any species that has been put into an inhospitable environment, they die off, at least in the shape they were.

¶669. Hegel does say that there is (or there are the conditions for) a true, self-conscious and existing conciliation, an *Ausgleichung*, and there is a necessity to all this. It seems to be that in the second-person addresses between the two "characters" (acting and judgmental), the

way in which one confesses to the other gives the other the chance
to reconcile with the first. The moralistic world in which we are all
holding ourselves and each other to impossible standards and continually in the process of shaming each other and laying on the guilt cannot
last, especially since we are all, in the terms of this way of living, invisible to each other and to ourselves. But self-conscious life continues,
and we are all just passing through. He also says that "the wounds of
the spirit heal and leave no scars behind," which seems, well, a bit opti-
mistic, but the idea is that through mutual forgiveness of our wrongful
deeds, we are capable of overcoming the wounds they open up and
eventually putting them behind us. Ultimately, the hard heart has to
break. But how is this *necessary*? Why can't the hard heart just sulk in
its corner and live out its solitary, friendless, moralistic life? (Slavoj
Žižek has taken this passage to mean that we just change our perspective, and the wound—self-consciousness—*is* the healing.)

¶670. Hegel's answer to this question is, roughly, his theory of subjectivity (of agency) itself. It is in the I that is We, the We that is I, built
out of the second-person address, that "a self-consciousness is (exists)
for another self-consciousness." The dialectical conception of self-
consciousness is given first in ¶177: "the experience of what spirit is,
this absolute substance which constitutes the unity of its oppositions in
their complete freedom and self-sufficiency, namely, in the oppositions
of the various self-consciousnesses existing for themselves: The *I* that is
We and the *We* that is *I*." The unity of the "universal" and the "singular"
is the concept of self-conscious life that has to make itself real (actual)
over the course of history. The awareness of this is not a purely theoretical matter but something that at this stage of the dialectic is intuited,
or so Hegel says—thereby setting aside the Kantian opposition of intuition and concept. We intuit this unity in a conceptualized intuition. (Hegel will later use this idea of a conceptualized intuition and
an intuitive concept to provide an account of how both art and religion can be about deep truths of self-conscious life without themselves
having to be completely philosophical.) Second-person knowledge is
knowledge of other wills that *cannot* be articulated as a universal judgment applied to an empirical case. It is a special form of knowledge,
in which the generality of a practice (or in this case, the generality of
self-conscious life) shows itself in the specific act. It is also manifested

or exhibited, as Aristotle argued, in justice. We can only do that in language ("Language is the existence, *Dasein*, of spirit") The kind of recognitive, communicative relation is more basic than any purely monological self-relation. The monological conception of subjectivity simply can't make sense of forgiveness, except as an isolated act by one, acceptance or rejection by another.

In the paragraph, Hegel continues his theologically inflected language. He speaks of a reconciliation (*Versöhnung*) between the two. In German, that has a linguistic resonance with the reconciliation of God and man in Christianity. He says that the word (forgiveness) of reconciliation is the existing (*daseiende*) spirit that is a pure knowledge of itself as a universal essence in its opposites, as both universal and as singularly individual. This has a surprising twist to it: the conceptual problem of the relation between the universal and the particular is solved at first not in theory but in the practice of reconciliatory forgiveness. What looked like a conceptual gap between the universal (the moral law) and the individual is here resolved in practice. Now it remains to capture what that practice is in theory.

¶671. We get the penultimate statement of this phenomenology of *Geist*'s appearances in actual history. As a result of working its way out from Greece and ethical life, then on through the alienated spirit and up through morality, we now have a potentially reconciled shape of life (reconciled *in itself* but maybe not yet *to itself* in a way that the reconciliation would thereby be present in the *for-itself* of each subject). Self-conscious life now is knowing that its pure knowing is the absolute essence. There is nothing behind the appearances of *Geist*, except *Geist* making sense of itself in historical time. It knows itself as "the universal" and as the singular individual recognizing other singular individuals. Hegel says, "Each of these self-certain spirits has no other end than their pure self and has no other reality and existence other than just this pure self. However, they are still different, and the difference is absolute because it is posited as lying in this element of the pure concept." We now have a statement of *Geist* as the *Mitte*, the medium in which the generality of the practice and the individuality of the act are united (as two sides of the dialectical coin, as the generic universality of the practice "showing itself" in the practical act, which is not an instantiation of the generality nor an application of a rule but the way in which the members of the practice "manifest" in a singular way that generality). This is a key takeaway, as it were, of the *Phenomenology*. So it will turn out, *Geist* ultimately just *is* the appearance of its essence, which is itself as developing in historical time, but that is still yet to be shown.

The problem for the two beautiful souls is thus that they are invisible to each other (as in the Isaiah 47:10 passage), but each takes himself to be fully on view to himself in his own inwardness. As it were, one of them (the acting consciousness) says that since every case involves a lot of complicated facts, he never acts until he has all the facts available, and thus even if things turn out badly, he always does what is pure and right in the circumstances. The judging consciousness says he never acts until he has all the facts, but he never has all of them, so he never acts but only judges. Each claims a purity that is invisible to the other, each accuses the other of evil or hypocrisy. But since there actually is a way of making ourselves visible—language is the *Dasein* of *Geist*—there is the possibility of a reconciliation. (We might even go so far as to say that language is the being-in-the-world of *Geist*.) In this formulation, the "I" is actual, not just a quasi-geometrical "point" in an alienated world.

The conclusion of this chapter is intriguing, but we'll have to go into the depths of the "Religion" chapter to understand it. Hegel says that the reconciling Yes in which both let go of their opposed existence—think of the last sentence in Joyce's *Ulysses*—is the existence of the I extended into twoness (*Zweiheit*, the second person) which remains that same and has the certainty of itself in the complete relinquishing of itself. This almost completes the movement first initiated in ¶177 by the second-person and first-person singular and plural that appeared there. This way of using the second-person confession and forgiveness for the "I" extended into "twoness" leads to the statement that it is itself *der erscheinende Gott*—the appearing God, the phenomenal God, depending on how you translate it. Keep in mind that *Erscheinung* for Kant is the *appearance* of things in themselves but *not* as they are in themselves. This appearance is in the midst of those who know themselves as pure knowing (that is, knowing what the essence is, what is the actual form of the world as we find it). Hegel is setting up a major Hegelian point here. The breakdown of beautiful souls declaring each other to be evil or hypocritical points to one of Hegel's basic theses. The *geistig* inner and the outer are not separable "things" but should be conceived in the same way that a language *shows itself* in the linguistic activities of its speakers, and the speakers *manifest* the language in their linguistic behavior.

In this case, the moralism inherent in the moral worldview appears in the way it applies the moral principles, as it were, from on high, which only leads to the kind of judgmental moralism that in turn breaks down under that pressure but which is put in its proper place by the more direct encounter with each other by the more "bottom up" acts of reconciliation and forgiveness. As it were, the moral worldview imposes its principles legalistically from on high, whereas the "experience" (*Erfahrung*) of the moral worldview shows it to be livable only in terms of the "bottom up" practices of reconciliation and forgiveness. However, the appeal to "forgiveness and reconciliation" sounds religious in character. So is the *erscheinende Gott* the way God really is, or the appearance of something else, deeper, not the same as its appearance? (Is God the hidden essence "behind" the appearance?) We can by now pretty well guess what the answer will be.

14

Religion

¶672. Hegel begins by summing things up. Up until now, he says, religion did indeed make an appearance, but only as consciousness of the absolute essence, not in and for itself. It is there "only as consciousness," so he says. It is put into the first-person, subject-object picture of things—me, my consciousness, the object of my consciousness, me wondering if I really am aware of the object I take myself to be aware of. Of course, we know by now that all consciousness is self-consciousness, that self-consciousness is social and recognitive, and that it determines itself concretely in "forms of life." Hegel does not speak of it in this paragraph, but one of his key ideas is that consciousness of the absolute first occurs in a thoughtful way in religion, and it occurs first in religion as a kind of sentiment or feeling (*Empfindung*). Only later is it taken up by philosophy. Religion, he will say, approaches the absolute as representation (*Vorstellung*). It thus operates within a subject-object picture (at least at first): the absolute is represented as an independent object or as something that is diffuse enough to make sense (or seem at first to make sense) of the infinite. One of the things we see in this chapter is Hegel's inclination to a more literary way of stating his theses, a mode to which he rarely returns in his later writings. It's his way, crucial to his system, of arguing for the ineradicability of nondiscursive modes of thought, even if discursive thought (philosophy) will end up having absolute priority over them.

¶673. More summing up: how we got from consciousness to self-consciousness to *Geist*. We immediately see one of Hegel's key theses repeated here. Already in "consciousness," we are driven to the thought of the supersensible, and the supersensible is (obviously) only available to thinking subjects. This is a key thesis of Hegel's idealism. He's often been thought to be saying that everything is somehow mental or spiritual. The rocks, planets, stars, trees, you and me, are all emanations or predicates (or something) of a large, enveloping cosmic being

Hegel's Phenomenology of Spirit. Terry Pinkard, Oxford University Press. © Oxford University Press 2023.
DOI: 10.1093/oso/9780197663127.003.0014

(*Geist*, God, whatever). His point is rather that in consciousness, we get the idea of infinity (in which one more can always be added or subtracted). You can't touch, taste, or see infinity, but you can think it. Aristotle said that infinity was that which cannot be traversed, but that "cannot" only appears to a kind of reflective thought, not to an intuition. So when in "Force and the Understanding," the concept of infinity is introduced and said to be "self-consciousness" itself, Hegel seems to be saying: individual objects, even the whole of nature, exist without thought, but we have the idea of infinity only because we are self-conscious thinking beings. We make the move from Consciousness to Self-Consciousness not by changing the topic, waving our hands, or looking for presuppositions. The chapter on consciousness finds itself confronting the problem of infinity and, in doing so, does not so much introduce the concept of self-consciousness as find that the topic has already been introduced. In self-consciousness, we have not merely purposes but purposes *as* purposes, not merely truths but truths *as* truths. We thus have reasons *as* reasons, and with that the thought of infinity begins as the chain or reasons, truths, and so forth begin spreading out into, well, infinity. (Remember that passage: *"As infinity is finally an object for consciousness, and consciousness is aware of it as what it is, consciousness is thus self-consciousness"* [¶163].)

This is why he says that at first the absolute essence is at first a supersensible devoid of self. We are just "aware" of the thought that the absolute has no end—is *unendlich*. The unhappy consciousness has only an otherworldly beyond—infinity as always just out of our reach. Likewise, "reason" in its immediate existence has no religion in its shapes, even if "reason" leads us to infinity. ("The understanding" is happy enough with finitude.)

¶674. In the ethical world (that of *Sittlichkeit*, the Greek world, Antigone), we have the concept of the absolute as a "fate" that has no self. Antigone, Oedipus, Agamemnon, Orestes, all suffer a fate that seems unintelligible. Eventually the Greek gods themselves seem to be subject to the same kind of fate. It's "the night devoid of consciousness," the "I don't know what" guiding all things. However, the fate, Hegel has told us, is really just the logic of this shape of life developing itself in which individuality is claiming a place for itself, with all of this turning out to be incompatible with Greek *Sittlichkeit* as it existed.

The species-being (*Geist*), self-conscious life, thought it flourished in Greek life in the polis, but it turned out to be unbearable. It turned out that what we thought we really were is not what we really were. We were really something else, and as things worked out, that turned out to be Romans.

¶675. More summing up: faith as emotionalist religion develops its content in thought, but without working it out conceptually, and finds itself caught in the "religion within the limits of pure reason alone" of the Enlightenment. Enlightenment at least is satisfactory for consciousness in its this-worldly aspect. Rationalist Enlightenment sees the infinite as simply an intellectual conundrum, not something to make a big deal about in any religious way.

¶676. Not finished with summing up: in the religion of morality ("natural religion" as it was called in the Enlightenment), the content is positive, but still otherworldly (as atemporal moral truth or as a postulate of the harmony of morality and nature).

¶677. Still summing up: all prior shapes of spirit are spirit in its consciousness (a claim which is difficult to make out, given both the table of contents and Hegel's own views on self-consciousness) confronting its world. In religion, spirit is self-consciousness, transparent to itself. It seems that Hegel means that up until now (where we are considering religion), *Geist* kept finding that it wasn't what it thought it was (or, rather, its thoughts about what it really was kept falling apart). In religion, it takes itself to be what it is, self-consciousness. Now it finds its self-consciousness *as* self-consciousness falling apart.

¶678. From one point of view, religion appears as just one more set of activities and pursuits in the world—the kind of thing studied in the sociology or psychology of religion. In its incomplete form, it is an actuality that doesn't reach the point it is supposed to reach in terms of its concept, that of spirit fully conscious of itself. Instead, it comprehends itself representationally and thus sees itself as one more finite activity among other finite activities (hunting, fishing, critiquing), instead of understanding its special role in the comprehension of the absolute.

¶679. Hegel gives us a methodological statement. The moments of *Geist* (consciousness, self-consciousness, etc.) shouldn't be *represented* in time. Only the whole of *Geist* is in time. So we shouldn't be tempted to say that force and the understanding come before self-consciousness, so the ancient Persians were conscious of forces but only the later Greeks were self-conscious. Nor should we think that because wealth versus state power has an earlier place in the book, we should think that wealth and state power precede religion in history. *Geist* realizes itself in singular individuality (in actuality) only with each of these moments as its middle term. Hegel says that in religion's relation to these moments (which he reiterates are the chapter titles: "*consciousness, self-consciousness, reason,* and *spirit*"), religion "is their *simple* totality, or their absolute self." Religion, as the self-conscious comprehension of what it means to be *Geist,* is the totality, the whole in which the various contending moments of each of these spheres is to be united.

This is part of the thought that we can characterize *Geist* as a species of self-conscious life; then we realize we must characterize what conscious life is, what self-consciousness is; then, after we've understood that *Geist* is essentially a moving target in the way it changes its concept of itself, we have a fuller accounting of what it would be for *Geist* to be what it really is.

¶680. However, "religion" follows the same trajectory as other phases of this phenomenology: we look to the *appearances* of *Geist* (in this case, *Geist* in religion) at first to see how they disclose the hidden *essence,* only to find that there is no hidden essence in the sense of something lying "beyond" appearance. Thus, Hegel says that religion must move from immediacy to the knowledge of what it is in itself, that is, to where the trajectory of its concept is leading it in order for it to reach the point where its shape (in appearance, *Erscheinung,* the phenomenal, experienced world) is the same as its essence, and then it "intuits itself" as it is. (It will "intuit" it since it operates in terms of *Vorstellungen,* representations, not fully articulated conceptual comprehensions of the absolute, which only find their home in philosophy.)

¶681. Since Hegel is especially concerned with this phenomenology being understood to be a "science" (a *Wissenschaft*), he tells us why the arrangement of the moments of consciousness, self-consciousness, etc. have to appear now in a different order. (In other words, it's not an idiosyncratic rearrangement for, say, purposes of narrating but something required by the theory itself.) In the other shapes of spirit treated thus far, each moment (such as wealth and state power or the moral world-view) was a whole unto itself, and its own moments took on a depth of their own and were held in a unity by *Geist* taking the shape it took. That unity of *Geist* formed the social substance of all the various moments within that shape. Now, however, the substance that was spiritual unity is itself the topic under discussion, and we are to examine how it develops. That in turn asks what the substance is in itself—what is the "concept" of this substance, and what is its conceptual trajectory? All of the various aspects that were studied in the chapter on spirit are all now to be understood as elements along the way of the development of substance, of what basically holds self-conscious life together. They are all distinct, but (Hegel uses a strained metaphor here) they are united in a single coil (a *Bund*, a bundle). Hegel adds as a reminder that "what is solely at issue in spirit's actuality per se has to do . . . in which shape it knows its essence." Spirit is one, but it takes very different shapes.

¶682. However basic religion is supposed to be, it still appears first of all only in its concept but without that concept having fully realized itself. *Geist* first appears to itself as just one more fact in the world (as "being"), but as its concept of itself is put into practice and necessarily begins to shift around under the pressure from its own self-conceptions, it comes to see that idea of self-conscious life in terms of being one fact among many as more and more problematic. It comes to comprehend itself more and more as a problem and as incomplete, as not yet in reality what it really is.

¶683. We get a kind of preview of what is to come. The first actuality of religion will be that of natural religion, then art-religion, and then finally revealed religion, at which point spirit grasps the concept of itself as "we" (the readers informed by our wise guide) have grasped it, and its shape is spirit itself. At that point, it *almost* knows itself as what it really is, but only almost. It will take "absolute knowing" to fully arrive at that point.

A. Natural Religion

¶684. *Geist*, in knowing itself, is being-for-itself: it demarcates itself as an individual, a distinguishable shape of self-conscious life in terms of how it intuitively places itself in relation to the infinite. Hegel's basic thesis here is that all religions are aspects of religion per se, but they are all still different from each other. They are to be shown as in a progression from less complete to more complete. The completed forms, moreover, are higher (more "noble") and cannot be subsumed under the less complete ones. Religion also has a progressive self-development.

a. The Luminous Essence

¶685. The first form of religion is something like that of ancient Persian Zoroastrianism. The absolute, the infinite, is represented as "light." The idea is that, roughly, as self-conscious lives, we get an intuitive grasp of infinity, which we then seek to represent as an object. Light is an obvious stand-in. Hegel speaks of *Geist*'s creative secret, how this comes out of the "nighttime" of *Geist* as it seeks to express its grasp of infinity. The light lights up everything but itself.

¶686. This is a form of consciousness, awareness of an object, not yet self-consciousness *as* self-consciousness. This object looks like the appropriate representation of the infinity of self-consciousness (truths as truths, purposes as purposes, all spreading out into infinity) since, as shapeless, it "represents" the shapelessness of pure self-relating *Geist* itself. It is what it is in contrast with darkness (its "negative"). Since it is shapeless and therefore empty, its emptiness is to be filled somewhat arbitrarily by artifacts of imagination.

¶687. As it follows the trajectory of its concept, this becomes the "One" (i.e., pantheism). Subjectivity, as really grasping itself as grasping the infinite, can't really develop out of this (so Hegel thinks). The hopelessly abstract One implies nothing else, and thus its representation is arbitrarily ornamented with various natural forces.

¶688. *Geist* as self-consciousness must develop itself out of this. (It carries its "negativity" with itself.) As people engage in the practice of religiously celebrating the luminous essence ("Light") as the absolute, they are led to reflect on their own place in the greater order of things. Having done that, *Geist* moves on.

b. Plants and Animals

¶689. The religion of light leads to breakoffs from itself, each imaginatively constructing itself around some version of pantheism, of the "One." After all, "the infinite" includes everything. However, the peaceful unity of the "flower religion" of the One quickly yields up distinct religions at war with each other. Each religion takes its own god to be the infinite God, but what we have is simply a set of finite gods (mine, yours) pictured as in conflict with each other. From peaceful flower religions, we thus move to animal religions, with their practices of bloody sacrifice, and then to warring animal religions, where the people at war keep themselves at an animal level.

¶690. However, as they seek to determine their own religions negatively vis-à-vis other religions (as not-them), they also produce people who craft the representations of their object into images, carvings, and so forth.

c. The Artisan

¶691. Hegel here invokes a distinction made by Johann Joachim Winckelmann between artists and artisans, an immensely important and influential view in the late eighteenth and early nineteenth centuries. Artisans build things, but they express no deep truth. They're just good at what they do. The artisan, he says, is instinctive, like a bee building cells. It's the distinction between the crafts and the arts, where only the latter is taken to make a truth claim.

¶692. Artisanal work comes closer to self-consciousness, and self-consciousness starts to see itself in the work. When it does, at that point, the artisan gives way to the artist. The artisan can craft an excellent image of, for example, a duck-god. But the artist is seeking a way to portray the truth of the religion in a beautiful manner.

¶693. The artisan, the craftsman, transforms his material (as being-in-itself, as something with a meaning and thus by implication a trajectory to follow) and makes it into something to which he relates (as being-for-itself). That makes the in-itself objective. You can see it, feel it, hear it, taste it. This is also now working with the distinction of soul and body. What does the soul look like? Sound like?—as if soul and body were two different things (the conclusion to which "the understanding" in "representational thought" is usually driven). But the artisan and the work he creates are still attempting to shape for the senses what is understood to be a hidden essence. He is attempting to give sensuous shape to something invisible.

¶694. In doing so, the artisan comes to see the work as expressing a kind of self-knowledge, and he implicitly grasps himself as the essence existing-for-itself. He takes the organic plant form, transforms it into ornament, thereby bringing the organic forms nearer to universal forms of thought, and with that, he begins to make the straight line into curvature (the root of free architecture). He's on the way to becoming an artist. (Art originates in the crafts, but goes beyond them.)

¶695. After transforming plant life, the artisanal laborer turns to animal life and blends it with the shape of human life. It thereby becomes, as Hegel puts it, a hieroglyph of thought itself. Such are the forms of Egyptian statuary, but they still lack a self-articulation as having an inner meaning; they lack language, the existence of spirit. In a reference to the Memnon Collosi of Thebes, Hegel says the work needs the rays of the sun to have a sound. As reported by Herodotus, the Memnon Collosi of Thebes were huge ruins of Egyptian statues that would give off a kind of singing sound when the sun's rays hit them in the morning. As it turned out, this was due to imperfections in the statues (fissures apparently caused by an earlier earthquake). Perhaps not unsurprisingly, when the ancients "repaired" them, they also ceased to sing.

¶696. The other shape appears, announces it has an inner, but the inner is still formless. (Hegel seems to be thinking of early Egyptian temples without windows. Or he could be thinking of the mummies' sarcophagi.)

¶697. The statuary column tries to present the unity of inner and outer in a way that can be seen. It thus attempts a presentation of *Geist* as the unity of inwardness (the self-relation that is self-consciousness) and existence. It's a blending of shapes, a deeper but scarcely comprehensible wisdom. This (for Hegel in 1807) is still one step away from being art.

¶698. The artisan in making a work that has a self-articulating inner ceases to work instinctually. He now has to ask himself, more or less, What am I trying to say?—not just, How do I go about crafting this imposing piece? In this estranged consciousness, spirit encounters spirit. It embodies a self-reflective turn: self-consciousness *as* self-consciousness. The outer takes an inward turn, the inner expresses itself in a thought that gives birth to itself. With that, the artisan becomes an *artist*. (In his later lectures on aesthetics in Heidelberg in 1818 and in Berlin in the 1820s, Hegel replaced this with his theory of the "symbol." Discussion of that would take us far away from this commentary.)

B. The Art-Religion

¶699. The shape attained is the form of self-conscious activity. The artisan has moved on from being a craftsman and has become a spiritual laborer, which means he's now an artist, or almost one. *Geist* is now concerned to see itself, hear itself, etc. It has a new task: How do we portray, put on view, what it is to be a self-conscious life? In 1807, Hegel thought that question first appeared with the so-called Greek miracle. The art-religion will be something different from nature-religion. In the latter, we look to forms in nature, or specific natural things (plants or animals) to get, as it were, a "symbol" of the absolute or the infinite (as self-consciousness). In art-religion, it will be assumed that crafting (as artisanal) a beautiful work will be the key to comprehending what it is to be a self-conscious life (which makes it a matter of art). It's not that art will be religion (or its substitute). It's that true religion, at this stage, will also be art, and art that is not religious (i.e., involving the absolute) is simply not art but remains only craft. This will be Hegel's substantive view of art, which he will greatly refine in his later career in Berlin: art is the practice of producing works that will capture, in sensuous form, reflection on what it is to be a self-conscious life (*Geist*), and in its most exemplary cases, in doing so, it manifests an aesthetic, "spiritual" beauty and not just natural beauty. Natural beauty, while deeply pleasing, means nothing, whereas aesthetic beauty means something about the deeper nature of *Geist*.

¶700. In this phenomenology, there is a logical transition from artisan to artist that signals the move from a craftsman-like comprehension of things to a more nearly conceptual (although not yet fully conceptual) reflection on what it is to be a "spiritual" (*geistig*) being. For Hegel, this also happens to be embodied in the history of Egypt and Greece. Hegel asks: Which actual spirit realizes the logic of this move? (In this context, that is only an infinitesimal distance from a rhetorical question.) The religion of art is that of the Greek, the "ethical" *Geist*, the "true *Geist*" of the *Phenomenology*. The shape of *Geist* is the essence for the individuals, but it is their own essence and work. The ethos of the community is the substance of each individual, and each knows it as his will and deed. There's thus no essential alienation in agency.

¶701. The actuality of ethical substance in Greek life rests on the immediate unity between the mores, ethos, and individual agents. (E.g., Antigone knows immediately that she must perform the rites on her brother, and she knows immediately that she must obey Creon.) Each knows her station in life as committing her to certain things. The basic terms of this moral ethos are "motionless": they are, as it were, set in stone, not subject to revision, and they are the object of a kind of deep-seated trust in their motionless nature. This in turn rests on the idea that self-consciousness is not yet itself comprehended *as* self-consciousness. This is a *Geist* that is certain of itself, but it cannot last. Such self-consciousness as it appears in ethical life, in the moral ethos, undermines the immediacy of that ethical life.

¶702. "Absolute art" appears in this shape. This is art that presents the absolute without residue and without any necessary link to instrumental use. The work of art (or the inner purpose of producing art) is such that the sensuous beauty of the piece fully discloses the form of the world—as that form is taken to be by this shape of self-conscious life. Art and metaphysics, as it were, coincide. The inherent trajectory of art appearing as absolute art is to fully *show* the absolute without requiring any further conceptual specification. There's nothing for metaphysics (the concept) to say that the artist hasn't or couldn't say. After the collapse of ethical life, *Geist* is said to "go beyond art," but will have its concept for its shape so that concept and artwork know each other as one and the same, in the sense that they both have the same purpose. It will just turn out that art will never again be able to do what it knows its own inner purpose is to do: to present the absolute truth about what it is to be a self-conscious life. Art will end up standing in a lower priority than philosophy for that task although it will not be any less important in fulfilling its own role in the whole, which is self-conscious life reflecting on what it is to be self-conscious life.

¶703. The concept, the activity by which spirit engenders itself as object, is the night in which substance was betrayed and made itself into subject. (This is a little florid.) *Geist* is resurrected, he says, as a shape freed from nature. Although the language clearly alludes to the Christian story of the betrayal of Jesus, Hegel's point here is how the polytheism of the Greeks, perfectly expressed in their art, will ultimately give way to the monotheistic-Trinitarian Christian life, in which the absolute truth of *Geist* (what its trajectory of development really is, its "in itself") cannot be fully presented in a beautiful work. The Christian God cannot be fully grasped aesthetically. The truth even of a beautiful painting of Christ cannot express what needs to be expressed. The picture of this human (Jesus) can only be grasped by rational theology, which in its own development finds its fulfillment in philosophy. Thus, if in pre-Greek life self-consciousness was more or less absorbed in substance, and in post-Greek life it makes its break from substance, then there will forever be a gap between moral ethos and what one immediately ought to do or is required to do. In his later Berlin lectures in the 1820s on the philosophy of history, Hegel said that the passage from ancient Egypt and Persia to ancient Greece was the point where spirit took leave of nature.

¶704. As Greek life (ethical *Geist*) falls apart because of its own internal stresses, *Geist* has to wrestle with shapeless existence, turns its pathos into its own existence, and the unity emerges as a "work," an *Oeuvre*, universal spirit individualized and represented. Or: what *Geist* seeks is a personalized way of understanding the divine, and into this logical space Christianity enters. Hegel now turns to the development of the religion of art to make this case.

a. The Abstract Work of Art

¶705. The first work of art is immediate, abstract, singular—for example, statues of gods. Self-consciousness is now more fully distinguishing itself from itself, thereby producing a possible fissure within itself between its full absorption in its substance and its possible alienation from its substance. This happens within the early religious cults of the ancient Greeks as oriented around certain distinct gods. Here the trajectory of self-conscious life moves in the direction of sublating this difference from itself that it now finds within itself, and it engenders a work of art that brings itself *as* self-conscious into view. Men and gods start to see themselves as coordinated elements of a cosmic order, and the gods start to take a shape that is recognizable—not just as the shapeless infinite, but as individual gods who have an (almost) human shape.

¶706. This new, aesthetic religion differs from the other forms of nature-religion in the following way. The nature-religions culminated in various intriguing shapes (Egyptian crystals, pyramids, etc.), but that was because *Geist* itself was very unclear about what it was trying to say as it tried to make sense of itself. These religions end up in something like "sublimity" in which the absolute is grand but very mysterious. That kind of art simply ended there, with nowhere else to go from there.

¶707. In the conceptual series of religious experiences and practices (which in this case, so Hegel thinks, is also fairly close to its historical origin), we at first have gods in the shape of animals, but the god is the hidden and unrepresentable essence behind or underneath the animal shape. But there is a core element of conceptuality at work there: the essence of the god is the unity of the universal existence of nature and of self-conscious spirit, and at first the tensions between the two—before spirit has bid nature adieu—are submerged into a unity. As this concept develops, the gods take on a natural shape, and in art-religion, that shape becomes *human*. We have Apollo, Zeus, Athena, Aphrodite, et al. As these gods become human, their "nature aspect" is "transfigured" by thought. The conceptual development of the idea of the gods in art-religion is taken up by the poets—not by philosophers offering a different conceptual account—who tell a story about how these new human-gods emerged from the old nature-gods. This has its place in Greek mythology as the ancient gods, the Titans, are said to be replaced with the clear ethical spirits of a self-conscious people (the Olympians). Nonetheless, these singular humanlike gods are also restricted to a singular people, and only in that relation are they actual, really at work in the lives of those for whom they are the gods.

¶708. In their concept of themselves, a people with those gods see themselves as motionless. They have the identity of "a people" immune to revision. In distinction from this, there is the motion and unrest of all that goes on in the lives of this "people." Hegel says that the artist (of epic poems like the *Iliad*) gives himself no actuality as an individual, but instead empties himself and rises to pure abstraction—for example, the "author" of the *Iliad*, whom we call "Homer." Unlike the craftsman, the artist is not basking in his own serene craft. The artist is saying: behold the truth. The work and the artist—otherwise so closely conceptually connected—are now separated.

¶709. The artist can't see the work as the equal to himself. He has presented something higher than his own finite existence. Of course, he enjoys the admiration of the multitude for his craftsmanship, but the key element in his art is, oddly, his second-person address to his community: you! This is what the god looks like—behold!

¶710. The most original works of art are thus things like statues. But once this purpose is underway, it calls for its own refinement. The statue is not a representation of the god. In the religious ceremony, in the right setting, in seeing the statue one beholds the god himself (or herself, as with Athena). The god is not "hidden" and shapeless behind the statue, the god *appears* in the statue. But the gods are not just "things," stone works. They must also have another way of appearing to us. The higher element is language, which gives us the work of art as ensouled in itself. It has pure activity in its existence, since it requires a reading or a reciting. You can't just behold it as you can with the statue. You must read or listen to the hymns—the poems celebrating a specific god—which themselves are beautiful, sensuous manifestations of pure thought (i.e., thought of the absolute, not just thought of this or that), and this kind of thinking is an act of devotion, the spiritual stream in which each is aware of the same activity. It is communicative religion, the gods addressing us, our listening to the address, and our addressing each other. This gives the community a deeper connection to itself: in this form of its pure inwardness, *Geist* has its pure unity, its being for others, and the being-for-itself of the individuals. *Geist* shows itself in the practices, and the practices are exhibitions and manifestations of that *Geist*. The hymns are not just poems in our more modern, secularized sense—they are aesthetic religious activities. Moreover, given the aesthetic nature of the religion, they can't be replaced by more nonaesthetic statements about them. You can't substitute a prosaic description of Athena for the hymn. (There will be no catechism classes for the Greeks.) You get everything you need to comprehend the god from the hymn (or the work of art in general).

¶711. There is another language, Hegel says, of the god: the oracle. The oracle originally "speaks" in the sense that the "essence of nature" speaks, that is, speaks in a way that at this stage of religious life seems to make sense. The infinite is paradoxical, so it either speaks in paradoxes or speaks in a way that's not really speaking. This universal spirit is an individual self, appears at first sublime, very deep, but as religious thought progresses, this kind of religious manifestation comes to seem much less important or even meaningful at all.

¶712. To get beyond the idea of the absolute as that which can be shown but not said (in "normal" language), the artist has to get out of his immersion in the pure pathos of substance—in the great current of feeling that he has as a member of this "people"—and become its master (craftsman). Learning to speak more intelligibly, the artist knows that what exists "in itself" as the universal truth, the unwritten law of the gods—which, as Sophocles has Antigone say, are eternal and nobody knows from whence they came—and the god's own language is that of the oracle who knows the god's concerns. These universal truths vindicate *wissende Denken*, "knowingly thinking." Hegel even mentions Socrates's invocation of his own daemon to explain how he knows certain things. Given the indeterminacy of what the oracle "says," to know what to do is up to contingent matters (flights of birds in the sky, the rolling of dice, and so on). Those who consult their own intelligence are still just relying on contingent matters, so the individual who consults oracles is simply expressing the ethical disposition of indifference toward the contingent. Or you can move even higher: you can make your deliberation itself into your oracle.

¶713. The art whose medium is language is the most adequate art for showing what self-conscious life truly is. Language—the existence of spirit—is always in motion, changing, drawing new conclusions, and finding new ways to manifest spirit. This contrasts with the statuary column, which is motionless, at rest. However, the statue remains, while language is disappearing, like time itself. The bard sings the poem, and at the end, there is nothing thinglike left over.

¶714. The motionless statuary column and the speech about the god come together in a unity that is the practice of the "cult." The god "appears" to the members of the cult, and you must be in the cult to have the god appear. The god, as it were, descends to you, and as you behold it, the god comes into self-conscious actuality, that is, comes to be at work in the community's activities and inwardness.

¶715. In the development of the concept of the hymnal song, the concept of the cult is already there in that trajectory. The music and the words are the expression of the temporality of subjectivity itself. "This hymnal devotion is the immediate and pure satisfaction of the self through itself and within itself": Hegel's metaphors in this paragraph should be taken in this light. In the hymn, one experiences the structured flow of subjectivity itself but apart from all specific content. It is easy to see this as an experience of purification (which comes with the wordless power of music).

¶716. The (Greek) cult at first only imagines, or "represents" to itself in secret, this fulfillment. (The very nature of the cult is its secret nature, into which one must be initiated.) But merely represented fulfillment isn't real fulfillment. It becomes real in elevating the self into *pure* self-consciousness. Self-consciousness is now on the way to asking itself more explicitly what it means to be self-conscious. What is the object of this pure self-consciousness? Whatever it is, it must be the essence "behind" or "beyond" appearance which is somehow merging itself with the self-consciousness of the individual of the appearing world.

¶717. The essence behind appearance is nature, but nature isn't really the full essence. This requires transformation, sublation. The action of the cult does this. It is a *geistige* (minded, spiritual) movement. "Essence" is here an abstraction as that which is beyond or behind nature but which becomes actual (at work) only in nature and yet also serves to explain nature. For pure consciousness, the essence is that for which it sacrifices its sense of its own inessentiality. Like devotion, the cult engages in actions that transform the ordinary into the spiritual. The cult is on the way to becoming theatrical action put on by actors portraying characters.

¶718. Hegel gives a kind of metaphysically tinged interpretation of the rituals of Greek blood sacrifice. An animal is sacrificed: it is ritually killed, then roasted. The gods demand it. But one of the most commented-on sections of this ritual (commented on by the Greeks themselves, for example, by Herodotus) is that the gods only get the inedible parts (the bones and some fat, with wine also poured over the bones, which leads to lots of smoke rising), whereas the edible parts are served up in a communal meal. So what exactly has been *sacrificed* to the god? (The Greeks even had a mythical story they told about how this odd reversal came about.) Hegel gives it a decidedly pre-Christian interpretation. For this to make sense as a genuine religious practice, it must be that they take the animal to somehow embody the god (the essence), so that they are sacrificing the god himself, who must in itself have already sacrificed itself for the purpose of that action. The god also makes itself the fruit of the earth (i.e., wine).

¶719. The significance of the cult is its communal self-consciousness, and it gives a second-person aspect to the "we." What the "sacrifices" of the cult show us is that the self-relinquishing of the cult (giving oneself over to the mystical vision of oneness in devotion) is also a rather down-to-earth pragmatism (there's no sense in just burning up the animal; let's all eat it ourselves in a communal meal). The "people" of the cult are celebrating themselves and their communal self-consciousness as much as they are celebrating the god. Indeed, there is a unity to the two. Out of the otherworldliness of their predecessors, the Greek cults are thereby creating a more human form of religion and therefore implicitly laying the ground for a metaphysics of the form of the world in which self-conscious life has its proper place. The people and the gods exist in a form of reciprocity rather than that of ruler and ruled.

b. The Living Work of Art

¶720. Art-religion is at work in *Sittlichkeit*, the moral ethos of the polis, and thus the people know the polis as their own creation. They don't need to tell a full creation myth about some god founding it. Although they do tell stories about mythical heroes founding it, still in those stories, the "essence" and the people are still one with each other. It is people (albeit mythical) doing the founding. This sets up the worm in the apple in Greek *Sittlichkeit*, namely, the concept of individuality having a status that cannot be completely absorbed into social life or religious practice.

¶721. What this means is that rather than the abstract representation of the absolute as, say, light, there begins to be a more nuanced and determinate and differentiated representation of the absolute. This puts into motion a trajectory where the gods may be approached without the cult. Hegel says that, satisfied, self-consciousness leaves the cult, and the god takes up residence in self-consciousness. Nature thus acquires the possibility of a higher existence through the rituals of sacrificing to the god and sharing the meal. As silently powerful substance, nature purifies itself into the feminine principle of nurturance and the male principle of self-impelling force. (This is Hegel's take on a very Greek idea. The difference between the sexes is taken to have a cosmic significance, and it is indicative of the most powerful forces governing the cosmos.)

¶722. We begin to see the mystical for what it is (the mystical, the mysterious as the name the Greeks gave to the cults): it's not really a secret but is the self knowing itself to be at one with the essence, and the essence as thus revealed. The absolute is the self thinking of what it is to be a self. But it's not clear *to itself* that is what it is doing.

¶723. The luminous essence of the sunrise is revealed, emptied of its abstract being, and surrenders itself to self-consciousness—a "mob of madly rapturous women, the unrestrained frenzy of nature in a self-conscious shape." This seems to be a reference to Euripides's *The Bacchae* and perhaps also to Aristophanes's *The Women Celebrating the Thesmophoria* (which is also about the *Bacchae*). The Thesmophoria was a cult around planting-time made up of adult women, and there is some evidence that Greek men luridly fantasized about how it involved the women getting really out of hand when they were off on their own and away from male authority. Thus, Aristophanes's comedy about it.

¶724. What has been betrayed (revealed) to consciousness is only "absolute spirit," that is, self-conscious life thinking about what it means to be a self-conscious life. It seeks the essence behind the appearance to get at the truth of what self-conscious life means. At this stage, though, all it gets is the simple essence, the spirit of nature, not really *Geist* in itself. We do not yet have the higher gods. The mystery of bread and wine is not yet the mystery of flesh and blood. It's just one of nature's mysteries.

¶725. Greek life moves from the chaotic revel of the Dionysians to something more stable. (It has to do so, or so Hegel asserts.) Another cult must take center stage: the festival that man gives in his own honor. These are the sporting events which carried a kind of religious significance to the Greeks. The young men are seen as if they are somehow like, or are approximations to, the gods. Hegel also gives this a pre-Christian spin: this is on the way to seeing the gods (or god) as embodied in a human form, but it isn't there yet. The festival (the Olympic Games) only lays the ground for that revelation.

¶726. In Bacchanalian enthusiasm, the self is external to itself, or maybe the better translation would be "beside itself" (as when one says she is beside herself in joy). But in the Olympic games, the spiritual essence is the beautiful embodiment itself. Now, the inwardness of the Bacchanalian must be united with the clarity of the beautiful embodiment. How to do this? Language, as the unity of the inner and the outer, is the key. But it can't be the language of the oracle, nor that of the cultic hymn, nor the stammer itself of the Bacchanalian revel. It has to be a language with a universal content, which is not that of a single national spirit but of universal human existence. In bidding adieu to nature, *Geist* now relinquishes itself (an *Entäußerung*) into complete embodiment. The shapeless essence behind appearance (nature) is taking on the shape of appearance (and natural embodiment) itself.

c. The Spiritual Work of Art

¶727. The different spirits of different peoples unite into a pantheon. This yields a pure intuition of itself—not an empirical generalization but a kind of general, principled, unified "view" of itself that is not yet fully conceptually articulated—as universal humanity in a *Geist* that joins with others in a common undertaking. With that in mind, under the aegis of different gods, people unite into a common undertaking. (Agamemnon unites the various "peoples" of Greece in the voyage to Troy.) A single ethical life—that of "Greek" in general—is produced, but it is only "immediate," "intuited" and not yet articulated. The Greeks see themselves as "one" in a common project, and they also see themselves as "one" in a way analogous to that in which speakers of a language see themselves as a "we" who speak the language (and who know, without observation, how to form and understand intelligible sentences). The two—individuals, each an "I," in a common undertaking, a "we"—are clearly distinguishable, but at this stage have not yet been distinguished.

¶728. They combine under the command, but not sovereign rule, of one of them. (That is what enables it to be a common undertaking.) The return of the divine essence into self-consciousness contains the ground that forms the focal point for those divine forces. Everything seems to be one: the different tribes are becoming "Greeks," and the different gods themselves are seen as uniting to assist them.

¶729. This way of taking things creates a work of art that tells a story about men, women, and gods, such that at the end of the story, the unity of a people (the Greeks) has been created. This is the function of *epic*: a synthetic combination of self-consciousness and external existence. In the epic, a national identity is forged in opposition to, or exclusion of an other, where the "other" is only an abstract negation. For the Greeks, that "other" is Troy. What's their relation to Troy? There's no internal relation. It just happens to be the place to which Helen has been taken. The connection is thus "synthetic" (and not a priori). It is thus also a manifestation of "representational thinking," which tends to see elements as distinct and independent items instead of being related in terms of what they mean within a whole. Hegel says it portrays the universal content (what it means to be self-conscious life) as the completeness of the world and not yet the universality of (conceptual) thought. It's the story of the "Greeks" and how they come to see themselves as the bearers of "universal humanity." This story about how the Greeks became Greeks and, to themselves, the bearer of the human project is itself, of course, made up whatever its contested basis in history might be. It's a story. The bard (Homer—"Sing in me, muse") is the individual who creates this world. What is his pathos, the current of feeling that explains his whole character? It isn't nature, Hegel says (nor is it a hidden essence), but Mnemosyne (the goddess of memory), and thus his pathos is the memory of an earlier immediate essence. It has the elements of a syllogism: the universality (of the gods), the singularity (of the bard), mediated by the particularity (of the people in its heroes, who are merely represented, imagined). And why heroes? They're needed to stop the regress of authority, of that which must be recognized. So the series has to begin with something or someone who just *has* authority, and that's either a god or a mythical hero (sometimes of partially divine parentage).

¶730. Hegel says: what came about in itself in the cult, the trajectory that put on the agenda a new relation between the divine and the human, is now in the epic put on display. The content is the action of essence conscious of itself, which as self-conscious disturbs the substance and divides its simplicity. The action is taken by the "people," the Greeks, as a subject. (The Greeks attack Troy.) Of course, it is a collective action that is concretely carried out by individual people (and heroes). Hegel even uses an odd word to describe this collective action: he says it is *selbstisch*, self-y, self-ishy, or maybe self-like (but not merely selfish). To put it differently, it's an apperceptive "we." It is also a "universal" action in the sense that it has a singular meaning that is not just what all the individual Greeks happen to think they are doing. The "we meaning" comes from what the gods have in mind by getting people to perform this action. Hegel points out a real conceptual difficulty here. The gods direct everything, but it is people who act—the gods are not the puppeteers pulling their strings, but they are doing what they need to do to provoke the human actors into performing the actions they want from them. What the gods want to see accomplished can only come about through the people, so they are powerless without a people. However, it sometimes looks as if it's the same action being performed by gods and people.

¶731. Besides their implicitly contradictory relation to nature, these gods also face a conceptual issue: they don't need to show off, but they do show off. They get into trouble with each other without there being any real reason to do so. It's as if they forget who they are: immutable, eternal, etc. They can't, for example, really threaten each other. Hegel says that this forces the next move: What governs the gods? One answer might be: nothing. The play of the gods is whatever equilibrium the cosmos just happens to have. But instead he answers that the pure force of the negative appears as their final power, against which they have no recourse. If they hover over people's actions with their own motives, then it looks like some kind of indeterminate concept-less void (i.e., fate) hovers over them. (Richard Wagner picks up this idea in his opera *Götterdämmerung*.)

¶732. To the Greek imagination, this looks like an indeterminate fate, but it is really a matter of conceptual necessity pushing toward monotheism. In the play of the gods, the world makes no sense. (This is becoming clear in *Antigone*.) In fact, the play of the gods is itself played around the middle term of the "syllogism," the hero who mourns the early death he sees before him. This is of course a reference to Achilles's famous lament that he could either have a long and ordinary life or a short one full of glory, and he chooses the latter.

¶733. This pushes the Greeks away from the cult and the epic to the higher language: tragedy. In epic, the two sides (Greece, Troy) are externally related. In tragedy, the antagonists are internally related, or have inherent antagonisms within themselves. In tragedy, the hero is the speaker, the actor on a stage. We no longer have a bard singing of past glories. Instead, we have people on stage who take on the personae of the heroes. In their own real personalities they give life, as it were, to the mythical heroes whom they present. We know they aren't the people they embody, but we put that aside. (Under the influence of German idealists, Coleridge called it the suspension of disbelief.) When the actors succeed, we see a "universal individuality" in their presence (e.g., John Gielgud playing Hamlet, Laurence Olivier playing Hamlet, Benedict Cumberbatch playing Hamlet, Andrew Scott playing Hamlet . . .). The actor, Hegel says, is essential to his mask (his role).

¶734. In tragedy, the common people find their representatives in the powerless chorus, who can only look on and comment. For Hegel, the chorus has a sense of the conceptual development of the plot and character and expresses the common person's reaction (horror, satisfaction, etc.) at where things are going and have gone. They express the fear that accompanies knowing the terrible fate awaiting the characters, and they express (sometimes) compassion for the afflicted. They also acquiesce to the necessity involved. (Hegel is giving his own spin on what in his own day was becoming a widely accepted view of the role of the Greek chorus.)

¶735. There's the crowd watching this (in their suspension of disbelief) who see these powers or "universal essences" (which could also be rendered as "universal beings") represented in terms of actors on the stage. (Hegel speaks of "this spectatorial consciousness as the indifferent soil of representational thinking.") In the struggle of heroes against each other, self-conscious life sees reflectively how things are coming apart. Self-conscious life *as* self-conscious life appears at this point in such a phenomenology as the estrangement of the concept of self-conscious life itself. The threads holding together the common life—the "substance"—unravel, and it seems that the common life is itself ruled by two opposing powers. The common people, the spectators, now find themselves as actors in the play insofar as the chorus is giving voice to the common people, and we have a participatory theater.

¶736. In this form of religious reflection as art, self-conscious life is now reflecting more on itself and not just on straightforward objectives to be achieved (such as how to appease the gods). However, as pulled apart into two extremes, the unity of this form of life presents itself as the human law and the divine law. But insofar as this presents the substance as falling apart, the individuals in the audience begin to see themselves as falling apart. Individuals are pushed into thinking of themselves as merely superficial forms of the essence, which itself seems to be going its own way on its own trajectory.

¶737. The actor faces up to the object, the negative of the knowing subject. We get a quick overview of what the Oedipal play means. The gods tell Oedipus what will become of him, but they do it in such a way that he misinterprets the meaning. Thus, he knows in one sense what he is doing (what his action is) and where he is going, and in another sense, he does not know what he will have done. Oedipus will tell you: I'm marrying this very congenial woman. He does not know that the deed will be: you're marrying your mother. Oedipus's character, which is ethical essentiality, knows only one power of substance, but the other power is concealed from him. The Hegelian conception of action finds its expression here: there is what I am doing (with its three phases of purposiveness: my intention to do it, my act of doing it, my having done it), and there is the deed, what I have done. I can fail at this, and it need not be the case that my original inner mental intention was thwarted. I just failed, perhaps even without knowing that I failed. (That is different from failing because I was interrupted or changed my mind in the process, etc.)

¶738. The Hegelian distinction between my *action* as what I'm *doing* (marrying a woman in Thebes) and the *deed* (what my action turns out to be) is here characterized as the distinction between the action and "being" (action and deed). So the agent's self-certainty—the knowledge that this is what I'm doing—turns out to be in opposition to the ethical. Hegel says that the ethical (and not, rather, the ethical actor) learns that it has grasped only one power of the substance. Its law is only the law of its character. "The ethical" is the nominative for the entire practice and its associated principles, in the way that we might say that "the presidency" has shown us various ways to go wrong in politics. "The ethical has learned" is shorthand for "actors working in the practice have learned x, y, z, such that the practice itself has changed." But what this all reveals about the Greek conception of life (and thus its religion) is that there seems to be a fundamental opposition at work in it (an opposition between and among the gods). The lesser right of the netherworld enjoys equal status with the god who is revealed. The terrible consequences of this divine opposition get played out in our lives. Does that make sense? Or is the world such that we must accept fate and note that our world is simply unintelligible in that oppositions between divinities show up without any deeper rhyme or reason in our lives?

¶739. We have to see how representational thought (*Vorstellung*) pictures this. There's the substance of life (the normative order, practices, ethos) which splits into two parts (family and the public, women and men), and there's the distinction of knowing and not knowing, which sets itself up within each of us. This in turn is pictured as two distinct items: the revealed god and the hidden gods (the self-concealing Erinyes, the Furies, who come after Orestes as they do after anybody who has committed a grave injustice against the divine order). The shape of the substance as a separate represented entity, Zeus, is really the (conceptual) necessity of the relation of both to the other (but here as represented, *vorgestellt*). Representational thinking thus pictures three distinct essences: the revealed god, the lower deities of the Erinyes, and Zeus as holding them all together.

¶740. How does the tragic actor figure this out? By acting. The gods reveal a truth to him, he acts in light of it, and it turns out he's been subtly misled. In following one aspect of what the god revealed to him, the agent acts against the other element in the warning that he did not see, and he uncovers or unlocks the second part only in acting. Hegel then mentions some other figures from Greek tragedy along with figures that aren't Greek but are Shakespearean (witches in *Macbeth*, ghosts in *Hamlet*). Such is tragedy: the world is full of oppositions that bring down the best by virtue of what is best in them. In the Greek conception, the only absolution to this is Lethe, forgetfulness. Fate takes over, and the various spheres of divinity, Hegel says, return into the simplicity of Zeus as the chief god among them. But as we see, in this picture, even the chief god is not all powerful. Even he cannot completely steer things into a more rational order.

¶741. In fact, the way the Greeks tell the stories about this leads to an increasing disbelief in the individual gods themselves. This fate, or destiny, completes, he says, the depopulation of heaven. The gods are dead. The representation of the gods as humanlike with their own individual pathos begins to seem perfectly senseless. It looked like it had made sense, but in fact it didn't. At least at first, the death of the god(s) is brought about in tragedy. The philosophers of antiquity demanded the same thing, but their arguments seemed too detached until tragedy brought the senselessness closer to home. As the pantheon of gods disappears, the self-consciousness "represented" in tragedy seems in fact to know only one highest power, maybe Zeus, but whatever that higher power is, it is the universal now dwelling in concealment. What do the god(s) want from us? It's a mystery. The world makes little or no sense.

¶742. Hegel gives us another rundown on the relation between the spectator and the stage. At first, we spectators see ourselves in the chorus, and we see the actors really embodying a figure (Oedipus, Antigone, etc.). But as the death of the gods sinks in, the actors playing these roles come to seem less and less true because their characters seem less and less true. As Hegel puts it, the hero who appears before the spectators fragments into both his mask and the actor himself, and the union of the two seems to be something like a hypocrisy. The show starts to become, as we would now say, purely "theatrical" and, if so, phony.

¶743. Thus, the heroes (as self-consciousness itself) step out of their masks, show themselves to be the fate of the gods of the chorus, as well as that of the absolute powers themselves. They too join the chorus. The self-conscious break between actor and role, already there, is now a fully realized break. Formerly, we spectators watched a tragic play unfolding, and we were seeing something real (in the way that for a believer, the church, temple, or mosque rituals are not just playacting but moments with other participants in a divine ceremony, real). But now we say: My gosh, it's all just theater. We are all just the chorus.

¶744. With that, we arrive at *comedy*. The Greek word for comedy could be rendered as "revel in odes." When Hegel said in the Preface that the truth is the Bacchanalian revel, he may as well have been saying: comedy is the truth. Comedy is about failures that fail to matter, which in turn supposes that there really is something that does matter (the "substance"). As tragedy slides from the deeply religious Sophoclean to the more social-skeptical Euripidean mode, we, the audience, begin to wonder whether the fate of the gods displayed in the characters really is the fate of the gods. Maybe it's just bad luck? We now get Aristophanes and his comedies, in which sometimes he himself pauses the action, takes off his mask, tells the audience to vote for this play to win the award, and then puts the mask back on. (The chorus in *The Clouds* does that too. So do the birds in *The Birds*, which promise to poop on people's heads if they don't vote for the play.) Greek irony appears as the very theatricality of this makes itself clear. The actors in comedies are trying to take themselves seriously—"the irony of something that wants to be something for itself"—but it turns out that they are wrong about what really matters, and the whole thing is a matter for laughter, which reveals something more serious at stake.

¶745. The fact is, actual self-consciousness has turned out to be what was at work there, and this is what comedy treats. Individuality takes shape, the individual separates himself from the ethical order, and the result is comedic. The rise of the demos (the people) is also a topic, as the "people" can also seriously make decisions that are silly. With comedy, it may also look like things are falling apart.

¶746. Out of tragedy and comedy a new form emerges: rational thinking, trying to rationally put the pieces back together again. (This is going to become philosophy.) This is inherently dialectical, in that it takes certain oppositions to be ground-level (the oppositions of the gods, etc.) and tries to think them into a coherent unity. It thus arrives at complete abstractions—the beautiful and the good—which only turn out to be clouds of vapor (*Clouds*, a play by Aristophanes featuring Socrates as a Sophist running an academy called "The Thinkery"). These thoughts of the beautiful and the good are the consciousness of the disappearance of the absolute validity those more concrete maxims used to have. The comedy thus turns on itself: the comedian is also a comic figure for taking himself so seriously. The emerging philosophical thought takes the comedic play to be itself only an empty game, not worthy of the truth.

¶747. The art-religion completes itself in comedy. The individual self brought to the fore in comedy is itself the negative force by which the gods disappear. The real self of the actor coincides with the person he plays, and what takes on the form of essentiality is dissolved into the activities of self-consciousness. Life has its ups and downs, and it is best to inject laughter into the spectacle. This kind of comedy gives us a state of well-being which is not to be found outside of this comedy.

15

Revealed Religion

¶748. Hegel tells us what the nature is of the transition that has just been made, both conceptually and historically: in the art-religion, *Geist* leaves the form of substance and becomes the form of subject. We had been treating the essence of self-conscious life as something "behind" self-conscious life itself, as a substance of sorts to be represented as some kind of hidden thing. Now, we treat the "essence" as itself a kind of activity, indeed, the same kind of activity as subjectivity. But what kind? To start, Hegel gives us as an overview as a kind of "compare and contrast": the incarnation of the absolute begins in the statuary column, but the inner shape (that of the self) falls outside of the statue. We get no further, deeper insight into the "inner" life from the statuary column. In the cult, the inner shape and outer shape come together: the hymn (music and words) are the external shape of the cult, but they serve to bring the inner life into view and give it shape. (In music, the pure temporality of subjectivity becomes more determinate.) The carelessness and lightheartedness of the classical ideal leads to the idea that the self is the absolute essence. That leads to a first and provisional idea: behind all appearance, there is a "self" which is (somehow) bringing matters to light.

¶749. The proposition "The self is the absolute essence" belongs to actual, nonreligious spirit, and this blocks a move back to natural religion. Self-consciousness consciously relinquishes itself, but it is preserved in its self-emptying and remains the subject of this substance. That is, now that self-consciousness has itself *as* self-consciousness, it cannot return to a view where it is absorbed completely into the substance. It was the contradictions of that idea (of the self as a predicate of the substance) that pushed it onward to this point. What it has now is an uneasy tension between seeing substance as the product of self-conscious life, and seeing self-conscious life as a product of the

Hegel's Phenomenology of Spirit. Terry Pinkard, Oxford University Press. © Oxford University Press 2023.
DOI: 10.1093/oso/9780197663127.003.0015

substance. That tension sets up the view that they are equally essential, and neither is the pure product of the other.

¶750. The religion of art is that which fits the shape of *Sittlichkeit*, ethical life. That shape of spirit comes to an end in (Roman) legality, in which the self is abstracted out of its "thick" life within the democratic community and shifted instead into the status of a legal person in an empire. "Being a legal person" (or more abstractly, an "officeholder") is the "absolute essence" of self-conscious life in Roman life. In the empire that replaces the polis, the spirits of individual peoples are gathered into the pantheon of pure thought, of abstract universality, of powerless form. The gods of the pantheon are no longer at work and are merely represented powers. What that yields is the singular individual relating to himself (his being-for-itself). It is not that all customs, mores, and ethos have vanished. It's that the ground-level requirements are now set by what it takes to be a successful Roman, not what the older gods required. Roman life eclipses those mores. The individual becomes cut off from the unity of the community and, in Hegel's words, becomes the "spiritless self."

¶751. The self has set the content free—that is, has cut itself off from almost all essential content to itself—and thus the self is empty. It is the abstract "point" in the world, a mere point of view. It has gone from "thick" to "thin." This is the recognition of the self as an "officeholder," an empty abstraction. The self possesses only the thought of itself, which sets it on the trajectory to realizing itself only in stoicism, skepticism, and the unhappy consciousness.

¶752. The unhappy consciousness knows what this all amounts to and what the story behind it is, and it knows that this all counts as a complete loss. It itself is the loss that has become conscious of itself as a loss. At this point in this phenomenology we understand that the unhappy consciousness is simply the counterpart to the comic consciousness. (This is what is at work in the crying/laughing masks we see in the theater.) In comedy, we understand that the substance, the fabric holding the community together, has frayed or unraveled. The substance is somewhat like a worn-out fabric you can see through. The unhappy consciousness is thereby the tragic fate of the self-certainty that was supposed to exist in and for itself. That was "ethical life," in which you knew what you were doing in light of the "substance" that held everything together. But the division of the known/unknown, of the gods clashing with gods, etc. has eventually unraveled all that. The gods have died off, one by one. Now there's none left, even the abstraction of Zeus, and the feeling "God has died."

¶753. With that, we can no longer have Greek religion. It has been undone and replaced by the comic consciousness. (This is all the more curious since Aristophanes was in essence a cultural conservative in Greek terms.) The unhappy consciousness is the knowledge of this entire loss. The gods go silent, and the muse now longer has any force. Like his friend Hölderlin, Hegel felt that the collapse of the classical Greek world was a world-historical event of the highest importance and had to be rethought again and again. (In his lectures on the philosophy of history more than fifteen years later, he said that with the loss of this ancient religion, the world's heart was broken.) We, on the other hand, have to struggle if we are to grasp what the classical world meant for its participants. They aren't the fruit growing on the tree; they are the fruit broken off, and then comes an odd image, "in the way a young girl might present that fruit." Scholars debate what's meant there. It's likely a reference to the Hebraic myth that replaced the Greek myths of origin, that of the Garden of Eden. What we are left with is at best the *Erinnerung* (the inwardizing remembrance) of their alienated, cast-off spirit. What we still have is the spirit of the tragic fate that collects them all into one pantheon, that is, self-conscious spirit aware of itself as spirit but not yet putting its thoughts in order. This idea of self-conscious life *as* self-conscious life is still empty. It is also not quite actual, at least not yet.

¶754. At this point in the narration, we are still in antiquity in the Roman world, and Hegel notes that the conditions are all there for the move from thinking in terms of an essence hidden behind appearance to the conception of self-conscious life *as* self-conscious life. Hegel uses theological language here: *Geist* has been relinquishing itself, emptying itself, this has been the *Entäußerung* of *Geist*. All these previous forms of life, shapes of self-consciousness, are metaphorically standing around the birthplace of spirit becoming self-conscious. But metaphors aside, this is supposed to follow a kind of conceptual necessity. As self-conscious life becomes reflective about itself in tragedy and then in comedy (and afterward and because of that, in philosophy), it has come to see that what it previously took to fill out the contours of self-conscious life have evaporated. Reflection on them showed that they made no sense, even though for centuries we had thought they did. The resolution of these difficulties is, however, on the way by virtue of what the "in itself" of self-conscious life is, what the trajectory of that concept in its development is. The conditions are ripe for the trajectory to take a certain direction.

¶755. There are two sides of the same coin: "Substance" empties itself and becomes self-consciousness. We pass from full absorption in social life (a kind of thick "We") to a kind of personal self-distancing relation to the "We." On the other hand, self-consciousness empties itself and makes itself into thinghood, into the universal self, into the abstraction, "self-conscious life in general." In doing so, self-conscious life is now conscious of itself *as* self-conscious life. It has gone from *Geist* to more fully self-conscious *Geist*. Hegel says that if one wishes (in other words, metaphorically) one could use terms from natural life to describe this transition, and he is quite obviously bringing in Christian terms to describe it. It has an actual mother (the previous shapes of human history, especially the ancient Greek and Roman world) that has "given birth" to this new shape of life emerging (Christianity), but it only has a father existing-in-itself: the concept of *Geist* as what it really is, "in itself," is there, but it has not yet fully developed its concept.

¶756. There is a crucial difference between this new shape of self-conscious life and the Greek shape. Herodotus says that the poets and artists Homer and Hesiod, in effect, gave the Greeks their gods. (They transformed older deities into stories of the Greek gods.) But now (after Greek philosophy), such storytelling won't solve the problem. *Geist* needs a real solution. However thrilling the story, it was still just a story, a garment that doesn't really cover the nakedness (of the emptiness inside).

¶757. If the meaning of what is objective is not to be mere imagination, it must exist in itself, that is, have its source in the concept and emerge in its necessity. It isn't enough to say that something momentous happened in Bethlehem. What happened also has to make sense. It can't take the *form* of a new myth. If it is self-consciously seen as a myth, it won't have its force. There has therefore to be some kind of conceptual progression at work that can itself be discerned. This means, Hegel thinks, that the world-spirit, humanity as a whole, now taken abstractly as "self-conscious life on the planet Earth," has reached this knowledge of itself. (To reach this, Hegel has to run through all his machinery about immediacy, in-itself, unity, concept, etc. By now this shouldn't be as murky as it was when we first started the book.)

¶758. Absolute spirit—spirit concerned only with what it is to be spirit—has given itself the shape of self-consciousness in itself—this is where its trajectory has taken it—and that means that the "faith of the world" is now that *Geist* "exists there"—one of many places where Hegel plays on *Dasein* as existence, here literally *da ist* in the German— as an actual person. He's not imaginary, as a Greek god is. This actual person embodies the essence for which religious thought has been seeking. How does he embody it? How is he different from, say, a Greek god taking on human shape as, say, a disguise?

¶759. The Incarnation of the divine essence is the simple content of absolute religion—religion that is completely oriented to the purely spiritual question: What is it to be spirit? In absolute religion, the essence is not something hidden behind appearance or "beyond" in some otherworldly sphere. The essence is *Geist* itself in taking its self-consciousness *as* self-conscious. We are thus *almost* at the end of this "phenomenology" as the examination of how self-conscious life makes its appearance in the world as developmental over time, that is, in history. *Geist* is the activity, the *energeia* of maintaining its self-equality (its being identical with its concept without losing itself in its relation to what is other to it) throughout its various manifestations. Hegel says that "religion is the essence's consciousness of itself as being *Geist*, for *Geist* is knowing itself in its self-relinquishing." So if the divine is the "essence," and the essence is the logic contained in (the concept of) self-consciousness, then *the divine essence is for that reason revealed.* Prior to this stage in the phenomenology, it seemed as if the "essence," the very form of the world, was something "secret." But the idea that we might be conscious not merely of the objects in the world as we represent them but also conscious of the secret form of the world led to nonsense. One can deal with that nonsense by adopting Kantian transcendental idealism, or eschewing that kind of talk altogether and resigning oneself to its impossibility, or by constructing a dialectical approach. So Hegel says, "The self is the pure concept, pure thinking, or *being-for-itself*, immediate *being*, and thereby *being for an other*, and as this *being for an other*, it has immediately made an inward return into itself and is at one with itself; it is therefore what is truly and solely revealed. . . . The divine nature is the same as the human nature, and it is this unity which is intuited." The self is pure concept: there is a conceptual development that has followed a logic. It is being-for-itself: it is activity, establishing itself as a unity by virtue of its spontaneity and activity, not just finding itself as a thing in the world. It is immediate being: the self knows itself as this, here, now, constrained by its past, absorbed in its present, projecting itself to its future. It is being-for-another in that this activity is fundamentally at its root a second-person address that is a component of an I/We unity. As having made an inward turn (an *Insichgehen*, a turn into oneself), it knows itself as self-conscious individuality, a status it only has in the web of its second-person relations (the I extended into twoness, *Zweiheit* of ¶671), which shapes an I/We that discloses the form of the world to itself. As having made it this far, consciousness knows itself in that relationship; it is revealed to itself in that object, in its own self-certainty. (It now knows what it is doing and has been doing.)

¶760. The absolute essence is a being, a self-consciousness. It seems to have descended from its eternal simplicity—this is the older Neoplatonist interpretation of the absolute—but actually it's achieved its highest essence in becoming fully self-conscious life.

¶761. What has just been said in the preceding paragraphs is, of course, the philosophical exposition of what the religious consciousness is trying to say about what it has experienced. Hegel states his conclusion forcefully: "God is therefore here *revealed* as *He is*; He *is there* in the way that He is *in itself*; He is there as spirit. God is solely attainable in pure speculative knowing, He is only in that knowing, and He is only that knowing itself, for He is spirit, and this speculative knowing is revealed religion's knowing." Moreover, "The hopes and expectations of the preceding world pushed their way towards this revelation" as a matter of conceptual development. Hegel thinks that this exposition is therefore the exposition of the truth of Christianity.

¶762. The original people encountering Jesus of Nazareth only see a singular individual talking, preaching, and so on. They see a particular person, "*this singular self-consciousness* as contrasted with *universal* self-consciousness. It is the excluding One, which, for the conscious-ness *for which* it is there, still has the undissolved form of a *sensuous other.*" It takes thought to bring together the appearance of this particular person with the thought that he manifests the spirit that binds together everyone.

¶763. The singular individual person as the revealed absolute essence is the immediately present God. If God is disclosed in self-consciousness, then this person who bears the message of the presence of God (of the nature of self-consciousness) *reveals* this truth to us. Hegel compresses the Christian story into a few remarks—this person is seen, understood as manifesting the universal essence in himself and his acts, and then he is no longer present. Those who heard him now experience him in a religious community as the spirit that brings them together. (He has "arisen" as spirit.) This consciousness takes shape as a community (a *Gemeine*, a religious community) and is actual, *wirklich*, only as such a community. When Hegel says: "Spirit is not the singular individual for himself but the singular individual together with the consciousness of the community; and what the singular individual is for this community is the complete whole of spirit," he is restating the concept of spirit as the I that is a We and the We that is an I in the terms of the Christian community's understanding of this "speculative truth."

¶764. But let us remember that for this religious community, this is initially only *Vorstellung*, representational thinking, a way of "picturing" the relation of the community to God as that of two distinct "things" coming together.

¶765. This form of *Vorstellung*, representational thinking, is the determinateness within which spirit is conscious of itself in the religious community. It is not yet the fully achieved self-consciousness of spirit, and the spiritual, *geistige* essence is thus still encumbered with unreconciled estrangement into a this-worldly (*Diesseits*) aspect and the otherworldly beyond (*Jenseits*). Or to put it differently, this "pictures" God as a "thing" of sorts, or as a distinct person existing in the otherworldly beyond. However, if you make the infinite into a thing, you will make it into something finite, and that will make it into nonsense.

¶766. Hegel gives us another summing up, which basically says: conceptual thinking (philosophy) has shown us how the ways in which we had thought we had fully determined the essence of self-consciousness and the form of the world have in fact turned out to be lacking. The truth of absolute spirit—self-conscious life thinking about what it means to be a self-conscious life—is not just to be in a religious community, nor is it to be tracking the trajectory that community needs to take to develop itself into what it really is. It is to make itself into an actual community—"actual" in the sense of really being efficacious in the world. It is easy to think of this as getting back to some form of primitive Christianity as "authentic" Christianity, but that would be to confuse a historical origin with the simplicity of the concept. "Authentic" religion is not necessarily that religion at its historical origin since from any origin we have to work out what that concept is in itself—what its trajectory will be as it develops itself in time.

¶767. Hegel gives us another statement of the development of the concept of religion into the concept of absolute religion. In its conceptual development, *Geist* initially takes the form of pure substance as the otherworldly beyond. (In this case, its historical and its conceptual development fairly well coincide.) As the early Neoplatonists thought of it, it descended from eternity into time, into existence, individuality. But as the religious consciousness develops, it makes a return in general out of *Vorstellung*, representational thought, and it returns out of otherness, out of seeing itself standing in an additive relation to some other freestanding spiritual thing.

¶768. This content of religious consciousness has already appeared in the account as the unhappy consciousness and the *glaubenden* consciousness (the "faith" of the earlier chapter on self-alienated *Geist*). In the unhappy consciousness, *Geist* is not yet in itself its own content. It is still bound by representational thinking, and it pictures what it is yearning for as a distant distinct being of some kind. Hegel says that the content of this religious consciousness was "*engendered* from out of *consciousness*," that is, from out of the subject-object divide which is the province of representational thinking. Likewise, the "faithful consciousness" represents the essence of the world as a distinct, otherworldly beyond, a kind of distinct object far away from the actual world or distinct from it. In the true religious community, the content is its substance, its certainty of self, that is, the content of communal religious life is the thought of itself as a religious community united by its concern over the answer of what it truly means to be self-conscious life.

¶769. Spirit is at first *represented* as substance, as an essence that is separate from spirit. (That's more or less the Neoplatonist view.) But simple essence, because it is an abstraction, is the negative in itself, it is its becoming-other. The very concept of such a simple essence begins to crack apart when subjected to reflective pressure. It looked like it made lots of sense, but then it starts making little sense, and it finally makes no sense. In such representationalist thinking and in the forms of theological reflection in its wake, representational thinking (*Vorstellung*) is led to "picture" as an event what is really the necessity of the concept. The divine "one" creates an other which is really only a phase of itself. Thinking of this difference—divine essence and its other—is to grasp the trajectory of this difference as that of "reverting" back into itself. As a complex unity, it is, to use Hegel's terms, the difference that is no difference, elements that may be distinguished but are not separable— elements that are distinguishable but only work within a whole.

¶770. Three such moments are to be distinguished: first, essence; second, being-for-itself (self-consciousness) as the other of the essence and for whom the essence is said to be or to appear; third, being-foritself as self-knowledge in an other (self-consciousness as being possible only in relation to another self-consciousness, which might that of the "essence" itself). In the same terms, the (divine) essence intuits, that is, views itself as splitting into itself and a being conscious of itself in being conscious of the (divine) essence.

¶771. So how to make sense of that? Without the whole phenomenology behind it, all the talk of "absolute essence" would be just fluff, the "void" as Hegel calls it, and without this phenomenology, *Geist* would be just a word. Typically, the religious community uses *Vorstellung*, representation, "picture thinking" to make sense of this. It thus "pictures" the various conceptual "moments" as if they were individual "things" or "substances" ("isolated immovable substances or subjects instead of transitional moments," as Hegel puts it). It makes sense of these rather complicated concepts by picturing them in terms of natural relations, such as father, son. When that is done, then they are thereby not related as they genuinely are in conceptual comprehension.

¶772. All the talk of the abstract essence has to be straightened out. To understand spirit as the abstract essence of appearance is to see it as a simple unity, but simple unities generate their own others. Spirit in particular is the unity of an I that is a We and a We that is an I, and thus otherness necessarily follows from it in this phenomenology. Although the concept of spirit is comprehended only in purely conceptual thinking, spirit itself exists only as the unity of independent self-conscious lives. Hegel expresses this by saying that spirit "does not exist only in pure thinking; it is also *actual*, for lying in the concept of spirit is *otherness* itself." He even goes so far as to call it "love" since it is another manifestation of the difference (two people) that is no difference (in their unity as not opposed to each other).

¶773. Hegel states again the difficulty of understanding the speculative unity at stake here. *Geist* is the nonadditive unity of different self-conscious lives, and these different lives are real. They take an inward turn, oppose themselves to each other, and thus conceptual, "pure" thinking makes a transition into representational thinking.

¶774. Representational thought pictures the relationship between the unity of spirit and the various spirits (people) as that of one substance (abstract eternal spirit) creating a world full of such substances (self-conscious lives).

¶775. Using representational thought to make sense of itself, spirit pictures itself as thrown into the world. In doing so, it pictures itself as innocent (thus not yet good or evil). To be good or evil, it must become self-conscious—"It must just as much become an *other* to itself." The myth of the Fall in the Bible is the representational thought of this conceptual truth. It pictures it as an event without any conceptual necessity to itself. Although this individual (Adam) is innocent, he's not yet good. (He hasn't eaten the fruit of knowledge of good and evil yet.) Adam needs an "other" (Eve), who is both other and the same as himself. Once the two are together, they both taste the fruit and become self-conscious. *Geist's* coming to be other is the *in-sich-gehen* (taking the inward turn) of knowledge of the self-opposed thought of good and evil. Representationalist thought's picture, however, is that of two conscious beings, aware of each other, tasting the fruit, establishing a second-person awareness (in this case, a consciousness of their nudity), but this means that they can't go on in the way they had been going on. Their very act expels them from the garden. They are no longer "mere" animals but are now animals aware of themselves *as* animals.

¶776. With the loss of innocence (which was itself just a lack of self-consciousness), evil enters the world. Evil appears as the consciousness that has taken the inward turn. Why would they do it? The myth says it was something that happened to them by virtue of a creature set on tempting them with the aim of undoing their paradisical condition. Lucifer tempted them and succeeded. In response to the idea that we could nicely package all of this as thesis, antithesis, synthesis, Hegel points out the superficiality of such a packaging. Is this a two in one, or a three in one? It could be seen as four in one, five in one, etc. As he succinctly puts it, "*Counting* the moments can be viewed as altogether useless."

¶777. Good and evil can be "pictured" as two opposing "things," but that's a mistake. They are the ways in which self-conscious life now finds its existence. Once life becomes self-conscious life, it also becomes possibly evil just as it becomes possibly good. In trying to understand the meaning of self-consciousness for human life, representational thought has to take it that the expulsion from the garden has to be rendered as a kind of divine wrath at our disobedience. However, at that point representational thought has exhausted its resources. To really get at the truth of what self-consciousness ultimately means, it must cease its "fruitless struggle."

¶778. We see the typical case when we have these philosophical concepts of the unconditioned. For representational thought, it seems like we have two incompatible things, or it seems like we have a chicken/egg problem where we feel compelled to see which one produces the other. The divine essence has alienated itself into itself and its other (self-conscious life). Some will feel compelled to say that of the two, the "divine essence" is the actual, whereas natural existence is subordinate. Others will feel compelled to say that natural self-consciousness is what is actual, and the divine is somehow the unessential part of the view. (Hegel's student, Ludwig Feuerbach, later proposed that divinities were simple projections of human needs and self-consciousness into an otherworldly beyond.) What's common to both views is, of course, existence itself, but at least this far in the narration, that's fairly empty.

¶779. We do not "picture" the sublation of this opposition as we did with that between mastery and servitude, which involved a struggle over which one of the members was to emerge as the independent member. In truth, these are both necessary moments of the whole which is spirit, but when we picture them in representational thought, we see it instead as the divine side of the opposition as exercising a kind of free will, emptying or relinquishing itself to become flesh. The simple (the essence) goes to its death and reconciles the absolute essence with itself. Actuality and the divine essence have reconciled: in its death, the abstract essence is resurrected as *Geist*.

¶780. The individual self-consciousness of the "essence" as self-consciousness becomes a "universal self-consciousness." It's not just my self-consciousness, but the two-ness, the *Zweiheit*, of the end of the section on beautiful souls (and thus a second-person address), and it is a "We." With that, a religious *community* forms, and with that, the community begins a subtle move from representational thought (*Vorstellung*) into "self-consciousness as such." (This is a controversial Hegelian view: the rites, rituals, etc. of the religious community are a valid and more embodied way of thinking of some of the issues that philosophy pursues in its more bloodless form.) To the extent that the religious community remains within representational thinking, it "pictures" the divine essence taking on a human nature; and if it becomes human, it becomes self-conscious, so it also acquires what Kant called radical evil. That's a "moment" therefore of the divine essence. This is not saying that evil and good are the same (which would be senseless). The point is not that they are the same, nor that they are independent elements of the world, but that the very concept of self-conscious life, of *Geist*, is that it is a life in which good and evil are ineliminable aspects of the concept of self-conscious life itself. This kind of speculative thought—of what seem to be opposing concepts working as necessary elements of a whole that is effective, actual—is what representational thought—what Hegel here somewhat misleadingly calls "the spiritless '*is*' of the judgmental copula"—has trouble coming to terms with. Once it does come to terms with it, it starts the transition away from itself and toward philosophical, conceptual thinking.

¶781. What does this mean? *Geist* just is universal self-consciousness which is real as a religious community (the *Gemeinde*), and which in turn at least implicitly moves from its representationalist understanding of what it is trying to formulate to a more conceptualist understanding. The religious community does this by bringing forth where its own trajectory (in terms of its concept of itself as "in itself") has taken it. In Hegel's own words, "The dead divine man, or the human God, is *in itself* universal self-consciousness." The members of the religious community (the *Gemeinde*), confronted by death and trying to make sense of their own finitude, grasp this in the idea of the divine freely taking on a human form and dying. The dead divine man displayed that the kingdom was at hand, that the truth of *Geist* is now available to us.

¶782. Death is the fate of all natural things. A self-interpreting animal is a self-conscious life, and life is part of nature, and death is part of life. To come to terms with this, the self must pull back from itself, turn inward, which puts it on the trajectory that has good and evil as intrinsic to the concept of *self-conscious* life. But, again for representational thought, it seems that nature itself is the root of evil. We might think therefore (representationally) that we have two natures, a natural one and a rational one. The "roots" of evil would be our natural desires, since if we only followed our rational nature, we'd always do the right thing. Desires interfere with the normal working of rational nature, and therefore natural desires must be the explanation of evil action. This is the conclusion to be drawn from such representational thought of two natures as that of two substances in opposition to each other. The unity of self-conscious life is the key to comprehending the way in which, in the opposition of reason (as self-consciousness) and desire, both work as necessary elements in one life. Speculative thinking goes beyond the apparent dualism to see the deeper unity and the tensions that animate it.

¶783. The inwardizing, becoming-inward (*Innerlichwerden*) of natural self-consciousness was evil as existing, so inwardizing is the knowledge of evil as what lay in the trajectory ("in itself") of the concept of human existence (*Dasein*). The fruit in the garden did not just lead to a knowledge of good and evil, it was the provocation for the basis of all knowing itself. To die to sin (in the Christian sense) thus can't be rejecting the natural life (or rejecting our bodies) but rather the forsaking of immediacy, of living by instinct and then coming to see erroneously our natural desires as interfering with our divine (rational) natures. To "forsake immediacy" is to come to grips with the kind of tensions that are intrinsic to all self-conscious life. What seems puzzling about taking the inward turn is that it seems to presuppose itself as its own ground. However, as self-conscious *animals*, we see that nature itself has already taken this inward turn, and that turn, not yet fully comprehended, provides the ground for this inwardizing move.

¶784. The relation of representational thought to conceptual thought in the religious consciousness is the topic here. The two aspects of human self-conscious life as that of nature and that of "universal self-consciousness" as the domain of reason itself are already in principle reconciled. However, for the person trying to representationally comprehend this reconciliation, it is enough to think of it as an event happening among different substances. The divine essence empties itself (the *Entäußerung* of the divine), incarnates itself, and dies. In fully spiritual self-consciousness, "Death loses this natural significance" and we get a proper comprehension of our place in the larger scheme of things. A transfiguration occurs in which the singular individual dies, but the religious community (as the universality of *Geist*) is daily resurrected. Old actors leave the scene, new ones arrive. Life goes on.

¶785. The death of the mediator is only the sublation of his particular being-for-itself, which becomes universal self-consciousness. What dies when Jesus dies is the abstraction of the divine essence. The divine is not in some otherworldly beyond but is now reconciled with us. Still, for representational thought, what has happened is the painful feeling that God himself has died, that the earth has lost its mooring. The "nothingness" of all finite life is put before us. The unhappy consciousness has the agonized feeling that God is dead. Nihilism seems to loom ahead, but is cut short by a kind of inspiration, or a making spiritual of the world around us.

¶786. This almost moves to a completion of the trajectory already laid out in the concept of *Geist* itself. In the religious community that moved on from a representationalist view of the divine to a more nearly speculative (but not yet fully conceptual) view, *Geist* has become the *Geist* that knows itself as what it is, which is to exist in this knowledge of itself. *Geist* has managed to develop to an I that is a We, and a We that is an I, as the section on self-consciousness had initially promised, and it has taken the form of a religious community (an I and a We) collectively and individually participating in the thinking through of what it means to be a self-conscious life and how that life is to be lived—and it does this not as an imaginary community or one that exists only in poetic narratives but as an actual community, existent and at work in the world. Spirit moves itself, Hegel says, and as he later puts it in several of his lectures, spirit is its own product, its own purpose, and its own beginning. Here he puts it by saying, "What moves itself is spirit; it is the subject of the movement, and it is likewise [*the act of*] *moving*, or the substance through which the subject passes." Self-conscious life ultimately responds to its circumstances in terms of how it (spontaneously) thinks of itself. Hegel also explicitly links this to the very last paragraph of the chapter on spirit, in which forgiveness and reconciliation appear as essential to self-conscious life for it to do what it is required to do. He also takes this to fulfill the promise made in ¶17: "Everything hangs on grasping and expressing the true not just as *substance* but just as much as *subject.*"

¶787. But the religious community has not yet reached its culmination. The community remains at the stage of representational thinking. The content of the thought is representational (God as a father, etc.), although the trajectory of this content—the concept of the unity of the divine and the natural—is moving in the direction toward speculative-conceptual thinking. However, to the extent that the community has its tradition of thinking in terms of representational thinking, it will not be able on its own to make that move. Hegel says that at this turning point, self-consciousness empties itself of its natural existence and becomes pure negativity, that is, a kind of pure speculative thinking of the kinds of basic oppositions that this kind of phenomenology has laid out, and its religious consciousness takes on a different sense. For devotional consciousness, however, this "speculative" subjectivity is an other. Its satisfaction is still burdened with a *Jenseits*, an otherworldly beyond. Whereas Hegel proposed a few paragraphs ago (¶755) that the individual divine man has a father "in itself," but an actual mother, the religious community really has as its father its own activity, since it sets itself into motion, and for its mother it has eternal love, the form in which free, mutual, and equal recognition holds the community together. Its reconciliation thus exists in its heart but is still estranged from its consciousness. All it needs now is to comprehend what it has already done "in itself"—or, as we might say, it needs to comprehend the true meaning of what it has done. That will require something other than religious consciousness.

16

Absolute Knowing

¶788. Revealed religion, so it turns out, has not yet overcome its consciousness as such, so it is not the last word in this phenomenology. Revealed religion still sees things "representationally," although in its practice (its actual self-consciousness), it manifests a fully "speculative" comprehension of the absolute. It simply has not and cannot fully articulate that to itself, and thus its self-understanding remains at odds with its practice. The sole remaining issue, as Hegel puts it, is to bring the form of thinking about the absolute away from its "representational" mode and into the form of its more authentically "speculative" mode, and whether doing so will have any impact on what that content is. Since it is a phenomenology, it will have to show that this change of form is the result of a developmental process, and it will have to avoid being "one-sided" (as representational thinking often ends up being) and without succumbing to the temptation to give one or the other sides of a basic opposition priority over the other or ascribe to it some grounding or explanatory force over the other. Neither self-consciousness itself nor the objects of the world seem to take priority over the other. The object of religious consciousness is *Geist* itself, which the religious consciousness now posits—takes to be—a nullity, a nothingness (*Nichtigkeit*) of sorts, and since it is a nullity, so is the religious consciousness. But in this emptying or relinquishing of itself, it now has itself as a pure object, as negativity itself.

¶789. To the extent that this shape of consciousness is now reflecting on its own activities as a knower, it runs through all its previous shapes (from sensuous certainty, to perception, and all the way up to the I that is a We, and the We that is an I, here described as "the movement of the universal into singular individuality by way of determination, as well as the converse movement from singular individuality to the universal by way of sublated singularity, or determination").

Hegel's Phenomenology of Spirit. Terry Pinkard, Oxford University Press. © Oxford University Press 2023.
DOI: 10.1093/oso/9780197663127.003.0016

All of this consists in the different forms or shapes of life, that *we*—the readers of this book—are called to gather together under the guidance and supervision of our guide (with whom we, the readers, begin to fuse).

¶790. In doing so, we have made what seem to be two incompatible infinite (unconditional) judgments—in effect, two judgments about the absolute. First, there is the infinite judgment that the I is a thing. There is the world as I found it, and in that world, all one could find there was one's own body alongside other things. This is "spiritless"—the "I" as subjectivity goes missing. The world is all that is the case, what is the case are things concatenating themselves into facts, and the world is exhaustively explained by the sciences that explain factual things.

¶791. Second, we have the infinite judgment that the thing is the I. Things have no meaning outside of their relation to subjectivity (the "I"). (The world itself is meaningless outside of its relationship to the subject.) This came to the forefront in Enlightenment, where the meaning of things consisted only in their utility for humans.

¶792. In the moral worldview, what is ultimately real is the moral self-consciousness itself knowing itself as what it is. Nothing in the world can override the demands of duty. This becomes all the more clear in the self-conception of the moral agent as conscience.

¶793. Self-conscious life, *Geist*, is what it is only in knowing itself, that is, only in its self-consciousness, which itself requires language for its existence as spirit. Hegel rehearses the stages we have already been through: acting, which puts spirit's unity into question; recognition, which first appeared in mastery and servitude; and forgiveness, which manifests the unity among the singular agents by neither effacing their singularity nor their standing within the unity of the spiritual community.

¶794. This prompts a reflection on the relation between form and content in the concept of *Geist*. Hegel says: "The unification of both aspects [the two infinite judgments] has not yet been shown; that unification wraps up this series of shapes of spirit, for in it spirit arrives at the point where it *knows itself not only as it is in itself*, or according to its *absolute content*, and not only *as it is for itself* according to its *contentless form*, or according to the aspect of self-consciousness. Rather, it knows itself as it is *in and for itself*." So there is indeed a truth to be said about what it means to be a self-conscious life; that is its absolute *content*; that content has always been in the process of development. We didn't just make up the content out of whole cloth. It was there at the outset in *Geist's* trajectory, but not yet as developed. However, as self-interpreting creatures we did not have that content until we made it real, that is, developed it in the myriad circumstances of world history. There are two aspects to this: the development of self-conscious life and its self-interpretations across time, and the religious comprehension of this development. The two come apart at several points in this narrative, but in the end they are both "moments" of the same development. The form of this is self-consciousness, the distinctively human self-relation, which is itself "contentless."

¶795. The unification of consciousness (as awareness of objects it takes to be distinct from itself) and self-consciousness (as reflection on what its consciousness means) is carried out in religion, but not in its genuine form—in religion, the truth about *Geist* which is present in (Christian) practice is still not present in its proper speculative form but instead remains representationalist. The content of religion is true, but the form in which it puts that content distorts it. Religion puts *Geist* on the right trajectory (as "in itself"), but as representationalist, religion is at odds with the kind of conceptual thinking that is where the trajectory of self-consciousness thinking about what it means to be a self-conscious creature is going. This reaches a penultimate stage in the appearance of the "beautiful soul."

¶796. The "beautiful soul" is the concept in its purity as pure self-knowledge but only in the form of a pure negativity as shutting itself off from the world. This contrasts with the acting consciousness, which is the concept as existence, as *Dasein*. They present two sides of the concept of self-conscious life, and in their existential opposition to each other, we see the estrangement of the concept itself (which demands a kind of "speculative" unification of both without yet giving it). The reconciliation comes to be when the hard heart breaks and each side relinquishes its own idea of its self-sufficiency. The master sought self-sufficiency in dominating the slave. The stoics and skeptics sought self-sufficiency in their own thoughts. The beautiful soul sought a self-sufficiency in its own putatively absolute inwardness. None of those attempts at absolute self-sufficiency work, but they have prepared the way for this final reconciliation. The last full sentence of this section is a good summary of Hegel's stance.

¶797. What in religion was the content is now the self's own doing and its recognition of itself as universal, as one self-conscious life in a larger scheme and of each as radically evil (as having the potential and the motive to substitute self-love for what we should do). Our narrator tells us that "our" (not just "his") sole contribution here is to gather up all these shapes and see what, if anything, they mean, all the while holding fast both to the individuality of all these shapes and the universality of conceptual thinking. (Both the readers and the guide are equally necessary. We couldn't go through it without the guide, but we have to have also gone through the process all on our own.)

¶798. In gathering all these up, we reach the last shape of spirit, which turns out to have been our goal all along without our having known it at the beginning: absolute knowing, "spirit knowing itself in the shape of spirit, or it is *comprehending conceptual knowing.*" Certainty—the sense of where one runs out of further reasons in regarding the world and one's place in it—and truth come together. What guides the consciousness of this is *Wissenschaft*—a rigorous theory, not just a hunch or a grab bag of various observations and accounts.

¶799. The "speculative science" that we now have before us is the "science" of self-consciousness as I and We, that is, *Geist* itself: once more, the unity of the singular agent ("which is *this I* and no other") and the universal (the "We" or even "Reason" itself). As "pure negativity," it is self-consciousness in which I distinguish myself from myself while immediately holding on to the identity between myself as the object of my self-awareness and as the subject of this self-awareness. For Hegel, this is the paradigmatic, ground-level form of "speculative" thinking.

¶800. This kind of *Wissenschaft* cannot appear until its time has come, that is, it can only make its appearance when the world around it has changed such that the surrounding institutional, practical, and intellectual world has been shaped to make this kind of science of self-conscious life not merely possible but actual. Up until now, however, only the real possibility of such a "science" had been prepared.

¶801. The social shapes that support and maintain this kind of knowing (the "substance" of knowing) are there long before the science of self-conscious life makes its appearance in history. There have been many adumbrations of this science long before it appears (which is just now, 1807). However, long before "cognition" (*das Erkennen*) has worked itself out, the deeper ties to the social substance are richer than the more abstract claims of "cognition" and are already there and are following the trajectory of their own concept until they are taken up in the fulfilled science of self-conscious life. Time is the intuited concept, so Hegel says. The intuition or "viewing" of time is the intuition of infinity that has not fully conceptualized itself and is the unity of the "opposition" of the discrete and the continuous. Conceptual thinking attempts an erasure of time insofar as it seeks timeless truths, but time is the destiny of incomplete spirit, so Hegel says.

¶802. At this point, we can now conclude: *nothing is known that is not in experience* (*Erfahrung*)—that sense of "experience" in which we say, "We learn from experience that . . ." Hegel adds: "Nothing is *known* that is not available as *felt truth*." The picture of knowing that leaves out "felt truth" is the one-sided picture of the knower as the disembodied universal knower, the "We" detached from all the particular "I's." The more adequate picture, which is "speculative," holds both elements (I and We, singular and universal) together in one whole, where the tensions between the two are real, ineliminable, but not necessarily self-undermining. The better picture, Hegel says, is circular rather than purely linear. The "bad infinite" is represented as a straight line which, if one tried to follow it out, would have an unreachable endpoint. The "good" or "true" infinite is better pictured as circular: one can begin at a certain point, traverse the circle an infinite number of times but always arrive back at the point from which one started. If one starts with sensuous certainty and follows the book out until one arrives at the science of self-consciousness, one will realize that the "in itself" of sensuous certainty already established a trajectory in its concept that would lead one to the "science," and having reached that "science," one would realize that one would have to start with sensuous certainty to follow it out. As for the speculative truth about spirit, religion may get there first in history, "But it is science alone which is spirit's true knowing of itself."

¶803. The actual movement of history, what is really moving history forward, is *Geist*'s pursuit of self-knowledge—to know what it means to be a self-conscious life. It also involves the twoness, the *Zweiheit* of the reconciliatory "Yes" of ¶671. This takes its actual shape at first in the religious community, but we shouldn't romanticize that. The religious community is originally more harsh and barbaric, and the wars of religion have left a pile of corpses behind. It is now time, Hegel says, for *Geist*, as it were, to climb down out of the intellectual world (Kant's term for the world of in principle unknowable noumena) and take a more existential turn. To do this, he rehearses again the movement leading to utility, absolute freedom, and morality, and once again, we're reminded of his statement in the Preface that, "in my view, which must be justified by the exposition of the system itself, everything hangs on grasping and expressing the true not just as *substance* but just as much as *subject*" (¶17). If we relied on substance alone—on the given social world and its mores and modes of inquiry—we would find no necessity in this conceptual development. However, what we now grasp is that in our time (1807 or thereabouts), substance and subject have come together.

¶804. *Geist* is neither pure withdrawal into self nor pure absorption in substance. The "I" is not erased and absorbed into the "We" (as ethnic nationalisms tend to have it). Nor is the "We" just an additive sum, a heap, of individual "I's" otherwise external to each other (as modern "individualisms" tend to have it). We are reminded again of ¶47: "The true is the bacchanalian revel where not a member is sober, because, in isolating himself from the revel, each member is just as immediately dissolved into it."

¶805. *Geist* has brought to a close the movement of giving shape to itself. At long last, "Spirit has won the pure element of its existence, the concept." It is no longer representational thinking of itself, and it realizes that the additive conception of itself as a sum of different things otherwise indifferent to each other cannot be the full account of *Geist*. Now self-conscious life has a more explicitly conceptual, holistic grasp of itself. What had appeared as "shapes of consciousness" can now be understood somewhat metaphorically as the different concepts spirit forms of itself in its history. As such "concepts," they can also now be grasped not as adventitious sums of different things but as manifesting a logic that is only now becoming clear.

¶806. *Geist* can't be satisfied with just knowing about this, reading it in a book. It must live it (have it as a felt truth). "Science contains within itself this necessity to relinquish itself of the form of the pure concept and to make the transition from the concept into *consciousness*." But likewise, *Geist* can't be content with just "living it." It also has to *know* it. This is, moreover, not just a practical fact about us but part of the logic of a phenomenology of *Geist* about how the I and the We are distinguishable but not separable and part of why we must make the effort to go along this path in the first place.

¶807. "Knowing is acquainted not only with itself, but also with the negative of itself, or its limit." The limit, though, is not one side of a curtain, with *Geist* on one side and something else on the other side. As mentioned before, Wittgenstein said in the Preface to his *Tractatus*: "to set a limit to thought, we should have to find both sides of the limit thinkable (i.e., we should have to be able to think what cannot be thought)." We can't do that; we cannot think what cannot be thought. Instead, self-conscious life as a whole has to come to terms with the fact that it comes to be from out of nature and that it exists only insofar as all of us contingent beings also come to be.

¶808. The other aspect of spirit's coming to be: history. That can be seen as: "This coming-to-be exhibits a languid movement and succession of spirits, *a gallery of pictures*, of which each, endowed with the entire wealth of spirit, moves itself so slowly because the self has to take hold of and assimilate the whole of this wealth of its substance." We might read this as a kind of aesthetic statement, as if we were walking through a museum of world history, viewing the gallery of pictures (say, of Greece), then moving into the next hall (Rome, with the curators putting little signs up on the wall telling us how long Rome existed and what we should be looking at). What would the last room be? A hall of mirrors? This is, I think, part of the sense here. There is, however, a more expansive conception of "pictures" at work here. A picture in this sense is an overall view of what ultimately counts and does not count, and what ultimately makes sense and does not make sense within a particular shape of consciousness. Each of these shapes of spirit presents such a picture, and on Hegel's view, the picture is also not static. It's a "moving picture" in which there are also various speaking roles for the people in it. How did that history look? Hegel says that spirit's shapes appearing in the form of *contingency* is *history*. History didn't have to go the way it went. History as a series of contingent events does not necessarily follow any logic. However, the retrospective account of these events reveals that despite the contingency, history does have a kind of logic to it. Despite its ups and downs, it has, seen retrospectively, taken the shape of self-conscious life coming to an awareness of what ultimately matters to it. As that history is conceptually grasped, it is *erscheinende Wissen*, phenomenal knowing, or knowing in appearance. The two together—phenomenal knowledge and Hegelian conceptual knowledge—form *begriffne Geschichte* (a term hard to render—kind of "concept-ized history"), and that forms the "the *science* of *phenomenal knowing*," knowledge as it appears in the various strife-ridden worlds of self-conscious life. However, now that this task has been completed, this is a climb up to the Golgotha of spirit (its Calvary, the *Schädelstätte*, the place of skulls, where Jesus was crucified). Hegel then speaks of this as absolute *Geist's* throne. If it had not made this journey of self-consummating skepticism along the path of despair (¶78), it would, he says, be *lifeless* and *alone*. He then ends by misquoting lines from a poem by Schiller. Is it an accidental misquote or a deliberate one? And why end this book of philosophy with a line of poetry? The poem is from Schiller's "Friendship" ("Die Freundschaft").

Here's Hegel:

| Out of the chalice of this realm of spirits
Foams forth to him his infinity | aus dem Kelche dieses Geisterreiches
schäumt ihm seine Unendlichkeit. |

Schiller's original:

Friendless was the great master of the world,	Freundlos war der große Weltenmeister,
He felt a lack—and so he created spirits,	Fühlte Mangel—darum schuf er Geister,
Blessed mirrors of his own blessedness!	Sel'ge Spiegel seiner Seligkeit!
Already the highest being found no equal,	Fand das höchste Wesen schon kein gleiches.
From the chalice of the whole realm of souls	Aus dem Kelch des ganzen Seelenreiches
Foams forth to him—infinity	Schäumt ihm—die Unendlichkeit.

Hegel subtly changes Schiller's own poem. He changes souls (*Seelenreiches*) into spirits (*Geisterreiches*) in the last two lines, even though it is spirits that the *Weltenmeister* has created. Hegel makes the whole definite (this) instead of just "the whole." Schiller has infinity as such foaming up, but Hegel has "his" (maybe better rendered as "his own") infinity—in both cases, it's an image of sparkling wine foaming up out of a chalice into which it has been poured. Hegel also leaves out the dash mark before "[his] infinity."

In particular, the replacement of "infinity" (*die Unendlichkeit*) with "his [own] infinity" (*seine Unendlichkeit*) suggests that we can conceive of what it is for our self-consciousness to think of the infinite and for self-consciousness to be self-consciousness only in doing so. It is both that sense of one's "own" infinity (as infinite in thought but not in time or extension) and also its history (or concept-ized history, *begriffne Geschichte*) that prevent it from being lifeless and alone. Without this rich history behind it and without its being a "phenomenology" of that life and history, the "science of self-consciousness" would decline into a merely formal enterprise (would be "lifeless") and would have no real link to the rest of the form of life of which it is a part (would be "alone"). It would be a dry, dead (and "merely" academic) enterprise. We began with a consideration of indexicals, with an actual location in a "this," and we end with a "this" ("*this* realm of spirits," *dieses Geisterreiches*), that is, not just in any possible world, but the actual, human world.

The phenomenology of spirit, of self-conscious life, has been an investigation of how the logic of shapes of consciousness and shapes of spirit are manifested in the lived experiences of people in a "form of life"—in Hegel's sense of a *Gestalt des Lebens*. It has also brought forth the conceptual connections among those shapes themselves from out of the very investigation itself. It is a far more "existential" piece than Hegel was ever to write again. (There are more "existential" moments in the development of Hegel's philosophy, but they are not part of the warp and woof of his books and lectures as they are in this book.) The last paragraph speaks of the way in which the lesson to be drawn from this is that now that the basic tensions inherent in the concepts of the unconditioned have been drawn in the course of this phenomenology, the issue "foams up" into a kind of indeterminate concept of where we go next. As we know, Hegel thought that was to be his *Science of Logic*, which was not to appear until several years later; he admitted in a letter to his friend, Niethammer, that he had at that time no real idea about what it would look like. That book was to answer the logical-metaphysical question of what were unconditional concepts and how they were to be related to each other. It was not to be a phenomenology but a piece of logic-as-metaphysics. Having worked out his systematic "scientific" introduction to his system, he spent the rest of his career working out just what that system was to be.

Synopsis of the Chapters

For purposes of teaching (or for just curiosity's sake), I have included a short synopsis of the chapters of my commentary. Often only part of the book can be taught, and this is intended as a kind of stopgap for times when the whole commentary is not needed. It is not intended as a substitute for the commentary but as a kind of second best when only the parts and not the whole are on the table.

Chapter 1. The Preface

Hegel begins the book by stating why prefaces to this kind of work cannot really be written. The reason is that in this kind of book, there can be no preannounced lesson to be learned, and the idea is that whatever it is that one learns, one has to learn it for oneself in going through the model cases laid out in the book. Nonetheless, after disdaining prefaces for such a work, Hegel goes on to write a very lengthy preface that provides some real clues as to what the book is about. He makes it clear that he intends it to be a systematic work of philosophy and not anything "edifying," nor based on vague feelings or noncommunicable personal "views." Like the Romantics, he is after an understanding of what he and Schelling took to calling "the Absolute"—that is, what ultimately matters to us above all else—but, so he tells us, it takes patient hard work to get there. He stresses how our own time (ca. 1807) has within it a spirit of something important having been lost and yet it's also a time of new birth and new positive possibilities. This new world is gradually working up to a clearer conception of itself, and Hegel's book is supposed to be a participant in that activity. To that end, he says that in fact everything hangs on apprehending and expressing the true not merely as *substance* but also equally as *subject*. That "subject" is said to be "pure negativity," which estranges itself and then restores itself.

As it moves in that field of estrangement and restoration, it comes to understand that the true (what it seeks) is the whole and that it only comes into view as a result of what the book investigates. This is a purposive activity even if, for most of it, there is no full consciousness of just what this purpose is. New terms are needed for this: what this subject is "in itself" as distinguished from what it is "for itself." Moreover, this activity is itself the process of world history itself. Philosophical argument is thus not like mathematical or geometrical argument where the end result can be stated and comprehended independently of the proof needed to get to it. Philosophy is more dialectical in its approach.

Chapter 2. The Introduction

Where to begin? We should start, so it seems, with what we already know, but to do that, it seems we first need a criterion for distinguishing knowing from not-knowing, and it seems that we therefore also have to contend with the deep-seated skeptical doubt that our knowledge might be metaphysically cut off from what it is we claim to be knowing. The idea of getting behind all our presuppositions to a presuppositionless beginning, however, itself also comes with its own set of seemingly intractable presuppositions. The concept of knowledge, so Hegel intimates, itself must be developmental, so that the concept embodies in itself a trajectory along which it can develop, and our ordinary taken-for-granted concept of knowing will have to undergo that development. The nature of the development, however, is not straightforward but involves breakdowns and failures. It even involves the possibility that just like every other concept of knowing that is merely the "appearance" at some particular time of what that time takes itself to know, the whole idea of a science of this knowing (of philosophy) itself may be itself only an "appearance" of its own time and thus no more stable than what it critiques. Faced with that possibility, this approach thus seems required to take the path of skeptical doubt about the very possibility of knowledge and end up instead on a path of despair. However, ultimately, this kind of radical doubt is self-consummating and leads to a deeper doubt about itself. This developmental concept of knowing will eventuate in a science of the experience of consciousness as it discovers why it had to take the path of despair until it reaches its nondespairing culmination.

Chapter 3. Sensuous Certainty, Perceiving, Force, and the Understanding

Again: Where to begin? The answer seems to be something like, "Begin with what we know with certainty" and then build out from there. But what do we know with certainty? If we know something because it follows from something else, then our certainty is only as strong as the certainty of what it follows from. Is there therefore anything we know with certainty without its following from anything else? That would be, it seems, one's certainty of being aware of this, here, now, irrespective of what this, here, now is. There would be two individual things involved: this subject and this object of awareness. But our language itself shows this not to be the case, since it shows itself as more general than the sheer nonrepeatable individuality of *this* subject aware of *this* object. Perhaps it must therefore be nonlinguistic awareness: knowledge of "this" that cannot itself be linguistically rendered and is therefore ineffable. However, nothing ineffable can serve as the basis of a further inference. It seems like we could have performed a meaning-free reference or "pointing out" of a singular "this," but that turns out not to be possible since even the most elementary act of "pointing out" involves a wider context of significance.

That wider context is that not of purely meaning-free referential acts but that of perceiving singular objects with general properties. However, that itself turns out not to be self-sustaining as an account since it too involves intractable problems within the terms it sets for itself. The further wider context seems to be that of seeing the world as the observable appearance of a wider context of regularities (as the laws of appearance). However, what explains the regularities (the laws) is something else, a set of forces. The regularities are conditioned by the forces, but what is really at work in explaining them is something unconditioned, a set of unconditional basic forces that manifest themselves in the laws of appearance. It would seem, though, that from a priori considerations, there must be two such basic forces (such as attraction and repulsion), and they are the "inner" that expresses itself in the "outer" (the world of appearance). The unity of the two forces as one "simple" explanatory construct now has the appearing world as merely a semblance, a seeming-to-be of the real world behind it. This "simple" substrate of the appearing world must therefore on a priori grounds be such as to divide itself into two opposing forces (e.g., attraction and repulsion). We end up with this dialectic leading us to an inverted world: in our world, what tastes sweet in the other world tastes sour, good actions in this world are bad in the other world, and so on. This topsy-turvy inversion of ordinary conceptions leads us to the concept of infinity, as that which cannot be traversed but which appears as an object of thought to consciousness, and with that, consciousness becomes self-consciousness. In that move, something new is introduced, and we are finally in a position to see that the paradigm of a single subject aware of an object led to the idea of a "curtain" of appearance hiding the real world—except that when we pull the curtain of appearance back, what we see are ourselves and our own activities looking back.

Chapter 4. Self-Consciousness and Self-Sufficiency: Mastery and Servitude

In "consciousness," the subject is aware of something that is external to its awareness of it. In "self-consciousness" the subject is aware of itself and thus not of anything external to it. Self-consciousness is thus a "difference that is no difference." Since organisms of a higher sort are marked by desire—the awareness, however inchoate, of a lack of something needed or demanded by the organism, self-consciousness is also desire. What it lacks is a unity with itself. As a creature constrained by its past, absorbed in its present, and projecting itself to a future marked by its nonexistence (death), it lacks a unity to that projection, at least thus far in the progression of the "path of despair." Our genus (self-conscious life) is a genus that is aware of itself as a genus, and thus our concept "in itself" marks out a not completely determinate trajectory for development. We shift our shape as we move along the development. It needs something authoritative to fix its development as going better in one direction rather than another, and it cannot do that on its own (for reasons similar to why it cannot have a "private language" on its own). Thus, for self-consciousness to be satisfied with itself, it needs another self-consciousness that would have the unconditional authority to lay down what counts as its development. This sets the stage for imagining two such self-conscious agents coming into a disagreement over who has the authority to set the terms of life. Where there is a fundamental disagreement on this, and a struggle for recognition occurs—a struggle over who sets the terms of authority— and both of them claim that in fact this unconditional authority they seek is more valuable to them than life itself, a struggle to the death comes on the scene. We then imagine that although both have staked out an unconditional claim to be recognized as "the" authority, one of them (out of the fear of death, the absolute lord and master of all) renounces that claim and thus recognizes the unconditional authority of the other, thereby becoming his slave or vassal. However, the slave soon comes to understand that the master's putative unconditional authority is really conditional on the slave's continued recognition of that unconditionality and thus isn't really unconditional at all. We thus end up having generated the concept of *Geist*, spirit, out of the idea of self-consciousness, which Hegel defines as an "I that is We and a We that is I," that is, a first-person apperception that is both singular and plural. This will form the basis of all the other further development in the *Phenomenology* since the basic question will now be how to maintain the full independence of the individual subject ("I") in the context of its existence as a member of a collective subject ("We") which it requires for its own self-consciousness. The necessity to understand two such opposed terms within a proper whole will be the basis of the dialectic of the *Phenomenology*.

Chapter 5. Freedom: Stoicism, Skepticism, Unhappy Consciousness

The dialectic of mastery and servitude showed that the inchoate impulse to be fully independent (that is, self-sufficient) failed. This has landed the subject of the book in the situation in which he now sees the independence he sought more truly consisting of freedom. At first, this seems to be freedom (or full independence) in thought and not in bodily existence. Although I may sit on the throne and be constrained by my duties and the plottings of my court, or although I may be a slave in chains, I am free in thought. In thought, nothing commands me except me myself, and I am thus at one with myself (*bei mir selbst*) only in thought. This mode of thinking about freedom took shape in the slave societies of the ancient Mediterranean world as the lived philosophies of Stoicism and skepticism. Each of these fails because in each the individual "I" wants to speak with the authority of the whole behind it (the authority of the "We" taken as humanity as a whole) but instead finds in each case that there is really nothing there that would entitle him to that. With that, in a time of universal fear and high cultural achievement (the Greek and Roman worlds), a different form of freedom takes shape as the "unhappy consciousness"—unhappy in the sense that the freedom it seeks (individuals speaking with the authority of the We)—is unattainable although abstractly conceivable. We imagine a "beyond" where the "One," the "unchangeable," views the temporal world timelessly as a whole, and we imagine what it would be like to assume that point of view (what Thomas Nagel memorably called the view from nowhere). From its early philosophical statement in Neoplatonism up to the early Christianity of the Roman Empire that itself became the ruling power of feudal Europe, this "unhappy consciousness" gradually worked off its despair about itself and its own self-abnegation in the face of the "unchangeable," and it affirmed its desire to attain a universal point of view that would keep its own singular self-consciousness intact. With that, it made the move from thinking of the general point of view as that of universal self-consciousness (a "We") to that of "Reason" itself as uniting both the "I" and the "We."

Chapter 6. Reason: First Part

Hegel prefaces this section with a somewhat puzzling discussion of some issues in Kantian, Fichtean, and Schellingian philosophy. To the extent that the "unhappy consciousness" has worked its way to its proper conclusion, it takes the stance of a "We" that is "Reason" itself.

This would be the self-consciousness that has emerged from all this which takes its thought to be "all reality." Hegel does not mean that it thinks that everything only exists in this self-consciousness itself but that all that ultimately matters (the "absolute") lies in this self-consciousness itself. There is no "other"—no master, no otherworldly beyond—that is entitled to command it. The relation to otherness as having to do with what ultimately matters is now set by self-consciousness itself, not by the "other" setting the terms for self-consciousness. The model of this relation to otherness is cognitive. There is nothing in principle unknowable by self-consciousness, and it is the world's knowability that ultimately matters to self-consciousness. This, Hegel says, is idealism. It should be the case that this idealism could derive the baselines of what it needs both to know and do from its own constitution, but it (so far) has failed to do so, and it has failed to do so because of the abstractness of its conception of reason. To fill itself in, reason becomes observing reason, determined to closely observe in a scientific manner the workings of the world. To do that, it sets about discovering laws as regularities of appearance. However, what it really seeks is what is "actual" (*wirklich*), what is really doing the explanatory work in the scientific observation of nature. It runs into trouble as it tries to apply the concept of "law as regularity" in doing this. While such a conception works reasonably well for physics, it runs into trouble explaining organic matter since there seem to be functions and purposes in organic life that are not mere matters of regularity. Observing reason thus finds itself doing more than just observing. It seeks to explain the unity of nature in ways that go beyond observation. It especially runs into trouble when it tries to explain the role of *Geist* in nature, since the whole in which *Geist* develops is world history, not just the development of organic life per se. Thus, when observing reason turns to psychological explanation, it is led to some particularly absurd conclusions since its methodological commitments exclude its seeing that what is at work in the realm of self-conscious life are various matters of justification and evaluation and not just regularities. Hegel take two such manifestly absurd models at work in his own day to illustrate this point: physiognomy (determining one's character from the shape of one's face) and phrenology (determining character based on the bumps on one's skull).

Chapter 7. Reason: Second Part

The immediate faith that reason was "all reality" did not work out as that faith thought it would. Although observing reason had limited success with the natural sciences, it met with absurd failure in the human sciences. Whereas it had thought it already had the resources to guide human action through the careful observation of so-called facts of human existence (even if absurdly, as in physiognomy and phrenology), it now realizes that it must in fact establish (or actualize) reason's guidance for action rather than just read it off the results of the naturalistic scientific study of the human. It must, that is, both individually and collectively establish the rationality of conduct, and doing this amounts to the realization of rational consciousness through itself. How to integrate the concerns of the "I" with those of the "We" forms the basic question around which all this turns. The first idea that arises has to do with how *particular* people can strive through their own powers to become free *individuals*, and with whether that requires that they distinguish themselves from the crowd of other particular people. If so, this must involve possession of some special knowledge. In this shape, the others in the "We" at issue are mostly just means for the end of self-realization of the particular agent seeking to become a free individual. One shape of subjectivity involves the particular individual taking himself to be in search of his own pleasure and to be the master of this quest. If this requires using others as means to the realization of oneself as an individual standing apart from (or over and above) the crowd of merely particular people, so be it. Hegel explores two myths, that of Don Juan (involving sexual mores and seductive skills) and Faust (forbidden knowledge that exceeds what humans ought to strive for). Both fail, and both myths land their respective protagonists in a kind of tragedy of their own making. Next is the figure of the "law of the heart and the madness of self-conceit" in which the agent does not seek to use the others as his stepping stone to self-realization as an individual apart from the pack. Instead, he claims to speak for them, that is, to speak on his own as the free individual he seeks to be with the authority of the voice of the whole and thereby to lead those others into actualizing their own full individuality. However, the self-realizing individual of the "law of the heart" runs up against other such individuals, each of whom is also seeking to be the legislator of mankind but to be legislating her own law, not his. The "law of the heart" is driven into a kind of fury in which he sees all of this as the result of some conspiracy (as nothing else seems fully explanatory of why his own law for humanity is not accepted by all). This slightly "Jena Romantic figure of legislating for all mankind" falls into a metaphorical war of all against all, that is, into madness. With that failure, the law of the heart shape-shifts into a knight of virtue, upholding the good (the universal) against the wickedness of the way of the world and thereby asserting his "true" individuality over and against the corrupted individuality of those who in the "way of the world" differ from his own virtue-inflected view of it. The knight of virtue, of course, loses his battle against the way of the world since he is just throwing around words, claiming to be a defender of an ancient ethics in a world that has changed so much that those ethics no longer have a place. He looks more like Don Quixote, and the way of the world—that of modern bourgeois life—has already won the day. With that, Hegel moves on to a view of the world where the agents are not any more seeking to *become* individuals but start with the premise that they always already *are* such individuals, and this results in the "spiritual kingdom of animals." In this (modern) world, there are no knights of virtue; there are instead the various individuals of the modern world jousting with each other over what it is that really matters (*die Sache selbst*). As such individuals, however, they do not see themselves as "jousting" at all but simply as expressing their own, individual conceptions of what really matters while being indifferent and maybe even blithely tolerant of others expressing their own and differing views of what really matters. This of course is all pretense and deception. These individuals take themselves to require no recognition from others, but everything they do operates in a public space, and thus each finds his own expression of what really matters not only taken up by others but also deeply contested. This is a deeply self-deceived mode of sociality, but it foregrounds what really does matter, which is *Geist* as a form of collective self-conscious life. This shape of consciousness does not immediately realize this and takes two shortcuts to preserve a sense of itself as a collective of independent rational individuals and not a deeply intertwined social form of life. It tries to see its sociality as the result of a kind of rational legislation of laws for a kingdom of ends, but that fails in the way it turns out to be too formal and abstract to be action-guiding, and, taking note of that, it then tries to see its sociality as the result of each individual testing laws formed elsewhere for their rational universality, but that too fails since the very tests suppose the kind of background horizon of what really matters in order to determine the salience of things in the immediate context of action. With that, the "Reason" chapter concludes and a new chapter, "Spirit" itself, opens.

Chapter 8. Spirit

Hegel had originally intended to end "The Science of the Experience of Consciousness" with the chapter on virtue and the way of the world, but, as Eckart Förster has shown, under the influence of Goethe's *Metamorphosis of Plants* and the course he was teaching at the time on the history of philosophy, he changed his mind and decided to write instead the *Phenomenology of Spirit*, thereby almost doubling the book in size. The new chapter was to be entitled simply "Spirit" (*Geist*), and it was to be more thoroughly historical in its dialectic. It begins with what Hegel calls "true spirit," which is basically that of archaic Greece with its democratic polis. It is true spirit because in it, the substance of collective life (the set of habits, dispositions, expectations, and formation of character in a collective form of life) and self-consciousness (with its inherent negativity and thus potential separation from such substance) are at one with each other. Substance as the "We" does not swallow up the "I," nor does the "I" break itself off from substance in its compulsion to actualize a true version of its individuality. This is, Hegel says, a kind of aspirational moral ethos, a *Sittlichkeit* (standardly translated into English as "ethical life"). Hegel gives a general overview of how this plays out in familial life and government in such "true spirit" to show that in each of these kinds of practices, the individual is both fully absorbed (and therefore fully "in" all the relevant actions of the practice) and fully reflectively self-conscious about it. It is a social order in which if each does what is socially required of him or her, then the whole will always harmonize with itself. "True" as it may be, it is also doomed to fall apart, and the Sophoclean tragedy of Antigone manifests this situation and hints at why it is ultimately self-destructive. As belonging to the family of Oedipus, Antigone watches her brothers quarrel over who has the right to the kingship inheritable from their father and end up at war over it, with the result of the death of both brothers. Her uncle, Creon, takes over and declares one of them cannot have the normal sacred burial rituals performed for him, whereas the other is to be given full honors. As her brother's sister, Antigone has an absolute requirement to perform those rituals, and as a young woman and subject to the new king's rule, she has an absolute requirement to obey Creon's orders. To this double bind is added a third constraint. that she is under an absolute requirement not to make up her own mind about what her requirements are, since the basic ones are set not by humans but by the divine nature of things, and this is especially true for women. This kind of triple bind is fatal for the community, and since Antigone must be punished for the wrong she has committed, the very intelligibility of the form of life of "true spirit" is put into question. That form of life generates the kind of individuality that is at odds with its ethical aspiration to full absorption and self-consciousness, all uniting with each other into a harmonious whole. The Greek polis had to depend on good luck in keeping all that together, and the small size of the communities together with their constant quarrels with each other over glory meant that when a larger, better-organized polity came up against them, their luck would run out. That power was Rome, and it replaced the full absorption of the polis with a community united around religious formalities and legal rules. Its lack of ethical life meant that it could sustain a democratic life itself only for a short period and, having no deeper ties of *Sittlichkeit* to hold its various contesting factions together, by its own logic fell into the shape of an empire ruled over by an emperor who in turn could have no real moral ethos governing him. Under those conditions of legalistic unity imposed by force, Rome itself lasted only until its luck also ran out.

Chapter 9. Self-Alienated Spirit

The collapse of the Roman Empire thus left what remained of it without anything to hold it together except its own still weak commitment to Christianity. Collective self-conscious life (*Geist*) now became subject to laws not seemingly of its own making and without any good reason to become absorbed in the larger, warring political order around oneself. *Geist* knows that Christianity has taught it that all are free and equal in the eyes of God, but it is abundantly clear that we are not all free and unequal in the eyes of our rulers. Thus, *Geist* enters a long period of alienation from itself (as caught in the contradiction of being free and unfree). In this world, there is no thick essence to human life (as there was in Greece) even if there may be one in the next world. In this constellation of self-conceptions, individuals by the time of the late Renaissance aspire to becoming the best alienated souls they can be, and they now conceive of themselves as being educated and educating themselves to being men (and, to a lesser extent, women) of cultivation, good judgment, and good taste. This creates a "type" for one to bend oneself into becoming. It creates a world ideally composed of three estates, each serving a different function and each embodying a different form of self-cultivation and character—in its French form as "I fight for you" (the military aristocracy), "I pray for you" (the ecclesiasticals), and "I work for you" (commoners). This eventuates in the early modern runup to absolute monarchy in which subjectivity becomes shaped into two types, those who self-interestedly work for wealth (the merchant bourgeoisie) and those nobles who selflessly work for "state power" (for the glory of the king or the state). But in the new dispensation arising out of the "way of the world," those merchants, as if led by an invisible hand, promote state power more than the courtiers whose self-image has to do with their exclusive role in promoting state power. The courtiers in turn feed off the wealth of the merchants and the patronage of the monarch, to which they relate through flattery. As Hegel puts it, the earlier heroism of silent service turns into the heroism of flattery, and the merchants and aristocratic courtiers both turn into each other. To the extent that the grand courts of absolute monarchy rested on the sharp distinction of those two roles, the system of "estates" and of absolute monarchy itself was severely undermined. An overall system of patronage displaces the old order, and the shape of spirit fragments into various actors confusedly seeking their own place in the world. The trope of the time for these alienated figures is that of the vanity of all things and even the vanity of all vanity. All is false, but I'm at least better for knowing that it's all false, except that this knowledge is itself only a piece of vanity.

Chapter 10. Faith, the Enlightenment, and the Truth of the Enlightenment

Unable to find themselves in this fragmented, confused world, these actors reshape themselves in terms of an emotionalist faith. If this world is fragmented, then the unity of the world and the hope of a nonalienated place in it must be placed into an otherworldly beyond. The vanity of this alienated world vanishes in that realm. In this world of emotionalist faith, the individual has everything he needs within himself to become aware of what really matters as the absolute, the deity. The world of the vanity of vanities threw individuals back on their own resources, and they found it in their emotional connection with this otherworldly beyond. What the faithful have that the alienated souls of the existing world lack is a kind of "pure insight" into what really matters. That "pure insight" is taken up in a different way by those who wish to hold on to or to resurrect the appeal to reason itself as distinct from convention or mores. Those of faith seek illumination from the otherworldly beyond, and those following out the secularized "pure insight" seek illumination from the *lumen naturale*, the light of nature, of pure reason itself. Those dedicated to the light of nature come to describe themselves variously as the "illuminated" and finally by the term "the Enlightenment." The Enlightenment sees faith not so much as religion as just superstition, and the two get into a dispute over who is illuminated by what. In fact, the idea on which both rely—a kind of unencumbered insight illuminated by some other source which illuminates all but itself—is hopelessly abstract, and the dispute is rather empty. However, as soon as Enlightenment can lure faith into defending itself, it has faith playing by the rules of a game that Enlightenment itself has written, and faith is destined to lose that game. However, Enlightenment is not enlightened about itself. It calls for rational defense of what needs to be defended, but it takes as a given that its illumination by the *lumen naturale* is all in order. It shows in its actions that to which Enlightenment commits itself, but it cannot say what it is that illuminates that path.

Chapter 11. Absolute Freedom and Terror

Enlightenment puts all its weight on ahistorical, unencumbered reason carried out by ahistorical unencumbered individuals illuminated by the light of nature. These individuals, each an "I," claim to speak with the authority of the whole, as a "We," and the "I" and the "We" fuse into one. At first, these rational individuals are led into the concept of utility (as producing the maximal amount of goodness, taken to be human happiness) as its criterion for what it should pursue. However, utility proves to be too much of a constraint on such a conception that is now that of "absolute freedom" as constrained by nothing but itself. This new individual as embodying the oneness of the "I" and the "We" itself shifts its shape into that of the "Nation" as the sovereign will that makes all other law. As the Revolution comes to be directed by the Committee of Public Safety headed by Robespierre (the virtuous), it takes on the task of governing the whole (the unity of "the Nation") guided only by its own sense of virtue. Divided into those who are "of" the Nation and those who oppose the laws of the Committee, the whole now turns on itself to expunge its pathological members that threaten the health of the whole, and the Reign of Terror sets in, a "wholly *unmediated* pure negation," as Hegel calls it. The result are the executions carried out in such a clinical manner that they are meaningless, of no more emotional significance than chopping off a head of cabbage. Under Robespierre, heads were to roll, and eventually his did too. The unifying abstraction of "absolute freedom" simply could not take the differences among individuals seriously. Once the Revolution was over, things settled down, and the unnerving experience of "absolute freedom" led the individuals, initially formed by faith and pure insight, thinning themselves out further into "absolute freedom," and then reshaping themselves into a new form of life, not of the "ethical" life of Greece but that of the "moral" life of the modern postrevolutionary world.

Chapter 12. Spirit Certain of Itself: Morality

What holds the new substance of collective self-conscious life together is an "I" that speaks for the whole (the "We"), but, as reflected out of it, as being the separate and distinct individual it is, its basic experience of that whole is its sense of duty as arising out of its own "pure consciousness," not from any especially individual desire or aim. This forms a worldview, which goes something like the following. Nature is indifferent to our moral duties in terms of either their content or our motivations to obey them, but morality (the realm of duty) is absolute, and when duty commands, we are motivated to obey it. Duty is done for its own sake, not for the sake of some natural ends such as happiness. In this worldview, since morality is actual—it is what is really at work in this new shape of collective "substance"—we must postulate that nature and morality harmonize even though we cannot prove that they do. Nor could it be the case that our own sensibility (as desire or inclination) could make it impossible to do our duty, so we must also postulate that nature and duty can harmonize. Since they can be in tension with each other, each of us has a duty to strive to bring them into a fuller harmony, a task which is infinite and thus which cannot be completely fulfilled. Moreover, since there are many different duties, some of which have the semblance of conflict with each other, there must be a single, "holy" duty from which they all follow and which is sanctified by some other postulated consciousness (which is itself authoritatively capable of sanctifying this). In morally perfect world, happiness would be distributed to each according to his own virtue (his propensity to fulfill his duties), and this too is the goal of an infinite and therefore incompletable task. That worldview leads to various contradictions when it is put into practice. It thus leads to an odd form of self-deception, *Verstellung*, a kind of dissemblance and playacting. Amid the contradictions that arise in this worldview, the actors simply shift from one side to the other, not avoiding the contradiction so much as avoiding dealing with it. If nothing else, the idea of the infinite task means that none of these are doable, and the idea that one can nonetheless get closer to the completion is off-base since no matter how close you get to infinity, you are still infinitely far away. Thus, in essence, the moral worldview is not a coherent whole but rather only a syncretism of the contradictions engendered by itself. If it becomes aware of its own dissemblance, then it cannot help but view itself as hypocrisy in its claims to be absolute and pure but in fact being only partial and self-involved.

Chapter 13. Beautiful Souls

The individual moral agent as crystallized in the moral worldview is, first, the result of a history of agency that has progressively thinned itself out; and second, sees itself and its moral projects as the only fixed point in an indifferent nature and an almost chaotic world. This "moral individual" now finds its truth in the picture of itself as directed by its conscience. In its own eyes, the individual moral agent takes it on himself to do the right thing because it is right, consults his conscience about it (weighing all the reasons, being honest with himself, and so on), and having done so, realizes himself as having acted out of duty. The agent acting out of conscience in this sense is a concrete individual, and the abstractions of the moral worldview become more focused and concrete when seen in that light. What holds the whole together is a shared view among such individuals of there being a moral world order (expressed as a "We") that is actualized by each individual attending to his own "conscience" in acting. When this whole functions according to its own concept, each knows what is salient in the myriad concrete circumstances surrounding him, sees clearly what he is unconditionally required to do in that situation, and as appealing to his own conscience is fully motivated to carry out the right action. This is the trajectory of the concept of the moral agency of conscience as it is "in itself." In this moral world order, each does what he has to do (as a matter of duty) and demands recognition from others as having acted out of conscience, that is, rightfully, even when others take umbrage at his decision. Of course, many of the older problems with the moral worldview now reappear in this supposed resolution of those problems, in particular, the tension between the asserted individuality of the "I" and the universal standpoint of the "We." The logic of this is to bestow a moral autarky on each of the members of the community of conscience. Hegel claims (not for the first time in the book) that "language is the existence of spirit"—that spirit remains merely an abstract, nonexisting "idea" until it is manifested in concrete actions within a linguistic community—and that this particular use of language itself manifests the tensions inherent in such a self-conception on the part of the community of conscience. Although the language of this form of life is such that in principle there should be no gap between the acting agents and the universal moral world order, in fact it necessarily opens up a gap given the inadequate comprehension of the relation between the "I" and the "We" here. This sets the stage for these people to turn even further inward and claim for themselves a status for which Hegel, adopting an older term, calls "the beautiful soul." This status quickly further bifurcates itself into two mutually accusatory self-conceptions. One person says that since every case involves a lot of complicated facts, he never acts until he has all the facts available, and thus even if things turn out badly, he thus always does what is pure and right in the circumstances. The other says he never acts until he has all the facts, but since he never has all of them, he never acts but only judges. Each claims a purity that is invisible to the other, and each accuses the other of evil or hypocrisy. Here the point at issue becomes not only the paradigmatic "I/We" relation, but the second-person "I/Thou" relation. This sets the stage for each of them recognizing themselves second-personally in the other through mutual forgiveness and reconciliation. Hegel strangely calls this enriched form of Spirit the "appearing God in their midst," thus setting the stage even further for a discussion of religion.

Chapter 14. Religion

"Absolute spirit" has to do with the reciprocal recognition obtained in reconciliation and forgiveness. Spirit thinking about what it means to be spirit (to be self-conscious life) is absolute in that it is mediating itself. Religion is one of the basic forms of such reflexive thinking. (Another is philosophy.) As with the other shapes of self-consciousness, religion exhibits a kind of progressive development of itself. The "in itself" of the concept of *Geist* shows a trajectory that now, in retrospect, was headed for the kind of pure reflection by self-conscious life on what it means to be self-conscious life. This project was only partly fulfilled by the aspects of spirit that had been drawn out to this point in the book. Spirit begins with natural religion, which sees "the One" of the universe in terms of metaphors such as light and dark. Thus, religion begins as pantheism. It develops into opposing religions as it differentiates itself in terms of metaphors of animals and plants. As people in those religions carve out more determinate images and sing more determinate songs about those deities, they produce artisans as the craftsmen for their particular religions. Artisans become artists when they come to concern themselves not merely with the well-made object but have to ask themselves what is meant by these objects and what they, as artists, are trying to say. Ancient Greece shifted this into an art-religion in which the religious truths that are trying to find expression can only be expressed in forms of beauty. This itself develops progressively from the abstract art of the early Greek statuary, Greek cults and their hymns, and oracles further to the more developed form of the creation of epics (the *Iliad* and the *Odyssey*) in which the people (as different tribes or clans or communities) come to see themselves as a unified people ("the Greeks"). From there it develops into theatrical presentations of tragedy and comedy. In epic, the "people" confront an other (Troy) that has no internal relation to their own form of life. In tragedy, the other they confront is themselves and the tensions in their own collective lives as lived out in the intense experiences of stylized individuals (mythical figures, ancient and partially mythological heroes) who are encountered often in defining historical events. To the extent that individuals see their own collective lives falling apart as the tragedies manifest the contradictions buried deeply in their form of life, they see themselves as falling apart as individuals. As this sets in, the theatrical tragedy becomes conceived as merely theatrical, as just a show, and with that, Greek comedy makes its appearance as the presentation of failures that fail to matter but which itself supposes that there is something that does really matter. As the actors become seen as just actors, as the laughter sets in, the individual self that is brought to the fore in comedy is itself the negative force by which the ancient Greek gods gradually disappear.

Chapter 15. Revealed Religion

The art-religion of ancient Greece manifests the fundamental and world transforming shift from explanation and justification by appeal to "substance" to the same as equally involving "subject." The order of the social world is now to be understood not in terms of the usually hidden laws of "substance" but as involving equally as much the activities of self-conscious life. The breakdown of Greek ethical life and its subsumption into imperial Roman rule had a profound consequence. Whereas in the Greek alternative, the Greeks received their gods from the poets (as Herodotus claimed), in the new dispensation, the problems facing the Roman and post-Roman form of life could not solved aesthetically but only realistically. Into that logical space, Christianity entered. Jesus is not imaginary as is Apollo or Zeus. He is real, he preaches, and he is condemned to death. In his presence and teachings, God is disclosed to us. However, this is originally taken by the newly formed Christian community in the form of *Vorstellung* (representational thinking) as being a relation between two independent individuals which can be pictured as standing in relations such as father and son. The myth of the Fall illustrates this, since Adam and Eve are pictured as living in complete innocence until they eat from the tree of knowledge of good and evil. That they immediately clothe themselves shows that the transition being mythically portrayed is from that of animal life to self-conscious life. The gap in ourselves which opened up with self-consciousness is what religion now concerns itself with. The very meaning of *Geist* is to be a problem to itself, and this is articulated in the Christian community as a communal self-reflection on self-conscious life and death, although not yet as a fully conceptual, philosophical reflection on it. In particular, Christian religion as the "absolute religion" places contingency, death, and ethics at the forefront of its reflections and it uses myth and rite to express this. The death of Jesus is its signal moment since it embodies the hope that *Geist* itself will never die even if individuals do. However, the "absolute religion" is still in the form of *Vorstellung*, and there is thus one more step to be taken.

Chapter 16. Absolute Knowing

The activity of religious self-consciousness runs up squarely to the threat of nihilism—that nothing whatsoever ultimately matters—and tries to meet it with a doctrine of hope, reconciliation, and forgiveness. This sets the stage for the full resolution of the problems of self-conscious life. Self-consciousness is, taken apart from all else, inherently empty. No ultimate content is analytically implied by self-consciousness itself abstracted out of its concrete history and situation. However, there is an absolute content that develops itself from the concept of self-consciousness as existing in time (in history) and embodied in its full individual and communal life. To get at it, we must simply gather up all the shapes of self-conscious life and what they have been through that we have seen so far in the book. In the last analysis, nothing is really known except as "felt truth," and this kind of phenomenological "science" is the appropriate method for bringing that "felt truth" to light. What is really moving history (our development as a species, as *Geist*) are the flesh-and-blood struggles of individuals to grapple with the meaning of their lives as the members of the communities they have constructed and the terms under which they tried to understand themselves. This has led *Geist* to give shape to itself as "the concept," that is, as the attempt to provide a holistic conceptual understanding of itself as achieving itself through a developmental struggle over what it means to be a self-conscious life. To do this, it cannot simply have read it in a book. It had to have lived it, to have had whatever it came up with as a "felt truth." "We" had been looking for the hidden substance of which *Geist* was only the semblance, but now "we" see that *Geist* is not the expression of something hidden behind the curtain of appearance but just is the series of its appearances as it develops itself in time. As it now looks back over what has transpired, it finds it at first as if it were a gallery of pictures, as if it were walking slowly through a museum of its own past. In doing so, it changes its contingent history into a concept-ized history (*begriffne Geschichte*) and sees that although events do not necessarily follow a strict logic in their occurrences, the retrospective look at the "gallery of pictures" shows that nonetheless the logic of self-conscious life has emerged as having a particular trajectory even though few if any of the historical individuals were aiming at it. If it were merely a matter of disembodied philosophy in a book, we would have *Geist* proceeding to its own Calvary (its *Schädelstätte*), where on its throne, it would be "lifeless and alone." That is, without this rich concept-ized history behind it and without its being a "phenomenology" of that life and history, the "science of self-consciousness" would become a merely formal enterprise (would be "lifeless") and would have no real link to the rest of the form of life of which it is a part (would be "alone"). It would be a dry, dead (and "merely" academic) enterprise. We began with a consideration of indexicals, with an actual location in a "this," and we end with a "this" ("this realm of spirits," *dieses Geisterreiches*), that is, not just in any possible world, but the actual, human world.

Notes

Prelude

1. I will, on the whole, not refer to my own discussion in T. P. Pinkard, *Hegel's Phenomenology: The Sociality of Reason* (Cambridge: Cambridge University Press, 1994). The account here supplements and in some cases substantially corrects that discussion, but I will ignore those differences. Over the last two decades or so, I have changed my mind about some passages, how to take them, and about the shape of some parts of the book, but a comparison of these different interpretations with the earlier book would be out of place here. Those who would be interested in that comparison (all three of you) will not find it here.

Chapter 1

1. G. W. F. Hegel, *The Science of Logic*, trans. G. Di Giovanni (New York: Cambridge University Press, 2010).
2. R. Brandom, *A Spirit of Trust: A Reading of Hegel's "Phenomenology"* (Cambridge, MA: Belknap Press of Harvard University Press, 2019).
3. The phrase "making sense of making sense" is taken from A. W. Moore, *The Evolution of Modern Metaphysics: Making Sense of Things* (New York: Cambridge University Press, 2012).

Chapter 2

1. L. Wittgenstein, *Philosophical Investigations = Philosophische Untersuchungen*, trans. G. E. M. Anscombe (New York: Macmillan, 1953), §217.
2. Ibid., §325.
3. Ibid.

4. This distinction, like the earlier one about making sense of making sense, is also taken from A. W. Moore, *The Evolution of Modern Metaphysics: Making Sense of Things* (New York: Cambridge University Press, 2012).

Chapter 6

1. See the important set of historical notes by Wolfgang Bonsiepen to the critical edition of the *Phenomenology*. G. W. F. Hegel, *Phänomenologie des Geistes*, ed. H.-F. Wessels and H. Clairmont (Hamburg: F. Meiner Verlag, 1988).

Chapter 7

1. E. Förster, *The Twenty-Five Years of Philosophy: A Systematic Reconstruction* (Cambridge, MA: Harvard University Press, 2012).; and T. P. Pinkard, *Hegel: A Biography* (Cambridge: Cambridge University Press, 2000).

Chapter 9

1. "So sage ich nun und bezeuge in dem HERRN, daß ihr nicht mehr wandelt, wie die andern Heiden wandeln in der Eitelkeit ihres Sinnes, deren Verstand verfinstert ist, und die entfremdet sind von dem Leben, das aus Gott ist, durch die Unwissenheit, so in ihnen ist, durch die Blindheit ihres Herzens; welche ruchlos sind und ergeben sich der Unzucht und treiben allerlei Unreinigkeit samt dem Geiz" (Ephesians 4:17–19). The King James Version uses "alienate" ("being alienated from the life of God"). Wycliffe uses "aliened."

Chapter 13

1. See the discussion of these people in T. P. Pinkard, *German Philosophy, 1760–1860: The Legacy of Idealism* (Cambridge: Cambridge University Press, 2002).

Further Reading

There are several English language studies of the full *Phenomenology of Spirit*, some of which take alternative viewpoints to the ones presented here and some of which follow this line of thought in some points and not in others. I haven't discussed any of them here (alas) since that would make this into a much more "scholarly" book than a normal "reader's guide," but nonetheless they are all worth reading. I have not listed any books dedicated to a study of only selected ideas or themes in the *Phenomenology*, and (with one exception) only fairly recent books are listed. It surely goes without saying that these do not exhaust all the books on Hegel's thought that provide essential insight into his philosophy.

Brandom, R. *A Spirit of Trust: A Reading of Hegel's "Phenomenology."* Cambridge, MA: Belknap Press of Harvard University Press, 2019.

Collins, A. B. *Hegel's Phenomenology: The Dialectical Justification of Philosophy's First Principles.* Montreal: McGill-Queen's University Press, 2013.

Harris, H. S. *Hegel's Ladder.* Indianapolis: Hackett, 1997.

Houlgate, S. "G. W. F. Hegel: The Phenomenology of Spirit." In *The Blackwell Guide to Continental Philosophy*, edited by R. C. Solomon and D. L. Sherman, 8–29. Malden, MA: Blackwell, 2003.

Hyppolite, J. *Genesis and Structure of Hegel's "Phenomenology of Spirit."* Translated by Samuel Cherniak and John Heckman. Evanston, IL: Northwestern University Press, 1974. Originally published in French in 1947.

Pinkard, T. P. *Hegel's "Phenomenology": The Sociality of Reason.* Cambridge: Cambridge University Press, 1994.

Russon, J. E. *Reading Hegel's "Phenomenology."* Bloomington: Indiana University Press, 2004.

Siep, L. *Hegel's "Phenomenology of Spirit."* New York: Cambridge University Press, 2014.

Stern, R. *Routledge Philosophy Guidebook to Hegel and the "Phenomenology of Spirit."* New York: Routledge, 2002.

Stewart, J. *The Unity of Hegel's "Phenomenology of Spirit": A Systematic Interpretation.* Evanston, IL: Northwestern University Press, 2000.

Works Cited

Brandom, R. *A Spirit of Trust: A Reading of Hegel's "Phenomenology."* Cambridge, MA: Belknap Press of Harvard University Press, 2019.

Förster, E. *The Twenty-Five Years of Philosophy: A Systematic Reconstruction.* Cambridge, MA: Harvard University Press, 2012.

Hegel, G. W. F. *Phänomenologie des Geistes.* Edited by H.-F. Wessels and H. Clairmont. Hamburg: F. Meiner Verlag, 1988.

Hegel, G. W. F. *The Science of Logic.* Translated and edited by G. Di Giovanni. New York: Cambridge University Press, 2010.

Moore, A. W. *The Evolution of Modern Metaphysics: Making Sense of Things.* New York: Cambridge University Press, 2012.

Pinkard, T. P. *German Philosophy, 1760–1860: The Legacy of Idealism.* Cambridge: Cambridge University Press, 2002.

Pinkard, T. P. *Hegel: A Biography.* Cambridge: Cambridge University Press, 2000.

Pinkard, T. P. *Hegel's: Phenomenology": The Sociality of Reason.* Cambridge: Cambridge University Press, 1994.

Wittgenstein, L. *Philosophical Investigations = Philosophische Untersuchungen.* Translated by G. E. M. Anscombe. New York: Macmillan, 1953.

Index

For the benefit of digital users, indexed terms that span two pages (e.g., 52–53) may, on occasion, appear on only one of those pages.

334   INDEX